*Compliments of your*
*Pfizer Laboratories Representative*

**LABORATORIES DIVISION**
PFIZER INC., NEW YORK, N.Y. 10017

SPECTRUM PUBLICATIONS, Inc.
175-20 Wexford Terrace, Jamaica, N.Y. 11432

**Library of Congress Cataloging in Publication Data**

Main entry under title:

Phenomenology and treatment of depression.
    "Proceedings of a symposium on the phenomenology
and treatment of depression, held in Houston,
Texas on December 4-5, 1975 . . . sponsored by the
Department of Psychiatry and the Office of
Continuing Education of Baylor College of Medicine
in Houston."
    Bibliography: p.
    Includes index.
    1. Depression, Mental–Congresses. I. Fann,
William E. I. Baylor University, Waco, Tex.
College of Medicine, Houston. Dept. of Psychiatry.
III. Baylor University, Waco, Tex. College of
Medicine, Houston. Office of Continuing Education.
[DNLM: 1. Depression. WM170 P541]
RC537.P47        616.8'9        76-48046
ISBN 0-89335-001-X

# Phenomenology and Treatment of Depression

*Edited by*

**William E. Fann, M.D.**
**Ismet Karacan, M.D., (Med) D.Sci.**
**Alex D. Pokorny, M.D.**
**Robert L. Williams, M.D.**

*all of the*

Department of Psychiatry
Baylor College of Medicine
Houston, Texas

S P Books Division of
**SPECTRUM PUBLICATIONS, INC.**
New York

# Contributors

HILDE BRUCH, M.D.
Professor of Psychiatry
Baylor College of Medicine
Houston, Texas

DAVID BURNS, M.D.
Fellow, Foundations' Fund for Research
in Psychiatry
University of Pennsylvania
and
Veterans Administration Hospital
Philadelphia, Pennsylvania

BETSY S. COMSTOCK, M.D.
Assistant Professor of Psychiatry
Baylor College of Medicine
and
Director, Psychiatric Outpatient Clinic
Ben Taub Hospital
Houston, Texas

JOHN M. DAVIS, M.D.
Professor of Psychiatry
University of Chicago School of
Medicine
and
Director of Research, Illinois State
Psychiatric Institute
Chicago, Illinois

NORMAN DECKER, M.D.
Assistant Professor of Psychiatry
Baylor College of Medicine
and
Director, Psychiatric Liaison Services
Veterans Administration Hospital
Houston, Texas

GEORGE M. FAIBISH, Ph.D.
Clinical Associate Professor of
  Psychiatry
Departments of Psychiatry and
  Neurology
Baylor College of Medicine
Houston, Texas

WILLIAM E. FANN, M.D.
Professor of Psychiatry
Associate Professor of Pharmacology
Baylor College of Medicine
  and
Chief, Psychiatry Service
Veterans Administration Hospital
Houston, Texas

MAX FINK, M.D.
Professor of Psychiatry
Director, Psychopharmacology Research
  Laboratory
State University of New York at
  Stony Brook
School of Medicine
Stony Brook, New York

JAMES C. FOLSOM, M.D.
Director, Rehabilitative Medicine
  Service
United States Veterans Administration
Washington, D. C.

CHARLES M. GAITZ, M.D.
Clinical Associate Professor of
  Psychiatry
Baylor College of Medicine
  and
Chief, Gerontology Research Section
Texas Research Institute of Mental
  Sciences
Houston, Texas

ALEXANDER GLASSMAN, M.D.
Associate Professor of Clinical Psychiatry
College of Physicians and Surgeons
Columbia University
New York, New York

FRANCIS J. KANE, M.D.
Professor of Psychiatry
Baylor College of Medicine
  and
Director, Psychiatry Service
The Methodist Hospital
Houston, Texas

SHEPARD J. KANTOR, M.D.
Instructor in Psychiatry
College of Physicians and Surgeons
Columbia University
New York, New York

HOWARD B. KAPLAN, Ph.D.
Professor of Psychiatry
Baylor College of Medicine
Houston, Texas

ISMET KARACAN, M.D. (Med)
  D.Sci.
Professor of Psychiatry
Baylor College of Medicine
  and
Associate Chief of Staff for Research
Veterans Administration Hospital
Houston, Texas

ISHAM KIMBELL, Jr., M.D.
Clinical Associate Professor of
  Psychiatry
University of Texas Southwestern
  Medical School
  and
Chief, Psychiatry Service
Veterans Administration Hospital
Dallas, Texas

JOE MENDELS, M.D.
Professor of Psychiatry
Chief, Depression Research Unit
University of Pennsylvania
  and
Veterans Administration Hospital
Philadelphia, Pennsylvania

JAMES M. PEREL, Ph.D.
Assistant Professor of Psychiatry
College of Physicians and Surgeons
Columbia University
New York, New York

ALEX D. POKORNY, M.D.
Professor of Psychiatry
Baylor College of Medicine
Houston, Texas

ARTHUR J. PRANGE, M.D.
Professor of Psychiatry
University of North Carolina School of
    Medicine
Chapel Hill, North Carolina

RUBEN D. RUMBAUT, M.D.
Associate Professor of Psychiatry
Baylor College of Medicine
    and
Director, Psychiatric Day Hospital
Veterans Administration Hospital
Houston, Texas

PATRICIA J. SALIS, M.A.
Research Assistant Professor of
    Psychophysiology
Department of Psychiatry
Baylor College of Medicine
Houston, Texas

JOSEPH C. SCHOOLAR, M.D., Ph.D.
Professor of Pharmacology and
    Psychiatry
Baylor College of Medicine
    and
Director, Texas Research Institute of
    Mental Sciences
Houston, Texas

JUDITH M. SHERMAN, M.D.
Assistant Professor of Psychiatry
Baylor College of Medicine
    and
Director, Psychiatric
    Crisis-Evaluation Clinic
Veterans Administration Hospital
Houston, Texas

MICHAEL SHOSTAK, M.D.
Instructor in Psychiatry
College of Physicians and Surgeons
Columbia University
New York, New York

JOHN R. STAFFORD, M.D.
Assistant Professor of Psychiatry
Baylor College of Medicine
    and
Director, Drug Abuse Treatment Clinics
Veterans Administration Hospital
Houston, Texas

JEANINE C. WHELESS, B.A.
Evaluation Coordinator
Psychiatry Service
Veterans Administration Hospital
Atlanta, Georgia

ROBERT B. WHITE, M.D.
Professor of Psychiatry
University of Texas Medical Branch at
    Galveston
    and
Training and Supervisor Analyst
Houston-Galveston Psychoanalytic
    School
Houston, Texas

ROBERT L. WILLIAMS, M.D.
D.C. and Irene Ellwood Professor and
    Chairman
Department of Psychiatry
Baylor College of Medicine
Houston, Texas

WILLIAM W. K. ZUNG, M.D.
Professor of Psychiatry
Duke University Medical Center
Durham, North Carolina

Financial support of the symposium on The Phenomenology and Treatment of Depression, conducted at Baylor College of Medicine, December 4-5, 1975, was provided by the following pharmaceutical manufacturers:

Geigy Pharmaceuticals
Hoechst-Roussel Pharmaceuticals, Inc.
Lederle Laboratories
Merck Sharpe & Dohme
Merrell-National Laboratories
Pennwalt Pharmaceuticals
Roche Laboratories
Sandoz Pharmaceuticals
Schering Corporation
USV Pharmaceutical Corporation

The editors and conference participants are most grateful to these organizations for their valuable assistance and for their dedication to the continuing education of physicians and other health care professionals.

# Acknowledgment

This volume originated in a symposium on The Phenomenology and Treatment of Depression, held at Baylor College of Medicine in Houston, Texas, on December 4-5, 1975. The symposium was one in the College's annual series of conferences devoted to the study of major psychiatric disorders.

The success of the conference, and the strength of the present volume, are largely attributable to the hard and competent work of several individuals whose enormous contributions are not necessarily apparent from scanning the table of contents or the list of invited guests.

Dr. Fred Taylor, Ms. Margaret Klug, and Ms. Christine Sartori of the Baylor Office of Continuing Education arranged and administered the conference impeccably; we are most grateful for the efforts and expertise of this outstanding group.

Dr. Harris Busch, Chairman of Pharmacology, and Dr. José Garcia, Assistant Professor of Psychiatry, served as section chairmen and discussants. We appreciate their interest and support.

Ms. Tommie Brackendorff, Ms. Nancy Berry, Ms. Elaine Miller and Ms. Katie Destouet worked on the arrangement of the conference and on the preparation of the manuscript.

Mr. Bruce Richman, Adjunct Instructor in Scientific Communication, served as managing editor of the volume.

To each of these individuals we express our most sincere gratitude.

# Foreword

This volume represents the proceedings of a symposium on The Phenomenology and Treatment of Depression, held in Houston, Texas, on December 4-5, 1975. The conference was sponsored by the Department of Psychiatry and the Office of Continuing Education of Baylor College of Medicine in Houston.

Our intention in conducting the conference was to bring together scientists and clinicians for a mutual exchange of ideas concerning the nature and treatment of depression, generally recognized as the most commonly occurring psychiatric malady. Despite the frequency with which depressed individuals are present in emergency rooms and in the private offices of psychiatrists and general practitioners, the causes and care of depressive disorders are imperfectly understood. Although we were aware that a comprehensive analysis of depression was not possible within the confines of a single conference or volume, we did attempt to assemble a series of papers which would indicate in some sense the breadth and difficulty of the subject while providing answers to some important practical questions.

Papers by Drs. Prange, Davis, and Burns and Mendels suggest a biological etiology in some cases of depression. Dr. Kane suggests the possibility of depressive reaction to prescribed medication. At the other end of the theoretical spectrum, Drs. Kaplan, Rumbaut, and White discuss depression in the context of psychodynamics. Each of these papers presents cogent evidence implicating specific factors in the genesis of depression, but at no time is there a suggestion that any single element or entity is identifiable as the sole cause of depressive disorder.

Drs. Bruch, Gaitz, Karacan, Decker, Pokorny, and Stafford address their papers to particular characteristics of depression as they appear in a variety of populations. Dr. Bruch describes depressive features of obesity and anorexia nervosa. Dr. Gaitz discusses the phenomenology of depression in elderly individuals and finds that this group is at special risk for development of depressive symptoms. Dr. Karacan evaluates the frequent presence of sleep disturbance in neurotic depressed patients and the response of these patients to drug therapy. Dr. Pokorny explores the issue of suicide, a factor central to any examination of the symptoms and implications of clinical depression. Dr. Decker considers the distinction between suicide as related to depression and as a possibly rational wish to die in terminally or otherwise incurably ill individuals. Dr. Stafford examines the depressive features commonly seen in the drug- and alcohol-dependent individuals who now comprise a considerable percentage of patients brought to the care of psychiatrists.

The treatment of depression is as complex and various as its phenomenology. Drs. Zung and Faibish and Kimball discuss the first stage in the treatment process, proper diagnosis and assessment of the disorder. Dr. Schoolar, Dr. Glassman, and Dr. Fann discuss pharmacological treatment of depression and its subtypes, while Dr. Fink presents a careful consideration of what has become a scientifically and politically controversial issue in psychiatry, the use of electro-convulsive therapy in depression. Dr. Folsom presents the rationale and technique involved in the clinical use of the antidepressant regimen, a novel treatment procedure with which he has had considerable success. Drs. Sherman and Comstock present chapters which will be of significant interest to all clinicians, discussing the management of acute depressive crisis and the proper care of depressed individuals outside the confines of the hospital.

Despite the rather extensive scope of this compendium and the considerable amount of research and clinical experience which it reflects, a definitive statement on the phenomenology and treatment of depression is not within the purview of this volume. Perhaps such a fully synthesized and universally adaptable sense of so complex a disorder is not possible, here or elsewhere. If the answers to our questions concerning depression do not exist in generalities, we must then approach the problems encountered through consideration of the issues individually, and it is our hope that this volume will provide a contribution to the study and care of depressive disorders within those necessary limitations.

WILLIAM E. FANN, M.D.
ISMET KARACAN, M.D., (Med) D.Sci.
ALEX D. POKORNY, M.D.
ROBERT L. WILLIAMS, M.D.

# Contents

1

# Patterns of Pituitary Responses to Thyrotropin-Releasing Hormone in Depressed Patients: A Review

ARTHUR J. PRANGE, JR.

Psychoendocrine inquiries have been addressed more intensively to depressive disorders than to other psychiatric conditions. This may be due in part to the observations of a sex-related difference in incidence (1), the suspicion that involutional changes may play a causal role (2,3), and the suggestion that mental changes related to a hormonally controlled phenomenon, the menstrual cycle, may represent a model of clinical depression (4). The availability of depressed patients may also contribute to the vigorous endocrine investigation this condition has received, for as strong a prima facie case could be made for endocrine involvement in anorexia nervosa, for example (3).

Various strategies for psychoendocrine study have been described (6). One or another of these approaches has yielded five findings in depressed patients which appear sufficiently founded to require interpretation. They are as follows:

1. Cortisol: some patients of both sexes are hypersecretors of this adrenocortical hormone (7,8,9): normal diurnal variation in plasma is often lost (8,9,10).
2. Growth hormone (GH) : postmenopausal patients secrete less of this anterior pituitary hormone in response to insulin hypoglycemia than do nondepressed controls (11,12).
3. Luteinizing hormone (LH) : this anterior pituitary hormone is found in diminished amounts in the plasma of postmenopausal women with unipolar depression (12,13).
4. Thyroid-stimulating hormone (TSH): the secretion of this anterior pituitary hormone in response to injection of thyrotropin-releasing hormone (TRH) is often deficient in depressed patients of both sexes.
5. Growth hormone: the secretion of this anterior pituitary hormone in response to injection of TRH is often increased in depressed patients of both sexes.

In addition, an alteration in prolactin (PRL) response has been described in depressed men and women, but results are preliminary and contradictory, as will be described, and cannot presently be interpreted. Our group has emphasized that a thyroid hormone, L-triiodothyronine (14,15,16), or for that matter TSH (17,18), can be used to accelerate the antidepressant action of imipramine in depressed women. While the former finding has been broadly confirmed (19,20,21) and is often utilized, neither of these findings is cogent to our present concern, the endocrine state of depressed patients, for the observation that a hormone exerts a beneficial effect only suggests, while surely failing to prove, its prior insufficiency.

In this brief review I plan to discuss the basis for the fourth and fifth findings listed above and then to explore what we may learn from them, especially when they are viewed in the context of the other endocrine findings.

Thyrotropin-releasing hormone (TRH) is a tripeptide, pyroglutamyl-histadyl-proline amide (22,23). It is found in the hypothalamus and other parts of brain (24,25,26). From the hypothalamus it is secreted into the portal venous system and transported to the anterior pituitary gland, where it releases into the general circulation TSH (27), PRL (28), and, in acromegalic patients, GH (29). Our interest in this substance is an extension of our traditional interest in the thyroid axis in depression and was piqued by the finding that TRH is active in mice in the pargyline-DOPA test (30), which has proven useful as a screening procedure for putative antidepressants (31).

TRH administration allows the simultaneous employment of two psychoendocrine strategies. First, does its administration cause a change in the depressed state? Second, in depression are pituitary responses to TRH altered? In our original paper we offered an affirmative answer to the first question (32). In a more detailed presentation of the same results we emphasized that in women with the unipolar form of the disorder the antidepressant action of TRH, though rapid and reliable, was also brief and partial (33). In the same communication we drew attention to a diminished TSH response in our patients.

Whether TRH exerts even a brief partial antidepressant effect continues to be a matter of controversy. We have recently reviewed 24 studies that pertain to this point and have discussed the contradictory findings (34). However, the theme to be developed presently is not the possible mental changes after TRH but rather the concatenation of findings that has issued from the study of the pituitary response of depressed patients to TRH administration.

We stated that in our 10 unipolar women both peak TSH response and area under the TSH response curve were diminished as compared to population norms (33). Later we studied 10 normal women and found the differences between them and the unipolar depressed patients just short of acceptable levels of statistical significance (35). Still more recently, additional data from patients and controls have attested to the statistical significance of both findings. In any case, the remarkable aspect of our original data was the almost total absence of a TSH response in 2 of our 10 patients. While an absent response is sometimes seen in a series of normals (36), it is quite uncommon. Ozawa and Shishiba (37) reported an absent TSH response in the case study of a man with Klinefelter's syndrome.

Not all investigators who have examined TRH for a putative antidepressant effect have studied pituitary responses, and conversely, a few investigators who have examined pituitary responses have not attended to psychological effects. The workers who have examined pituitary responses to TRH challenge in depression are listed in Table 1. Twelve studies involving 153 patients have reported one or another order of fault in TSH response. Two studies involving 4 patients have found none.

Table 2 offers a more detailed analysis of those studies whose authors have tried to establish the context of the TRH fault. Some investigators have tried to relate the finding to one or another clinical aspect of depression; some have tried to relate it to other aspects of pituitary response. The former considerations can be dealt with quickly. Previous drug intake seems unimportant. The TSH response deficit seems unrelated to type of depression, and this generalization holds whether the unipolar-bipolar dichotomy is employed (38) or whether a more elaborate system is used (39). The fault is probably not related to severity of depression, for there are four negative

Table 1.  TSH Response to TRH Challenge in Depression

| Authors | N | Results and Comments |
|---|---|---|
| DIMINISHED RESPONSE FOUND | | |
| Prange et al., 1972 | 10 | All responses borderline low or absent. Thyroid state normal. |
| Kastin et al., 1972 | 5 | Four showed diminished responses. |
| Coppen et al., 1974 | 16 | Four of 16 showed no response. Thyroid state normal. |
| Chazot et al., 1974 | 30 | Fifteen showed diminished responses. (Seven of 13 showed positive GH responses). |
| Kirkegaard et al., 1974 | 8 | Group tended toward diminished responses, with recovery of responses after ECT. Elevated free thyroxine could influence initial diminution. |
| Ehrensing et al., 1974 | 8 | Three patients showed diminished responses. Prolactin responses also diminished. |
| Hutton, (1974) | 1 | Baseline TSH as well as TSH responses diminished. |
| Takahashi et al., 1974 | 36 | See text. |
| Ban et al., 1975 | 6 | Diminished in all patients. All patients euthyroid. No GH responses occurred. |
| Kirkegaard et al., 1975 | 10 | See text. |
| Widerlov and Sjostrom, 1975 | 10 | Baseline TSH as well as TSH responses lower than in hospitalized, non-depressed controls. |
| Maeda et al., 1975 | 13 | See text. |
| NORMAL RESPONSE FOUND | | |
| Shopsin et al., 1973 | 2 | Responses normal. |
| Dimitrikoudi et al., 1974 | 2 | Responses normal. |

findings on this point opposing one positive finding. On the other hand, Takahashi and co-workers (39) suggest that duration of illness correlates positively with the occurrence of the deficit. They supported this finding, obtained in their total population, by following three patients for an extended period. Two unipolar patients who had shown normal responses after

Table 2. Concordance of Pituitary and Clinical Findings

| Authors | TSH Depressed | TSH Recovered | PRL Depressed | PRL Recovered | GH Depressed | GH Recovered | Previous Drugs | Diagnosis | Severity | Duration |
|---|---|---|---|---|---|---|---|---|---|---|
| | | | | | | | Is the TSH Finding Related To: | | | |
| Prange et al., 1972 | Absent 2/10 | — | — | — | — | — | No | All Unipolar | No | — |
| Ehrensing et al., 1974 | ↓3/8 | — | ↓4/8 | — | — | — | — | No | Yes | — |
| Chazot et al., 1974 | ↓15/30 | — | — | — | ↑8/13 | — | — | — | — | — |
| Coppen et al., 1974 | Absent 4/16 | No change after 3 weeks | — | — | — | — | — | No | No | — |
| Takahashi et al., 1974 | ↓12/36 | — | — | — | — | — | — | No | No | Yes |
| Maeda et al., 1975 | ↓7/13 | 2/7 | ↑8/13 | No change | ↑8/13 | All normal | — | No | No | — |
| Kirkegaard et al., 1975 | ↓6/10 | 3/6 | — | — | — | — | — | No | — | — |
| Ban et al., 1975 | ↓5/6 | — | — | — | No positive response | — | — | All Unipolar | — | — |

8 and 16 months of illness showed deficient responses 9 months later, as illness progressed without remission.

Is a deficit in TSH response related to the state of being depressed or to the trait of having been depressed (or at high risk for future depression)? Data are inadequate to provide a definitive answer to this question, but it would appear that most patients who demonstrate this fault during depression do not correct it upon clinical recovery. This, it must be admitted, seems partly in conflict with the suggestion by Takahashi and his colleagues (39) that the fault develops as the consequence of prolonged illness.

Table 2 shows that two groups have studied PRL response to TRH. Ehrensing et al. (40) found that PRL response *decreased* in half their patients; Maeda et al. (38) found the response *increased* in slightly more than half, with no change upon recovery from depression. For the purposes of the present essay these contradictory findings will simply be set aside. The Japanese group were also at a loss to account for their contradiction of the findings by the New Orleans investigators.

Unlike the findings pertaining to PRL responses, the data pertaining to GH responses are consistent. Independently, Chazot et al. (41) and Maeda et al. (38) reported striking and nearly identical findings. In 8 of 13 depressed patients both groups of investigators found an acromegalic-like GH response to TRH—i.e., release of the pituitary hormone. Maeda and his colleagues found that this always normalized with recovery from depression.

Next we must attempt to sort out the relationships between the various pituitary responses to TRH. Ehrensing et al. (40) found PRL response decreased whenever TSH response was decreased; in addition, the former was decreased in one patient in whom the latter was normal. Chazot et al. (41) did not report the relationship of their TSH and GH findings. Maeda et al. (38) offered a detailed presentation of the interrelationships of their pituitary findings, and these have been simplified somewhat for presentation in Table 3. First, it can be seen that no pituitary finding or combination of findings relate to diagnosis, sex, age, or severity of illness. Among pituitary findings, relationships are equally obscure. Every possible combination of the typical changes is represented, though no patient is normal in every respect.

Before the significance of these findings can be assessed they must be criticized on purely endocrinological grounds. Here it is convenient to limit the discussion to the most widely confirmed finding—the frequent diminution of TSH response after TRH injection.

Hyperthyroidism is the most frequent cause of a diminished TSH response to TRH. However, all authors whose work is represented in Table 1 were careful to exclude this endocrinopathy. Nevertheless, some degree of thyroid activation is sometimes seen in depression (42,43), and it is conceiv-

Table 3. Concordance of Pituitary and Diagnostic Findings

| | Age | Severity | Responses to TRH | | |
| | | | TSH | PRL | GH |
| --- | --- | --- | --- | --- | --- |
| Unipolar Patients | | | | | |
| Women | 22 | Marked | N | ↑ | ↑ |
| | 25 | Marked | N | ↑ | ↑ |
| | 32 | Mild | N | ↑ | N |
| Men | 46 | Marked | ↓ | N | N |
| | 49 | Mild | ↓ | N | N |
| | 45 | Mild | N | N | ↑ |
| | 22 | Mild | ↓ | N | ↑ |
| | 38 | Mild | ↓ | ↑ | N |
| Bipolar Patients | | | | | |
| Women | 59 | Marked | N | N | ↑ |
| | 54 | Marked | ↓ | ↑ | ↑ |
| | 49 | Marked | ↓ | ↑ | N |
| | 38 | Marked | N | ↑ | ↑ |
| Men | 36 | Mild | ↓ | ↑ | ↑ |

Data from Maeda et al. (1975), *J. Clin. Endocrinol. Metab.* 40:501-505.

able that heightened thyroid state even within the usually cited normal range could damp TSH response through enhanced negative feedback on the anterior pituitary. Kirkegaard and her colleagues (44) were especially attentive to this possibility, but authors generally have found no consistent correlation in depressed patients between thyroid indices (all in the normal range) and TSH response. Takahashi et al. (39) provided telling evidence on this point when they showed that patients with *low* free thyroxine indices "paradoxically" also showed the most blunted TSH responses. One can submit the tentative conclusion that not all the blunted TSH responses seen in depressed patients can be accounted for by thyroid activation. Possibly some can, but not all.

Another potential explanation for the main finding, also based on changes in function in a peripheral endocrine gland, cannot presently be easily dismissed. It has been shown that chronically elevated cortisol levels interfere with the pituitary TSH response to TRH (45), though lowered cortisol levels, as in Addison's disease, have no effect (46). The most venerable endocrine finding in depression is elevated cortisol. However, certain considerations render it unlikely that elevated cortisol accounts for many, if any, cases of diminished TSH response: elevated cortisol tends to be related to severity of illness rather than to duration (47); diminished TSH response appears to be related more to duration than to severity (39). It becomes imperative, nevertheless, to examine cortisol levels in patients when TSH response to TRH is to be measured.

Let us assume that not all instances of the main finding can be set aside as a consequence of changes in function of the thyroid gland or of the adrenal cortex. The finding can then be discussed from two aspects: its value for clinical psychiatry as an empirical event and its heuristic value for understanding the biological basis for depression. In regard to the first consideration, it should be noted that Kirkegaard and her colleagues (44) found clinical relapse to be common when recovery of TSH response did not accompany clinical recovery. When pituitary recovery occurred along with clinical improvement, relapse was uncommon. All their patients were treated with ECT, and it appears possible that recovery of the TSH response may be an indicator of the sufficiency of treatment. Recently, with Loosen's leadership, we have studied the TSH responses to TRH of five men early in the course of the alcohol withdrawal syndrome (48). Only two men demonstrated normal responses. One showed a borderline low response; two showed virtually absent responses. Testing has not yet been carried out after patients have shown full recovery from the syndrome. Thus, the state/trait question is unresolved. Nevertheless, it is tantalizing to speculate that a pituitary response may help to illuminate the postulated genetic relationship between alcoholic patients and a subtype of depressed patients (49). In line with this reasoning, it would be interesting to examine psychiatrically and genealogically those few normal subjects who show a deficient TSH response.

Whatever the resolution of the above matters, it remains necessary to determine the neurobiological implications of the finding. If the fault does not reside in thyroid or adrenocortical function, then pituitary and hypothalamic function must be scrutinized. In pituitary hypothyroidism, the TSH response to TRH is deficient (50). However, in this disorder there is clear evidence of hypothyroidism, and no such evidence has been reported in the depressed patients studied. There is a rare disorder known as hypothalamic hypothyroidism, wherein hypothalamic TRH may be deficient. In this condition, as in pituitary hypothyroidism, there is evidence of diminished thyroid activity. Moreover, in hypothalamic hypothyroidism, pituitary TSH response to TRH is normal, not diminished (50). Thus, in depression one is left with an endocrine finding for which there is no ready explanation. Like most other authors, one can only state in a general way that it is evidence for a disruption of hypothalamic-pituitary integration.

The importance of brain biogenic amine function in psychiatric disturbance is so well established that there is a tendency to interpret new biological findings in terms of their implications for central amine function. The interpretation of endocrine data in this way is fraught with difficulty. It is true that levels of most peripheral hormones are influenced by pituitary hormones, whose levels are influenced by hypothalamic releasing factors, which are influenced by biogenic amines (51). However, relationships are complex. For example, some pituitary hormones (e.g., TSH) can be influenced by two hypothalamic releasing factors [THR and somatostatin (52)]. Some releasing factors may influence more than one pituitary hormone [somatostatin inhibits the release of GH (53) and TRH (52); luteinizing hormone-releasing hormone stimulates the release of LH (54) and follicle stimulating hormone (55)]. These complexities take one only to the hypothalamic releasing hormone level. If one wishes to extrapolate through this web to the biogenic amine level, one must appreciate that each releasing factor is more or less complexly influenced, positively or negatively, by one or more biogenic amines and perhaps by acetylcholine (51). This is an enormous field of inquiry in itself, and it is presently subject to contradictions and the complicating feature of species difference (56). Despite these difficulties, Sachar (6) has proposed some ingenious way to sort these matters out. Nevertheless, it appears premature to force the interpretation of present endocrine data more cephalad, as it were, than the level of hypothalamic releasing factors.

Interpretation at the releasing factor level may in fact have its own order of validity and importance. In a series of review statements we have marshaled the evidence that supports the view that releasing factors have intrinsic behavioral effects, quite apart from their acknowledged effects on pituitary tropic hormones (57,58,59,60).

How can endocrine data in depression be interpreted from the point of view of hypothalamic hormone function? One now encounters a limitation of the data that hampers their interpretation in any framework: in a given patient there is usually only one finding. [The study by Maeda et al. (38) is an elegant exception.] The most one can do, and this only tentatively, is to consider together the two findings pertaining to pituitary response in depression that seem best established. These are the diminished GH response to insulin hypoglycemia in postmenopausal depressed women (11,12), and the diminished TSH response to TRH in a wide variety of depressed patients. These defects must sometimes occur together, and when they do, one may postulate excessive hypothalamic activity of somatostatin (61). At the hypothalamic level this is the most parsimonious explanation of the two most prominent findings. Somatostatin, it will be recalled, inhibits the release of GH and inhibits the TSH response to TRH.

Animal studies are consistent with the formulation suggested above. Segal and Mandell (62) gave somatostatin to rats by slow intraventricular infusion and noted marked inhibition of spontaneous activity, while TRH had an opposite effect. In the course of work directed mainly toward endocrine changes, Siler et al. (63) gave large doses of somatostatin to monkeys and noted tranquilization. As we have suggested before (61), it would be of great interest to study the somatostatin-treated rat as a possible model of depression. One would examine such animals for the two endocrine responses typically altered in depression and for correction of the behavioral state by antidepressant drugs and TRH.

It is unlikely that the above formulation or any formulation like it will finally be found to describe all depressed patients. For example, Table 2 shows that some depressed patients have an *enhanced* growth hormone response to TRH. Table 3 records three patients who have a decreased TSH response (suggesting enhanced somatostatin activity) and an increased GH response (suggesting diminished somatostatin activity). Obviously there are depressed patients whose altered pituitary responses cannot be attributed to changes in somatostatin activity alone.

What are needed to promote our understanding of endocrine changes in depression are data from more than one kind of challenge to endocrine response—for example, insulin administration on one occasion and TRH administration on another. Repetition of studies when patients are in remission would also be valuable. Little is known as to whether endocrine findings in depression pertain to cause or consequence or are merely parallel findings.

Basic neurobiology is making rapid strides, and workers in the field can be depended upon to clarify the relations between biogenic amines, hypothalamic releasing factors, and pituitary tropic hormones. It is a challenge for clinical science to apply these findings to the clarification and treatment of mental illness.

**REFERENCES**

1. Silverman, C. *The Epidemiology of Depression*. Baltimore: The Johns Hopkins Press, 1968.
2. Kendell, R. E. The problem of classification, in A. Coppen and A. Walk, eds., *Recent Developments in Affective Disorders*. Ashford, Kent. 1968, pp. 15-26.
3. Winokur, G., and Cadoret, R. The irrelevance of the menopause to depressive disease,

in E. J. Sachar, ed., *Topics in Psychoendocrinology*, Seminars in Psychiatry, New York: Grune & Stratton, 1975, pp. 59-66.

4. Coppen, A., and Kessel, N. Menstruation and personality. *Brit. J. Psychiat.* 109:711-721, 1963.

5. Katz, J. L. Psychoendocrine considerations in anorexia nervosa, in E. J. Sachar, ed., *Topics in Psychoendocrinology*, Seminars in Psychiatry. New York: Grune & Stratton, 1975, pp. 121-134.

6. Sachar, E. J. Endocrine factors in psychopathological states, in J. Mendels, ed., *Biological Psychiatry*. New York: Wiley-Interscience, 1973, pp. 175-197.

7. Sachar, E. J., and Coppen, A. Biological aspects of affective psychoses, in G. Gaull, ed., *Biology of Brain Dysfunction*, Vol. 3. New York: Plenum, 1975, pp. 215-245.

8. Sachar, E. J. Corticosteroids in depressive illness. I. Reevaluation of control issues and the literature. *Arch. Gen. Psychiatry* 17:544-553, 1967.

9. Carroll, B. J. Plasma cortisol levels in depression, in B. Davies, B. J. Carroll, and R. M. Mowbray, eds., *Depressive Illnesses: Some Research Studies*. Springfield, Ill.: Charles C. Thomas, 1972, pp. 69-86.

10. Sachar, E. J., Hellman, L., Roffwarg, H. P., Halpern, F. S., Fukushima, D. K., and Gallagher, T. F. Disrupted 24-hour patterns of cortisol secretion in psychotic depression. *Arch. Gen. Psychiatry* 28 (1) :19-24, 1973.

11. Gruen, P. H., Sachar, E. J., Altman, N., and Sassin, J. Growth hormone responses to hypoglycemia in postmenopausal depressed women. *Arch. Gen. Psychiatry* 32 (1) : 31-33, 1975.

12. Sachar, E. J. Neuroendocrine abnormalities in depressive illness, in E. J. Sachar, ed., *Topics in Psychoendocrinology*, Seminars in Psychiatry. New York: Grune & Stratton, 1975, pp. 135-156.

13. Altman, N., Sachar, E. J., Gruen, P. H., Halpern, F. S., and Eto, S. Reduced plasma LH concentration in postmenopausal depressed women. *Psychosom. Med.* 37 (3) :274-276, 1975.

14. Prange, A. J., Jr., Wilson, I. C., Rabon, A. M., and Lipton, M. A. Enhancement of imipramine antidepressant activity by thyroid hormone. *Amer. J. Psychiat.* 126:457-469, 1969.

15. Wilson, I. C., Prange, A. J., Jr., McClane, T. K., Rabon, A. M., and Lipton, M. A. Thyroid-hormone enhancement of imipramine in nonretarded depressions. *New Eng. J. Med.* 282:1063-1067, 1970.

16. Prange, A. J., Jr., Wilson, I. C., Breese, G. R., and Lipton, M. A. Hormonal alteration of imipramine response: a review, in E. J. Sachar, ed., *Hormones, Behavior, and Psychopathology*. New York: Raven Press (in press) .

17. Prange, A. J., Jr., Wilson, I. C., Knox, A. E., McClane, T. K., Breese, G. R., Martin, B. R., Alltop, L. C., and Lipton, M. A. Thyroid-imipramine clinical and chemical interaction; evidence for a receptor deficit in depression. *J. Psychiat. Res.* 9:187-205, 1972.

18. Prange, A. J., Jr., Wilson, I. C., Knox, A., McClane, T. K., and Lipton, M. A. Enhancement of imipramine by thyroid stimulating hormone: clinical and theoretical implications. *Amer. J. Psychiatry* 127 (2) :191-199, 1970.

19. Earle, B. V. Thyroid hormone and tricyclic antidepressants in resistant depression. *Amer. J. Psychiatry* 126 (11) :1667-1669, 1970.

20. Coppen, A., Whybrow, P. C., Noguera, R., Maggs, R., and Prange, A. J., Jr. The comparative antidepressant value of L-tryptophan and imipramine with and without attempted potentiation by liothyronine. *Arch. Gen. Psychiatry* 26:234-241, 1972.

21. Wheatley, D. Potentiation of amitriptyline by thyroid hormone. *Arch. Gen. Psychiatry* 26:229-233, 1972.
22. Burgus, R., Dunn, T. F., Desiderio, D., and Guillemin, R. Structure moleculaire du facteur hypothalamique hypophysiotrope TRF d'origine ovine: mise en evidence par spectrometrie de mass de la sequence PCA-His-Pro-NH$_2$. *C. R. Acad. Sci. Paris*, 269: 1870, 1969.
23. Boler, J., Enzmann, F., Folkers, K., Bowers, C. Y., and Schally, A. V. The identity of chemical and hormone properties of the thyrotropin releasing hormone and pyroglutamyl-histadyl-proline-amide. *Biochem. Biophy. Res. Comm.* 37:705, 1969.
24. Jackson, I. M. D., and Reichlin, S. Thyrotropin releasing hormone (TRH) : distribution in the brain and urine of the rat. *Life Sci.* 14:2247-2257, 1974.
25. Jackson, I. M. D., and Reichlin, S. Thyrotropin releasing hormone (TRH) : distribution in hypothalamic and extrahypothalamic brain tissues of mammalian and submammalian chordates. *Endocrinology* 96:854-862, 1974.
26. Winokur, A., and Utiger, R. D. Thyrotropin-releasing hormone: regional distribution in the rat brain. *Science* 185:265-267, 1974.
27. McCann, S. M., Fawcett, C. P., and Krulich, L. Hypothalamic hypophysical releasing and inhibiting hormones in *MTP Int. Rev. Sci. Series I Physiol. Vol. 5, Endocrine Physiols*, London: Butterworths, 1974.
28. Mueller, G. P., Chen, H. J., and Meites, J. In vivo stimulation of prolactin release in the rat by synthetic TRH. *Proc. Soc. Exp. Biol. and Med.* 144 (2) :613-615, 1973.
29. Irie, M., and Tsushima, T. Increase of serum growth hormone concentration following thyrotropin-releasing hormone injection in patients with acromegaly or gigantism. *J. Clin. Endo. Metab.* 35:97-100, 1972.
30. Plotnikoff, N. P., Prange, A. J., Jr., Breese, G. R., Anderson, M. S., and Wilson, I. C. Thyrotropin releasing hormone: enhancement of DOPA activity by a hypothalamic hormone. *Science* 178:417-418, 1972.
31. Everett, G. M. The DOPA response potentiation test and its use in screening for antidepressant drugs. Proceedings of the First International Symposium on Antidepressant Drugs, Excerpta Medica International Congress Series No. 122, Milan, 1966.
32. Prange, A. J., Jr., and Wilson, I. C. Thyrotropin releasing hormone (TRH) for the immediate relief of depression: a preliminary report. *Psychopharmacologia* 26:82, 1972.
33. Prange, A. J., Jr., Wilson, I. C., Lara, P. P., Alltop, L. B., and Breese, G. R. Effects of thyrotropin-releasing hormone in depression. *Lancet* ii:999-1002, 1972.
34. Prange, A. J., Jr., Nemeroff, C. B., Breese, G. R., Cooper, B., Lipton, M. A., and Wilson, I. C. Behavioral effects of polypeptide hormone, in S. H. Snyder, L. L. Iverson, and S. D. Iverson, eds., *Handbook of Pharmacology*. New York: Plenum (in press) .
35. Prange, A. J., Jr., Wilson, I. C., Lara, P. P., Wilber, J. F., Breese, G. R., Alltop, L. B., and Lipton, M. A. TRH (Lopremone) : psychobiological responses of normal women. *Arch. Gen. Psychiatry* 29:28-32, 1973.
36. Frontiers of Hormone Research, Vol. I, *Thyrotropin Releasing Hormone*, R. Hall, I. Werner, H. Holgate, and M. Marois, eds. Basel: S. Karger, 1971.
37. Ozawa, Y., and Shishiba, Y. Lack of TRH-induced TSH secretion in a patient with Klinefelter's syndrome: a case report. *Endocrinol. Japan.* 22 (3) :269-273, 1975.

38. Maeda, K., Kato, Y., Ohgo, S., Chihara, K., Yoshimoto, Y., Yamaguchi, N., Kuromaru, S., and Imura, H. Growth hormone and prolactin release after injection of thyrotropin-releasing hormone in patients with depression. *J. Clin. Endocrinol. Metab.* 40:501-505, 1975.

39. Takahashi, S., Kondo, H., Yoshimura, M., and Ochi, Y. Thyrotropin responses to TRH in depressive illness: relation to clinical subtypes and prolonged duration of depressive episode. *Folia Psychiatrica et Neurological Japonica* 28 (4) :355-365, 1974.

40. Ehrensing, R. H., Kastin, A. J., Schalch, D. S., Friesen, H. G., Vargas, J. R., and Schally, A. V. Affective state and thyrotropin and prolactin responses after repeated injections of thyrotropin-releasing hormone in depressed patients. *Amer. J. Psychiatry* 131 (6) :714-718, 1974.

41. Chazot, G., Chalumeau, A., Aimard, G., Mornex, M., Garde A., Schott, B., and Girard, P. F. Thyrotropin releasing hormone and depressive states: from agroagonines to TRH. *Lyon Med.* 231 (9) :831-836, 1974.

42. Dewhurst, K. E., El Kabir, D. J., Harris, G. W., and Mandelbrote, B. M. A. review of the effect of stress on the activity of the central nervous-pituitary-thyroid axis in animals and man. *Confin. Neurol.* 30:161-196, 1968.

43. Whybrow, P. C., Coppen, A., Prange, A. J., Jr., Noguera, R., and Bailey, J. E. Thyroid function and the response to liothyronine in depression. *Arch. Gen. Psychiatry* 26:242-245, 1972.

44. Kirkegaard, C., Norlem, N., Lauridsen, U. B., Bjorum, N., and Christiansen, C. Protirelin stimulation test and thyroid function during treatment of depression. *Arch. Gen. Psychiatry* 32 (9) :1115-1118, 1975.

45. Otsuki, M., Dakoda, M., and Baba, S. Influence of glucocorticoids on TRF mediated TSH response in man. *J. Clin. Endocrin.* 36:95-102, 1973.

46. Woolf, P. D., Gonzalez-Barcena, D., Schalch, D. S., Lee, L. A., Arzac, J. P., Schally, A. V., and Kastin, A. J. Lack of effect of steroids on thyrotropin-releasing hormone (TRH) mediated thyrotropin (TSH) release in man. *Neuroendo.* 13:56-62, 1973/74.

47. Gibbons, J. L. Cortisol secretion rate in depressive illness. *Arch. Gen. Psychiatry* 10: 572-575, 1964.

48. Loosen, P. T., Wilson, I. C., Lara, P. P., Prange, A. J., Jr., and Pettus, C. Treatment of depressive state in alcohol withdrawal syndromes by thyrotropin releasing hormone. *Arzneimmillel-forschung* (in press) .

49. Winokur, G. Diagnostic and genetic aspects of affective illness. *Psychiatric Annals* (3) 2:6-15, 1973.

50. Pittman, J. A., Jr. Thyrotropin-releasing hormone. *Adv. Int. Med.* 19:303-325, 1974.

51. Frohman, L. A. Neurotransmitters as regulators of endocrine function. *Hospital Practice* 54-67, 1975.

52. Siler, T. M., Yen, S. S. C., and Guillemin, R. Inhibition of somatostatin on the release of TSH induced in man by thyrotropin-releasing factor. *J. Clin. Endo. Metab.* 38 (5) : 742-745, 1974.

53. Brazeau, P., Vale, W., Burgus, R., Ling, N., Butcher, M., Rivier, J., and Guillemin, R. Hypothalamic polypeptide that inhibits the secretion of immunoreactive pituitary growth hormone. *Science* 179:77-79, 1973.

54. Kastin, A. J., Schally, A. V., Zarate, A., Arimura, A., Gonzales-Barcena, D., Medeiros-Neto, G. A., and Schalch, D. S. Analysis of clinical studies with natural and syn-

thetic luteinizing hormone-releasing hormone in man. *Israel J. Med. Sci.* 10:1305-1313, 1974.

55. Malacara, J. M., Bowers, C. Y., Gomez, F., Hernandez, S., Change, J., and Folkers, K. Stimulation of LH and FSH release by pGlu-His-Trp-Ser-Tyr-Gly-Leu-Arg-Pro-Gly-NH$_2$ in normal subjects by rapid i.v. injection and by 8 hour infusion, in C. Gaul and E. Rosemberg, eds., *Hypothalamic Hypophysiotropic Hormones: Physiological and Clinical Studies.* Amsterdam: Excerpta Medica, 1973, pp. 291-298.

56. Reichlin, S. Regulation of somatotrophic hormone secretion, in R. O. Greep, E. B. Astwood, E. Knoline, W. H. Sawyer, and S. R. Geiger, eds., *Handbook of Physiol. Endocrinology IV, Part 2.* Washington, D. C.: Amer. Physiology Soc., 1974, pp. 405-447.

57. Prange, A. J., Jr., and Wilson, I. C. Behavioral effects of thyrotropin releasing hormone in animals and man: a generic hypothesis. *Psychopharmacology Bulletin* 11:22-24, 1975.

58. Prange, A. J., Jr., Wilson, I. C., Breese, G. R., and Lipton, M. A. Behavioral effects of hypothalamic releasing hormones in animals and men, in W. H. Gispen, Tj. B. van Wimersma Greidanus, B. Bohus, and D. de Wied, eds., *Hormones, Homeostasis and the Brain,* Progress in Brain Research 42. The Netherlands: Elsevier, 1975, pp. 1-9.

59. Prange, A. J., Jr., Breese, G. R., Wilson, I. C., and Lipton, M. A. Brain behavioral effects of hypothalamic releasing hormone: a generic hypothesis, in W. E. Stumpf and L. D. Grant, eds., *Anatomical Neuroendocrinology.* Basel: Karger (in press).

60. Prange, A. J., Jr., Breese, G. R., Wilson, I. C., and Lipton, M. A. Pituitary and suprapituitary hormones: brain-behavioral effects, in E. J. Sachar, ed., *Topics in Psychoendocrinology,* Seminars in Psychiatry. New York: Grune & Stratton, 1975, pp. 105-119.

61. Prange, A. J., Jr., Breese, G. R., Jahnke, G. D., Martin, B. R., Cooper, B. R., Cott, J. M., Wilson, I. C., Alltop, L. B., Lipton, M. A., Bissette, G., Nemeroff, C. B., and Loosen, P. T. Modification of pentobarbital effects by natural and synthetic polypeptides: dissociation of brain and pituitary effects. *Life Sci.* 16:1907-1914, 1975.

62. Segal, D. S., and Mandell, A. J. Differential behavioral effects of hypothalamic polypeptides, in A. J. Prange, Jr., ed., *The Thyroid Axis, Drugs, and Behavior.* New York: Raven Press, 1974, pp. 129-133.

63. Siler, T. M., VandenBurg, G., Yen, S. S. C., Brazeau, P., Vale, W., and Guillemin, R. Inhibition of growth of hormone release in humans by somatostatin. *J. Clin. Endo. Metab.* 37:632-634, 1973.

64. Kastin, A. J., Ehrensing, R. H., Schalch, D. S., and Anderson, M. S. Improvement in mental depression with decreased thyrotropin response after administration of thyrotropin-releasing hormone. *Lancet* ii:740-742, 1972.

65. Coppen, A., Montgomery, S., Peet, M., and Bailey, J. Thyrotropin-releasing hormone in the treatment of depression. *Lancet* ii:433-434, 1974.

66. Kirkegaard, C., Norlem, N., Birk Lauridsen, U., and Bjorum, N. Thyrotropin-releasing hormone and depression. *Lancet* ii:722, 1974.

67. Hutton, W. N. Thyrotropin-releasing hormone in depression. Lancet ii:53, 1974.

68. Ban, T. A., Lehmann, H. E., Nair, N. P. V., Pecknold, J. C., and Orbach, L. Clinical studies with TRH, 17th National Meeting of APhA Academy of Pharmaceutical Sciences, New Orleans, November 10-14, 1974.

69. Widerlov, E., and Sjostrom, R. Effects of thyrotropin releasing hormone on endogenous depression, *Nordisk Psykiatrisk Tidskrift* (in press).

70. Shopsin, B., Shenkman, L., Blum, M., and Hollander, C. T3 and TSH response to TRH: newer aspects of lithium-induced thyroid disturbance in man. *Psychopharmacology Bulletin* 9:29, 1973.
71. Dimitrikoudi, M., Hanson-Norty, E., and Jenner, F. A. T.R.H. in psychoses. *Lancet* ii:456, 1974.

2

# Central Biogenic Amines and Theories of Depression and Mania

## JOHN M. DAVIS

I will first try to outline the possible role of biogenic amines in current theories of depression and then summarize the theoretical developments which have appeared more recently. Then I will consider the practical implications of the theory and give a critique of it. The theories involving biogenic amines in depression derive from the observation that there are three types of organic treatment for depressive disorders: (1) the tricyclic antidepressants, (2) the monoamine oxidase inhibitors and (3) the electroshock treatment (ECT); and also from clinical evidence that a number of drugs can precipitate depression in the predisposed individual. These include reserpine, alpha methyl dopa, and propanolol. Historically, as early as 1958 the innovative pharmacologists Everett and Toman (1), working at Abbott Laboratory, noted many of the pharmacological clues suggesting that the MAO inhibitors functionally increased biogenic amines, etc., and hence raised the question as to whether a deficit in biogenic amines could be to some degree related to depression. Working independently at about the same time, the British investigators Pare and Sandler (2) in effect formulated the same biogenic amine theory and tested it by administering dopa, which should be converted to dopamine and norepinephrine by depressed patients. Working independently in Boston, Schildkraut, Klerman and their co-workers (3) tested the same hypothesis based on the therapeutic response to dopa. The existence of three types of treatment which may increase nor-adrenergic function, and the fact that drugs which lower brain norepine-phrine through different mechanisms caused depression, suggested that per-haps a deficit in norepinephrine was somehow related to depressive disease. Bunney and I (4) reviewed this evidence and formulated it into the catecho-lamine hypothesis. Schildkraut (5) also drew together the same information in a review paper very similar in content to ours. It should be noted that much the same evidence applies to serotonin—namely, the tricyclic anti-depressants and the MAO inhibitors may in some sense potentiate serotonin, and reserpine lowers brain serotonin. Hence, the same hypothesis could be applied to depression. Evidence was compiled for this serotonin theory of depression by a number of British workers such as Alec Coppen (6).

The principal evidence for the biogenic amine theory of depression lies in the pharmacologic studies of the drugs which aggravate or relieve depres-sion. The tricyclic antidepressants are probably the most effective drug treat-ment of depression. All the tricyclic antidepressants inhibit the uptake of biogenic amines. There is some difference in the potency of the various drugs with respect to their relative ability to inhibit the uptake of norepine-phrine or serotonin, but a common property shared by all these drugs is their ability to inhibit the uptake of biogenic amines. Platelets have been used as a model for the nerve endings which possess a membrane pump for serotonin. In addition, studies of platelets from patients taken at baseline and again when therapeutic concentrations of the tricyclics have been reached (7) in-dicate that at therapeutic concentrations, their membrane pump is inhibited. There are similar data available based on studies in patients off and on tricyclic antidepressants with respect to the blood pressure raising effects of tyramine and norepinephrine which indicate that the membrane pump is inhibited peripherally with clinical doses (8). It often takes from three or four days to several weeks before the antidepressant effect of the drug is clinically observed. The membrane pump is inhibited almost immediately. There is no adequate explanation for the lag period between the physiolog-ical effect and the therapeutic response. It takes a week or so to achieve a steady tricyclic level, and the lag period may be partially explained by this, but the exact and complete explanation of the lag period remains an enigma.

The tricyclic antidepressants exert prophylactic properties by prevent-ing recurrence of depression. This raises the possibility of a different type of biochemical-clinical comparison. If tolerance developed to the uptake-inhibiting properties of the tricyclics, then it would be difficult to explain the long-lasting effect of the tricyclic. In this laboratory we have shown that the uptake-inhibiting properties persist over the course of many days, and apparently tolerance does not develop to this.

The monoamine oxidase inhibitors block the intracellular deamination of catecholamines, thus raising levels of biogenic amines in the brain. There is a substantial lag period after initiation of treatment with MAO inhibitors and biochemical response. There is some evidence from autopsy brain studies that it takes several weeks before sufficient MAO inhibition is actually achieved. Hence the time course of the clinical response to MAO inhibitors is consistent with the pharmacologic evidence.

Parenthetically, it should be mentioned that tranylcypromine (Parnate) inhibits the membrane pump as well as MAO, and so it is not a useful drug for theory building. Other drugs such as iproniazid or phenelzine are primarily MAO inhibitors and it is on the therapeutic action of these drugs that the theory rests. Clinically, it has been suggested that a subtype of depressed patients—namely, hysterical outpatients with secondary depression —may respond better to the MAO inhibitors than to the tricyclics. This clinical observation has not been extensively investigated, and additional empirical evidence is required for its confirmation. It is relevant to note that there has been a recent series of studies comparing the MAO inhibitor phenelzine (Nardil) to placebo in depressed outpatients. This body of literature provides substantial evidence for the efficacy of phenelzine in this population. This is a uniform finding, emerging clearly from several studies of outpatient depressions (9). There is some evidence from inpatient studies that phenelzine is not a particularly useful drug in schizophrenics with secondary depression. It is also relevant to note that phenelzine is only effective when adequate degrees of MAO inhibition are achieved. Donald Robinson and his co-workers in Vermont show that 30 mg of phenelzine is ineffective; it is effective only when 60 mg or more is given. Another study found that 90 mg/day was effective only in patients who were slow metabolizers of the drug and hence would have higher plasma levels, but that this dose was ineffective in fast metabolizers (10). This would indicate that the correct dose of phenelzine for many patients is in the range of 60 to 90 mg, although some may require higher dosages than this. In addition to providing evidence relevant to the biogenic amine theory of depression, the MAO inhibitors are an effective class of antidepressants. Some patients who fail to respond to tricyclic drugs may have a therapeutic response to MAO inhibitors, and there is clearly a place for MAO inhibitors in psychiatry.

Studies of animals given ECT indicate that the synthesis of norepinephrine is increased by ECT, an increase which persists after the series of convulsive treatment is terminated. This raises the question whether ECT increases catecholamine synthesis in humans. The rate-limiting enzyme in the synthesis of dopamine and norepinephrine is tyrosine hydroxylase. If ECT increased synthesis through an enzymatic mechanism, therefore, it would be expected that if catecholamine synthesis is increased by ECT, the synthesis of dopamine as well as norepinephrine should be increased. Recently, Dysken and his co-workers in our group have been able to confirm the initial observation of Lebensohn that patients who have Parkinson's disease experience an improvement in their parkinsonian symptoms as well as depression after treatment with ECT. We also observed that the time course of improvement of the parkinsonian symptoms as well as the depressive symptoms coincided. This would be evidence that ECT does increase catecholamine synthesis in man. Drugs which lower adrenergic functions seem to cause depression in predisposed individuals (4). For example, reserpine can cause depression in as high as 15% of some series of hypertensive patients treated with the compound. These same patients often have episodes of depression unrelated to reserpine, so a predisposition to depression is apparently involved. Hypertensive patients often are treated with a variety of antihypertensive agents throughout their lifetime. Many patients who have had reserpine depressions also experience depression when given alpha methyl dopa (4). In addition, patients who have had reserpine depression may also experience depressions when given propanolol in higher than normal doses. Both reserpine and alpha methyl dopa lower brain norepinephrine levels, although they do so through different mechanisms. Propanolol is a beta blocker and so may interfere with adrenergic transmission through its blockade of beta receptors. The propanolol depressions are not as well established as the alpha methyl dopa and reserpine depressions in that depression was only observed in one report when higher than usual doses of propanolol were used. Thus there is a substantial body of evidence suggesting that potentiating norepinephrine may alleviate depression and lowering norepinephrine may cause depression. This concept is based on noradrenergic function and does not necessarily mean a physical lowering or raising of the amount of norepinephrine in the brain. It could be a deficit in one or a number of areas, including synthesis, storage release, reuptake, receptor site level, and feedback level. Although it is convenient in discussing the catecholamine hypothesis to refer to high or low brain norepinephrine, we would emphasize that the theory does not necessarily imply changes in levels but speaks more generally of noradrenergic function; abnormal functioning may not necessarily be paralleled by an abnormality in levels.

Lithium is the drug of choice in treating mania. Does its pharmacology provide a clue to the biochemistry of depression? There is no consensus on how lithium produces its antimanic effect (11). In our laboratory we have found that lithium increases the rate of norepinephrine uptake into a rat nerve-ending preparation (12,13). Thus, in a descriptive sense, lithium would have the opposite action of the tricyclics. By increasing the rate of reuptake, lithium would remove norepinephrine from the receptor site and thus exert an anti-norepinephrine effect on function. The tricyclic anti-depressants, by retarding the reuptake of norepinephrine, leave more nore-pinephrine available to stimulate the receptor and thus potentiate central norepinephrine. This effect has been replicated in several other laboratories and tends to confirm our own observations.

The next question to ask would be whether or not lithium does in fact increase the action of the membrane pump in man. Murphy, Colburn, Davis, and Bunney (14) showed that treatment with lithium increases the uptake of serotonin by the platelet membrane pump above the uptake level at baseline. Since the platelet membrane pump is similar to the nerve membrane pump, the evidence is consistent that at clinically used concentrations of lithium, the rate of uptake of the membrane pump is augmented. When norepinephrine is infused, there is a transitory increase in blood pressure. This increase in blood pressure is terminated by the membrane pump; the norepinephrine stimulates the smooth muscles of the arteries, producing the elevation in blood pressure. As the norepinephrine is taken up and stored by noradrenergic nerve endings in the blood vessels, this increase in blood pressure is terminated, because the membrane pump removes norepinephrine from its site of action. If lithium increases the rate of norepinephrine uptake, then one would expect a lower blood pressure response in patients on lithium. Dr. Fann, in an elegant experiment, observed this by measuring the pressure response to norepinephrine at a baseline period and after lithium administration to hypomanic patients (15). Lithium may also act through other mechanisms; it may act directly on the receptor site. Although there is no consensus about how lithium produces its therapeutic action, the above experiments are consistent with the catecholamine theory of depression.

There is no direct test of the hypothesis, since norepinephrine does not pass the blood-brain barrier. Infusion of peripheral norepinephrine should not benefit depression. In addition, urinary excretion of norepinephrine only reflects peripheral pools of norepinephrine, and is not relevant in any direct way to central norepinephrine function. Work at the Illinois State Psychiatric Institute indicates that the norepinephrine metabolite 3-hydroxy-4-methoxy phenyl glycol (MHPG) is largely produced in the brain and may provide a marker for brain norepinephrine. Urinary epinephrine and normetanephrine reflect only the storage of norepinephrine in the periphery. Metanephrine reflects adrenal epinephrine urinary metanephrine originating in the adrenal medulla. Some MHPG originates from the periphery, but a fair amount originates in the brain. Just what percentage of the urinary excretion of MHPG comes from the brain or the periphery is not known at the present time. Though it does not provide a perfect measure of brain norepinephrine turnover, however, MHPG does to some degree reflect norepinephrine synthesis in the brain and does provide an observable marker for brain norepinephrine. Low urinary MHPG's would therefore reflect low brain norepinephrine synthesis. It is of considerable interest that the workers at the Illinois State Psychiatric Institute have shown that primary depressed patients excrete low amounts of urinary MHPG (16,17). Not all depressions excrete low MHPG's, only some. This finding would be consistent with the hypothesis that those depressed patients who have low MHPG have low norepinephrine synthesis in their brain. It is also of interest that manic patients have high urinary MHPG levels in comparison to their excretion in a normothymic period or when depressed. This also is consistent with a catecholamine hypothesis.

Another strategy which has been used to investigate whether or not there is a functional abnormality of biogenic amines in the brain is the endocrine technique. The secretion of peripheral hormones such as cortisol or growth hormone is ultimately under central control of biogenic amines in the brain mediated by releasing factors which initiate a chain of command to ultimate secretion of a given hormone. Techniques for measuring the releasing factors in man are still in the developmental stages, but the actual hormones at the end of the chain of regulation can be measured in blood and/or urine. Thus hormonal abnormalities could reflect abnormalities in the biogenic amines that control the secretion of releasing factors at the central level. It is therefore of interest that many depressed patients have an abnormality of cortisol regulation. They excrete excessively high amounts of cortisol and furthermore have a disorder of the regulation of cortisol in that they fail to suppress cortisol secretion when given exogenous steroids (16-20). One of the central biogenic amines which governs cortisol regulation is norepinephrine, and the direction of this regulation is consistent with the norepinephrine hypothesis—namely, low norepinephrine centrally is consistent with high peripheral cortisol. It has also been shown that some depressed patients have abnormally low release of growth hormone following insulin stimulation (23). Since there is control centrally of growth hormone by norepinephrine in the direction which would be consistent with low growth hormone, this evidence is also consistent with the catecholamine hypothesis. Like most physiologic functions, hormones are under the control of multiple homeostatic systems, so that although the evidence is consistent with the norepinephrine theory, it is not definitive; it depends on the assumption that the hormonal systems which govern the release of these releasing

**Table 1. Pharmacological Evidence
Evidence in the Norepinephrine (NE) Theory of Depression**

|  | Mechanism | Therapeutic |
|---|---|---|
| Tricyclic Antidepressant | Potentiate norepine-phrine (NE) by inhibiting uptake pump | Benefit depression |
| MAO inhibitors | Potentiate NE by inhibiting its destruction | Benefit depression |
| ECT | Increase NE synthesis | Benefit depression |
| Reserpine | Lower brain NE by decreased storage | Cause depression |
| $\alpha$ methyl dopa | Lower brain NE by displacement | Cause depression |
| Propanolol | Blocks $\beta$ receptor | Cause depression |

factors have the same deficit as the hormonal systems governing affect. Since many amines could be involved in the regulation of hormones, this evidence, although definitely supporting the catecholamine theory, is not definitive. Recently, Garver, Hengeveld, Pandey, Dekirmenjian, and I have been investigating the endocrine strategies and correlating this with urinary MHPG.

Much the same story can be told for serotonin. The MAO inhibitors block the destruction of serotonin; the tricyclic antidepressants block the re-uptake of serotonin; reserpine lowers brain serotonin levels. Indeed, the serotonin theory of depression has been particularly popular in England, whereas the norepinephrine theory of depression has been much more discussed in the United States. Presumably this relates to the interest of investigators in the United Kingdom in serotonin rather than to the possibility that Americans have norepinephrine depressions and the British have serotonin depressions. It is possible that depression is truly caused by low norepinephrine and there is only minimal abnormality of serotonin levels in depression. It is also possible that depression could be caused by low serotonin levels, with norepinephrine playing either a minor or negligible role. There are several other possibilities, however. These have been elaborated in two ways: one is the so-called permissive theory of depression and mania, and the other is the two-disease theory. The permissive theory was suggested by Kety (24) and Prange (25) and suggests that an abnormality in two trans-

**Table 2. Laboratory Evidence for Depression**

1. Low urinary MHPG (NE metabolite) in primary depression.
2. High cortisol production and factors to suppress dexamethasone.
3. Low insulin stimulated growth hormones.

mitters may be involved in depression—namely, when a patient has any affective disorder (either depression or mania), his brain serotonin level is invariably low.

The permissive theory is similar to the norepinephrine theory of depression in that it postulates that low norepinephrine is associated with depression and high norepinephrine is associated with mania. The new departure of the permissive theory is the suggestion that serotonin may be low in both mania and depression. Clinically, it is a widespread observation that manic patients can be depressed to some degree at the same time. Many manic patients show a good deal of depressive affect at the same time they are displaying a manic flight of ideas, euphoria, grandiosity, and associated symptoms. Some manic patients have episodes of depressive affect, crying, and sadness, intermixed with mania. Although most of the time they may be showing many features of mania, for short periods of time, often only 30 or 60 seconds, they may suddenly feel very depressed and start crying. The term permissive refers to the fact that low serotonin must be present in order for patients to have an affective disturbance of either mania or depression. This is illustrated in Table 2. Since low serotonin and high norepinephrine accompanies mania, the raising of brain serotonin should benefit mania. This can be accomplished by giving serotonin's precursor, tryptophan, using the precursor loading strategy. The precursor loading strategy is based on administering the precursor of serotonin: tryptophan or 5-hydroxy tryptophan. Tryptophan is particularly relevant, since it passes the blood-brain barrier and is partly converted to serotonin. There is some evidence that brain serotonin levels are controlled by brain tryptophan levels and brain tryptophan levels are controlled by *total* plasma tryptophan, although other substances in plasma which compete with tryptophan for transport within the brain can affect the brain control of serotonin by blood tryptophan levels. The permissive theory has been tested by Prange and his associates (25), who administered tryptophan to manic patients and found that tryptophan had a considerable antimanic property; it was essentially the equivalent of neuroleptics. If this work is cross-validated, it would be an important step in our attempts to build a theory of affective disorders. Dr. Mendels has reviewed in

Table 3.

---

**NOREPINEPHRINE THEORY OF AFFECTIVE DISEASE**

Depression = low NE

Mania      = high NE

**SEROTONIN THEORY OF DEPRESSION**

Depression = low serotonin

Mania      = high serotonin

**PERMISSIVE THEORY**

Depression low NE, low serotonin

Mania high NE, low serotonin

**TWO-DISEASE THEORY**

| NE Type | Serotonin Type |
|---|---|
| Depression—low NE, normal serotonin | Depression—low serotonin, normal NE |
| No specific theory of mania | No specific theory of mania |

---

his volume the precursor loading strategy of affective disturbance. Evidence that serotonin may be low in depression rests primarily on the indirect evidence of the biogenic amine hypothesis and also on the observations that depressed patients do tend to have low or mean 5-hydroxy indoleacetic acid levels in their cerebrospinal fluid at baseline and also following probenecid treatment (26-31). In addition, we and others have found low brain serotonin and/or 5-hydroxy indoleacetic acid in autopsy brains (32). These differences are not large, but they are a fairly consistent finding from study to study. Indeed, if tryptophan benefits mania, it would indicate that serotonin plays a somewhat paradoxical role with respect to affective disturbance. Low levels of serotonin are present in some depressed patients' brains/CSF. Tryptophan may help some depressed patients, although the evidence of this is controversial. Mendels discusses it in some detail. The fact that tryptophan may help mania implies that mania may in part also be caused by low serotonin levels. The permissive theory holds that a deficit or other functional disturbance of the transmitter agent of both the norepinephrine and serotonin systems causes mania and depression.

This is conceptually distinct from the theory which postulates that there are norepinephrine depressions and there are serotonin depressions. Thus the subtype or two-disease theory of depression holds there are two types of depressive disease. One subtype is the result of low levels of norepinephrine, and the other subtype results from low levels of serotonin. The permissive theory, in contrast, holds that all patients with depression have low levels of norepinephrine and serotonin.

In considering the two-disease theory, evidence that there are serotonin depressions derives from the fact that *some*, but not all, depressed patients have low levels of 5-hydroxy indoleacetic acid in their cerebrospinal fluid, either at baseline or after probenecid treatment (26-31). Furthermore, it is this subtype, in those patients with low levels of CSF 5HIAA, that responds to tryptophan. This work is discussed in the chapter of this volume by Burns and Mendels in more detail. There is also evidence that some but not all depressed patients have a deficit of norepinephrine. The fact that this is present in only some patients suggests that only a subtype of depressed patients may have low norepinephrine depressions. More precisely, Maas, Dekirmenjian, Jones, and Fawcett (33-34) at the Illinois State Psychiatric Institute have shown that some, but not all, depressed patients excrete low levels of MHPG. These low MHPG excretors tend to respond to the tricyclic antidepressants, imipramine and desipramine. Further, on detailed diagnostic examination, the low MHPG depressions tend to be diagnosed as primary depressions by the Research Diagnostic Criteria and similar diagnostic schemes. It has also been observed clinically that some patients will respond to imipramine and not to amitriptyline, and other patients respond to amitriptyline and not to imipramine. Furthermore, amitriptyline may not be a good inhibitor of norepinephrine or norepinephrine uptake (35,36,37). We mentioned above that although all the tricyclic antidepressants inhibit the uptake of biogenic amines to some degree, there are clear differences in their ability to inhibit uptakes. Imipramine and amitriptyline are more effective in inhibiting serotonin uptake, while desmethyl derivatives such as nortriptyline or desipramine are more effective at inhibiting norepinephrine uptake. This is further complicated by the fact that imipramine and amitriptyline are metabolized in the body to desipramine and nortriptyline. However, imipramine primarily metabolizes to desipramine, whereas amitriptyline is converted to nortriptyline to a much lesser extent. Since imipramine is largely converted to desipramine, it will strongly inhibit norepinephrine. Since the predominant compound after amitriptyline administration is still amitriptyline, it would be more effective in inhibiting serotonin uptake. Moreover, there may be a difference in the potency of the two drugs with respect to norepinephrine and serotonin, amitriptyline being most effective in inhibiting serotonin uptake, while imipramine, desipramine, or nortriptyline is more effective in inhibiting norepinephrine uptake. The two-amine theory of depression combines this evidence and states that some depressions are caused by low norepinephrine. These patients are helped by imipramine,

desipramine, nortriptyline, or protriptyline, which are most effective in inhibiting the reuptake of norepinephrine. Other depressions are caused by
low levels of serotonin, and these patients are helped by amitriptyline, which
is particularly effective in inhibiting the reuptake of serotonin. This theory
has not been directly tested, since no investigator has as yet randomly assigned patients to imipramine or amitriptyline and measured urinary
MHPG and CSF 5-hydroxy indoleacetic acid prior to treatment.

The two-disease theory would suggest that some individuals would have
low MHPG and normal 5HIAA and hence would have low-norepinephrine
depressions. It would also suggest that some patients have low 5HIAA with
normal MHPG, and would have low-serotonin depressions. Low-norepinephrine depressions should respond to imipramine, desipramine, nortriptyline, or protriptyline, and low-serotonin depressions should respond differentially to amitriptyline. We are at present engaged in a random assignment
double-blind study to test this hypothesis in collaboration with four other
centers: Yale, University of Pennsylvania, Cornell, and Washington University. It is absolutely essential in such a study to have random assignment of
patients to the imipramine or amitriptyline group after the initial assessment
of urinary MHPG or CSF 5HIAA. I will not review in detail here the evidence for and against these hypotheses or the limitations of both types of
evidence. In my judgment, however, the two-disease concept is interesting
and there is some evidence supporting it, but it is not definitive. It is nevertheless important to discuss how these theories may be relevant to practice.

According to the original biogenic amine theory, whether it be the norepinephrine or the serotonin variety, all the tricyclic drugs have the same
basic pharmacologic action, the inhibition of uptake of the biogenic amines.
It would follow that if a patient failed to respond to one tricyclic, he might
not respond to another tricyclic. From this point of view, the single-disease
theories would have the same implication for treatment as the permissive
theory in the sense that one would assume that if a patient failed to respond
to adequate doses of one tricyclic, he would not respond to another. The
two-disease theory has a different implication for treatment. If a patient fails
to respond to amitriptyline, he might have a norepinephrine depression
which would respond to imipramine or to the other norepinephrine uptake
inhibitors. On the other hand, if a patient fails to respond to one of the
norepinephrine uptake inhibitors, he might respond to amitriptyline, a serotonin uptake inhibitor. The two-disease theory is not proven, however. Of
course, prior to the two-disease theory there was no empirical evidence indicating that if a patient didn't respond to one tricyclic, other tricyclics
would also fail. There was no verified evidence that trying a second tricyclic
would be useless. With the two-disease theory there is a pharmacologic ra-

tionale for prescription of a second tricyclic in a nonresponder to a first. Although this theory is unproven, the evidence for it so far would indicate that it is not an unreasonable strategy for treatment. Furthermore, if one decides to try a second tricyclic, it would make sense to switch groups, from a norepinephrine uptake inhibitor to a serotonin or vice versa. In that case, if the patient failed to respond to desipramine, imipramine, nortriptyline, or protriptyline, then amitriptyline would be indicated. If he failed to respond to amitriptyline, one of the four others would be indicated. There would be no particular indication, however, to go from nortriptyline to desipramine, two demethylated compounds, since these are very similar drugs. Given the premise that a trial of a different tricyclic indicated the theory suggests information relevant to choice of tricyclic. It has been my clinical observation and that of other clinicians that some patients who fail to respond to tricyclic drugs do respond to MAO inhibitors. There is a substantial body of evidence which shows that 50% of patients who fail to respond to tricyclic drugs will respond to electroconvulsive therapy. It follows that patients who do not respond to one form of therapy for depression should be tried on others. Occasionally a combination of drugs can be useful.

To complicate things further, there is evidence that there may be cholinergic factors in mania and depression. Most physiologic functions are controlled by a balance between transmitter substances. For example, most endocrine functions are controlled by a central balance between transmitters that govern the secretion of the releasing factors in the brain. Basic physiologic functions like hunger and thirst are controlled by balances of transmitters. The movement disorder of Parkinson's disease is also controlled by a dopamine-acetylcholine balance. The peripheral autonomic nervous system, the parasympathetic and sympathetic system, involves a balance between acetylcholine and norepinephrine. It is thus reasonable to ask whether cholinergic factors can play a role in mania and depression. We have reviewed the evidence relevant to the role of the cholinergic system, and there is substantial evidence that altering the cholinergic system alters mood in a direction which suggests there may be high cholinergic function in depression and low levels of function in mania (37). To test this hypothesis, we administered physostigmine, a drug which increases central acetylcholine levels, to manic patients and showed that it converts their mania into a depression (39). Physostigmine also makes depressed patients more depressed (39). We would conceptualize acetylcholine as a modulator of affect, not a prime mover, but we suggest that part of the neuropharmacologic correlations of mania and depression may involve a modulatory role for acetylcholine such that mania would be associated with low acetylcholine levels of function, and depression associated with high acetylcholine levels of function.

It should be emphasized that the biogenic amine theories have not been proven. There is much evidence consistent with them, but there is also evidence inconsistent. For example, lithium helps mania but prevents the recurrence of both bipolar depression and unipolar depression. This is hard to explain with a theory which is basically an up-down model: high norepinephrine function equals mania, low norepinephrine function equals depression.

The drug iprindole is neither a tricyclic antidepressant with uptake inhibiting properties nor an MAO inhibitor. Nevertheless, it has a therapeutic effect in depression. It does have a tricyclic structure. We have studied it in both rats and humans and found it not to be a membrane pump inhibitor. The observation that this drug helps depression without altering norepinephrine is inconsistent with the biogenic amine theory of depression. Of course, if new evidence on iprindole and norepinephrine is discovered, the picture could change radically.

It may be argued that since the biogenic theories of depression are not proven, it is impossible to specify their exact relevance to psychiatric practice. Understanding of the underlying biologic mechanisms does have special practical relevance, however, particularly in understanding side effects. We discussed at some length above the effects of tricyclic drugs in inhibiting the uptake of norepinephrine. This is relevant to a clinically important drug-drug interaction. Guanethidine, an antihypertensive drug, is concentrated inside the neuron by the norepinephrine membrane pump. Once guanethidine reaches its intracellular side of action, it produces its therapeutic hypotensive effect in the hypertensive patient. If the membrane pump is inhibited, then guanethidine can no longer be concentrated inside the neuron by the membrane pump and hence is rendered therapeutically ineffective. The tricyclic antidepressant in effect keeps guanethidine from reaching its therapeutic site of action. For example, Fann and his co-workers (41,42) have shown that guanethidine is an ineffective agent when used in patients treated with 200 to 300 mg per day of the tricyclic antidepressant, doxepin. In addition, the drug chlorpromazine, which incidentally has a tricyclic structure, does inhibit the membrane pump. Fann, Janowsky, Oates and I (43) have shown that chlorpromazine also interferes with the therapeutic action of guanethidine. Furthermore, all of the tricyclic antidepressants do interfere with the therapeutic action of guanethidine. Thus much of the research undertaken from a purely basic point of view to understand the underlying pharmacologic mechanisms and from a clinical viewpoint associated with a theory of disease process has produced important interim findings applicable to the more precise prescription of psychotropic compounds.

## SUMMARY

In this paper we have reviewed the biogenic amines theory of depression. We have first briefly stated the norepinephrine theory of depression and then the competing serotonin theory of depression. These theories suggest that either low norepinephrine or low serotonin is associated with depression. We then briefly reviewed the permissive theory of depression—which holds that low norepinephrine and low serotonin are both required for depression— and finally the two-disease theory, which contends that depression is not a homogeneous disease, but rather a group of diseases, one subtype of which consists of a low-norepinephrine depression and the other subtype a low-serotonin depression. We briefly discussed also a critique of these theories, the possible role of acetylcholine, and the clinical implications. There is a very large body of evidence relevant to these theories. We focused on a brief statement of the theory comparing and contrasting these various theoretical formulations and made no attempt to deal in a comprehensive manner with all the relevant information. The main purpose was a clear statement of these theories and a discussion of some implications for treatment.

## REFERENCES

1. Everett, G. M., and Toman, J. E. P. *Biol. Psychiat., Proc. Sessions Soc. Biol. Psychiat., San Francisco*, Vol. I. New York: Grune & Stratton, 1959, p. 75.
2. Pare, C. M. B., and Sandler, M. A clinical and biochemical study of a trial of iproniazid in the treatment of depression. *J. Neurol. Neurosurg.* 22:247, 1959.
3. Klerman, G. L., Schildkraut, J. J., Hasenbush, L. L., et al. Clinical experience with dihydroxyphenylalanine (Dopa) in depression. *J. Psychiat. Res.* 1:289-297, 1963.
4. Bunney, W. E., Jr., and Davis, J. M. Norepinephrine in depressive reactions. *Arch. Gen. Psychiat.* 13 (6) :483-494, 1965.
5. Schildkraut, J. J. The catecholamine hypothesis of affective disorders (A review of supporting evidence) . *Amer. J. Psychiat.* 122:509, 1965.
6. Coppen, A. The biochemistry of affective disorders. *Brit. J. Psychiat.* 113:1237-1264, 1967.
7. Murphy, D. L., Colburn, R. W., Davis, J. M., and Bunney, W. E. Imipramine and lithium effects on biogenic amine transport in depressed and manic depressive patients. *Amer. J. Psychiat.* 127:339-345, 1970.
8. Mitchell, J. R., Cavanaugh, J. H., Arias, L., and Oates, J. A. Guanethidine and related agents: III Antagonism by drugs which inhibit the norepinephrine pump in man. *J. Clin. Invest.* 49:1596-1604, 1970.
9. Tyrer, P., Candy, J., and Kelly, D. A study of the clinical effects of phenelzine and placebo in the treatment of phobic anxiety. *Psychopharmacologia*, 32:237-254, 1973.

10. Johnstone, E. C., and Marsh, W. Acetylator status and response to phenelzine in depressed patients. *Lancet,* 1:567-570, 1973.

11. Davis, J. M., and Fann, W. E. Lithium: A review. In *Annual Review of Pharmacology* 11:285-302, 1971.

12. Davis, J. M., Goodwin, F. K., Bunney, W. E., Jr., Murphy, D. L., and Colburn, R. W. Effects of ions on uptake of norepinephrine by synaptosomes. *Pharmacologist* 9 (2) : 184, 1967.

13. Colburn, R. W., Goodwin, F. K., Bunney, W. E., Jr., and Davis, J. M. Effects of lithium on the uptake of noradrenaline by synaptosomes. *Nature* 215 (5108) :1395-1397, 1967.

14. Murphy, D. L., Colburn, R. W., Davis, J. M., and Bunney, W. E., Jr. Lithium stimulation of monoamine uptake in human platelets. *Life Science* 8 (1) :1187-1193, 1969.

15. Fann, W. E., Davis, J. M., Janowsky, D. S., Cavanaugh, J. M., Kaufmann, J. S., Griffith, J. D., and Oates, J. A. Effects of lithium on adrenergic function in man. *Clin. Pharm. and Therap.* 13:71-77, 1972.

16. Fawcett, J. A., and Bunney, W. E., Jr. Pituitary adrenal function and depression. An outline for research. *Arch. Gen. Psychiat.* 16:517-535, 1967.

17. Carroll, B. J. Hypothalamic-pituitary function in depressive illness: Insensitivity to hypoglycemia. *Brit. Med. J.* 3:27-28, 1969.

18. Carroll, B., in B. Davies, B. Carroll, and R. M. Mowbray, eds., *Depressive Illness: Some Research Studies.* Springfield, Ill.: Charles C. Thomas, 1972.

19. Carroll, B. M., and Davis, B. M. Clinical associations of 11-hydroxycorticosteroid suppression and nonsuppression in severe depressive illnesses. *Brit. Med J.* 1:789-791, 1970.

20. Carroll, B. J., Martin, F. I. R., and Davies, B. M. Resistance to suppression by dexamethasone of plasma 11-OHCS levels in severe depressive illnesses. *Brit. Med. J.* 3:285-287, 1968.

21. Sachar, E. J., Heliman, L., Fukushima, D. K., and Gallagher, T. F. Cortisol production in depressive illness. A clinical and biochemical clarification. *Arch. Gen. Psychiat.* 23:289-298, 1971.

22. Mendels, J. Endocrine factors in psychopathological states, in J. Mendels, ed., *Biological Psychiatry.* New York: Wiley, 1973, pp. 175-197.

23. Sachar, E. J., Finkelstein, J. J., and Hellman, L. Growth hormone responses in depressive illness. I. Response to insulin tolerance test. *Arch. Gen. Psychiat.* 25:263-269, 1971.

24. Kety, S., B. T. Ho and W. M. McIsaac, eds., *Brain Chemistry in Mental Disease.* New York: Plenum Press, 1971, p. 237.

25. Prange, A. J., Jr., and others. Enhancement of imipramine by thyroid stimulating hormone: Clinical and theoretical implications. *Amer. J. Psychiat.* 127:191-199, 1970.

26. Asberg, M., Bertilsson, L., Tuck, D., Cronholm, B., and Sjoqvist, F. Indoleamine metabolites in the cerebrospinal fluid of depressed patients before and during treatment with nortriptyline. *Clin. Pharmacol. Ther.* 14:277-286, 1973.

27. Bowers, M. B., Henninger, G. R., and Gerbode, F. Cerebrospinal fluid 5-hydroxyindoleacetic acid and homovanillic acid in psychiatric patients. *Int. J. Neuropharm.* 8:255-262, 1970.

28. Coppen, A. J., Prange, A. J., Jr., Whybrow, P. C., and Noguera, R. Abnormalities of indoleamines in affective disorders. *Arch. Gen. Psychiat.* 26:474-478, 1972.

29. Mendels, J. A., Frazer, S., Secunda, S., and Stokes, J. Biogenic amine metabolites in

the cerebro-spinal fluid of depressed and manic patients. *Science* 175:1380-1382, 1972.

30. Van Praag, H. M., Korf, J., and Putte, J. 5-hydroxyindoleacetic acid levels in the cerebro-spinal fluid of depressive patients treated with probenecid. *Nature* 225:1259-1260, 1970.

31. Van Praag, H. M., and Korf, J. Endogenous depressions with and without disturbances in the 5-hydroxytryptamine metabolism: A biochemical classification? *Psychopharmacologia* 19:148-152, 1971.

32. Bourne, H. R., Bunney, W. E., Jr., Colburn, R. W., Davis, J. M., Davis, J. N., Shaw, D. M., and Coppen, A. J. Noradrenaline, 5-hydroxytryptamine, and 5-hydroxyindoleacetic acid in hindbrains of suicidal patients. *Lancet* 2 (7572) :805-808, 1968.

33. Maas, J. W., Dekirmenjian, H., and Fawcett, J. A. MHPG excretion by patients with affective disorders. *Int. Pharmacopsychiat.* 9:14-26, 1974.

34. Maas, J. W., Dekirmenjian, H., and Jones, F. The identification of depressed patients who have a disorder of NE metabolism and/or disposition, in E. Usdin and S. Synder, eds., *Frontiers of Catecholamine Res.* New York: Pergamon, 1973, pp. 1091-1096.

35. Schildkraut, J. J. Biogenic amines and affective disorders. *Ann. Rev. Med.* 25:333-348, 1974.

36. Schildkraut, J. J. Depressions and biogenic amines, in D. Hamburg, ed., *American Handbook of Psychiatry*, Vol. 4. New York: Basic Books (in press).

37. Schildkraut, J. J., Keeler, B. A., Grab, E. L., and Kantrowich, J. MHPG excretion and clinical classification in depressive disorders. *Lancet* 1:1251-1252, 1973.

38. Janowsky, D. S., El-Yousef, M. K., and Davis, J. M. Parasympathetic suppression of manic symptoms by psysostigmine. *Arch. Gen. Psychiat.* 28:542-547, 1973.

39. Janowsky, D. S., El-Yousef, M. K., Davis, J. M., and Sekerke, H. J. A cholinergic-adrenergic hypothesis of mania and depression. *Lancet* 1:632-635, 1972.

40. Fann, W. E., Davis, J. M., Janowsky, D. S., Kaufman, J. S., Griffith, J. D., and Oates, J. A. Effect of iprindole on amine uptake in man. *Arch. Gen. Psychiat.* 26:158-162, 1972.

41. Oates, J. A., Fann, W. E., and Cavanaugh, J. H. Effect of doxepin on the norepinephrine pump: A preliminary report. *Psychosom.* 10:12-13, 1969.

42. Fann, W. E., Cavanaugh, J. H., Kaufmann, J. S., Griffith, J. D., Davis, J. M., Janowsky, D. S., and Oates, J. A. Doxepin: Effects on transport of biogenic amines. *Psychopharmacologia*, 22:111-125, 1971.

43. Janowsky, D. S., Fann, W. E., Davis, J. M., and Oates, J. A. Chlorpromazine reversal of the antihypertensive action of guanethidine. *Amer. J. Psychiat.* 133 (4) :808-812, 1973.

3

# Biogenic Amine Precursors and Affective Illnesses

DAVID BURNS
JOSEPH MENDELS

## INTRODUCTION

Considerable attention has been directed to the possible role of biogenic amines in the genesis of the affective disorders. It has been suggested that depression is associated with a functional deficiency of norepinephrine (NE) or serotonin (5-hydroxytryptamine) (5HTP) at some site in the brain. The evidence for these hypotheses has been extensively reviewed and will not be repeated here (1-5). Direct validation of the biogenic amine hypothesis is difficult, and consistent results that are compatible with it have not been forthcoming (6-11).

As the amines themselves do not cross the blood-brain barrier, it is not possible to directly test their effectiveness in depression. An alternative approach involves the administration of precursors which, after penetrating into the brain, are converted into the amines.

The interpretation of findings when this strategy is used depends on a number of assumptions regarding the fate of the precursor: (1) the precursor (usually administered orally) must be absorbed from the gastro-intestinal tract; (2) it must not be inhibited in its transport across the blood-brain barrier; (3) it should attain a physiological distribution in the brain; (4) the necessary enzymatic systems must be operating so as to convert the precursor into the relevant amine; (5) the precursor or newly synthesized amine must not alter the activity of other neurotransmitter systems; and (6) the release of the newly synthesized transmitter must occur normally so as to elicit a physiological postsynaptic response. As will be discussed later, all these criteria are not adequately met for the various precursors used. Nevertheless, considerable attention has been focused on this strategy. This is perhaps due to the success observed with the catecholamine precursor, L-dihydroxyphenylalanine (L-dopa), in the treatment of Parkinson's disease.

## SEROTONIN PRECURSOR STUDIES

### I. Tryptophan

The amino acid tryptophan is converted into 5-hydroxytryptophan, which in turn is converted into serotonin. The results of trials in which tryptophan was administered in an effort to alter the clinical features and course of a depression are summarized in Tables 1-6. The findings noted here are conflicting.

### Uncontrolled Studies (Table 1)

In 1970, Bowers (12) administered 2-8 grams of L-tryptophan daily to nine depressed patients as well as to a schizophrenic control group. He reported that tryptophan did not alleviate either depression or insomnia in the group of depressed patients. In the same year, Broadhurst (13) reported on the effects of 6 grams L-tryptophan daily in 36 patients with chronic relapsing depression. Twenty-eight of these patients improved with tryptophan administration with recurrence of the depressive mood swings when tryptophan was discontinued. In a single case study, Winston (14) reported that a 5-gram dose of L-tryptophan per day was effective in a severe refractory patient who relapsed when supplemental pyridoxine was added. The withdrawal of pyridoxine resulted in subsequent clinical remission. These were all uncontrolled studies and therefore difficult to evaluate.

### Controlled Studies

The antidepressant effect of tryptophan has been compared with several known and effective treatments for depression.

## Table 1. Tryptophan (L-TP) in Depression: Uncontrolled Studies

| Study | No. of Patients | Investigators' Diagnosis | Duration (Days) | Design | Daily Dose | Comment |
|-------|-----------------|--------------------------|-----------------|--------|------------|---------|
| Bowers (12) | 9 | 8 depressive 1 manic depressive | 8-18 | Open; schizophrenic control group | 2-8 gm L-TP 100 mg pyridoxine | Neither depressive symptoms nor insomnia were significantly relieved in depressive group |
| Broadhurst (13) | 36 | Chronic relapsing depressive illness; patients had not previously responded to ECT or anti-depressants | >28 | Open | 6 gm L-TP | 28 of these patients improved; depressive mood swings on discontinuation of L-TP |
| Winston (14) | 1 | Unremitting treatment refractory depression | 6 mos. | Open | 5 gr L-TP with or without 50 mg pyridoxine | The patient responded to L-TP, relapsed when pyridoxine was added, and responded again when pyridoxine was withdrawn. |

## 1. Comparison With Electroconvulsive Therapy (Table 2)

In an early report, Coppen et al. (15) suggested that 5-7 grams/day of DL-tryptophan was as effective an antidepressant as electroconvulsive therapy (ECT), suggesting that tryptophan is itself an effective antidepressant. However, Carroll et al. (16) were unable to confirm Coppen's findings. In this study, patients were randomly assigned to two treatment groups: ECT or 7 grams L-tryptophan daily. Eleven of twelve tryptophan patients did not improve and subsequently required electroshock therapy. In two more recent comparisons of L-tryptophan and ECT, L-tryptophan was ineffective in one (17) and reported to be actually superior to electroconvulsive therapy in another (18). The comparison of tryptophan with electroshock therapy is difficult to evaluate because of the non-blind nature of these studies.

## 2. Comparison With Tricyclic Antidepressants (Table 3)

In two studies (13,20), L-tryptophan was as effective as 150 mg imipramine daily, while Gayford et al. (21) were unable to confirm this. Insofar as we can tell from the reports, these studies were apparently non-blind.

The findings from two double-blind comparisons of L-tryptophan with tricyclics were that L-tryptophan was either as effective as (22), or nearly as effective (23) as tricyclics.

Those investigators who found that L-tryptophan was as effective as imipramine (3,20,22,23) argued that imipramine is more effective than placebo, and that therefore L-tryptophan must also be superior to placebo. This assumption, however, is open to question. In a recent interview, Baldessarini (24) has argued that the efficacy of tricyclic antidepressants is sometimes exaggerated and has suggested that they may be only 10 or 20% more effective than placebo. Burrows et al. (25) have pointed out that while many studies have demonstrated the superiority of imipramine over placebo, it cannot be assumed that imipramine will be of equal value in every treatment setting, because many controlled trials have not been able to show its superiority over placebo. Carroll et al. (26) have cautioned: "We have become so impressed by the effects of nonspecific factors on the patients' responses in a teaching and research unit that we regard comparison with an inert substance as a necessary requirement in the assessment of antidepressant drugs." Therefore, the improvement described for both L-tryptophan and imipramine in several investigations (19,20,22-23), while suggestive, cannot be taken as proof that either treatment was superior to placebo.

## 3. Comparison With Placebo (Table 4)

Bunney et al. (27) and Murphy et al. (28,29) have reported on the effects of up to 9.6 grams of L-tryptophan daily as compared with placebo in

**Table 2. Tryptophan Compared with Electroconvulsive Therapy**

| Study | No. of Patients | Investigators' Diagnosis | Duration (Days) | Design | Daily Dose | Comment |
|---|---|---|---|---|---|---|
| Coppen et al. (15) | 22 | Severe unremitting depression | 28 | Single-blind; ECT control group | 5-7 gr DL-TP 100 mg pyridoxine | L-TP as effective as ECT; MAO-inhibitor enhanced response to L-TP |
| Carroll et al. (16) | 24 | Severe primary depressive illness | 21 | Non-blind raters; random assignment to ECT or L-TP | 7 gm L-TP; 170 mg pyridoxine | L-TP ineffective in treatment of depression; 11 L-TP patients subsequently required ECT |
| Harrington et al (17) | 43 | Severe primary depression | 28 | Open; random assignment to ECT or L-TP | 8 gm L-TP; 100 mg pyridoxine | ECT superior to L-TP after 2 weeks. L-TP group remained moderately depressed on Beck and Hamilton tests. |
| MacSweeney (18) | 27 | Severe unipolar depression | 28 | Open; ECT control group | 3 gr L-TP; 1 gr nicotinamide | After the 10th day, L-TP was superior to ECT on the Beck scores, and this was statistically significant after day 21. Both groups improved. L-TP group received nicotinamide. |

## Table 3. Tryptophan Compared with Tricyclics

| Study | No. of Patients | Investigators' Diagnosis | Duration (Days) | Design | Daily Dose | Comment |
|-------|----------------|--------------------------|-----------------|--------|------------|---------|
| Broadhurst (13) | ~16 | Active primary depressive illness | ≥28 | Open; imipramine control group | 6 gm L-TP; 60 mg pyridoxine | L-TP as effective as 150 mg imipramine hydrochloride |
| Coppen et al. (22) | 15 | 12 unipolar depressives; 3 bipolar depressives | 28 | Double-blind; imipramine control group | 9 gm L-TP; 180 mg ascorbic acid; some also received 25 mg liothyronine | L-TP as effective as 150 mg imipramine; L-TP had no effect on sleep |
| Gayford et al. (21) | 10 | Endogenous depressive illness | 14 | Open; 3 control subjects received 175 mg amitriptyline and 2 receiving plus 60 mg phenelzine | 6 gm L-TP 60 mg pyridoxine | No improvement in 9 of 10 patients, who then responded to ECT; L-TP plus MAO-inhibitor caused hypomania in 2 patients; 3 amitriptyline patients responded |
| Kline and Shaw (20) | 34 | Depressive illness | 42 | Apparently open; control group received 225 mg imipramine | 3-6 gm L-TP | 60% of patients in each group improved, utilizing a 3-point global rating system, suggesting that imipramine and tryptophan were equally effective |
| Jensen et al. (23) | 42 | Endogenous depression, unipolar and bipolar. Psychotic or chronic patients were excluded | 21 | Double-blind; control group received 150 mg imipramine | 6 gm L-TP | Both groups showed improvement, but imipramine worked more rapidly. The mean Hamilton score was still 16.5 at day 21 in the TP group |

**Table 4. Tryptophan Compared with Placebo**

| Study | No. of Patients | Investigators' Diagnosis | Duration (Days) | Design | Daily Dose | Comment |
|---|---|---|---|---|---|---|
| Bunney et al. (27) Murphy et al. (28, 29) | 24 | Bipolar and uni-polar depression | 20 | Double-blind placebo substitution crossover design | 9.6 gm L-TP; 50 mg pyri-doxine; 100 mg ascorbic acid | 1. No significant antidepressant effect in 16 unipolars; evidence of increased peripheral and central serotonin metabolism in these patients; strikingly few behavioral effects; patients did respond to other treatments. 2. 5 of 8 bipolar patients showed partial improvement, with 3 of these relapsing with placebo substititution |
| Mendels et al. (30) | 15 | Bipolar and uni-polar depression | 42 | Double-blind; placebo substitution | 16 gm L-TP; 50 mg pyri-doxine | No significant improvement on Beck, Hamilton or nurses' rating scales |
| Dunner and Fieve (31) | 11 | Bipolar and uni-polar depression | 10-18 | Double-blind | 9 gr L-TP; 150 mg pyri-doxine; 900 mg ascorbic acid; 5 patients also received 4.5-6.0 gm L-dopa | 1 of 6 L-TP patients responded; 1 of 5 L-TP plus L-dopa patients responded. Pyridoxine may have interfered with L-dopa |

24 bipolar or unipolar depressed patients. There was no antidepressant effect in 16 unipolar patients. However, 5 of the 8 bipolar patients showed partial improvement, and 3 of these relapsed with placebo substitution.

We (30) have compared up to 16 grams of L-tryptophan daily with either 8 grams L-dopa or placebo under double-blind conditions. There was no significant benefit from the tryptophan.

Recently, Dunner and Fieve (31) administered 9 grams L-tryptophan alone, or in combination with 5-6 grams of L-dopa in a double-blind study of unipolar and bipolar patients. Only 1 of the 6 tryptophan and 1 of 5 tryptophan-dopa patients responded. These patients also received pyridoxine, which may have increased the peripheral decarboxylation of L-dopa, with less entering the central nervous system (CNS).

## 4. Tryptophan Plus MAO Inhibitors (Table 5)

The administration of tryptophan together with a monoamine oxidase inhibitor (MAO inhibitor) has been shown to be superior to either agent alone in five studies (15,32-35), including several double-blind, controlled investigations. There is also a report of two patients treated with this combination who became hypomanic in association with very high blood serotonin levels (21). This could have been the result of excessive treatment.

## 5. Tryptophan Plus Tricyclics (Table 6)

The potentiation of tricyclic antidepressants by tryptophan has been evaluated in four double-blind studies, with no potentiation being found in two (33,36-37), equivocal results in one (38), and superior results in one (39) study. In the one successful trial (39), 6-7 grams of DL-tryptophan were used with chlorimipramine in the treatment of 24 depressed women. This combination was superior to chlorimipramine alone.

## 6. Tryptophan in Mania (Table 7)

Two double-blind, controlled studies of tryptophan in mania have been reported. Murphy et al. (29) reported that 7 of 10 patients had significant reductions in mania while on L-tryptophan. Some of these patients also had significantly elevated depression ratings while in the manic phase, and the depression ratings also decreased significantly while they were receiving L-tryptophan. Three of the responders subsequently relapsed with placebo substitution, suggesting that the improvement may have been a true drug effect. Prange et al. (40) reported that 6 grams of L-tryptophan was somewhat more effective than 400 mg of chlorpromazine per day in controlling mania (not statistically significant). More pronounced anti-manic effects might have been observed had larger doses of tryptophan been used.

## Table 5. Tryptophan plus MAO-Inhibitors: Effect in Depression

| Study | No. of Patients | Investigators' Diagnosis | Duration (Days) | Design | Daily Dose | Comment |
|---|---|---|---|---|---|---|
| Coppen (32) | 24 | Profound depression | 28 | Open; MAOI plus placebo controls | 13 gm DL-TP; 20 mg pyridoxine | L-TP accelerated and enhanced the response to tranylcypromine (30 mg) |
| Pare (33) | 14 | Previously depressed patients who relapsed when dose of MAOI was lowered | not stated | Double-blind; placebo substitution | 7.5 to 15 gm L-TP; various MAOI's | 6 out of 14 patients showed a "striking improvement" 2-3 days after L-TP was added, and relapsed when placebo was substituted |
| Coppen (15) | 19 | Endogenous or reactive depression | 28 | Open; 22 additional patients received tranylcypromine alone | 5-7 gm DL-TP; 100 mg pyridoxine; some patients received potassium and carbohydrate supplements | Tryptophan as effective as ECT by day 28; TP plus 30 mg tranylcypromine was slightly better than TP alone |
| Glassman and Platman (34) | 20 | Serious endogenous depression | 21 | Double-blind; MAOI plus TP or placebo | 12-18 gm DL-TP; 30 mg phenelzine | 6 of 10 TP patients and 2 of 10 placebo patients were discharged by 3 weeks. |
| Gutierrez and Alino (35) | 30 | Endogenous depression | 20 | Double-blind; MAOI plus TP or placebo | 6 gm DL-TP; 500 mg IV or IM nialamide | TP accelerated and increased the response to nialamide |
| Gayford et al. (21) | 2 | Endogenous depression | 14 | Open; control groups received L-TP alone or amitryptiline | 6 gm L-TP; 60 mg pyridoxine | Both patients became hypomanic in association with very high blood serotonin levels. Treatment was withdrawn. L-TP alone ineffective. |

Table 6. Tryptophan plus Tricyclics: Effect in Depression

| Study | No. of Patients | Investigators' Diagnosis | Duration (Days) | Design | Daily Dose | Comment |
|---|---|---|---|---|---|---|
| Pare (33) | 10 | Relapsed depressives | not stated | Double-blind | 7.5 to 15 gm L-TP plus 225 mg amitriptyline, imipramine or placebo | L-tryptophan or placebo were given to patients who had relapsed when their dose of imipramine or amitriptyline was lowered. Only 1 of 10 patients was "much improved." |
| Shaw et al. (36, 37) | 54 | Unipolar affective disorder | 28 | Double-blind | 175 mg chlorimipramine alone; or 6 gm L-TP plus 225 mg desipramine | 6 grams L-tryptophan daily did not potentiate antidepressant action of chlorimipramine. Desipramine plus L-tryptophan was not superior to chlorimipramine alone |
| Alino et al. (38) | 30 | Depressive illness | 30 | Double-blind | 3 gm L-TP plus 150 mg amitriptyline or placebo | Patients receiving L-tryptophan with amitriptyline improved more than a control group receiving amitriptyline alone (not statistically significant) |
| Walinder et al. (39) | 24 (women) | Depression | 21 | Double-blind | 150 mg chlorimipramine plus 6-7 gm DL-TP or placebo | Tryptophan plus chlorimipramine was statistically superior to chlorimipramine alone |

**Table 7. Tryptophan in Mania**

| Study | No. of Patients | Investigators' Diagnosis | Duration (Days) | Design | Daily Dose | Comment |
|---|---|---|---|---|---|---|
| Murphy et al. (29) | 10 | Bipolar in manic phase | 20 | Double-blind; placebo substitution crossover design | 9.6 gm L-TP; 50 mg pyridoxine; 100 mg ascorbic acid | 7 of 10 patients exhibited significant reductions in mania ratings; hypomanics responded better; in 8 of 10 patients, depression ratings decreased significantly; 3 of 7 responders relapsed on placebo |
| Prange et al. (40) | 10 | Bipolar depression in manic phase | 35 | Double-blind; CPZ substitution crossover design | 6 gm L-TP; 50 gm pyridoxine | TP rapidly reduced hyperactivity, was more effective than chlorpromazine, 400 mg/day (not statistically significant) |

It should be noted that L-tryptophan has significant sedative effects in man (41-48). We have recently found that the acute intravenous administration of 3-10 grams L-tryptophan to normal subjects has profound sedative effects. Thus it is important to determine whether the symptomatic improvement seen in the manic patients given L-tryptophan is the result of a true anti-manic effect or a nonspecific sedative action of the tryptophan.

## II. 5-Hydroxytryptophan

The immediate serotonin precursor, 5-hydroxytryptophan (5-HTP) has been given to depressed patients either alone or in combination with an MAO inhibitor or a peripheral decarboxylase inhibitor (Tables 8-10).

### 1. 5-Hydroxytryptophan Alone (Table 8)

Persson and Roos (49) administered 5HTP to a refractory patient who remitted in five days in conjunction with a doubling of lumbar spinal fluid 5-hydroxy-indoleacetic acid (5HIAA) levels. Van Praag et al. (50,51) administered up to 3 grams a day of DL-5HTP to five depressed patients in a double-blind placebo controlled study. Three of the five 5HTP patients improved, whereas none of the placebo patients improved. The 5HTP responders were characterized by subnormal CSF levels of 5HIAA after probenecid administration, raising the possibility that the 5HTP may have specifically corrected a CNS serotonin deficiency. Recently, these investigators (52) reported the potentiation of the antidepressant action of chlorimipramine by 5HTP in a small group of refractory depressed patients. The data are too preliminary to allow for any conclusions to be formed.

Sano (53) reported a dramatic response within 14 days in 69% of 107 unipolar and bipolar patients treated with 5HTP. Unfortunately, this report is in Japanese, and details of the procedures are not available to us. Fujiwara and Otsuki (54) treated 20 unipolar, bipolar, and involutional depressives with 50-200 mg L-5HTP daily. Seventeen patients received L-dopa, and 7 patients received both compounds in a crossover study. They reported that 5HTP was effective in 10 of the 20 patients. The responders were characterized by agitation, insomnia, and low CSF and urinary 5HIAA concentrations. L-dopa was effective in 5 of the 17 patients, who were characterized by psychomotor retardation.

### 2. 5-Hydroxytryptophan Plus MAO Inhibitors (Table 9)

Pare and Sandler (55) administered small doses of DL-5HTP intravenously to depressed patients who had been pretreated with the MAO in-

Table 8. 5-Hydroxytryptophan in Depression

| Study | No. of Patients | Investigators' Diagnosis | Duration (Days) | Design | Daily Dose | Comment |
|---|---|---|---|---|---|---|
| Perrson and Roos (49) | 1 | Severe recurrent depression not responding to ECT and tricyclics | 14 | Open | A total of 150 mg 5-HTP I.V. | Remission in 5 days continuing for 2 months; CSF 5HIAA doubled |
| Van Praag et al. (50, 51) | 5 | Endogenous depression suitable for ECT | 21 | Double-blind; placebo substitution | 3 gm DL-5HTP | 3 of 5 and no placebo patients improved. 5HTP responders had subnormal 5HIAA increase after probenecid |
| Sano (53) | 107 | Unipolar and bipolar depression | 28 | Not in English | Not in English | "Dramatic response; 69% were cured or improved by day 14." |
| Fujiwara and Otsuke (54) | 20 | Unipolar, bipolar and involutional | 7-28 | Open; an additional 17 patients received L-dopa | 50-200 mg L-5HTP | L-5HTP "effective" in 10 of 20 patients. L-dopa effective in 5 of 17 patients. 5HTP responders had more anxiety, agitation and insomnia than L-dopa responders, and had decreased CSF and urinary 5HIAA levels. 5HTP was associated with several days of severe insomnia followed by sudden clinical remission |

**Table 9. 5-Hydroxytryptophan plus MAO-Inhibitors**

| Study | No. of Patients | Investigators' Diagnosis | Duration (Days) | Design | Daily Dose | Comment |
|---|---|---|---|---|---|---|
| Pare and Sandler (55) | 7 | Depression suitable for ECT | Repeated single injections at intervals of at least one day | DL-5HTP or DL-dopa were given in a randomized order to patients on iproniazid | 12.5 mg DL-5HTP or DL-dopa I.V. | No alleviation of depression |
| Kline and Sacks (56) | 20 | Depression | 1 or 2 injections | Open | 10 to 50 mg DL-5HTP I.V. various MAOI's | 18 of 20 patients responded within 24 hours |
| Kline et al. (57) | 49 | Primary depression | 1 or 2 injections | Double-blind | 25 or 50 mg DL-5HTP I.V. after 3 days on various MAOI's | Approximately 30% of primary depressions had some improvement. No placebo group. |

hibitor, iproniazid, with no benefit to the patients. Using a similar approach, Kline and Sacks (56) reported that 18 out of 20 patients responded to a small dose of intravenous 5HTP after MAO inhibitor treatment. They were unable to replicate these findings when they repeated the study under double-blind conditions (57).

These early studies of intravenous 5HTP with MAO inhibitors do not provide any convincing evidence of an antidepressant effect for 5HTP. This may be due in part to the fact that very small doses of the DL-isomer of 5HTP were used. As only the 5HTP can be utilized for serotonin formation by the brain, it is probable that significant serotonergic stimulation was not achieved.

There is a general problem in the interpretation of studies using 5HTP. The enzyme, L-aromatic amino acid decarboxylase, which converts 5HTP to serotonin, has a nonspecific distribution in the brain. As a result, the administration of high doses of 5HTP results in the formation of serotonin in catecholaminergic as well as in serotonergic neurons (58). Although 5HTP does increase whole brain serotonin, it is uncertain whether it increases it significantly in serotonergic neurons (59). Furthermore, the regional distribution of serotonin and 5HIAA appears to be abnormal after large-dose 5HTP administration (60,61). These findings suggest that the serotonin formed after 5HTP administration may not function physiologically.

## 3. 5-Hydroxytryptophan Plus a Peripheral Decarboxylase Inhibitor (Table 10)

An alternative approach involves the administration of lower doses of 5HTP in conjunction with a decarboxylase inhibitor. This reduces peripheral conversion of 5HTP, allowing proportionately more to cross the blood-brain barrier and enter the CNS (62). However, the decarboxylase inhibitor itself does not cross the blood-brain barrier. Thus it may be possible to have more 5HTP enter the CNS with fewer gastrointestinal side effects. Using this strategy, Brodie et al. (63) conducted a double-blind, placebo controlled, 14-day study of seven patients with severe refractory depressions. Only one of the seven showed a modest response, in spite of significant increases in CSF 5HIAA. In contrast, Matussek et al. (64) administered this combination to fifteen unipolar depressives as well as 5HTP alone to eight patients. They reported that six of the fifteen patients who received 5HTP plus RO4-4602 did improve, whereas 5HTP alone was ineffective. This was apparently an open study.

Recently, Trimble et al. (65) have administered intravenous 5HTP after peripheral decarboxylase blockade to nondepressed patients with neurologic problems such as the myoclonic syndrome. One of the eight patients

**Table 10. 5-Hydroxytryptophan plus Peripheral Decarboxylase Blockade**

| Study | No. of Patients | Investigators' Diagnosis | Duration (Days) | Design | Daily Dose | Comment |
|---|---|---|---|---|---|---|
| Brodie et al. (63) | 7 | Severe refractory depression | 20 | Double-blind | 500 mg L-5HTP plus 200 mg Mk-486; or 3.25 gm L-5HTP alone | 1 of 7 patients showed a modest response. CSF 5HIAA increased after 5HTP |
| Matussek (64) | 23 | Mostly unipolar depression | 14 | Open | 100-300 mg L-5HTP; some patients also received RO4-4602 | 6 of 15 patients improved somewhat |
| Trimble et al. (65) | 8 | Myoclonic syndrome or other neurologic disorders | 1 | Open | 100-300 mg L-5HTP in I.V. infusion; most patients pre-treated with carbidopa | 1 patient became depressed in 1-2 hours; 7 others became euphoric, garrulous and disinhibited |

**Table 11.  Serotonin Precursors in Affective Illness — Summary**

|  | Effective | Not Effective | Equivocal |
|---|---|---|---|
| 1. Tryptophan in Depression | | | |
| Uncontrolled Studies | 2 | 1 | 0 |
| TP vs. ECT | 2 | 2 | 0 |
| TP vs. Tricyclics | 3 | 1 | 1 |
| TP vs. Placebo | 1 (Bipolar) | 4 | 0 |
| Total: | 8 | 8 | 1 |
| 2. Tryptophan + MAOI in Depression | 5 | 0 | 1 (hypo-mania) |
| 3. Tryptophan + Tricyclics in Depression | 1 | 2 | 1 |
| 4. 5HTP in Depression | 5 | 2 | 2 |
| 5. Tryptophan in Mania | 2 | 0 | 0 |

became significantly depressed within 1 to 2 hours of 5HTP. Seven others became euphoric, garrulous, and disinhibited. It is not known whether intravenous 5HTP would have similar effects in depressed patients.

## OVERVIEW OF SEROTONIN PRECURSOR STUDIES

The effects of serotonin precursors administered to patients with affective illness are summarized in Table 11. Tryptophan when given alone to depressed patients has been reported to be an effective antidepressant in eight studies, ineffective in eight, and equivocal in one study. Those studies which compared tryptophan with ECT are conflicting, with two positive and two negative reports (Table 2), while most of tryptophan-tricyclic comparisons are positive (Table 3). However, in the three studies where L-tryptophan was compared with placebo under double-blind conditions, there was no evidence for an antidepressant effect in unipolar depressives, with the suggestion of some beneficial effects in bipolar patients (Table 4). Thus the more encouraging findings in some tricyclics or ECT comparison studies may have been the result of the lack of adequate controls in these investigations.

Tryptophan plus MAO inhibitor has been reported to be effective in nearly all studies, while the evidence that tryptophan potentiates tricyclics is not strong. 5HTP has been reported to be an effective antidepressant in five studies, ineffective in two, and equivocal in two. However, most of the 5HTP studies were not well controlled and involved very small numbers of patients. In double-blind evaluations of 5HTP, there was one positive (51), one negative (63), and one equivocal report (57). In manic patients, L-tryptophan has been reported to be somewhat effective in two controlled studies.

## CATECHOLAMINE PRECURSOR STUDIES

L-dopa is converted into dopamine and norepinephrine. It has been given to a variety of depressed patients either alone or in combination with an MAO inhibitor or a decarboxylase inhibitor.

### Uncontrolled Studies

The results of five uncontrolled studies of L-dopa in depression are summarized in Table 12. These studies do not provide any convincing evidence for an antidepressant effect for L-dopa. However, the dose of L-dopa in most of these studies was relatively small.

### Controlled Studies

The double-blind placebo controlled studies of L-dopa in depression are summarized in Table 13. The first of these was conducted in 1963 (43). All seven patients in the study had no significant response to small doses of L-dopa. In a double-blind, placebo controlled, crossover study using up to 7 grams of L-dopa or smaller doses of L-dopa with a decarboxylase inhibitor, Goodwin, Murphy, and their associates (67,68) reported some improvement in four of eleven retarded depressives, whereas no agitated depressives responded. Some activation was seen in all patients, with the nonresponding depressives becoming increasingly depressed and paranoid. The patients who received more than 4 grams of L-dopa manifested increased anger. The five bipolar patients in the study became hypomanic or manic, but with no decrease in their depression rating scale scores. These bipolar patients excreted more urinary dopamine than unipolar patients who did not develop these symptoms, suggesting differences in the metabolism of L-dopa between these groups of patients.

Matussek (69) reported partial improvement in 12 of 18 retarded depressives treated with L-dopa and a decarboxylase inhibitor. There was no significant difference in the changes in the depression rating scale scores produced by L-dopa as compared with placebo, even in the retarded depres-

**Table 12. L-Dopa in Depression: Uncontrolled Studies**

| Study | No. of Patients | Investigators' Diagnosis | Duration (Days) | Design | Daily Dose | Comment |
|---|---|---|---|---|---|---|
| Pare and Sandler (55) | 3 | Suitable for ECT | 2 | Open | 275 mg I.V. (single injection) | No alleviation of depression |
| Ingvarsson (55A) | 3 | 2 endogenous 1 uncertain | 1 | Open | 40-50 mg I.V. (single injection) | Definite improvement in 2 patients within 30-90 min. of injection |
| Fujiwara and Otsuki (54) | 17 | Unipolar, bipolar and involutional | 7-28 | Open; an additional 20 patients received 5HTP | 600-1800 mg | Effective in 5 of 17 patients |
| Persson and Walinder (70) | 5 | Depressive symptoms | not stated | Open | 2-4 gm L-dopa | 4 patients had initial improvement, but effect waned over time; changing dosage at this time was without effect; these patients were resistant to both usual and unusual treatment |
| Nahunek (71) | 30 | Endogenous or involutional | Mean of 20 (3-56) | Open | 1.15 gm L-dopa 10 patients also received alpha-methyl-dopa; 20 patients also received di-hydralazine | 6 patients had full remissions; best response on motor activity with little effect on other symptoms of depression |

## Table 13. L-Dopa in Depression: Double-Blind Placebo Controlled Studies

| Study | No. of Patients | Investigators' Diagnosis | Duration (Days) | Design | Daily Dose | Comment |
|---|---|---|---|---|---|---|
| Klerman et al. (66) | 7 | Endogenous, moderate-severe | 15-72 | Single or double-blind | 80-120 mg DL-dopa | No response |
| Goodwin et al. (67) Murphy et al. (68) | 16 | Unipolar and bipolar | up to 50 | Double-blind; placebo crossover substitution design | 7.2 gm L-dopa or 750 mg L-dopa plus decarboxylase | 1. 4 of 11 retarded patients responded; placebo substitution caused relapse in 3 of 4; 0 of 5 agitated depressives responded.<br>2. L-dopa produced anger<br>3. Bipolars became hypomanic or manic<br>4. Activation seen in all patients<br>5. Non-responding psychotic depressives became more depressed and paranoid<br>6. Bipolar patients who develop mania excrete more urinary dopamine |
| Matussek (69) | 31 18 taking active medication 13 taking placebo | Retarded depressive | 18 | Double-blind | 150 mg L-dopa plus decarboxylase inhibitor | 12 of 18 receiving dopa improved, 4 discharged; 5 of 13 taking placebo improved, 1 discharged |
| Mendels et al. (30) | 6 | 3 unipolar 3 bipolar | 42 | Double-blind | 8 gm L-dopa | 1 out of 6 improved; mean depression ratings not different from placebo group |

**Table 14. L-Dopa: Summary of Clinical Studies**

|  | Effective | Not Effective | Equivocal |
|---|---|---|---|
| L-DOPA in Unipolar Depression | 1 | 6 | 1 |
| L-DOPA in Bipolar Depression | 0 | 2 | 0 |
| L-DOPA plus MAOI in Depression | 0 | 1 | 0 |
| Total: | 1 | 9 | 1 |

sive subgroup, and only four of the eighteen patients improved sufficiently to be discharged.

We (30) administered up to 8 grams of L-dopa per day to six depressives. An additional nine patients received either L-tryptophan or placebo (*vide supra*). Only one of six patients receiving L-dopa improved.

### L-Dopa Plus MAO Inhibitors

There are two reports of patients receiving a combination of L-dopa plus an MAO inhibitor while depressed. Pare and Sandler (55) administered 12.5 mg of intravenous L-dopa or DL-5HTP in randomized order to three patients who were previously unresponsive to iproniazid. Neither amino acid appeared to alleviate the depressive symptoms, but only small doses of the DL-isomers were administered, making the results difficult to interpret. Klerman et al. (66) reported that three of five patients receiving daily doses of 120-800 mg DL-dopa plus phenelzine had severe hypertensive crises associated with anxiety attacks.

### OVERVIEW OF CATECHOLAMINE PRECURSOR STUDIES

The studies using L-dopa in depressive illness are summarized in Table 14. On the basis of these findings it seems reasonable to conclude that L-dopa is not an effective antidepressant in most depressed patients. Even when some improvement was noted (67,69-71), it was usually not sufficient to allow the patient to leave the hospital. There are reports, however (67,68), that L-dopa does result in psychomotor activation, which can result in an intensification of unipolar depression or the induction of manic symptoms in bipolar depressives.

## DISCUSSION

### Catecholamine Precursor Studies

The catecholamine hypothesis of affective disorders suggests that there is a reduction in the functioning of central dopamine or norepinephrine systems in depression. If it could be assumed that the L-dopa administered in these studies adequately stimulates these systems, then the findings from these studies would be evidence against this hypothesis.

Therefore, it is important to determine whether or not the administration of L-dopa leads to increased turnover of either dopamine or norepinephrine in the brain. L-dopa (100 mg/kg) intravenously administered to rats produces only minimal effects on the electrical activity of striatal dopaminergic neurons, and dopamine concentrations increase only slightly (72). If this can be extrapolated to apply to man, then 6-7 grams L-dopa may not have significant electrical or biochemical effects on these dopamine systems in the brain.

On the other hand, it has been reported (72) that when L-dopa (50 mg/kg) is given to rats in conjunction with a decarboxylase inhibitor, there is a 40-90% decrease in dopamine neuron firing rates in association with significant increases in striatal dopamine levels. Therefore, it might be that in those clinical trials in which L-dopa was administered with carbidopa, there were significant effects on central dopamine systems. The lack of antidepressant effects in such studies indicates that increases in central dopamine levels are in themselves not sufficient for clinical remissions in most patients. However, the dopamine elevations may have been responsible for the reported activating effects of L-dopa (67,68). If, as has been suggested (11), motor activation can trigger improvement in other aspects of depressive symptomatology, this could account for the partial improvement noted in some retarded depressives treated with this amino acid. In this regard, it should be noted that retarded depressives may also have a decrease in the turnover of brain dopamine (73).

A further difficulty in evaluating these studies arises from the finding that the administration of L-dopa in large amounts may lead to dopamine formation in non-dopaminergic neurons in the brain and to the displacement of serotonin from neurons and non-neuronal tissues (76-80). Thus, there are reports of decreased platelet serotonin (77) and urinary and CSF 5HIAA in man during L-dopa administration (78-80). Recent animal studies indicate that if L-tryptophan is administered with L-dopa, the decrease in brain serotonin can be prevented (76). However, when L-tryptophan and L-dopa were administered together to depressed patients (31), there was no significant improvement. Thus the ineffectiveness of L-dopa as an antidepressant is probably not due to interference with the brain's serotonergic systems.

The effects of L-dopa on norepinephrine levels and turnover in the brain are less clear than its effects on the dopamine system. Many investigators have been unable to document significant increases in brain levels of norepinephrine or its metabolites after L-dopa administration (81-86), and in man no more than 5% of the administered dose of L-dopa appears as urinary norepinephrine or its metabolites (79,87-89). There is a report of an increase in urinary 3-methoxy-4-hydroxyphenylglycol in one patient receiving L-dopa (67). One report noted an initial increase in norepinephrine turnover in rat brain after L-dopa administration, which was followed by an inhibition of norepinephrine turnover in a few hours (75). Thus there is no convincing evidence that L-dopa produces significant and long-lasting stimulatory effects on norepinephrine levels and synthesis rates. This implies that the administration of L-dopa does not provide a definitive test of the hypothesis of diminished noradrenergic function activity in depression. Its beneficial effect in some retarded depressives suggests that this form of depression *may be* associated with a functional dopamine deficiency. The induction of manic or hypomanic symptoms in some bipolar patients (67,68) suggests that excess dopaminergic activity may play a role in the bipolar form of this disorder.

## Serotonin Precursor Studies

The indoleamine hypothesis of affective disorders suggests that there is a reduction in central serotonergic activity in depression. L-tryptophan may be expected to correct such a deficit, since the rate of brain serotonin turnover in laboratory animals appears to depend on the availability of intraneuronal L-tryptophan (90-95). This in turn correlates with fluctuations in plasma tryptophan concentrations and variations in dietary intake (92,93, 96-100).

## Unipolar Depression

The results of the studies in which L-tryptophan was administered to unipolar depressed patients are conflicting. These discrepancies may be due to methodologic differences in experimental designs, and to biochemical or diagnostic heterogeneity in the patients studied. Uncontrolled studies or open comparisons with ECT are quite vulnerable to observer bias, and positive and negative reports using these strategies are about evenly divided. The comparison of L-tryptophan with tricyclics may provide false positive results, because of the possibility of placebo responders in these studies.

The double-blind comparison of L-tryptophan with placebo in unipolar depression yielded negative results in three of three investigations (27-31). This design is probably the most rigorous test of L-tryptophan's efficacy, and these data raise doubt that this agent has any significant effects in unipolar depression.

There are some suggestions of an antidepressant effect with 5HTP, but too few patients have been included in placebo-controlled double-blind evaluations to permit a definite conclusion. It is of interest that in two reports (51,54), 5HTP responders were characterized by low CSF 5HIAA levels, suggesting there may be a biochemically identifiable subgroup of patients with an abnormality in serotonin metabolism. In one of these reports (54), the patients with low CSF 5HIAA concentrations were characterized by more anxiety, agitation and insomnia than were another group of patients who responded to L-dopa. It is of interest that 5HTP-response in this study occurred several days after the development of insomnia which may have been produced by the 5HTP. There are reports (101) that sleep deprivation per se may produce significant improvement in depressives, and it is therefore possible that this may have contributed to the apparent 5HTP response.

The studies with 5HTP are difficult to interpret because of the complex effects on various brain systems noted below. The more recent strategy of combining low dose 5HTP with peripheral decarboxylase blockade may result in more selective CNS serotonin potentiation, and further studies of this type will be of interest.

The important question to be answered in evaluating L-tryptophan's apparent ineffectiveness in unipolar patients is whether it results in selective activation of the serotonin systems in the brain. Winston (14) has suggested that the lack of an antidepressant effect with L-tryptophan in some studies might be due to the simultaneous administration of pyridoxine, which would increase the peripheral utilization of L-tryptophan, making it less available to the brain. Pyridoxine is a co-factor in the hepatic metabolism of L-tryptophan to kynurenic acid, anthranilic acid, xanthurenic acid, and 3-hydroxyanthranilic acid (102). There is evidence that some of these metabolites decrease the uptake of L-tryptophan by rat brain slices, resulting in a decrease in the brain serotonin (103). However, we (104) have shown that the concomitant administration of pyridoxine does not increase the urinary excretion of these compounds after L-tryptophan administration in man. Furthermore, pyridoxine does not inhibit the increase in serotonin and 5HIAA in rat brain after L-tryptophan administration *in vivo* (105), and therefore the absence of an antidepressant effect with L-tryptophan cannot be explained by the concomitant administration of pyridoxine.

**Table 15.  Tryptophan-Pyridoxine Interactions in Affective Illness**

|  | Tryptophan Effective | | Tryptophan Ineffective | |
|---|---|---|---|---|
|  | Pyridoxine Added | No Pyridoxine | Pyridoxine Added | No Pyridoxine |
| TP in Unipolar Depression | 2 | 3 | 7 | 0 |
| TP in Mania or Bipolar Depression | 3 | 0 | 0 | 0 |
| TP and MAOI in Depression | 2 | 3 | 0 | 0 |
| Total | 7 | 6 | 7 | 0 |

Table 15 summarizes the reported tryptophan-pyridoxine interactions in depressed patients. It is apparent that pyridoxine was used in all of the studies where tryptophan was found to be ineffective. However, as can be seen in the table, pyridoxine was also administered in seven studies where tryptophan was reported to be effective, especially in bipolar illness or when tryptophan was combined with an MAOI. Thus there is no clear clinical or biochemical evidence that pyridoxine blocks the purported antidepressant effects of tryptophan.

An alternative explanation for the ineffectiveness of tryptophan in some studies is the possibility that it may activate the hepatic pyrrolase enzyme. This could increase the peripheral metabolism of tryptophan, making less available for transport into the brain (106). There is evidence from animal studies (107-109) that either nicotinamide or allopurinol may block *in vivo* pyrrolase activity, so it has been suggested (106) that one of these agents should be administered with tryptophan in order to inhibit any excess hepatic shunting and perhaps enhance the antidepressant effects. Consistent with this hypothesis, nicotinamide plus L-tryptophan were found to be significantly more effective than unilateral electroshock treatments in one open study (18).

However, blood levels of free and bound plasma tryptophan increase enormously after oral tryptophan administration (110). Total plasma tryptophan increases by a factor of 10 and free plasma tryptophan increases by a factor of over 30 within two hours of a 5-gram oral dose of tryptophan to normal volunteers (110). It would therefore require a very large induction in pyrrolase activity with chronic tryptophan administration to lower these high levels of tryptophan. It is therefore unlikely that the ineffectiveness of L-tryptophan in unipolar depressed patients is due to hepatic pyrrolase induction.

Data dealing with the question of whether the administration of large doses of tryptophan leads to increased brain serotonin turnover in depressed patients is conflicting. Bowers (111,112) reported less of an increase in CSF 5HIAA levels after L-tryptophan loading in depressive than in schizophrenic patients. Ashcroft et al. (113,114) found no difference in CSF 5HIAA levels of depressed patients as compared with neurologic control subjects 8 hours after 50 mg/kg DL-tryptophan. Dunner and Goodwin (115) have reported a two- to threefold increase in the probenecid induced accumulation of CSF 5HIAA after an L-tryptophan load in depressed patients. Thus it cannot be assumed that a defect in blood-brain tryptophan transport or in brain serotonin synthesis is the basis for L-tryptophan's ineffectiveness as an antidepressant in unipolar patients.

It is not clear whether the serotonin formed in the brains of these patients is functionally active. Thus the administration of L-tryptophan to rats is followed by an *inhibition* of the firing rate of brain stem raphe neurons (116,117). This slowing may be due to a compensatory feedback inhibition from a postsynaptic neuron or to a direct effect of serotonin on presynaptic receptors. If this occurs in the patients receiving tryptophan, it would indicate that the functional output of serotonergic neurons might not be increased after the administration of L-tryptophan.

Another possible explanation for the relative ineffectiveness of L-tryptophan in unipolar depressed patients may be because they have an abnormality in serotonin release or postsynaptic receptor sensitivity. Thus while L-tryptophan has a sedative effect in normals, insomniacs, and manic patients (41-48), it does appear to increase sleep time in depressed patients (30). This could be due to an abnormality of serotonin release or receptor sensitivity in these patients. It is also necessary to remember that several indole compounds other than serotonin are formed after L-tryptophan loading. These include tryptamine (119), 5-methoxytryptamine (120), melatonin (120), and possibly others (121-123). Any of these may have neurotransmitter activity (120) and may affect the activity of serotonin.

The equivocal results of L-tryptophan alone in unipolar patients are quite puzzling in light of the fact that many studies have confirmed that L-tryptophan accelerates and intensifies the effects of MAO inhibitors, as compared with MAO inhibitors alone. One possible explanation for this may be that the serotonin formed after L-tryptophan alone is degraded intraneuronally by the monoamine oxidase system, and may not be released into the synapse in sufficient amounts to have significant postsynaptic effects. This

#### Table 16. Tryptophan and Lithium: Similarities

|  | L-tryptophan | Lithium |
|---|:---:|:---:|
| *Biochemical* | | |
| Stimulation of high affinity tryptophan uptake by brain synaptosomes | X | X |
| Acute stimulation of brain serotonin turnover | X | X |
| Chronic compensatory inhibition of tryptophan hydroxylase | ? | X |
| *Behavioral* | | |
| "Serotonergic syndrome" in rats pretreated with MAOI | X | X |
| *Clinical* | | |
| Equivocal effects in unipolar depression | X | X |
| Probable effects in bipolar depression | X | X |
| Anti-manic effects | X | X |
| Potentiation of MAOI | X | Probable |

obviously will not occur with the concurrent administration of an MAO inhibitor. In this regard, rats treated with L-tryptophan plus an MAO inhibitor develop a syndrome of hyperactivity that is not seen after L-tryptophan alone (118). It may be that the high levels of serotonin produced by this drug combination result in a "spillover" of free serotonin into the synapse with enhanced serotonergic activity that does not occur with tryptophan alone. Thus the effects of tryptophan plus MAO inhibitors in depressed patients are consistent with a role for serotonin in the modulation of mood.

## Bipolar Illness

There is some evidence that L-tryptophan may be beneficial in the manic (29,40), and depressed (27-29) phases of bipolar illness, in contrast with the findings with unipolar depressives. This is of interest because of several similarities between L-tryptophan and lithium (Table 16). Both L-tryptophan and lithium stimulate the high affinity tryptophan uptake system of rat brain synaptosomes (124). This correlates with increased brain serotonin turnover after both acute lithium and tryptophan administration. Chronic lithium administration seems to be associated with a return of brain serotonin synthesis to normal or below-normal levels (131). Knapp and Mandell (132) have reported that this decline in turnover rate is due to a compensatory inhibition of tryptophan hydroxylase, which occurs with chronic lithium administration. They have proposed (132) that the combination of increased tryptophan uptake and decreased tryptophan hydroxylation results in a "stabilization" of the serotonin system which may be related to the clinical effects of the drug. It is not known whether chronic L-tryptophan administration is also associated with a compensatory inhibition of tryptophan hydroxylase, but this information would be of considerable interest.

In addition, L-tryptophan and lithium have some striking similarities in their effects on animal behavior. Tryptophan plus an MAO inhibitor or lithium plus an MAO inhibitor both produce a typical "serotonergic syndrome" in the rat, consisting of hyperactivity and reciprocal forepaw treading (125). In both instances, this syndrome has been correlated with an increased rate of brain serotonin synthesis (125).

Clinically, the effects of both lithium and tryptophan on unipolar depression are controversial, and it appears that at most a small number of unipolar depressives will respond to these agents (133), while both may have antidepressant effects on some bipolar depressive patients (133). Both agents may potentiate the antidepressant effects of MAO inhibitors.

Thus it is possible (but unproven) that the beneficial effects of lithium are mediated through the brain's serotonin system. This leads to several predictions: (1) chronic L-tryptophan administration may stabilize mood oscillations in manic-depressive patients; (2) lithium may accelerate the antidepressant effects of monoamine oxidase inhibitors, as compared with monoamine oxidase inhibitors alone; and (3) lithium in combination with tryptophan may be superior to either agent alone.

## CONCLUSION

The data reviewed in this report suggest that L-dopa, alone or in combination with MAO inhibitors or peripheral decarboxylase blockade, is not a clinically effective antidepressant. However, L-dopa administration may not have a significant effect on CNS norepinephrine turnover, so that the finding does not have any significant implications for the hypothesis that decreased brain noradrenergic activity exists in some depressed patients. The activating effects of L-dopa in some depressed patients suggests that abnormalities of central dopaminergic activity may at least play a role in some aspects of the symptomology of affective illness. There is no conclusive evidence that the serotonin precursors tryptophan and 5HTP have a significant antidepressant effect in unipolar patients. However, there is evidence that L-tryptophan does potentiate the antidepressant effects of MAO inhibitors, which is compatible with the indoleamine hypothesis of depression. In addition, there are some preliminary reports that acute intravenous 5HTP has significant mood-elevating effects in individuals pretreated with decarboxylase inhibitors.

There are reports that L-tryptophan has antimanic and antidepressant effects in bipolar patients and evidence that L-tryptophan and lithium may have similar effects on CNS serotonergic systems. These data are consistent with the hypothesis of abnormalities of central serotonergic activity in both mania and depression, and require further investigation.

## REFERENCES

1. Prange, A. J., Jr. The pharmacology and biochemistry of depression. *Dis. Nerv. Syst.* 25:217-221, 1964.
2. Schildkraut, J. J. The catecholamine hypothesis of affective disorders: A review of supporting evidence. *Am. J. Psychiat.* 112:509-522, 1965.
3. Coppen, A. The biochemistry of affective disorders. *Br. J. Psychiat.* 113:1237-1264, 1967.
4. Davis, J. M. Theories of biological etiology of affective disorders, in *International Review of Neurobiology*, C. C. Pfeiffer and J. R. Smythies, eds., New York: Academic Press, Inc. 1970, Vol. 12, pp. 145-175.
5. Mendels, J., and Stinnett, J. Biogenic amine metabolism, depression and mania, in *Biological Psychiatry*, J. Mendels, ed., New York: Interscience-Wiley, 1973, pp. 99-131.
6. Robins, E., and Hartman, B. K. Some chemical theories of mental disorders, in *Basic Neurochemistry*, R. W. Albers, G. J. Siegel, R. Katzman, et al., eds., Boston: Little, Brown, 1972, pp. 607-644.
7. Carroll, B. J. Monoamine precursors in the treatment of depression. *Clin. Pharmacol. Ther.* 12:743-761, 1971.
8. Post, R. M., Kotin, J., Goodwin, F. K., et al. Psychomotor activity and cerebrospinal fluid amine metabolites in affective illness. *Am. J. Psychiat.* 130:67-72, 1973.
9. Mendels, J. Biological aspects of affective illness, in *The American Handbook of Psychiatry*, S. Arieti, ed., New York: Basic Books, 1974, pp. 448-479.
10. Mendels, J., and Frazer, A. Brain biogenic amine depletion and mood. *Arch. Gen. Psychiat.* 30:447-451, 1974.
11. Mendels, J., Stern, S., and Frazer, A. Biological concepts of depression, in *Depression: Behavioral, Biochemical, Diagnostic and Treatment Concepts*, D. Gallant and G. Simpson, eds., New York: Spectrum, 1976, pp. 19-74.
12. Bowers, M. B., Jr. Cerebrospinal fluid 5-hydroxyindoles and behavior after L-tryptophan and pyridoxine administration to psychiatric patients. *Neuropharm.* 9: 599-604, 1970.
13. Broadhurst, A. D. L-tryptophan versus ECT. *Lancet* 1:1392-1393, 1970.
14. Winston, F. Treatment of unipolar depression. *Lancet* (letter) i:868, 1975.

15. Coppen, A., Shaw, D. M., Herzberg, B., and Maggs, R. Tryptophan in the treatment of depression. *Lancet* 2:1178-1180, 1967.
16. Carroll, B. J., Mowbray, A. M., and Davies, B. Sequential comparison of L-tryptophan with ECT in severe depression. *Lancet* 1:967-969, 1970.
17. Harrington, R. N., Bruce, A., Johnston, E. C., et al. Comparative trial of L-tryptophan and E.C.T. in severe depressive illness. *Lancet* 2:731-734, 1974.
18. MacSweeney, D. A. Treatment of unipolar depression. *Lancet* (letter) ii:510-511, 1975.
20. Kline, N. S., and Shaw, B. K. Comparable therapeutic efficacy of tryptophan and imipramine: Average therapeutic ratings versus "true" equivalence: An important difference. *Curr. Ther. Res.* 15:484-487, 1973.
21. Gayford, J. J., Parker, A. L., Phillips, E. M., et al. Whole blood 5-hydroxytryptamine during treatment of endogenous depressive illness. *Br. J. Psychiat.* 122:597-598, 1973.
22. Coppen, A., Whybrow, P. C., Noguera, R., et al. The comparative antidepressant value of L-tryptophan and imipramine with and without attempted potentiation by liothyronine. *Arch. Gen. Psychiat.* 26:234-241, 1972.
23. Monro, J .Tryptophan/imipramine in depression. *Lancet* ii:920, 1975.
24. Baldessarini, R. J. Biogenic amine hypothesis in affective disorders, in *The Nature and Treatment of Depression*, F. F. Flack and S. C. Draghi, eds., New York: Wiley, 1975, pp. 347-385.
25. Burrows, G. D., Mowbray, R. M., and Davies, B. A sequential comparison of doxepin (Sinequan) and placebo in depressed patients. *Med. J. Aust.* 1:364-366, 1972.
26. Carroll, B. J., Mowbray, R. M., and Davies, B. L-tryptophan in depression. *Lancet,* 1:1228, 1970.
27. Bunney, W. E., Jr., Brodie, H. K. H., Murphy, D., et al. Studies of alpha-methyl-paratyrosine, L-DOPA, and L-tryptophan in depression and mania. *Am. J. Psychiat.* 127:872-881, 1971.
28. Murphy, D. L., Baker, M., Kotin, J., et al. Behavioral and metabolic effects of L-tryptophan in unipolar depressed patients, in *Serotonin and Behavior*, J. Barchas and E. Usdin, eds., New York: Academic Press, 1973, pp. 529-537.
29. Murphy, D. L., Baker, M., Goodwin, F. K., et al. L-tryptophan in affective disorders: Indoleamine changes and differential clinical effects. *Psychopharmacologia (Berl.)* 34:11-20, 1974.
30. Mendels, J., Stinnett, J. L., Burns, D., et al. Amine precursors and depression. *Arch. Gen. Psychiat.* 32:22-30, 1975.
31. Dunner, D. L., and Fieve, R. R. Affective disorder: Studies with amine precursors. *Am. J. Psychiat.* 132 (2) :180-183, 1975.
32. Coppen, A., Shaw, D. M., and Farrell, J. P. Potentiation of the antidepressant effect of a monoamine-oxidase inhibitor by tryptophan. *Lancet* 1:79-81, 1963.
33. Pare, C. M. B. Potentiation of monoamine oxidase inhibitors by tryptophan. *Lancet* 2:527-528, 1963.
34. Glassman, A. H., and Platman, S. R. Potentiation of monoamine-oxidase inhibitor by tryptophan. *J. Psychiat. Res.* 7:83-88, 1969.
35. Gutierrez, J. L. A., and Alino, J. J. L.-I. Tryptophan and a MAOI (nialamide) in the treatment of depression. *Int. Pharmacopsychiat.* 6:92-97, 1971.
36. Shaw, D. M., Johnson, A. L., and MacSweeney, D. A. Tricyclic antidepressants and tryptophan in unipolar affective disorder. *Lancet* (letter) ii:1245, 1972.

37. Shaw, D. M., MacSweeney, D. A., Hewland, R., et al. Tricyclic antidepressants and tryptophan in unipolar depression. *Psychol. Med.* 5:276-278, 1975.
38. Alino, J. J. L.-I., Gutierrez, J. L. A., and Iglesias, M. L. M. Tryptophan and amitriptyline in the treatment of depression: A double-blind study. *Int. Pharmacopsychiat.* 8:145-151, 1973.
39. Walinder, J., Skott, A., Nagy, A., et al. Potentiation of antidepressant action of clomipramine by tryptophan. *Lancet* i:984, 1975.
40. Prange, A. J., Jr., Wilson, I. C., Lynn, G. W., et al. L-tryptophan in mania. *Arch. Gen. Psychiat.* 30:56-62, 1974.
41. Smith, B., and Prockop, D. J. Central nervous system effects of ingestion of L-tryptophan by normal subjects. *New Eng. J. Med.* 267:1338-1341, 1962.
42. Griffiths, W. J., Lester, B. K., Coulter, J. D., et al. Tryptophan and sleep in young adults. *Psychophysiology* 9:345-346, 1972.
43. Hartmann, E. L. The effect of L-tryptophan on the sleep-dream cycle in man. *Psychosom. Sci.* 8:479-480, 1967.
44. Hartmann, E. L. L-tryptophan as a physiological hypnotic. *Lancet* 1:807, 1971.
45. Hartmann, E., Chung, R., and Chien, C. P. L-tryptophan and sleep. *Psychopharmacologia* 19:114-127, 1971.
46. Hartmann, E., and Chung, R. Sleep-inducing effects of L-tryptophan. *J. Pharm. Pharmacol.* 24:252:253, 1972.
47. Wyatt, R. J., Engelman, K., Kupfer, D. J., et al. Effects of L-tryptophan (a natural sedative) on human sleep. *Lancet* 2:842-846, 1970.
48. Mendels, J., and Chernik, D. A. The effect of L-tryptophan on sleep in man, in *Sleep Research*, M. H. Chase, W. C. Stern, and P. L. Walter, eds., Los Angeles: Brain Information Service/Brain Research Institute, 1972, p. 66.
49. Persson, T., and Roos, B-E. 5-Hydroxytryptophan for depression. *Lancet* 2 (2) :987-988, 1967.
50. Van Praag, H. M., Korf, J., Dols, L. C. W., et al. A pilot study of the predictive value of the probenecid test in application of 5-hydroxytryptophan as antidepressant. *Psychopharmacologia (Berl.)* 25:14-21, 1972.
51. Van Praag, H. M., and Korf, J. 5-Hydroxytryptophan as an antidepressant. *J. Nerv. Ment. Dis.* 158 (5) :331-337, 1974.
52. Van Praag, H. M., and Korf, J. Zur Diskussion: Central monoamine deficiency in depression: Causative or secondary phenomenon? *Pharmakopsych.* 8:322-326, 1975.
53. Sano, I. L-5-Hydroxytryptophan- (L-5-HTP) Therapie. *Fol. Psychiat. Neurol.* 26 (1) : 7-17, 1972.
54. Fujiwara, J., and Otsuki, S. Subtype of affective psychoses classified by response on amine precursors and monoamine metabolism. *Fol. Psychiat. Neurol.* 28 (2) : 93-99, 1974.
55. Pare, C. M. B., and Sandler, M. A clinical and biochemical study of a trial of iproniazid in the treatment of depression. *J. Neurol. Neurosurg. Psychiat.* 22:247-251, 1959.
55A. Ingvarsson, C. G. Orientierende klinische versuche zur wirkung des dioxy phenylalanins (L-Dopa) bei endogener depression. *Arzneimittel-forschung.* 15:849-852, 1965.
56. Kline, N. S., and Sacks, W. Relief of depression within one day using an M.A.O. inhibitor and intravenous 5-HTP. *Am. J. Psychiat.* 120:274-275, 1963.
57. Kline, N. S., Sacks, W., and Simpson, G. M. Further studies on: One day treatment of depression with 5-HTP. *Am. J. Psychiat.* 121:379-381, 1964.

58. Fuxe, K., Butcher, L. L., and Engel, J. DL-5-Hydroxytryptophan-induced changes in central monoamine neurons after peripheral decarboxylase inhibition. *J. Pharm. Pharmacol.* 23:420-424, 1971.

59. Aghajanian, G. K., and Asher, I. M. Histochemical fluorescence of raphe neurons: Selective enhancement by tryptophan. *Science* 172:1159-1161, 1971.

60. Dahlstrom, A., and Fuxe, K. Evidence for the existence of monoamine-containing neurons in the central nervous system: I. Demonstration of monoamines in the cell bodies of brain stem neurons. *Acta Physiol. Scand.* 62: 1-55, 1964.

61. Moir, A. T. B., and Eccleston, D. The effects of precursor loading in the cerebral metabolism of 5-hydroxyindoles. *J. Neurochem.* 15:1093-1108, 1968.

62. Korf, J., Venema, K., and Postema, F. Decarboxylation of exogenous L-5-hydroxytryptophan after destruction of the cerebral raphe system. *J. Neurochem.* 23:249-252, 1974.

63. Brodie, H. K. H., Sack, R., and Siever, L. 1. Clinical studies of L-5-hydroxytryptophan in depression, in *Serotonin and Behavior*, J. Barchas and E. Usdin, eds., New York: Academic Press, 1973, pp. 549-560.

64. Matussek, N., Angst, J., Benkert, M., et al. The effect of L-5-hydroxytryptophan alone and in combination with a decarboxylase inhibitor (Ro 4-4602) in depressive patients. *Adv. Biochem. Psychopharmacol.* 11:399-404, 1974.

65. Trimble, M., Chadwick, D., Reynolds, E. H., et al. L-5-hydroxytryptophan and mood. *Lancet* i:583, 1975.

66. Klerman, G. L., Schildkraut, J. J., Hasenbush, L. L., et al. Clinical experience with dihydroxyphenylalanine (DOPA) in depression. *J. Psychiat. Res.* 1:289-297, 1963.

67. Goodwin, F. K., Murphy, D. L., Brodie, H. K. H., et al. Levodopa: Alterations in behavior. *Clin. Pharmacol. Ther.* 12:383-396, 1971.

68. Murphy, D. L., Goodwin, F. K., Brodie, H. K. H., et al. L-dopa dopamine, and hypomania. *Am. J. Psychiat.* 130 (1) :79-82, 1973.

68A. Murphy, D. L. L-dopa, behavioral activation and psychopathology. *Neurotrans.* 50: 472-493, 1972.

69. Matussek, N. L-DOPA in the treatment of depression, in *Advances in Neuropharmacology*, O. Vinar, Z. Votava, and P. B. Bradley, eds., Amsterdam: North Holland Publishing Co., 1971, pp. 111-119.

70. Persson, T., and Walinder, J. L-DOPA in the treatment of depressive symptoms. *Br. J. Psychiat.* 119:277-278, 1971.

71. Nahunek, K., Svestka, J., Kamenicka, V., et al. Preliminary clinical experience with L-DOPA in endogenous depressions. *Act. Nerv. Super. (Praha)* 14:101-102, 1972.

72. Bunney, B. S., Aghajanian, G. K., and Roth, R. H. Comparison of effects of L-dopa, amphetamine and apomorphine on firng rate of rat dopaminergic neurones. *Nature New Biol.* 245 (143) :123-125, 1973.

73. Van Praag, H. M., and Korf, J. Retarded depression and the dopamine metabolism. *Psychopharmacologia* 19:199-203, 1971.

74. Ng, K. Y., Chase, T. N., Colburn, R. W., et al. L-dopa-induced release of cerebral monoamines. *Science* 170:76-77, 1970.

75. Wurtman, R. J., and Romero, J. A. Effects of levodopa on nondopaminergic brain neurons. *Neurol.* 22 (5) :72-81, 1972.

76. Fahn, S., Snider, S., Prasad, A. L. N., et al. Normalization of brain serotonin by L-tryptophan in levodopa-treated rats. *Neurol.* 25 (9) :861-865, 1975.

77. Murphy, D. L. Amine precursors, amines, and false neurotransmitters in depressed patients. *Am. J. Psychiat.* 129 (2) :55-62, 1972.

78. Goodwin, F. K., Dunner, D. L., and Gershon, E. S. Effect of L-dopa treatment on brain serotonin metabolism in depressed patients. *Life Sci.* 10 (1) :751-759, 1971.
79. Tyce, G. M., Muenter, M. D., and Owen, C. A., Jr. Metabolism of L-dihydroxyphenylalanine by patients with Parkinson's disease. *Mayo Clin. Proc.* 45:645-656. 1970.
80. Brune, G. G., and Pflughaupt, K. W. Effects of L-DOPA treatment on indole metabolism in Parkinson's disease. *Experientia* 27:516, 1971.
81. Everett, G. M., and Borcherding, K. W. L-DOPA: Effect on concentrations of dopamine, norepinephrine and serotonin in brains of mice. *Science* 168:849-850, 1970.
82. Constantinidis, J., Bartholini, G., Tissot, R., et al. Accumulation of dopamine in the parenchyma after decarboxylase inhibition in the capillaries of brain. *Experientia* 24:130-131, 1968.
83. Bartholini, G., and Pletscher, A. Cerebral accumulation and metabolism of C14-dopa after selective inhibition of peripheral decarboxylase. *J. Pharmacol. Exp. Ther.* 161: 14-20, 1968.
84. Reis, D. J., Moorhead, D. T. II, and Merlino, N. Dopa-induced excitement in the cat: Its relationship to brain norepinephrine concentrations. *Arch. Neurol.* 22:31-39, 1970
85. Breese, G. R., and Prange, A. J., Jr. Chronic dopa treatment: Effect on the concentration of norepinephrine in the hearts and brains of rats. *Eur. J. Pharmacol.* 13:259-261. 1971.
86. Chalmers, J. P., Baldessarini, R. J., and Wurtman, R. J. Effects of L-dopa on norepinephrine metabolism in the brain. *Proc. Nat. Acad. Sci. U.S.A.* 68:662-666, 1971.
87. O'Gorman, L. P., Borud, O., Khan, I. A., et al. The metabolism of L-3, 4-dihydroxyphenylalanine in man. *Clin. Chim. Acta* 29:111-119,1970.
88. Morgan, J. P., Bianchine, J. R., Spiegel, H. E., et al. Metabolism of levodopa in patients with Parkinson's disease: Radioactive and fluorometric essays. *Arch. Neurol.* 25:39-44, 1971.
89. Goodall, M., and Alton, H. Metabolism of 3, 4-dihydroxyphenyl-ala-nine (L-dopa) in human subjects. *Biochem. Pharmacol.* 21:2401-2408, 1972.
90. Jequier, E., Loverberg, W., and Sjoerdsma, A. Tryptophan hydroxylase inhibition: The mechanisms by which p-chlorophenylalanine depletes rat brain serotonin. *Mol. Pharmacol.* 3:274-278, 1967.
91. Lovenbert, W., Jequier, E., and Sjoerdsma, A. Tryptophan hydroxylation in mammalian systems. *Adv. Pharmacol. Chemother.* 6:21-36, 1968.
92. Fernstrom, J. D., and Wurtman, R. J. Brain serotonin content: Physiological dependence on plasma tryptophan levels. *Science* 173:149-152, 1971.
93. Fernstrom, J. D., and Wurtman, R. J. Effect of chronic corn consumption on serotonin content of rat brain. *Nature (New Biol.)* 234:62-64, 1971.
94. Tagliamonte, A., Tagliamonte, P., Perez-Cruet, J., et al. Effect of psychotropic drugs on tryptophan concentration in the rat brain. *J. Pharmacol. Exp. Ther.* 177: 475-480, 1971.
95. Costa, E. Appraisal of current methods to estimate the turnover rate of serotonin and catecholamines in human brain, in *Advances in Biochemical Psychopharmacology*, M. Ebadi, and E. Costa, eds., New York: Raven Press, 1972, vol. 4, pp. 171-183.
96. Lin, R. C., Costa, E., Neff, N. H., et al. *In vivo* measurement of 5-hydroxy-C14-tryptophan to C14-5-hydroxytryptamine. *J. Pharmacol. Exp. Ther.* 170:232-238, 1969.

97. Neff, N. H., Spano, P. F., Gropetti, C. T., et al. A simple procedure for calculating the synthesis rate of norepinephrine, dopamine and serotonin in rat brain. *J. Pharmacol. Exp. Ther.* 176:701-710, 1971.

98. Fernstrom, J. D., and Wurtman, R. J. Brain serotonin content: Increase following ingestion of carbohydrate diet. *Science* 174:1023-1025, 1971.

99. Fernstrom, J. D., Larin, F., and Wurtman, R. J. Daily variations in the concentrations of individual amino acids in rat plasma. *Life Sci.* 10:813-819, 1971.

100. Fernstrom, J. D., Larin, F., and Wurtman, R. J. Correlations between brain tryptophan and plasma neutral amino acid levels following food consumption in rats. *Life Sci.* 13:517-524, 1973.

101. Editorial: Depression and curtailment of sleep. *Brit. Med. J.* 4:543 1975.

102. Adams, P. W., Rose, D. P., Folklord, J., et al. Effect of pyridoxine hydrochloride (vitamin B₆) upon depression associated with oral contraception. *Lancet* 1:899-904, 1973.

103. Green, A. R., and Curzon, G. The effect of tryptophan metabolites on brain 5-hydroxytryptamine metabolism. *Biochem. Pharmacol.* 19:2061-2068, 1970.

104. Frazer, A., Pandey, G. N., and Mendels, J. Metabolism of tryptophan in depressive disease. *Arch. Gen. Psychiat.* 29:528-535, 1973.

105. Carroll, B. J., and Dodge, J. L-tryptophan as an antidepressant. *Lancet* 1:915, 1971.

106. Young, S. N., and Sourkes, T. L. Antidepressant action of tryptophan. *Lancet* ii: 897-898, 1974.

107. Badawy, A. A.-B., and Evans, M. Tryptophan plus a pyrrolase inhibitor for depression? *Lancet* ii:1209-1210, 1974.

108. Fernando, J. C., Joseph, M. H., and Curzon, G. Tryptophan plus a pyrrolase inhibitor for depression? *Lancet* i:171, 1975.

109. Badawy, A. A.-B., and Evans, M. Tryptophan plus a pyrrolase inhibitor for depression. *Lancet* ii:869, 1975.

110. Greenwood, M. H., Lader, M. H., Kantameneni, B. D., et al. The effects of oral tryptophan in human subjects. *Br. J. Clin. Pharmac.* 2:165-172, 1975.

111. Bowers, M. B., Jr. Cerebrospinal fluid 5-hydroxyindoles and behavior after L-tryptophan and pyridoxine administration to psychiatric patients. *Neuropharmacol.* 9:599-604, 1970.

112. Bowers, M. B., Jr. 5-HT metabolism in psychiatric syndromes. *Lancet* 2:1029, 1970.

113. Ashcroft, G. W., Blackburn, I. M., Eccleston, D., et al. Changes on recovery in the concentrations of tryptophan and the biogenic amine metabolites in the cerebrospinal fluid of patients with affective illness. *Psychol. Med.* 3:319-325, 1973.

114. Ashcroft, G. W., Crawford, T. B. B., Cundall, R. L., et al. 5-Hydroxytryptamine metabolism in affective illness: The effect of tryptophan administration. *Psychol. Med.* 3:326-332, 1973.

115. Dunner, D. L., and Goodwin, F. K. Effect of L-tryptophan on brain serotonin metabolism in depressed patients. *Arch. Gen. Psychiat.* 26:364-366, 1972.

116. Aghajanian, G. K. Influence of drugs on the firing of serotonin-containing neurons in the brain. *Fed. Proc.* 31:91-96, 1972.

117. Aghajanian, G. K., and Haigler, H. J. Direct and indirect actions of LSD, serotonin and related compounds on serotonin-containing neurons, in *Serotonin and Behavior*, J. Barchas and E. Usdin, eds., New York: Academic Press, 1973, pp. 263-266.

118. Grahame-Smith, D. G. Studies *in vivo* on the relationship between brain tryptophan,

brain 5-HT synthesis and hyperactivity in rats treated with a monoamine oxidase inhibitor and L-tryptophan. *J. Neurochem.* 18:1053-1066, 1971.

119. Saavedra, J. M., and Axelrod, J. Effect of drugs on the tryptamine content of rat tissues. *J. Pharmacol. Exp. Ther.* 185:523-529, 1973.

120. Koslow, S. H., and Green, R. A. Analysis of pineal and brain indole alkylamines by gas chromatography-mass spectrometry, in *Advances in Biochemical Psychopharmacology*, E. Costa and B. Holmstedt, eds., New York: Raven Press, 1973, vol. 7, pp. 33-43.

121. Aghajanian, G. K., and Asher, I. M. Histochemical fluorescence of raphe neurons: Selective enhancement by tryptophan. *Science* 172:1159-1161, 1971.

122. Bjorklund, A., Falck, B., and Slenewi, V. Classification of monoamine neurons in the rat mesencephalon: Distribution of a new monoamine system. *Brain Res.* 32: 269-285, 1971.

123. Gal, E. M. Hydroxylation of tryptophan and its control in brain. *Pavlovian J.* 10 (3) : 145-160, 1975.

124. Knapp, S., and Mandell, A. J. Short- and long-term lithium administration: Effects on the brain's serotonergic biosynthetic systems. *Science* 180:645-646, 1973.

125. Grahame-Smith, D. G., and Green, A. R. The role of brain 5-hydroxytryptamine in the hyperactivity produced in rats by lithium and monoamine oxidase inhibition. *Br. J. Pharmac.* 52:19-26,1974.

126. Schubert, J. Effect of chronic lithium treatment on monoamine metabolism in rat brain. *Psychopharmacologia (Berl.)* 52:19-26, 1974.

127. Segawa, T., and Nakano, M. Brain serotonin metabolism in lithium treated rats. *Japan. J. Pharmacol.* 24:319-324, 1974.

128. Perez-Cruet, J., Tagliamonte, A., Tagliamonte, P., et al. Stimulation of serotonin synthesis by lithium. *J. Pharmacol. Exp. Ther.* 178 (2) :325-330, 1971.

129. Tagliamonte, A., Tagliamonte, P., Perez-Cruet, J., et al. Effect of psychotropic drugs on tryptophan concentration in the rat brain. *J. Pharmacol. Exp. Ther.* 177 (3) : 475-480, 1971.

130. Iwata, H., Okamoto, H., and Kuramoto, I. Effect of lithium on serum tryptophan and brain serotonin in rats. *Japan. J. Pharmacol.* 24:235-240, 1974.

131. Ho, A. K. S., Loh, H. H., Craves, F., et al. The effect of prolonged lithium treatment on the synthesis rate and turnover of monoamines in brain regions of rats. *Eur. J. Pharmacol.* 10:72-78, 1970.

132. Knapp, S., and Mandell, A. J. Effects of lithium chloride on parameters of biosynthetic capacity for 5-hydroxytryptamine in rat brain. *J. Pharmacol. Exp. Ther.* 193 (3) :812-823, 1975.

133. Mendels, J. Lithium in the treatment of depression. *Am. J. Psychiat.* 133:373-378, 1976.

4

# Iatrogenic Depression
# in Women

FRANCIS J. KANE

The noted clinical pharmacologist Dr. Louis LaSagna has coined the term "the diseases of medical progress" (1) for those illnesses which occur as a result of our new therapies, especially those involving pharmacologic agents which we currently use to treat our patients. The main focus of this review will be those illnesses, especially depression, which occur with the use of the oral contraceptive agents. The early clinical studies of hormonal oral contraceptives stressed their high degree of clinical efficacy in controlling reproduction, associated with a fairly low incidence of side effects of all kinds (2). The passage of time and a concomitant broadened base of experience make possible a more accurate appraisal of the role of these agents in our "diseases of medical progress." The currently available clinical evidence indicates that: (1) as many as 50% of women using oral contraceptives will experience mild to moderate depression, irritability, tiredness and emotional lability; (2) psychotic reactions have been reported, including two reports of psychosis upon withdrawal of medication; (3) decreased sexual drive and capacity for orgasm is a frequent occurrence; (4) patients with a previous history of psychiatric illness were more at risk for such reactions; (5) these reactions seem to be related to higher progestin content of the drug; (6) possible causative mechanisms probably include (a) hormone-induced alterations of the neurohormones norepinephrine and serotonin (b) altered vitamin metabolism, especially pyridoxine, folic acid, and $B^{12}$ (c) altered corticosteroid metabolism (d) impaired psychological defenses (e) activation of psychological conflicts as a result of drug use.

Our observation of the first reported psychotic reaction, a withdrawal psychosis (3), prompted a pilot study (4) which yielded data considerably at variance with then-reported studies, with a substantial incidence of depression and impaired libido. Our own experience with five cases of psychosis (5,6) (2 sequential and 3 combination agents) and two other reported cases (7,8) showed that 6 of the 7 patients had previous histories of psychiatric morbidity. Four of the 6 reported significant postpartum reactions. In a second study of 139 women without a history of psychiatric care and 64 women with such a history, 52% of the normal women and 75% of those with a psychiatric history reported adverse change with use of these drugs (9). Depression and irritability were most often reported by both groups, while 10% reported feeling better while taking drugs. Those most at risk for such reactions had reported increased menstrual disability and lessened frequency of sexual activity, supporting the premise that these agents enhanced already present neurotic traits in these women. Several Swedish studies reported similar results. Nilsson et al. (10) reported the results of a questionnaire study of 313 women who had received an oral contraceptive during the year of 1964: 53% of the sample reported new symptoms of emotional disturbance or worsening of previous symptoms of emotional disturbance; 9% reported improvement in symptoms of emotional disturbance. The women at greatest risk for development of psychiatric symptoms were (1) those with a previous psychiatric history, (2) those with psychiatric symptoms of severe nausea and vomiting during previous pregnancy and (3) overweight women. Ten times more women experienced a decrease in sexual interest than had an increase. In 1968, Nilsson and Almgren reported a prospective study of 168 women (11). Fifty-four pill users were compared with 104 using other contraceptive means. After two to four months, pill users had a significant increase in (1) psychiatric morbidity, (2) depressive symptoms (feelings of depression, sleep disturbance, inferiority feelings, and difficulty in starting work), (3) neurasthenic symptoms (increased fatiguability, increased emotional lability, and irritability) and (4) weight gain.

Lewis and Hóghughi (12) reported similar data in a study using psychiatric evaluations and a Hamilton Rating Scale for Depressive Symptoms.

Women who were taking oral contraceptives had significantly more clinical depression (2 were suicidal) and had a significantly higher score on the Hamilton Rating Scale. Patients with a previous history of depression were found to be more at risk to develop depression. There was a trend toward higher depression scores with longer time period of use, and higher dose of progestin.

Herzberg et al. (13) showed that 6.6% of their group showed significant evidence of depression severe enough to require discontinuing contraceptive medication versus 2% of controls. The women who developed depression and irritability as side effects had higher neuroticism scores and an increased incidence of moderate or severe depression before starting the pill.

Culberg et al. (14) reported a study of 99 pill takers and 99 controls which showed 14% reporting mental or sexual disturbances during the first six months, but no abnormal mental symptoms after six months. In a study of 215 patients utilizing psychiatric evaluation inventories and rating scales, Peterson (15) reported 46% of his patients to show strong adverse reactions, mostly of the depressed type. He also reported that the gestagen-dominant preparations showed more psychic symptoms. Grounds et al. (16), in a double-blind study with 10 women over two cycles using fairly comprehensive psychiatric and psychological evaluation, showed that 9 of 10 patients were depressed during the first months when taking the pill, while the control groups had only 2 of 10 patients depressed. In addition, he reported decreased sexual interest in 8 of 10 patients. In 1971, Silbergeld et al. (17) in a double-blind crossover placebo study four cycles long, involving eight patients, showed very significant tranquilizing effects. Self-rated anxiety was also increased.

Culberg (18), in a double-blind study of 299 women, showed that 14% more individuals reported adverse mental changes in the interview ratings of the gestagen-dominated medication groups in comparison with a placebo group. Estrogen-dominated pills showed 18% more negative reactions than the placebo groups. These differences were significant at the .05 level. The mental symptoms were generally mild and mostly of a depressive dysphoric type. In his study, Culberg showed that women who had more premenstrual irritability tended to have reactions more than those without premenstrual symptoms.

Huffer (19) et al. compared 16 patients who experinced adverse psychological symptoms with 23 who had none. Of those who had difficulty, 11 showed depressive reactions and 5 had loss of sexual interest and pleasure not related to depression. All developed these symptoms while on the oral contraceptive and lost them after discontinuance. Two factors tended to correspond with the development of adverse reactions: the use of combined as opposed to sequential type of contraceptive pill, and age of subject.

Bakke (20) in a double-blind study of an estrogen alone, an estrogen-progestin mixture, and placebo in 32 hysterectomized postmenopausal women has also documented irritability and moodiness in 9 of 32 patients. Increased and decreased libido were reported, and he also noted mood changes and insomnia accompanying withdrawal of both estrogen and estrogen-progestin medications.

There have been some reported negative studies. Herzberg and Coppen (21), in a one-year study of 218 pill takers and 54 IUD users using psychiatric evaluation and rating scales, demonstrated no clear significant difference between the groups. Goldzieher et al. (22), using a double-blind crossover method utilizing placebo, reported some increased nervousness in the first-treatment cycle with one preparation. They also reported that estrogen-dominant preparations showed psychic symptoms in contrast to gestagen-dominant preparations. In a number of studies, Kutner (23) has been unable to support a relationship between oral contraception and depression. He found no evidence that oral contraceptives aggravated a depressive history, but a history of depression in relation to pregnancy did seem to be associated with discontinuance of the drug. The strength of his data lies in the use of objective rating instruments such as the MMPI Depression Scale, a large sampling of patients (5,151), and its existence as part of a multiphasic health screening.

There is now a considerable body of clinical and experimental data indicating that alterations in the metabolism of biogenic amines, especially noradrenaline and serotonin, may be crucial to the development of depressive and manic illnesses. Much research in the United States has focused on the hypothesis that lower levels of noradrenaline at central noradrenergic receptor sites accompany depression, while mania is believed to be characterized by an excess of noradrenaline at these sites (24). These hypotheses are supported by clinical evidence showing that drugs which deplete noradrenaline are associated with clinical depression (reserpine, disulfiram, alpha methyl dopa), especially in those who have had previous significant depressive episodes. Drugs which antagonize the effects of reserpine in animals (MAO inhibitors, tricyclic antidepressants) have been shown to be effective antidepressants in man.

Another area of considerable research interest, especially with regard to depressive states in psychiatric patients, concerns the possibility that alterations in the metabolism of tryptophan and its subsequent metabolism to serotonin (5-hydroxytryptamine) may be important in the genesis of depressive illness. Studies in depressed patients have revealed that they excrete less tryptamine when depressed, and when they recover, tryptamine excretion is increased. The administration of tryptamine also has beneficial effects upon the disturbed sleep of depressed patients, and the administration of tryptamine plus psychotropic drugs has been shown by some to have beneficial effect upon the course of depressive illness.

There is a considerable body of evidence, mainly in animals, showing that the hormones of the type used in estrogen-progestin mixtures may be dependent for their action in brain upon biogenic amines. Myerson (25), for example, has shown that estrous behavior in ovariectomized animals, normally activated by estrogen and progesterone, will also be activated by estrogen in combination with amine depletors tetrabenzine and reserpine. In previous experiments, he had shown that estrogen plus monoamine oxidase inhibitors inhibited sexual behavior. He sees this as most easily explained by the assumption of monoamine-dependent pathways mediating heat inhibition. Increased levels of monoamine produce decreased sexual response, while a decrease in biogenic amines increases the heat response. His work seemed to suggest that progesterone may act by altering amine levels in brain or receptor response to amines in some way. A recent report confirmed the influence of gonadal hormones in either sex or norepinephrine metabolism in the brain of rats (26). Other experimenters have shown that there were alterations in biogenic amines and MAO activity in brain related to the estrous cycle of the rat (27,28). Biogenic amine values and MAO activity were maximum in proestrus and lowest at estrus. Work of this kind is relatively sparse in humans. We reported (29) a one-month psychophysiological double-blind study of 3 patients which revealed (1) diminished sexual desire in all 3 subjects; (2) objective and subjective evidence of mild depression in 2 of the 3 subjects; (3) sleep decrease was reported by 2 subjects; (4) remembered dreams doubled during the drug period; (5) there was a decrease in basal resting heart rate; and (6) there was a decreased excretion of catecholamine metabolites. In another study (30) 7 female subjects were studied on a single-blind basis. Two subjects received only a combination oral contraceptive while 5 other subjects received the most commonly used estrogen, mestranol, for 2 weeks, followed by a combined hormone pill containing mestranol and a progestin.

Two subjects who received the higher dose of progestin reported depression with a decreased level of urinary metabolites during the drug period as compared to their normal luteal phase. The 5 subjects who received a lower dosage showed, as the most consistent finding, an increase in normetanephrine excretion.

Other research has focused upon alterations in vitamin metabolism, many of which are co-enzymes in neurohormone metabolism. The changes described above may be related to functional pyridoxine deficiency. Mason et al. (31) have examined several vitamin B[6] dependent enzyme systems in the tryptophan kynurenine pathway and suggest that estrogen conjugates compete with pyridoxal phosphate for binding sites on several apoenzymes, notably kynureninase and kynuernine transaminase. In view of the fact that estrogen has been shown to inhibit 5-hydroxytryptophan decarboxylase in vitro (32), it is not unreasonable to suppose that a similar situation may exist along the indole pathway, reducing levels of tryptamine and serotonin, the synthesis of which is pyridoxine dependent. Since dopa decarboxylase is thought to be the same enzyme as 5-hydroxtryptophan decarboxylase and is also pyridoxine-dependent, levels of catecholamines may be similarly affected. It has been shown that up to 25 mg pyridoxine are required daily to correct tryptophan metabolism along the kynurenine pathway in women taking oral contraceptives (33). As the usual human dietary requirement is approximately 2 mg daily, this seems to be evidence that oral contraceptives markedly interfere with the proper use of, or increase the need for, pyridoxine. In view of the many decarboxylase and transaminase reactions that are pyridoxine-dependent, it is unlikely that such a situation would manifest itself with one clinical symptom such as depression, and consideration must be given to the possibility that a functional pyridoxine deficiency is contributory to other side effects of oral contraceptives. An oral contraceptive manufactured in Spain, which contains 25 mg pyridoxine, is reported to have fewer side effects (34).

Another possible contributor to the phenomena observed may relate to alterations in folate metabolism. Shojania et al. (35) have recently reported a significant lowering of plasma folate levels in oral contraceptive users. In his study, 30% of the values of those using contraceptives were below the lowest of the nonusers. Folate deficiency and megaloblastic anemia have recently been reported associated with the use of oral contraceptives. Streiff et al. (36) described five women taking oral contraceptives in whom folate deficiency and megaloblastic anemia developed who did not respond hematologically to a normal hospital diet but did respond to the oral administration of 250 micrograms of folic acid daily even though they continued to take oral contraceptives. Two additional patients had a hematologic response following discontinuation of oral contraceptive agents without the need for folic acid supplementation. Folate absorption studies in nine women taking oral contraceptive agents appeared to show a reduction in absorption of folate polyglutamate but not the monoglutamate form. Prior treatment with folic acid abolished the malabsorption of folate polyglutamate.

Another contribution to the understanding of this abnormality was reported by da Costa and Rothenberg (37), who showed the presence of a macromolecular factor with binding determinants for unreduced and partially reduced folates to be present in the leucocytes of patients who were pregnant and those taking oral contraceptives. This binding capacity reduced by 90% at the end of the pregnancy.

Wertalik et al. (38) have shown a significant reduction of serum vitamin $B^{12}$ levels in women taking oral contraceptives. This reduction can occur within five months, and serum levels may fall to values indistinguishable from other forms of vitamin $B^{12}$ deficiencies. In spite of the drastic reduction in serum levels in some women, no anemia or evidence of tissue depletion was detected. They also confirmed the presence of a reduction of serum folates. The authors were unable to explain this phenomenon, since absorption seemed normal as evidenced by normal Shilling tests in two subjects and an increase in vitamin $B^{12}$ serum level when a small oral dose was administered. Lowered folic acid levels may interfere with biogenic amine metabolism, since folic acid has been shown to give an important co-factor in the rate-limiting step in the biosynthesis of norepinephrine. Reynolds et al. (39,40) studied serum folate and vitamin $B^{12}$ levels in 101 patients with depressive illness. Subnormal folates were found in 24% and subnormal $B^{12}$ levels in .2% of the patients. Patients with subnormal folate levels were found to have significantly higher depressive scores and significantly lower validity scores on the Mark Nyman Temperament Scale on admission and discharge. Vitamin $B^{12}$ deficiency (40) has been shown to be important in producing many types of psychological disturbance, including depression, confusion, and psychotic pictures.

Metabolic studies have also shown alterations in the metabolism of vitamin A and vitamin C as well. A significant increase in plasma levels of vitamin A has been shown in women taking the oral contraceptive pills when compared with controls studied under similar conditions (41). None of the pill subjects have values approaching toxic levels. In another study, Kalesh et al. (42) showed that women taking oral contraceptives exhibited significantly lower platelet ascorbic acid levels than controls two weeks after both had been placed on a low vitamin C diet. While most investigators have stressed that these findings do not necessarily connote pathology, it is of interest that in a recent study (43) in the *American Journal of Clinical Nutrition*, physical findings related to vitamin deficiency have been described, especially in the lower socioeconomic groups who use oral contraceptive agents. Such findings as dry skin, easily plucked hair, angular lesion of the mouth, caries and debris of teeth, marginal redness, swelling, and bleeding of the gums, filiform papillary atrophy, fungiform papillary hypertrophy of the tongue and glossitis, and scaling of the skin were seen more often in these groups. Most vitamin deficiency states have a component of depression, and these findings suggest that in some patients this may well be a variable to be concerned about.

Another area in which further research is needed concerns the altered steroid level seen in patients who use these medications. The rise in total plasma corticosteroids is substantial, though most investigators believe these to be in bound form. Other (45,46) investigators have cast doubt upon this, with one report citing a two and a half fold increase in unbound steroids at the tissue level. Thus a relative state of hypercorticism may exist in at least some of the patients. Psychiatrists are familiar with the increased morbidity associated with the use of exogenous corticosteroids. This may be the underlying mechanism in the 2 cases of withdrawal psychosis which have been reported, and may also account for the mild withdrawal symptoms reported by patients when they stop the pill every month.

Another explanation for some of these undesirable side effects of the oral contraceptive agents may be explained by so-called nonspecific paradoxical reactions to drugs which have been observed often with agents which cause tranquilization or central nervous system depression. Progesterone has central nervous system depressant properties and has been used as an anesthetic agent (46). Many of the symptoms described by the patients could also be seen as relating to these tranquilizing effects. The major tranquilizers have been observed to cause similar paradoxical reactions: when given to emotionally disturbed patients they seemed to make the situation worse rather than better. DiMascio and Klerman (47) studied the effects of such drugs on normal subjects. They identified two groups of patients with different clusters of personality characteristics. One type, labeled type A, was an athletically oriented type whose personality integration was dependent upon a great deal of motor activity and interaction with the environment. The other group of subjects, called type B, represented an aesthetic, intellectually oriented, passive type of individual. In a number of studies utilizing drugs with sedative and nonsedative properties, the athletic subjects tended to react in a paradoxical fashion to drugs with pronounced sedative actions—in this case secobarbital and chlorpromazine. They manifested this by expressing irritability, apprehension, and increased anger, and by becoming more agitated and showing thought confusion with impairment of learning. On the other hand, the aesthetic subjects showed improvement on tests of intellectual functioning, reported no negative feeling toward the drug, became more calm, and showed an increase in rapport after the same dose of sedative drugs. Similar findings were found with the use of minor tranquilizers in normal subjects classified as high or low anxious on the basis of scores on an anxiety scale (48). They found that these drugs were helpful in lowering anxiety levels in the high anxious subjects, while in the low anxious subjects an increase in anxiety was noted. In a similar design, patients with high and low depressive scores in a normal population were given 150 mg of imipramine and showed a decrease in depression. Those with high scores showed a decrease in depression, while those with low depression scale scores tended to have increasing depression (49). These experiments clearly demonstrate the importance of the basic normal personality in the evaluation of any kind of drug response, especially those with tranquilizing properties. It is quite likely that such factors have accounted for at least some of the depression in the clinical groups described.

Another variable contributing to the overall adjustment to oral contraceptive agents is the use to which they may be put in the complex relationship between huband and wife. Zell and Crisp (50) have categorized the fears associated with drug use as follows:

1) Fears about bodily damage. While there can be some legitimate concern about such a possibility, these may also be a more superficial manifestation of resentment related to feminine role conflict. Anything that might provoke physical change would be seen as a threat, especially if it were more likely to remind the woman of her deprived female status. Such drugs might also tend to diminish the possibility of using sexuality to manipulate a relationship with a man.

2) Fear of loss of control of sexual impulses and latent fantasies of prostitution. Such fears may account for some of the loss of sexual desire and capacity for orgasm seen in our sample, as a further defense against the feared sexual impulses which can no longer be suppressed or otherwise controlled by concerns about pregnancy. These had previously been useful as a defense against guilt-provoking sexual experiences.

3) Fears about future fertility. Here again, a seemingly realistic fear may reflect concern about interference with an important source of self-esteem for all women—their ability to bear children. In certain cultural groups, this is an important source of self-esteem to the woman and her partner and has actually contributed to the nonuse of any method of contraception, often where they are most needed. The fears about menopause may also be related to such an unconscious attitude. This is a factor of importance in middle-life depressions and has been shown to be an important source of morbidity in reaction to other kinds of contraceptive or operative procedures on the female genital tracts involving the loss of procreative function, whether intentional or not. Similar considerations apply to those women who have strong unconscious wishes for children and respond to the thwarting of these wishes with depression and other manifestations of psychological conflict.

In summary, the data seem to show an increased risk of development of mild to moderate symptoms of depression and loss of sexual interest and capacity for orgasm in a considerable number of women. Those most at risk would seem to be those with a history of previous psychiatric illness, especially postpartum disorders. Those with a history of severe premenstrual symptoms would also seem to be more at risk. The only menstrual symptom not shown to be associated with neuroticism is cramps during the menses. This is of some importance because of the oral contraceptive agents are sometimes used to treat severe dysmenorrhea. The use of vitamin supplements, especially in the poorly nourished, would seem to be indicated to counter the possibility of the deficiency states described. The persistence of symptom reactions with the use of other contraceptive measures would indicate the need for an exploration of possible intrapsychic factors in the user.

The many biochemical abnormalities which have been shown to occur must now be shown to be related to the altered mood and behavioral changes cited, since few of the studies reviewed have been conducted with special attention to concomitant behavior change.

## REFERENCES

1. LaSagna, L. The disease drugs cause. *Perspect. Biol. Med.*, 7:457, 1964.
2. Glick, I. D. Mood and behavioral changes associated with the use of oral contraceptive agents. *Psychopharmacol.* 10:363-374, 1967.
3. Keeler, M. H., Daly, R., and Klee, F. J. An acute schizophrenic episode following abrupt withdrawal of Envoid in a patient with previous postpartum psychiatric disorder. *Amer. J. Psychiat.* 120:1123-1124, 1964.
4. Kane, F. J., Daly, R. J., Ewing, J., and Keeler, M. Mood and behavior changes with progestational agents. *Br. J. Psychiat.* 113:265-268, 1967.
5. Daly, R. J., Kane, F. J., and Ewing, J. A. Psychosis associated with the use of a sequential oral contraceptive. *Lancet* 2:444-445, 1967.
6. Kane, F. J. Psychosis associated with the use of oral contraceptive agents. *South. Med. J.* 62:190-192, 1969.
7. Idestrom, C. M. Reaction to norethisterone withdrawal. *Lancet* 1:718, 1966.
8. Sturgis, S. H. Oral contraceptives and their effect on sex behavior. *M. Aspects Hum. Sex.* 2:4-9, 1968.
9. Kane, F. J., Treadway, R., and Ewing, J. Emotional change associated with oral contraceptives in female psychiatric patients. *Comp. Psych.* 10:16-30, 1969.
10. Nilsson, A., Jacobson, L., and Ingemanson, C. A. Side effects on an oral contraceptive with particular attention to mental symptoms and sexual adaptation. *Acta. Obst.-Gynecol. Scand.* 46:537-556, 1967.
11. Nilsson, A., and Almgren, P. E. Psychiatric symptoms during the postpartum period as related to use of oral contraceptives. *Brit. Med. J.* 2:453-455, 1968.
12. Lewis, A., and Hóghughi, M. An evaluation of depression as a side effect of oral contraceptives. *Brit. J. Psych.* 115:697-701, 1969.
13. Herzberg, B., Johnson, A. L., and Brown, S. Depressive symptoms and oral contraceptives. *Brit. Med. J.* 4:142, 1970.
14. Culberg, J., Gelli, M., and Jonsson, C-O. Mental and sexual adjustment before and after six months' use of an oral contraceptive. *Acta. Psy. Scan.* 45:259-276, 1969.
15. Peterson, P. Psychiatrische und psychologische aspekte der familienplanung bei oral Kontrazeption. Stuttgart: Georg Thieme Verlag, 1969.

16. Grounds, D., Davies, B., and Mowbray, R. The contraceptive pill, side effects, and personality—Report of a controlled double blind trial. *Brit. J. Psychiat.* 116:169-172, 1970.
17. Silbergeld, S., Brast, N., and Noble, E. P. The menstrual cycle—A double blind study of symptoms, mood, and behavior, and biochemical variables using Envoid and placebo. *Psychosom. Med.* 33:411-428, 1971.
18. Culberg, J. Mood changes and menstrual symptoms with different gestagen/estrogen combinations: A double blind comparison with a placebo. *Acta Psy. Scan. Suppl.* 48: 236, 1972.
19. Huffer, V., Levin, L., and Aronson, H. Oral contraceptives: Depression and frigidity. *J. Nerv. and Ment. Dis.* 151:1, 35-41, 1970.
20. Bakke, J. L. A double-blind study of a progestin-estrogen combination in the management of the menopause. *Pacific Med. Surg.* 73:200-205, 1965.
21. Herzberg, B., and Coppen, A. Changes in psychological symptoms in women taking oral contraceptives. *Br. J. Psychiat.* 116:161-164, 1970.
22. Goldzieher, J. W., Moses, L. E., Averkin, E., Scheel, C., and Taber, B. Z. Nervousness and depression attributed to oral contraceptives—A double blind, placebo controlled study. *Am. J. Ob. Gyn.* 111:8, 1013-1020, December 15, 1971.
23. Kutner, S. J., and Brown, W. L. Types of oral contraceptives, depression, and premenstrual symptoms. *J. Nerv. and Ment. Dis.* 15:3, 153-169, 1972.
24. Schildkraut, J. J., and Kety, S. S. Biogenic amines and emotion. *Science* 156:21-30, 1967.
25. Myerson, B. Estrus behavior in spayed rats after estrogen or progesterone treatment in combination with reserpine or tetrabenazine. *Psychopharmacol.* (Berlin) 6:210-218, 1964.
26. Anton-Tay, F., and Wurtman, R. J. Norepinephrine turnover in rat brains after gonadectomy. *Science* 159:1245, 1968.
27. Kuwabara, S. Hypothalamic biogenic amines, monoamine oxidase (MAO) and the estrus cycle. 49th Meeting of the Endocrine Society, Miami Beach, Florida, 1967.
28. Stefano, F. J. E., and Donoso, A. Norepinephrine levels in the rat hypothalamus during the estrus cycle. *Endocrin.* 81: 1405-1406, 1967.
29. Marcotte, D., Kane, F. J., Lipton, M., and Obrist, P. Psychophysiologic changes accompanying oral contraceptive use. *Br. J. Psychiat.* 116:165-167, 1970.
30. Kane, F. J., Lipton, M. A., Krall, A. R., and Obrist, P. A. Psychoendocrine study of oral contraceptive agents. *Amer. J. Psychiat.* 127:85-92, 1970.
31. Mason, M., Ford, J., and Wu, H. L. C. Effects of steroid and non-steroid metabolites on enzyme conformation and pyridoxal phosphate binding. *Proc. N.Y. Acad. Sci.* 166:170, 1969.
32. Mason, J., and Schirchi, L. Inhibition of B6 enzymes by free and conjugated estrogens. *Fed. Proc.* 20:200, 1961.
33. Luhby, A. L., Davis, P., Murphy, M., Gordon, M., Brin, M., and Spiegel, H. Pyridoxine and oral contraceptives. *Lancet* II:1083, November 21, 1970.
34. Otte, J. Oral contraceptives and depression. *Lancet* II:498, 1969.
35. Shojania, A. M., Hernady, G., and Barnes, P. H. Oral contraceptives and serumfolate levels. *Lancet* I:6, 1376, 1968.
36. Lewis, A., and Hóghughi, M. An evaluation of depression as a side effect. *Br. J. Psychiat.* 115:697, 1969.
37. daCosta, Maria, and Rothenberg, S. P. Appearance of folate binder in leukocytes and serum of women who are pregnant or taking oral contraceptives. *J. Lab and Clin. Med.* 83:2, 207-214, February, 1974.

38. Wertalik, Metz, E. N., Lobuglio, A. F., and Bolcerzak, S. P. Decreased serum B[12] levels with oral contraceptive use. *J.A.M.A.* 221:12, 1371-1374, 1972.
39. Reynolds, E. H., Preece, J. M., Bailey, J., and Coppen, A. Folate deficiency in depressive illness. *Br. J. Psychiat.* 117:287-292, 1970.
40. Reynolds, E. H., Milner, G., Matthews, D. M., and Chanarin, I. Anticonvulsant therapy, folic acid, and Vitamin B[12] metabolism and mental symptoms.
41. Gal, I., Parkinson, C., and Craft, I. Effects of oral contraceptives on human plasma Vitamin A levels. *Br. Med. J.* 2:436-438, May 22, 1971.
42. Kalesh, A. G., Mallikarjuneswara, V., and Clemetson, C. A. Effects of estrogen-containing oral contraceptives on platelet and plasma ascorbic acid concentrations. *Contraception* 4:3. 183-192, September, 1971.
43. Prasad, A. S., Oberleas, D., Lei, D. Y., Moghissi, K. S., et al. Effect of oral contraceptive agents on nutrients: I. Minerals. *Amer. J. Clin Nutrition* 28:377-384, April 1975.
44. Wynn, V., and Doar, J. W. H. Some effects of oral contraceptives on carbohydrate metabolism. *Lancet* 2:715-719, 1966.
45. Plager, J. E., Schmidt, K. G., and Staubitz, W. J. Increased unbound cortisol in the plasma of estrogen-treated subjects. *J. Clin. Invest.* 43:1066-1072, 1964.
46. Merryman, W. J. Progesterone 'anesthesia' in human subjects. *J. Clin. Endocr.* 14: 1567, 1954.
47. Klerman, G. L., DiMascio, A., Greenblatt, M., and Rinkel, M. The influence of specific personality patterns on the reactions of phrenotropic agents. In *Biological Psychiatry*, J. Masserman, ed. New York, Grune & Stratton, pp. 224-242.
48. DiMascio, A., and Barrett, J. Comparative effects of oxazepam in "high" and "low" anxious student volunteers. *Psychosomatics*, 6:298-302, 1965.
49. DiMascio, A., Meyer, R. E., and Stiffler, L. Effects of imipramine on individuals varying in level of depression. *Amer. J. Psychiat.* In press.
50. Zell, J., and Crisp, W. E. A psychiatric evaluation of the use of oral contraceptives. *Obst. Gynec.* 23:657, 1964.

5

# Gender and Depression: A Sociological Analysis of a Conditional Relationship

HOWARD B. KAPLAN

One of the more consistent findings concerning correlates of depression is the report that this disorder is more prevalent among females. Silverman (1), for example, asserts: "There appears to be no exception to the generalization that depression is more common in women than in men, whether it is the feeling of depression, neurotic depression, or depressive psychosis." Kendell (2) notes that "the greater liability of women to depression is one of the few facts that is established beyond question." This conclusion appears to be warranted whether it is based upon studies of hospitalized patients or investigations of general populations and (among the latter category) whether depression is defined in terms of psychiatric syndromes or scores on depression scales. Illustrative of studies of patient populations (3,4) is that of DeFundia and his associates (5) in which, among samples of hospitalized psychiatric patients in Argentina and the United States, women were more likely to have received diagnoses of depression than men. With regard to differential prevalence rates of clinical depression in the general population Dohrenwend (6), referring to earlier reviews of "true prevalence" studies (7,8), notes the consistently higher female rates of neurosis (28 of 32 relevant studies) and manic-depressive psychosis (18 of 24 relevant studies) "with their *possible common denominator of depressive symptomatology* ..." (my italics). Other studies, while not reporting on sex-related differences in depressive diagnosis, did report that in general populations, females scored significantly higher than males on measures of depressed mood (9,10).

The relationship between sex and depression is consistent with any of a number of explanations. First, numerous attempts have been made to implicate female endocrine-physiologic processes in the genesis of depression (1,11,12).

The observation of greater prevalence of depression among females is also consistent with the view that females are more likely than males to experience stresses that lead to depression and other psychological responses. The implication is that were men to experience a like number of stresses of equal intensity that depression would be as prevalent among males as among females. Gove and Tudo (13) consider several reasons why it may be assumed that because of the roles they occupy, women are more likely than men to have emotional problems. They point to the restriction to a single major social role that implies the absence of major alternative sources of gratification; the requirements to perform frustrating and low prestige instrumental activities; the unstructured and invisible role requirements of the housewife that permits her to brood over her troubles; the less prestigious position of the married working woman and the greater number of hours that she must work at her combined household and occupational chores; and the unclear and diffuse expectations confronting women.

In support of the argument that it is the social role of the married woman rather than biological characteristics of females which increases the probability of mental illness among women relative to men, studies report married women to have noticeably higher rates of mental illness than married men, although when single women are compared with single men, divorced women with divorced men, and widowed women with widowed men, there is no significant distinction by sex in the rate of mental illness. Indeed, what small difference does exist suggests that women within these categories have lower rates of mental illness than men (14).

A third point of view, also consistent with the male-female differential in depression, is that, regardless of whether the sexes differ in number and kind of stresses, the two sexes are prone to employ different (in the extreme) pathological response patterns consequent to the experience of severe and persistent stress. Males or females are not necessarily more likely to experience psychiatric disorder. Rather, given the predisposition to psychiatric disorder, females are more likely to experience certain types of disorder (such as depression) while males are more likely to experience other disorders (for example, sociopathic patterns), perhaps as extensions of normal modes of adapting to stress (15,5). Dohrenwend (6) generalizes from studies of true prevalence and states the issue as follows:

> The major sex differences that we have found in the results of the "true" prevalence studies center on the consistently higher female rates of neurosis and manic-depressive psychosis with their *possible common denominator of depressive symptomatology*, and the consistently higher male rates of personality disorder with its possible common denominator of irresponsible and anti-social behavior. The issue these differences raise is: what is there in the endowments and experience of men and women that push them in their different deviant directions? [my italics: p. 369.]

These views are not necessarily mutually exclusive. The research objective here, therefore, is not to demonstrate that only one point of view is true, but rather to consider the tenability of one of the explanations whether or not the other explanations have merit. The present study is devoted to consideration of the third point of view.

In the formulation that guided this analysis it is postulated that the "stresses" referred to in the last two explanations are all interpretable as circumstances that threaten the person's positive self-evaluation and thereby evoke self-rejecting attitudes (16).

Depression is viewed here as the affective response to such negative self-attitudes. In response to persistent and severe self-devaluing experiences, the individual is unable to deflect blame from the self, by directing the blame (for the blameworthy experience) outward, by denying the occurrence of a blameworthy event, by counterbalancing the experience of self-blame with self-enhancing experiences, or by employing any of a number of other adaptive, coping, or defense mechanisms. The inability to avoid self-blame (that is, the loss of self-esteem) evokes depression as its affective component. Although depression as a response to loss of self-esteem (and to the implicit inability to consistently turn blame away from the self in blameworthy circumstances) is interpreted primarily as the emotional expression of subjective distress, it is also interpretable as a somewhat effective mechanism for restoring a degree of self-esteem. This distinction parallels that made by Bibring (17) between the basic mechanism of depression, "fall in self-esteem due to awareness of one's own real or imaginary, partial or total, insufficiency or helplessness," and the secondary uses of depression that may be made consciously or unconsciously, such as gaining narcissistic gratification by receiving affection and attention.

Elements of this concept of depression (the central role of loss of self-esteem, the relationship between depression and inner-directed anger, the distinction between depression as the emotional expression of loss of self-esteem and as an attempt to restore self-esteem) are consistent with any of a number of psychoanalytic, broader psychological, and sociocultural theories of depression, and empirical studies stimulated by those theories (17,18,19).

The frequently observed sex difference in the prevalence of depression is said to be a consequence of differential socialization experiences which decrease the probability that females will employ mechanisms that permit deflection of blame away from self in the face of self-devaluing circumstances and increase the probability of self-rejecting responses in such circumstances. The socialization experiences were such that the adoption of mechanisms that would otherwise permit turning blame away from self by females is regarded as inappropriate. Thus the adoption of such mechanisms in an attempt to avoid self-devaluation and consequent depression could only be accomplished at risk of further loss of self-esteem entailed by the adoption of proscribed patterns.

Among the female socialization experiences that would inhibit successful deflection of blame away from self in blameworthy circumstances are the proscription against externalization (hostile-aggressive) type responses by females and the greater dependence of the female upon others for satisfaction of personal needs. In the former case, the female would (if successfully socialized) experience self-reproach as a consequence of externalization of blame. In the latter case, the female would risk loss of interpersonal gratification by hostile-aggression responses to others (on the assumption that these responses would evoke negative sanctions toward the subject by the object of these extra-punitive responses) and might also be expected to inhibit avoidance responses, since the range of affectional needs is in large measure dependent upon her interpersonal communication with other group members.

The formulation presented here is supported in both child development literature and in the literature dealing with sex-related differences in ego-defense mechanisms.

Kagan (20), reviewing research literature, evaluates the proposition that the basic motivation for sex-role identification is the desire to conform to an internal standard. Apparently sex-role standards consisting of culturally approved characteristics for males and females do in fact exist. Children at a very early age (4 years) frequently become aware of these standards. The extent to which the individual regards himself or herself as masculine or feminine constitutes sex-role identity. The sex-role identity is established and maintained by the individual's expectations of affection and acceptance and the prevention of social rejection by displaying the traits of the standard. Deviation from sex-role standards can produce anxiety and conflicts in view of the strong motivation to achieve congruence between an ideal representation of the self and everyday behavior. In the present context, then, the question arises as to what extent, if at all, are circumstances associated with the differential use of blame-deflecting mechanism aspects of sex-role identification processes. Apparently such circumstances are indeed closely associated with differential sex-role socialization. In support of this conclusion are the following categories of results:

First, females are consistently reported to be significantly less likely to display aggression than males regardless of the nature of the research design (21). Since the blaming of others is a major mechanism for avoiding self-blame, and since this mechanism involves expression of some degree of hostility, this finding is consistent with the assertion that females are less likely to be trained to deflect blame from self. In observational studies, McCandless and associates (22), observing pre-school-age children, noted that boys initiated significantly more conflicts than girls and showed less resistance to conflict. Girls tended to change the activity they were engaged in more frequently following conflict.

In rating studies, for example, Digman (23), in a study of rating of personality traits of first- and second-grade children, observed that boys tended to be rated as more negativistic, untrustworthy, aggressive, and noisy than girls. Toigo and associates (24) noted that boys received higher peer-nomination aggression scores than girls in a study of third-graders.

In experimental studies a number of investigators reported that nursery school or four-to-six-year-old boys were significantly more likely to manifest imitative and/or nonimitative aggression than similarly aged girls (25,26,27, 28,29,30). Moore (31) reported results for four-to-six-year-old children that indicated that boys were more likely to manifest direct aggression with less displacement of aggression following frustration. In this study the subjects played a card game in which they lost or won chips from cards which were either blank or which bore a drawing of a child of the subject's own sex. In the low frustration condition the child came out even winning from the child card. The child was then asked to play a shooting game where he could either shoot at the card with the figure of high or low similarity to the card used in the chip game.

Buss (32) reported for college student subjects that men were significantly more aggressive than women to a person associated with frustration. The subject was asked to act as the experimenter in a concept-learning task. Punishment was in terms of the subject-determined strength of shock to be administered. The subject was told that the reward he received would depend on how fast his victim learned the task. The victim always learned too slowly to earn the reward for the subject. Half the men and half the women subjects had a male victim and the other half a female victim. The results indicated that men were significantly more aggressive than females.

Studies employing projective tests generally showed similar sex differences. In a variety of age groups (5-14, 6-13, college men, 20-to-29-year-olds), using any of a variety of projective tests (TAT, Rosenzweig P-F Test, Sentence Completions, tachistoscopic recognition), men were generally noted to be more hostile or aggressive than females (33,34,35).

Studies utilizing self-report measures of aggression and hostility were also confirmatory of the general conclusion. In studies using a variety of adolescent and adult subject groupings, boys (men) manifested higher aggressive and hostile tendencies than women (36,37,38,39). In the few studies in which women or girls were higher on some measure of aggression or hostility they tended to be higher on pro-social aggression but lower on anti-social aggression relative to boys (40) or higher on covert hostility but lower on overt hostility than men (41).

Studies observing fantasy aggression in doll play also tended to note a greater tendency of boys relative to girls to be aggressive and hostile. Sears (42), observing children's aggressive acts in doll play where the dolls represented family members, noted that boys were significantly more likely to manifest aggressive acts than girls—in particular, direct bodily injury. Moore and Ucko (43) observed children during a structured-doll-play session in which the child was asked to tell what would happen in domestic situations such as children fighting, not enough food for the family, a lapse in toilet-training. Among the relevant observations for present purposes were those that boys tended to give more aggressive responses when tested at age four and again at age six. When they were anxious, boys were more likely to give aggressive responses, while the girls were more likely to give passive responses or to not respond at all (interpreted as avoiding the problem).

Throughout this discussion the assumption has been made that aggression for males serves as a more or less effective mechanism for restoring or maintaining self-esteem, and that, by virtue of the socialization process, females are deprived of this mechanism. This assumption is further supported by findings that reports of aggression toward fathers and measures of aggression on the Rorschach were related to the self-rated need for acceptance for boys but not for girls (37).

Second, if in fact females were socialized to inhibit extrapunitive responses, it would be expected not only that such responses would be less frequent among females, but also that females would display greater anxiety than males over aggression. When observations about anxiety and guilt associated with aggression are made separately for the sexes, it does appear to be the case that women are more likely to manifest guilt or anxiety when manifesting aggression. Sears (40), reporting on sixth-grade children, found that girls were indeed higher on aggression anxiety. In an experimental situation, Buss and Brock (44) observed that guilt (assessed by questionnaire following the experiment) was more likely to be observed in women than men. The experiment involved subjects who were known to be opposed to giving shocks being required to administer shocks to experimental subjects. Rothaus and Worchel (38), in an experimental situation involving the provocation of hostility, observed that women had higher aggression-anxiety scores (indicated by the amount of impersonal aggression expressed on the TAT). Wyer et al. (39), as in the previous two studies cited above, observed college students and again reported that males were less likely to manifest guilt over aggression. Cosentino and Heilbrun (45) reported that at the age of twenty, as at the age of twelve, rating of femininity was related to greater aggression anxiety for both males and females, and that within either sex a more feminine sex-role identity involved more than a latent disposition to respond with greater anxiety to aggression cues.

Third, as would be expected if females were socialized to be less aggressive than males, aggressive behavior by females tends to evoke negative sanctions from others.

In this connection, Sears and his associates (46) indicated that boys' mothers were more permissive of aggression toward parents and peers. In an experiment in which grade-school teachers rated hypothetical children as if they were children in their classroom, it was observed that teachers manifested a significantly greater liking for dependent girls than for aggressive girls, although there was no significant difference in their liking of dependent boys and aggressive boys (47).

Fourth, females are characteristically socialized to have a greater need for affiliation than males and therefore (by implication) a greater need to avoid disruption or attenuation of social relationships. With very few exceptions studies suggest that women and girls are observed to be significantly more likely to display a need for affiliation than men and boys (48,49,50,41,37). Congruent with the observations of these studies are reports by McClelland that when achievement motivation was aroused by introducing competition for social approval and acceptability women showed a significant increase in achievement motivation (by TAT responses) while men did not (51).

Compatible also with the presumed greater need for affiliation by females is the observation that females rather than males tend to display greater interest in, and positive feelings for, others. In a Classified Summary of Research in Sex Differences (21) some 22 studies are cited that with few exceptions support this conclusion. Since the female's affiliative needs are so strong it is unlikely that they would permit themselves to use guilt-deflecting mechanisms (extrapunitive and avoidance responses) that might evoke negative sanctions from positively valued others and/or would deprive the female of full participation in relationships that offer diffuse personal gratification.

Fifth, in support of this reasoning, the development in the course of the socialization process of a greater dependency upon interpersonal relationship on the part of females is reflected in the greater tendency for females relative to males to conform to peer-group judgments in experimental group pressure studies (52,53,54,55,56), as well as to endorse socially acceptable attitudes and to manifest acceptance of group standards in paper and pencil tests (57,58,36).

Finally, the relative inability of females to avoid self-blame and consequent depression, whether by blaming others or otherwise avoiding personal responsibility for blameworthy circumstances (including personal attributes and behaviors), is suggested by a number of studies dealing with ego-defense mechanisms which are employed by normal and clinical samples.

If females manifest higher depression because of the greater inability to deflect blame outward and/or a tendency to use self-blame as a defense, we would expect the literature to report just such tendencies on the parts of males and females. That is, males would be more likely to employ defenses which externalize blame and females would manifest greater tendencies toward self-blame.

Just such tendencies were reported by Gleser and Ihilevich (59). In college, general adult, and psychiatric samples, males appeared significantly more likely than females to manifest "turning against object" defenses (dealing with conflict through attacking a real or presumed frustrating object and including such defenses as identification with the aggressor and displacement). Males were also consistently higher on projection defenses in the three samples, although the differences were only significant in the student sample. Projection includes those defenses that "justify the expression of aggression toward an external object through first attributing to it, without unequivocal evidence, negative intent, or characteristics" (59). Females, on the other hand, were significantly higher on "turning against self" defenses. Included in this class are those defenses that deal with conflict by directing aggressive behavior toward the self. Certain of the findings were affirmed by Bogo and his associates (60) when they reported for their college student subjects that men demonstrated more of a tendency to use ego-defense mechanisms involving turning against an object and a lesser tendency to turn against the self than women. No sex differences were observed, however, for the mechanisms of reversal, principalization, or projection.

Consistent with these results are the results of a study of psychiatric symptomatology in hospitalized patients in Argentina and the United States.

In both countries, females were more likely than males to manifest symptoms that reflected the dominant role of turning against one's self (for example, guilt; self-accusation; self-critical, self-depreciatory ideas; suicidal ideas; fears of hostile impulses; apprehension; depression; insomnia; disturbed sleep), while men were more likely to manifest symptoms reflecting dominant roles of turning against others (assaultive threats; temper outbursts; excessive drinking; irresponsible behavior; assaultiveness; exhibitionism; etc.) or avoidance of others (excessive daydreams and fantasies; poor time, place, or person orientation; depersonalization; hallucinations; apathy; social isolation; etc.), although these trends appear to be more pronounced in Argentina than in the United States (5).

The self-punitive tendency of females is attested to by a number of studies from the child-development literature. For example, Sears and his associates (61) noted among the nursery school students a greater tendency for girls to show emotional upset where they believed that they had deviated from adult requests. Rebelsky and her associates (62), studying sixth-grade children, administered story completions in order to determine fantasy confessions to deviation. The story completions were administered before and after a game in which cheating was possible and necessary to win the game. Girls confessed in the story completions more than boys. Further, girls were more likely than boys to be reported by their mothers as having highly developed consciences (46) and to rate themselves as high in conscience as a determinant of behavior (63).

Given these findings, it is perhaps not surprising that for children age two to five brought to a clinic, parents tended to report significantly more hyperaggression among other symptoms for boys while girls were reported to have significantly more problems related to overdependence and emotional overcontrol as well as other symptoms (64).

A number of other reports are also interpretable as indicating that females (particularly those raised in the traditional female role) are less able to effectively defend against ego threat. Thus, Gump (65) reported from a study of college women data that suggest overall ego strength may be inversely related to conformity to a narrowly defined traditional female sex role. Further, Maccoby and Jacklin (12) note that "boys obtain higher scores on 'lie' scales and 'defensiveness' scales that are designed to measure the degree to which an individual disguises his actual evaluation of himself and attempts to present an entirely favorable picture of himself to the researcher." They make this observation in the context of noting that male self-concepts might indeed be lower than are reflected on self-report measures of self-concept. Nevertheless, these observations might also be taken as indicating that women are less able to deflect self-blame. Maccoby and Jacklin (12) cite a number of studies relevant to the presumed higher rate of defensiveness on the part of males.

However, although there is abundant literature supporting the assertions that females are more depressed than males and that the socialization experiences of the sexes are such that females are inhibited from responding in ways that would deflect blame from self, there are virtually no acceptable data indicating that the sex differences in depression hold only under circumstances that reflect such socialization outcomes.

In order to determine whether or not the sex differential in depression *is a function of* socialization experiences that inhibit (facilitate) deflection of blame from the self in blameworthy circumstances, a research strategy was adopted that is based on the concept of the conditional relationship. By this strategy, if a given explanation for an observed relationship is under consideration, a series of conditions are specified under which the observed relationship would hold or be strengthened *if the explanation in question is tenable.* If the relationship in fact holds only under the specified conditions, then the explanation under consideration is supported. While any one conditional relationship might be congruent with more than one explanation, it is not likely that a pattern of such conditional relationships would be supportive of multiple explanations. Indeed, if the same complex pattern of conditions were stipulated for different explanations to be appropriate, this would suggest that the "different" explanations were in fact the same explanation.

An earlier study successfully employed the strategy of conditional relationship analysis in an investigation of the association between social class and self-derogation (66).

## STATEMENT OF THE PROBLEM

This paper reports findings relating to a series of 15 hypotheses about the conditions under which a statistically significant relationship between sex and depressive affect will be observed. The hypotheses take the form: For subjects characterized by condition X, a statistically significant relationship between depressive affect and sex will be observed; for subjects characterized by condition X', no such relationship is hypothesized. In each instance where the relationship between sex and depressive affect was hypothesized, it was expected that females would be significantly more likely to manifest high depressive affect scores than males.

The conditions under which the relationship was hypothesized were those which are assumed to reflect circumstances that would facilitate the expression of self-derogatory attitudes to self-devaluing experiences and/or would inhibit alternative responses to such self-devaluing experiences. Such alternative responses would include externalization of blame and denial of the occurrence of the blameworthy (self-devaluing experiences). Insofar as depression is said to be the emotional concomitant of self-devaluing judgments (that is, loss of self-esteem), such conditions which would effectively increase the probability of self-derogating responses would increase the manifestations of high depressive affect.

If indeed the greater prevalence of depression among females is accounted for by differential socialization experiences for the two sexes such that females are inhibited from employing mechanisms that deflect blame from self (in blameworthy circumstances), any condition that would impose external constraints and/or would evoke internal inhibition against such mechanisms should permit observation of the sex differential in depression. To the extent that the sex differential in depression is consistently observed under the specified conditions but not in the absence of such conditions, support would be provided for the thesis that the sex differential in depression is a function of socialization experiences that inhibit or proscribe the use of mechanisms by females which would deflect judgments of self-blame in blameworthy circumstances.

Although the study was not initiated for this particular purpose, data collected in the course of a study of correlates of self-derogation in the general population permit an oblique investigation of the conditions under which the generally hypothesized associations between sex and depression would be observed.

## METHOD

Since the methodology of the investigation has been described in detail elsewhere (67), only a brief overview will be presented here.

### Sampling and Data Collection

The data were collected by personal interview with a sample of 500 respondents selected from the adult population of Harris County, Texas, which includes the city of Houston. The sample was selected by a three-stage probability sample design (Selection of a random sample of 500 blocks or identifiable geographical areas within the county and random selection of respondents from among eligible respondents in the selected households). "Eligible respondent" was defined as a person 21 years of age or older, if married. Of the preselected sample, 74.6 per cent were successfully interviewed. Eighteen per cent refused to be interviewed, 6.4 per cent could not be contacted after at least six attempts, and 1 per cent terminated during the interview. These 127 respondents were replaced by substitute respondents selected at random from adjacent households, thus ensuring that the replacements were from areas with adjacent socioeconomic characteristics similar to those of the preselected subjects.

The primarily structured 23-page schedule was administered to the respondents in their homes between July 18 and November 18, 1966. The interviews were conducted by a local marketing counsel and research firm. On the average, the interview lasted slightly over one hour.

## Operational Definitions

For the purposes of the present report, the relevant operational definitions were those relating to depressive affect and the "conditional variable."

*Depressive affect.* The Guttman scale and scoring procedure to indicate depressive affect were adopted directly from Rosenberg (68). The items and response categories are presented immediately below. The possible scores range from 0 to 6, with the subject receiving a positive score for any item if the response fell into one of the starred response categories. A higher score indicated greater depressive affect.

1. On the whole, how happy would you say you are?
      Very happy
      Fairly happy
      *Not very happy
      *Very unhappy
2. On the whole, I think I am quite a happy person.
      Agree
      *Disagree
3. In general, how would you say you feel most of the time—in good spirits or in low spirits?
      Very good spirits
      Fairly good spirits
      *Neither good nor low spirits
      *Fairly low spirits
      *Very low spirits
4. I get a lot of fun out of life.
      Agree
      *Disagree
5. I wish I could be as happy as others seem to be.
      *Agree
      Disagree

6. How often do you feel downcast and dejected?
   *Very often
   *Fairly often
   *Occasionally
   Rarely
   Never

For purposes of the present analysis, the distribution of depressive affect scores was distributed between "high" (scores of 2 or more) and "low" (scores of 0 or 1) depressive affect categories.

Although it is not asserted that this measure reflects clinical depression, it is associated with other constructs—most notably, self-derogation or loss of self-esteem—that are generally implicated in the phenomenology of clinical depression (68,67).

*Conditional variables.* Among the data collected in the course of a study of correlates of self-derogation in the general community (67) were some 50 items that referred to aspects of the adult subjects' childhood experiences. From these items, fifteen were selected which were interpreted as reflecting conditions that would impose variable degrees of constraint against (or in varying degrees would permit) the adoption of response patterns which would serve to deflect blame from self in the face of blameworthy circumstances. Insofar as the sex-related differences in depression are the result of sex differences in the adoption of such response patterns, the sex differences in depression should be increased where the conditional variables are present, since instances of the adoption of blame-deflecting patterns by females are in effect removed from consideration.

The conditional variables fall into five groupings. The first grouping of (four) variables refer to social positions that differentiate the subject according to age, race/ethnicity, nature of the community in which the subject was raised, and father's social class position. These variables were understood to reflect important dimensions of the (sub) cultural matrix in which the subject was raised, and/or subjective cues for the appropriateness of specific types of behavioral patterns. The second grouping of (three) variables refer to the nature and extent of the subject's relationships with his (sibling) peers. The third group of (two) variables refer to the nature and extent of the subject's relationship with his (nonsibling) peers. The fourth grouping of (three) variables reflects the nature of the subject's intrafamilial relationships. The fifth group of (three) variables was interpreted as indicating the subject's degree of embeddedness in the social relational system of the more inclusive community.

It should be emphasized that the decision to conduct the present analysis was made *following* the design and the execution of the study. Therefore, the variables selected were not face valid indicators of the conditions under which the relationship between sex and depressive affect was expected to be observed. Rather, the major criterion for selection of a variable was the *judgment* that the item was *interpretable* as an indicator of one of the conditions. The judgments were based upon the reasoning to be described below and, frequently, the awareness that such reasoning was congruent with releated research reports. The 15 conditional variables are described below in conjunction with presentation of the results.

## Analysis

The 15 hypotheses were tested using chi-square to test the hypothesis of no relationship. The .05 level of significance was the selected criterion for acceptance/rejection of the hypotheses. For each of the conditional variables it was hypothesized that among subjects manifesting the specified values, females would be significantly more likely than males to manifest high depressive affect scores. For subjects manifesting the remaining variable values, no such relationship was predicted.

## RESULTS

The results of the analysis are summarized in Table 1. In order to provide a basis for comparison, the initial row of data presents *for the total study group* the percentage of subjects of each sex who manifest high depressive affect scores.

Consistent with the studies cited above, females were significantly more likely to score high on the depressive affect scale than males. Thirty-three per cent (N = 274) of the females had scores of 2 or higher, compared with only 22 per cent (N = 226) of the males ($X^2 = 8.2$, df = 1, p < .005). Insofar as this difference is accounted for by the inability of the females to adopt response patterns that function to deflect blame from self, the 15 hypotheses specified below should be supported.

The relevant data appear in the 15 sets below the "All Subjects" row in Table 1. For each set of data, the conditional variable and the relevant variable values are presented in the left-hand column. Next to each value the row of entries indicates the percentage of subjects of each sex with "high" depressive affect scores. The parenthetical entries indicate the number of cell entries.

The specific value preceded by # (number sign) is understood to reflect or imply the condition under which the association between sex and depressive affect would be observed. That is, *for subjects characterized by the par-*

## Table 1. Percentage of Subjects with High Depressive Affect Scores by Sex and Selected Characteristics of Pre-Adulthood Experiences

|  | Males | Females |
|---|---|---|
| All Subjects**[1] | 22<br>(226)[2] | 33<br>(274) |
| **Age** | | |
| #[3] Below 30* | 10<br>(41) | 26<br>(68) |
| # 30 - 39** | 22<br>(74) | 45<br>(66) |
| 40 - 49 | 25<br>(52) | 27<br>(62) |
| 50 - 59 | 20<br>(30) | 31<br>(42) |
| 60 and older | 34<br>(29) | 36<br>(36) |
| **Race/Ethnicity[4]** | | |
| # White-Anglo* | 20<br>(188) | 31<br>(219) |
| Black | 33<br>(27) | 42<br>(40) |
| Latin American | 18<br>(11) | 40<br>(15) |
| **Place of Socialization ("Brought up mostly . . . ")[4]** | | |
| # Farm** | 20<br>(94) | 42<br>(87) |
| Town | 15<br>(40) | 29<br>(66) |
| Small City | 29<br>(34) | 33<br>(45) |
| Large City | 25<br>(56) | 27<br>(75) |
| **Father's Social Class[4]** | | |
| I - II (High) | 22<br>(23) | 18<br>(17) |
| III | 18<br>(28) | 17<br>(41) |

**Table 1. Percentage of Subjects with High Depressive Affect Scores by Sex and Selected Characteristics of Pre-Adulthood Experiences (cont.)**

|  | Males | Females |
|---|---|---|
| IV | 21<br>(71) | 28<br>(90) |
| # V (Low)*** | 21<br>(98) | 46<br>(120) |
| **How well subject got along with brothers and/or sisters[5]** | | |
| # Very well** | 18<br>(140) | 32<br>(172) |
| Less than very well | 28<br>(67) | 39<br>(76) |
| **Number of siblings** | | |
| 0 - 1 | 31<br>(49) | 27<br>(55) |
| 2 - 3** | 9<br>(58) | 27<br>(85) |
| # 4 or more** | 24<br>(119) | 40<br>(134) |
| **Sex distribution among siblings[5]** | | |
| all same sex as subject | 25<br>(28) | 21<br>(33) |
| # mostly same sex as subject*** | 16<br>(97) | 40<br>(101) |
| half of each sex | 25<br>(48) | 37<br>(54) |
| mostly opposite sex | 24<br>(37) | 30<br>(66) |
| **Played alone (relative to most of the children subject knew)[4]** | | |
| more | 26<br>(27) | 38<br>(40) |
| same | 23<br>(150) | 30<br>(167) |
| # less** | 14<br>(48) | 37<br>(65) |

96

Number of like-sex friends (relative to
  most other children subject knew)

| | | |
|---|---|---|
| more | 19 (58) | 23 (52) |
| # same** | 21 (155) | 34 (183) |
| fewer | 38 (13) | 41 (39) |

Amount of attention received from
  parents relative to attention received
  by brothers and sisters[5]

| | | |
|---|---|---|
| more | 18 (27) | 28 (32) |
| # as much** | 19 (160) | 34 (191) |
| less | 38 (21) | 50 (26) |

Afraid of being left alone[4]

| | | |
|---|---|---|
| # not at all* | 20 (184) | 31 (165) |
| somewhat | 25 (32) | 34 (53) |
| very much | 40 (10) | 40 (55) |

Family members (relative to families of
  most of the children subject knew) were[4]

| | | |
|---|---|---|
| # closer* | 19 (91) | 32 (135) |
| about the same | 23 (112) | 30 (125) |
| not as close* | 24 (21) | 61 (13) |

**Table 1. Percentage of Subjects with High Depressive Affect Scores by Sex and Selected Characteristics of Pre-Adulthood Experiences (cont.)**

| | Males | Females |
|---|---|---|
| How well subject did in life relative to siblings[5] | | |
| better | 25 (68) | 30 (60) |
| # about the same** | 16 (120) | 33 (150) |
| not as well | 42 (19) | 57 (37) |
| Family's standard of living relative to most of the families in the neighborhood[4] | | |
| higher | 30 (30) | 24 (38) |
| # about the same** | 17 (172) | 31 (210) |
| lower | 45 (20) | 64 (25) |
| Proportion of families in neighborhood of same religion as subject's family[4] | | |
| # more than half* | 20 (84) | 36 (115) |
| about half | 24 (66) | 35 (80) |
| less than half | 23 (48) | 25 (51) |

[1] Indicates probability levels chi-square analysis, df=1: * = p < .05, ** = p < .01, *** = p < .001.

[2] Parenthetical entries indicate N in cell.

[3] #Indicates conditional value under which the significant relationship between sex and depressive affect is hypothesized.

[4] Where N's do not total 226 and 274 for males and females respectively, data were missing.

[5] Item is not applicable to all subjects.

*ticular value* it is hypothesized that female subjects will be significantly more likely than male subjects to manifest high depressive affect scores. For subjects characterized by the other values, no such differences were hypothesized.

The findings relating to the 15 conditional variables will be presented in turn. For each variable the hypothesis will *first* be presented. The nature of the conditional variable and the specific values will become apparent in the statement of the hypothesis and examination of Table 1. The hypotheses will be stated in terms of the value for which females are expected to manifest a greater percentage of high depressive affect scores than males. Second, the reasoning behind the selection of the particular conditional variable will be discussed. Finally, the results will be presented.

Since except for the conditional variable the 15 hypotheses are identical, it will be necessary to state the common terms but once. *Female subjects will manifest a higher percentage of high depressive affect scores than males under the following conditions:*

1. *Where the subjects are in the below 30 and 30-39 age groups.*

The sex differential in depression was expected to be significant in these two groups only since it has been noted that sex typing is less extreme as individuals age (and, of course, is most extreme in the earlier years), with men becoming less aggressive and more affectionate and with women becoming more independent and assertive (69). As Neugarten (70) concludes from one study of women in their forties, fifties, and sixties, "women, as they aged, seemed to become more tolerant of their own aggressive, egocentric impulses; whereas men, as they age, of their own nurturant and affiliative impulses" (p. 71).

Insofar as women felt least free to use mechanisms that might mitigate self-blame and men felt most free to do so in earlier years, the sex differences in depression would have been greatest in those years. Furthermore, it was (particularly in the 30-to-39-year-old group) in these years that the woman's child-rearing role would be most likely to reflect the traditional female role, including dependence on the family as the primary source of affiliative satisfaction and the possession relatively little authority (69).

As hypothesized, the above observed difference in depressive affect between the sexes holds only for the youngest age groups. In the below thirty group 26 per cent of the females and only 10 per cent of the males scored 2 or higher on the depressive affect scale ($X^2 = 4.4$, df $= 1$, p $< .05$). In the 30-39 grouping 45 per cent of the females and only 22 per cent of the males scored 2 or higher on the depressive affect scale ($X^2 = 8.98$, df $= 1$, p $< .005$). For none of the other age groupings did the sex differences hold.

Markush and Favero (9) also report data that suggest that the sex differences in depression are greatest in the younger age groups. Similarly, a number of other studies cited by Kendell (2) demonstrate that the female predominance in depression is accentuated in young adults rather than in old age. Data from these studies

> all show that after the age of 65 depressive illnesses are almost as common in men as in women. In women the incidence is highest in the fourth decade and falls steadily thereafter, whereas in men the peak is not reached until the sixth decade. This difference between the age distributions of the two sexes is not shared by any other psychiatric disorder and is largely due to the low incidence of depression in men under the age of 40, precisely those who must readily resort to physical violence [2].

2. *Where the subjects were white.*

Since black households were reported to be wife-dominant in decision-making (71) it was expected that the above observed sex differences in depression would be diminished for the black and observed only for the white subjects. Given this black intrafamilial authority structure, the males would be less likely to employ (and the women would be better able to employ) extrapunitive defenses against self-blame, with the consequence of a lesser sex differential in depression.

As expected, the previously observed differences between the sexes with regard to depressive affect were observed only among the white subjects where 31 per cent of the females and only 20 per cent of the males scored 2 or higher on the depressive affect scale ($X^2 = 6.2$, df $= 1$, p $< .02$).

A similar trend was apparent in data reported by Markush and Favero (9) in an adult sample obtained from a probability sample of households in Kansas City, Missouri.

3. *Where the subjects were brought up mostly on farms.*

Insofar as sex differentials in depression are explainable in terms of the lesser ability of the female to employ extrapunitive and avoidance mechanisms in order to maintain or restore self-esteem, the differential should be greatest among subjects raised on the farm. In this setting the female would be most dependent on a small social group for satisfaction of affiliative needs. In the absence of a broad range of alternative primary relationships she would of necessity be unwilling to deprive herself of affectional satisfactions by either risking negative responses from other group members (by employing hostile-aggressive responses) or by leaving the group.

As hypothesized, the significant sex differences in depression observed above are accounted for by the subjects who were raised on the farm (or perhaps, in general, rural areas). Among subjects on the farm, 42 per cent of the females compared with only 20 per cent of the males received scores of 2 or more on the depressive affect scale ($X^2 = 10.5$, $df = 1$, $p < .005$). Considering subjects who were raised either on the farm or in a small town, 37 per cent of the females compared with 19 per cent of the males received scores of 2 or more on the depressive affect scale ($X^2 = 11.4$, $df = 1$, $p < .001$). There was an interaction effect observed between sex and place of socialization such that females raised on the farm were significantly more likely to be depressed as adults compared to females who were raised in other locations ($X^2 = 4.8$, $df = 1$, $p < .05$) or males who were raised on the farm.

It is not inconsistent with these findings that Dohrenwend (6) in his review of true prevalence studies notes that the manic-depressive subtype of psychosis in 3 of 4 studies in which relevant data were available was more prevalent in rural settings than in urban settings.

4. *Where the subjects were raised in the lowest social class.*

The index of social class employed in the present study is Hollingshead's Index of Social Position (72), based upon a weighted combination of father's occupation and education. Each subject received a score ranging from 11 (high social position) to 77 (low social position). The continuation of scores was then broken into a hierarchy of five score groups (using the score limits specified by Hollingshead) representing five social class positions ranging from I (highest) to V (lowest).

The sex differential was hypothesized for subjects raised in the lower class, since it is in this subculture that the female appears to be permitted the fewest alternatives to self-punitive responses in the face of blameworthy circumstances. In general, the white working class, relative to the more prestigious classes, is thought to be more bound to the traditional sex roles in which the male is more assertive and has greater situational power than the female. In conflict situations, the female tends to be subject to the male's authority (69).

Consistent with this position are research findings indicating that, particularly in the case of boys, lower socioeconomic children were more affected by sex typing in their standards and expectancies than higher socioeconomic status subjects (73); low socioeconomic girls were more severely punished for aggression to peers than high socioeconomic status girls (74); and, in an intelligence testing situation, lower socioeconomic status (Puerto Rican) girls were more likely to try hard to follow the tester's directions while the boys were more likely to ignore or forget the directions (75). It is particularly interesting to note that these sex differences were found only in the lower socioeconomic status Puerto Rican sample. Among the middle socioeconomic status United States sample no such sex differences were noted.

As hypothesized, controlling on social class of origin, it was observed that the tendency for females to manifest higher depressive affect than males held only for the lowest social class: among subjects raised in class V, 46 per cent of the females compared with only 21 per cent of the males manifested high depressive affect as adults ($X^2 = 14.1$, df $= 1$, p $< .001$). There was an interaction effect observed such that females raised in class V were significantly more likely to manifest high depressive affect than either females raised in any of the other classes ($X^2 = 14.6$, df $= 1$, p $< .001$) or males raised in class V.

These trends are similar to those apparent in data reported by Markush and Favero (9) for samples of the general adult population in Kansas City, Missouri, and Washington County, Maryland.

5. *Where the subjects indicated that they got along very well when they were growing up.*

The indication of close sibling relationships was interpreted as suggesting both that such relationships were sources of diffuse affective gratification for the subject and that there was an increased probability that where such relationships existed, there was an implicit proscription against the expression of negative affect toward other family members. If such proscription indeed had differential effects upon the two sexes (with appropriate consequences for depression) then the sex-related difference in depression would be expected to hold only under the conditions of close sibling relationships.

As expected, controlling on such judgments, it was observed that only among subjects who indicated that they got along very well with their siblings were females more likely to score higher on the depressive affect score than males: 32 per cent of the females compared with only 18 per cent of the males who indicated that they got along very well with their siblings scored two or more on the depressive affect score ($X^2 = 8.7$, df $= 1$, p $< .005$).

6. *Where the subjects grew up with a greater number of siblings.*

It was expected that where more siblings were present, the parents would find it more necessary to constrain overt expression of aggression. At the same time, the greater number of interpersonal relationships would make it difficult to use avoidance type mechanisms. The lessened ability to employ extrapunitive or avoidance mechanisms would increase the probability of self-blaming responses and thereby the use of depressive responses.

As expected, controlling on number of siblings, it is observed that the tendency for females to have higher depressive affect holds only for the 2 to 3 siblings and 4 or more sibling category. Considering subjects with 2 to 3 siblings, only 9 per cent of the males compared with 27 per cent of the females manifested high depressive affects as adults ($X^2 = 7.4$, df $= 1$, p $<$ .01). For subjects with 4 or more siblings, 24 per cent of the males compared with 40 per cent of the females manifested high depressive affect as adults ($X^2 = 6.6$, df $= 1$, p $<$ .01). For subjects with 0 or 1 sibling there was no significant sex difference in depressive affect. It should be noted that the difference in the "4 or more" category might reflect the influence of the social class factor noted above. However, this factor should not be as much of an influence upon the sex differential in depression observed for subjects with 2 or 3 siblings.

7. *Where the subjects grew up with siblings who were mostly of their own sex.*

It was reasoned that the predominance of like-sex siblings would increase the probability of traditional sex-role socialization (inhibition of aggression for females, etc.), since role models were available. Further, the implied presence of opposite sex siblings increases awareness of sex-role differentiation. This reasoning is consistent with a report by Rosenberg and Sutton-Smith (76) to the effect that sex of siblings was a significant influence on subject's femininity scores insofar as girls with sisters scored significantly higher than girls with brothers.

As hypothesized, only where siblings were mostly of the same sex were females observed to be significantly higher than males on depressive affect.

Considering only subjects in which the subject grew up with siblings who were mostly of the same sex, we observe that 40 per cent of the females compared with only 16 per cent of the males manifested high depressive affect as adults ($X^2 = 13.0$, df $= 1$, p $<$ .001).

8. *Where the subjects played alone more than most of the other children they knew when they were growing up.*

"Playing alone less" was taken as an indicator of effective socialization as females insofar as great affiliative need was associated with the female role. At the same time, the greater range of interpersonal affiliations would serve to inhibit the expression of extrapunitive or avoidance responses as mechanisms for raising or maintaining self-esteem, and would thereby increase the probability of depressive responses.

As expected, it was only among children who said that they played alone less than most of the children they knew that females scored higher than males on the depressive affect score: 37 per cent of the females in this category compared to only 14 per cent of the males in this category manifested high depressive affect scores as adults ($X^2 = 6.9$, df $= 1$, p $<$ .01).

It might be noted again that playing alone less might be a consequence of the larger families observed in the lower class, and therefore the present conditional relationship between sex and depression might not be independent of that observed above for subjects who grew up in the lower class.

9. *Where the subjects reported that they had about the same number of like-sex friends when they were growing up as most of the children they knew.*

Having the same number of like-sex friends (rather than more or fewer) was interpreted as a condition that implied at the same time the presence of role models for appropriate sex-role identification, a range of interpersonal affiliations, and the presence of opposite-sex friends that would facilitate sex-role discrimination. Appropriate role models and sex-role discrimination would increase learning such patterns as inhibition of aggression and affiliative needs which would decrease extrapunitive and avoidance type responses. The net effect would be an increased probability of intrapunitive (and consequent depressive) response patterns.

As hypothesized, it was observed that only among the "same" responders were females more likely than males to manifest high depressive affect scores as adults: 34 per cent of the females compared with only 21 per cent of the males in this category manifested high depressive affect scores ($X^2 = 7.1$, df $= 1$, p $< .01$).

10. *Where the subjects indicated that when they were growing up they received as much attention from their parents as did their siblings.*

This hypothesis as well as the next two hypotheses state conditions which are interpreted as reflecting benign parent-child relationship. Such relationships would on the one hand reflect an atmosphere conducive to appropriate sex-role socialization and on the other hand would inhibit extrapunitive and avoidance responses (out of a fear of disrupting or being deprived of gratifying relationships). Consistent with this position are research findings such as those reported by Lansky and his associates (37) to the effect that expressed criticism of mother among girls was related among other things to low concern with affiliation, low desire to be similar to mother, and minimal guilt about aggressive acts directed against a male authority. Girls who were critical of their fathers were rated low in conformity by the interviewers and had low scores on identification with mother on the self-rating inventory.

In the present hypothesis "as much" (rather than more or less) attention is taken as an indicator of mutually satisfying parent-child relationships.

As hypothesized, females (34 per cent) were significantly more likely than males (19 per cent) to score higher (two or more) on the depressive affect scale only among subjects who indicated that they received as much attention as their siblings ($X^2 = 9.4$, df $= 1$, p $< .005$).

11. *Where the subjects were not at all afraid of being left alone.*

This variable was taken as a second oblique indicator of benign parent-child relationship which for reasons stated above was expected to be a condition of a sex differential in depression.

As hypothesized females (31 per cent) were significantly more likely than males (20 per cent) to score high on the depressive affect scale only where the subjects were not at all (rather than somewhat or very much) afraid of being left alone ($X^2 = 5.4$, df $= 1$, p $< .025$).

12. *Where family members were described as closer to each other than was the case with the families of most of the other children they knew when they were growing up.*

As in the last two hypotheses close family relationships were expected to be preconditions for appropriate sex-role socialization and further inhibition of extrapunitive and avoidance responses in the service of the self-esteem motive.

As hypothesized, among subjects indicating that their family's members were closer (as opposed to about the same or not as close), 32 per cent of the females compared with only 19 per cent of the males manifested high depressive affect scores as adults ($X^2 = 5.3$, df $= 1$, p $< .025$). However, in addition, although this relationship was not hypothesized, females (61 per cent) were also significantly more likely than males (24 per cent) to manifest high depressive affect scores as adults ($X^2 = 4.8$, df $= 1$, p $< .05$) *among subjects who indicated that their childhood family relationships were not as close* as in the families of most of the other children that they knew. This relationship was apparently the result of observing a female-specific antecedent of depression. For females, but not for males, "not as close" childhood family relationships were apparently antecedents of adult depression ($X^2 = 5.00$, df $= 1$, p $< .05$). Thus while close family relationships were a condition for increasing the probability of feminine self-blame responses in the event that blameworthy circumstances should arise, the circumstances of disrupted family relationships (particularly given the more intense affiliative needs of females) increased the subsequently observed level of depression among females. In these relationships we observed simultaneously the relative sex-specific significance of social interdependence as a breeding ground for potential depressive responses to self-devaluing judgments *and* the actual induction of depression through the critical disruption of interpersonal relationships.

13. *Where the subjects perceived themselves doing as well in life as their siblings.*

This hypothesis as well as the two following hypotheses assert conditions which are said to reflect the degree to which the subject's childhood family was implicated in the more inclusive network of community relationships. It was assumed that such relational interdependence would intensify the already existing (by virtue of sex-role differentiation processes) tendency of females to eschew extrapunitive or avoidance responses to self-devaluing circumstances. To the extent that one is involved in a broad range of social relationships (whether for instrumental or intrinsically gratifying purposes), the less one is able to either risk disruption of, or leave, such relationships.

This position appears warranted in view of the apparent direct relationship between social participation and intrapunitive responses. Teele (77), for example, within a population of former mental patients, compared those who were suicidal at the time of their last admission to a mental hospital with those who were assaultive. The investigator observed a clear relationship between the patients' symptoms and their mothers' social isolation scores (participation in social hobbies, visiting with friends, and participation in voluntary associations). The socially isolated mothers were more likely to have assaultive children, while the socially participating mothers were more likely to have suicidal children.

In the hypothesis under consideration, doing as well in life was understood to imply continuity with a subculturally defined social structure, including acceptance of a system of sanctions that inhibits disruption of the network. On the other hand, upward or downward social mobility (doing better or not as well) implies less commitment to a set of relationships and, therefore, less constraint against extrapunitive or avoidance type responses (as alternatives to intrapunitive type responses).

As hypothesized, only among subjects who perceived themselves as doing about the same in life as their siblings were females significantly more likely than males to score higher on depressive affect: 33 per cent of the females compared with only 16 per cent of the males received high depressive affect scores among these subjects ($X^2 = 10.0$, df $= 1$, p $< .005$).

14. *Where the subjects indicated that their childhood family's standard of living was about the same as most of the families in the neighborhood.*

Such a circumstance implies the involvement of the subject in a range of interpersonal and associational relationships, dependence upon the instrumental and intrinsic gratifications provided by these relationships, and commitment to the normative order that defines the network of relationships. This situation precludes easy adoption of avoidance or extrapunitive type responses, responses that would be permitted by individuals who were more culturally apart from the local community, as would be indicated by a lower or higher standard of living than that characteristic of the neighborhood.

As hypothesized only among respondents indicating "about the same" standard of living were females significantly more likely than males to manifest high depressive affect scores: 31 per cent of the females compared with only 17 per cent of the males manifested high depressive affect ($X^2 = 9.2$, df $= 1$, p $< .005$) among these subjects.

15. *Where more than half of the families in the subject's childhood neighborhood were of the same religion as his own childhood family.*

This hypothesis was derived by precisely the same reasoning as suggested by the fourteenth hypothesis.

As hypothesized, among subjects who indicated that their family was of the same religion as more than half the families in the neighborhood, but not among other subjects, females (35 per cent) were significantly more likely than males (20 per cent) to manifest high depressive affect as adults ($X^2 = 5.6$, df $= 1$, p $< .02$).

## DISCUSSION

In general, then, the results support the conclusion that females tend to be more depressed than males because females in the course of their socialization experiences are inhibited from adopting patterns that would permit them to deflect blame from themselves in blameworthy circumstances. As a result, they experience loss of self-esteem and consequent depression.

This is not to say that males do not get depressed. Both males and females do get depressed. Indeed, the data reported above point to factors that are associated with high depressive affect in each of the sexes, although the pattern of correlates of depression appears to be different for each sex. For males, high depressive affect was significantly associated with being sixty or older, having either "0 or 1" or "4 or more siblings," reports of receiving less attention from his parents than his siblings received during childhood, having done either better or not as well in life as his siblings, and having had either a higher or lower standard of living than most of the other families in the neighborhood while growing up.

For females, high depressive affect tended to be significantly associated with being 30-39, having been raised on a farm, lowest social class position during childhood, having had four or more siblings, description of family members as not as close as the families of most of the children they knew, reports of not doing as well in life as their siblings, and having had a lower standard of living than most of the families in their neighborhood when they were growing up.

A number of other variables were unrelated to depression for either sex although they were conditions for observation of a significant sex differential in depression. These variables include race/ethnicity, sex distribution of children in childhood family, reports of playing alone during childhood, relative number of like-sex friends while growing up, fear of being left alone during childhood, and religious homogeneity of childhood neighborhood.

However, these patterns will not be discussed as such, since the purpose of the present study was not to report on sex-specific or general antecedents of depression but rather to account for the frequently observed sex differential in depression. This difference was explained in terms of differential sex-role socialization that inhibits the use of response patterns by females which would deflect their attribution of blame (in blameworthy circumstances) away from self. The fact that sex differences in depressive affect were observed only under conditions where greater requirement for inhibition of such responses might be expected provided support for this interpretation.

While the results are consistent with this conclusion several methodological issues require consideration. First, as in an earlier report (66), since the decision to analyze the data in order to test the proposal described above was made *following* collection of the data, the variables selected to reflect or imply the presence of the conditions could not, except by chance, be taken as direct, face-valid indices. Rather, at best, these variables were oblique indices of the conditions assumed to be present when social class position influenced the degree of the subject's self-derogation, selected only after making several sometimes tenuous assumptions.

Second, the sex differential in depression, it might be suggested, could reflect a greater tendency to admit to depression when in fact both sexes might experience the same degree of depression. This possibility has been suggested in other studies (10,78). However, if the results were a function of a greater tendency on the part of females to admit to (rather than, in fact, to experience) depression, then the relationship between sex and depressive affect should have been observed for each value of the conditional variables rather than for only the specified values as was generally observed. Further, data collected in the course of the study indicated that males were not significantly different from females in willingness to be reinterviewed. Eighty-six per cent of the males and 85 per cent of the females indicated a willingness to be reinterviewed. Thus differences between the sexes with regard to correlates of depressive affect were not likely to be accounted for in terms of self-disclosure tendencies.

A third issue concerns the independence of the conditional variables and the depressive affect measure. The possibility exists that the conditional variables are reflections of a depressed state rather than antecedent to (or otherwise independent of) depressive states. Thus females who are more depressed than males might be more likely (through such processes as retrospective distortion) to reflect their depression in their reports of certain conditional values. The variable would thus be a reflection rather than condition of the sex difference in depression. However, this issue does not appear to seriously compromise the interpretation of the data in the light of observations that (a) many of the conditional variables are not easily subject to perceptual distortion (age, race, place of socialization, number and sex distribution of siblings, father's social class), and (b) in the instances of other variables where perceptual distortion is more of a possibility, the sex differential in depression is generally noted for conditional values that are positively valued or affectively neutral rather than for negative values as would be expected if the conditional relationship were the result of perceptual distortion associated with depression. Further, as was noted above, there was no consistent tendency noted for more depressed subjects of either sex to report negatively valued attributes and experiences as characteristic of the childhood years.

Fourth, it should be recalled that the conclusions put forth here are based upon data collected in 1966 and therefore refer to socialization experiences at a much earlier point in time. Whether or not current socialization patterns will continue to inhibit deflection of blame from self on the part of females is problematic. To the extent that they do not continue to do so, the sex differential in depression may be expected to change dramatically.

In summary, there are few serious contraindications for the conclusion that the relationship between sex and depression is a conditional one—i.e., under conditions which might inhibit the deflection of blame away from self on the part of females the sex differential is observed. Under alternative conditions it is not observed. The pattern of results not only supports the thesis that females are more inhibited from deflecting blame from self (in blameworthy circumstances) than males, but also, given the reasoning by which the predictions were derived, suggests the validity of the more general hypothesis that mode of psychopathology is an extension of normal adaptive responses learned in the course of the socialization process and supports the interpretation of depression as an affective response to loss of self-esteem.

## REFERENCES

1. Silverman, C. *The Epidemiology of Depression*. Baltimore: Johns Hopkins Press, 1968, p. 70.
2. Kendell, R. Relationship between aggression and depression. *Arch. Gen. Psychiat.* 22: 308-318, 1970, p. 313.
3. Paykel, E. S., Klerman, G. L., and Prusoff, B. A. Treatment setting and clinical depression. *Arch. Gen. Psychiat.* 22:11-21, 1970.
4. Spicer, C. C., Hare, E. H., and Slater, E. Neurotic and psychotic forms of depressive illness: evidence from age incidence in a national sample. *Br. J. Psychiat.* 123:535-541, 1973.
5. DeFundia, T. A., Draguns, J. G., and Phillips, L. Culture and psychiatric symptomatology: a comparison of Argentine and United States patients. *Soc. Psychiatry* 6: 11-20, 1971.
6. Dohrenwend, B. P. Sociocultural and social-psychological factors in the genesis of mental disorders, in H. B. Kaplan and G. Warheit, eds., *Recent Developments in the Sociology of Mental Illness*. Special issue of *J. Health Soc. Behav.*, 16:365-392, 1975.

7. Dohrenwend, B. P., and Dohrenwend, B. S. Social and cultural influences on psychopathology. *Ann. Rev. Psychol.* 25:417-452, 1974.

8. Dohrenwend, B. P., and Dohrenwend, B. S. Sex differences and psychiatric disorders. *Am. J. Sociology.* In press.

9. Markush, R. E., and Favero, R. Epidemiologic assessment of stressful life events, depressed mood, and psychophysiological symptoms—a preliminary report, in B. S. Dohrenwend and B. P. Dohrenwend, eds., *Stressful Life Events: Their Nature and Effects.* New York: Wiley, 1974, pp. 171-190.

10. Blumenthal, M. D. Measuring depressive symptomatology in a general population. *Arch. Gen. Psychiat.* 32:971-978, 1975.

11. Hamburg, D. A. Recent research on hormonal factors relevant to human aggressiveness. *Int. Soc. Sci. J.* 23:36-47, 1971.

12. Maccoby, E. E., and Jacklin, C. N. *The Psychology of Sex Differences.* Stanford, Calif.: Stanford University Press, 1974.

13. Gove, W., and Tudor, J. Adult sex roles and mental illness. *Am. J. Soc.* 78:812-935, 1973.

14. Gove, W. The relationship between sex roles, marital status, and mental illness. *Soc. Forces* 51:34-44, 1972.

15. Kaplan, H. B. *The Sociology of Mental Illness.* New Haven, Conn.: College and University Press, 1972.

16. Kaplan, H. B. *Self-Attitudes and Deviant Behavior.* California: Goodyear Publishing Company, Inc., 1975.

17. Bibring, E. The mechanism of depression, in P. Greenacre, ed., *Affective Disorders.* New York: International Universities Press, Inc., 1953, pp. 13-48.

18. Izard, C. F. *Patterns of Emotions: A New Analysis of Anxiety and Depression.* New York: Academic Press, 1972.

19. Akiskal, H. S., and McKinney, W. T., Jr. Overview of recent research in depression. *Arch. Gen. Psychiat.* 32:285-305, 1975.

20. Kagan, J. Acquisition and significance of sex typing and sex role identity, in M. L. Hoffman and L. W. Hoffman, eds., *Review of Child Development Research,* Vol. I. New York: Russell Sage Foundation, 1964, pp. 137-167.

21. Maccoby, E. E., ed. *The Development of Sex Differences.* Stanford, Calif.: Stanford University Press, pp. 323-351.

22. McCandless, B. R., Bilous, C. B., and Bennett, H. L. Peer popularity and dependence on adults in pre-school age socialization. *Child Dev.* 32:511-518, 1961.

23. Digman, J. M. Principal dimensions of child personality as inferred from teacher's judgments. *Child Dev.* 34:43-60, 1963.

24. Toigo, R., Walder, L. O., Eron, L. D., and Lefkowitz, M. M. Examiner effect in the use of a near-sociometric procedure in the third grade classroom. *Psychol. Rep.* 11:785-790, 1962.

25. Bandura, A., Ross, D., and Ross, S. A. Transmission of aggression through imitation of aggressive models. *J. Abnorm. Soc. Psychol.* 63:575-582, 1961.

26. Bandura, A., Ross, D., and Ross, S. A. Vicarious reinforcement and imitative learning. *J. Abnorm. Soc. Psychol.* 67:601-667, 1963.

27. Bandura, A., Ross, D., and Ross, S. A. Influence of models' reinforcement contingencies on the acquisition of imitative responses. *J. Pers. Soc. Psychol.* 1:589-595, 1965.

28. Hartup, W. W., and Himino, Y. Social isolation vs. interaction with adults in relation

to *aggression in pre-school children. J. Abnorm. Soc. Psychol.* 59:17-22, 1959.

29. Hicks, D. J. Imitation and retention of film-mediated aggressive peer and adult models. *J. Pers. Soc. Psychol.* 2:97-100, 1965.

30. Jegard, S., and Walters, R. H. A study of some determinants of aggression in young children. *Child Dev.* 31:739-747, 1960.

31. Moore, S. G. Displaced aggression in young children. *J. Abnorm. Soc. Psychol.* 68: 200-204, 1964.

32. Buss, A. H. Physical aggression in relation to different frustrations. *J. Abnorm. Soc. Psychol.* 67:1-7, 1963.

33. Sanford, R. N., Adkins, M., Miller, R. B., et al. Physique, personality and scholarship. *Monogr. Soc. Res. Child Dev.* 8, 1943.

34. Sarason, I. G., Ganzer, V. J., and Granger, J. W. Self-destruction of hostility and its correlates. *J. Pers. Soc. Psychol.* 1:361-365, 1965.

35. Kagan, J., and Moss, H. A. *Birth to Maturity.* New York: Wiley, 1962.

36. Gill, L. J., and Spilka, B. Some nonintellectual correlates of academic achievement among Mexican-American secondary school students. *J. Educ. Psychol.* 53:144-149, 1962.

37. Lansky, L. M., Crandall, V. J., Kagan, J., et al. Sex differences in aggression and it correlates in middle-class adolescents. *Child Dev.* 32:45-58, 1961.

38. Rothaus, P., and Worchel, P. Ego-support, communication, catharsis, and hostility. *J. Pers.* 32:296-312, 1964.

39. Wyer, R. S., Weatherley, D. A., and Terrell, G. Social role, aggression and academic achievement. *J. Pers. Soc. Psychol.* 1:645-649, 1965.

40. Sears, R. R. Relation of early socialization experiences to aggression in middle childhood. *J. Abnorm. Soc. Psychol.* 63:466-492, 1961.

41. Bennett, E. M., and Cohen, L. R. Men and women: personality patterns and contrasts. *Genet Psychol. Monogr.* 59:101-155, 1959.

42. Sears, P. S. Doll play aggression in normal young children: influence of sex, age, sibling status, father's absence. *Psychol. Monogr.* 65: iv, 42, 1951.

43. Moore, T., and Ucko, L. E. Four to six: constructiveness and conflict in meeting doll play problems. *J. Child Psychol. Psychiatry* 2:21-47, 1961.

44. Buss, A. H., and Brock, T. C. Repression and guilt in relation to aggression. *J. Abnorm. Soc. Psychol.* 66:345-350, 1963.

45. Cosentino, F., and Heilbrun, A. B. Anxiety correlates of sex-role identity in college students. *Psychol. Repr.* 14:729-730, 1964.

46. Sears, R. R., Maccoby, E. E., and Levin, H. *Patterns of Child Rearing.* Evanston, Ill.: Row, Peterson, 1957.

47. Levitin, T. A., and Chananie, J. D. Responses of female primary school teachers to sex-typed behaviors in male and female children. *Child Dev.* 43:1309-1316, 1972.

48. Spangler, D. P., and Thomas, C. W. The effects of age, sex, and physical disability upon manifest needs. *J. Counseling Psychol.* 9:313-319, 1962.

49. Lagrone, C. W. Sex and personality differences in relation to fantasy. *J. Consult. Psychol.* 27:270-272, 1963.

50. Exline, R. V. Effects of need for affiliation, sex, and the sight of others upon initial communications in problem-solving groups. *J. Pers.* 30:541-556, 1962.

51. McClelland, D., et al. *The Achievement Motive.* New York: Appleton-Century-Crofts, 1953.

52. Allen, V. L., and Crutchfield, R. S. Generalization of experimentally reinforced con-

formity. *J. Abnorm. Soc. Psychol.* 67:326-333, 1963.
53. Crutchfield, R. S. Conformity and character. *Am. Psychol.* 10:191-198, 1955.
54. Nakamura, C. Y. Conformity and problem solving. *J. Abnorm. Soc. Psychol.* 56:315-320, 1958.
55. Steiner, I. D., and Rogers, E. D. Alternative responses to dissonance. *J. Abnorm. Soc. Psychol.* 66:128-136, 1963.
56. Iscoe, I., Williams, M., and Harvey, J. Modifications of children's judgments by a simulated group technique: a normative development study. *Child Dev.* 34:963-978, 1963.
57. Getzels, J. W., and Walsh, J. J. The method of paired direct and projective questionnaires in the study of attitude structure and socialization. *Psychol. Monogr.* 72, 1958.
58. McGuire, C. Sex role and community variability in test performances. *J. Educ. Psychol.* 52:61-73, 1961.
59. Gleser, G. C., and Ihilevich, D. An objective instrument for measuring defense mechanisms. *J. Consult. Clin. Psychol.* 33:51-60, 1969.
60. Bogo, N., Winget, C., and Gleser, G. Ego defenses and perceptual styles. *Percept. Mot. Skills* 30:599-604, 1970.
61. Sears, R. R., Ray, L., and Alpert, R. *Identification and Child Rearing.* Stanford, Calif.: Stanford University Press, 1965.
62. Rebelsky, F. G., Alinsmith, W., and Grinder, R. E. Resistance to temptation and sex differences in children's use of fantasy confession. *Child Dev.* 34:955-962, 1963.
63. Rempel, H., and Signoi, E. I. Sex differences in self rating of conscience as a determinant of behavior. *Psychol. Rep.* 15:277-278, 1964.
64. Beller, E. K., and Neubauer, P. B. Sex differences and symptom patterns in early childhood. *J. Child Psychiatry* 2:414-433, 1963.
65. Gump, J. P. Sex role attitudes and psychological well being. *J. Soc. Issues* 28:79-92, 1972.
66. Kaplan, H. B. Social class and self-derogation: a conditional relationship. *Sociometry* 34:41-64, 1971.
67. Kaplan, H. B., and Pokorny, A. D. Self-derogation and psychosocial adjustment. *J. Nerv. Ment. Dis.* 149:421-434, 1969.
68. Rosenberg, M. *Society and the Adolescent Self-Image.* Princeton: Princeton University Press, 1965.
69. Yorburg, B. *Sexual Identity, Sex Roles and Social Change.* New York: Wiley, 1974.
70. Neugarten, B. L. Age, sex roles, and personality in middle age: a Thematic Apperception study, in B. L. Neugarten, ed., *Middle Age and Aging.* Chicago: University of Chicago Press, 1968, pp. 58-71.
71. Blood, R. O., Jr., and Wolfe, D. M. Negro-white differences in blue collar marriages in a northern metropolis. *Soc. Forces* 48:59-64, 1969.
72. Hollingshead, A., and Redlich, F. *Social Class and Mental Illness.* New York: Wiley, 1958.
73. Stein, A. H. The effect of sex role standards for achievement and sex role preference on three determinants of achievement motivation. *Dev. Psychol.* 4:219-231, 1971.
74. Eron, L. D., Walder, L. O., Toigo, R., et al. Social class, parental punishment for aggression, and child aggression. *Child Dev.* 34:849-867, 1963.
75. Hertzig, M. E., Birch, M. G., Thomas, A., et al. Class and ethnic differences in the responsiveness of preschool children to cognitive demands. *Monogr. Soc. Res. Child Dev.* 33:117, 1968.

76. Rosenberg, B. G., and Sutton-Smith, B. Family interaction effect on masculinity feminity. *J. Pers. Soc. Psychol.* 8:117-120, 1968.
77. Teele, J. E. Suicidal behavior, assaultiveness, and socialization principles. *Soc. Forces* 43:510-518, 1965.
78. Phillips, D. L., and Segal, B. E. Sexual status and psychiatric symptoms. *Am. Sociol. Rev.* 34:58-72, 1969.

th

6

# Life Events, Change, Migration, and Depression

RUBEN D. RUMBAUT

## ON HUMAN BEINGS AS PART OF THEIR ENVIRONMENT

What are the boundaries of a living being? If we look around, it seems very easy to differentiate a fish, a bird, a horse, or a man from their respective environments. But is it, really? If the fish is taken out of water it dies almost immediately. In a biological sense, the water that surrounds the fish is therefore a part of it, because that water is an indispensable requisite of its life. Without water the fish not only cannot survive, but it cannot feed, reproduce, or otherwise function. The horse, as well as the human being, needs the soil, the air, the water. The oxygen that we breath is an indispensable part of us; in its absence we die in a matter of minutes. In sum: the immediate physical environment is absolutely necessary for living things to exist, to grow, and to function.

Experiments in sensory deprivation demonstrate that in only a few hours, disorientation, confusion and psychotic-like states (including hallucinations and delusions) can be induced in anybody. Thus human beings not

**115**

only need soil, air, water, food, and shelter; they also require constant sensory stimuli, an unending exchange of messages of all kinds between the "outside" and the "inside." Through the windows of our senses we reach the world and the world reaches us.

Nature does not exist "outside" ourselves. It is not a "thing," it is not "there," it is not static and stable. Nature is a process, in constant change, and we are a part of it. "Man" is not a special being apart from everything else, standing above. Nothing exists in complete isolation. "No man is an island, entire of itself; every man is a piece of the continent, a part of the main" (1). When plants and animals live together in a dynamic equilibrium, we call their physical environment a "habitat."

A human being's "habitat" and his "ecological niche" comprise much more, of course, than a physical environment. We are social beings, we depend upon one another: our families, our jobs, our cities, our friends, our culture, and our nation form much of what is indispensable for our survival, health, and well-being.

The concept of human beings as part of their environment began to gain currency early in this century. In a recent book, Salvador Minuchin quotes José Ortega y Gasset, world-renowned Spanish philosopher, who wrote in 1914: "I am myself plus my circumstance, and if I don't save it, I cannot save myself. This section of my circumstantial reality forms the other half of my person; only through it can I integrate myself and be fully myself" (2). Minuchin also quotes George Bateson's metaphor: "Consider a man felling a tree with an axe. Each stroke of the axe is modified or corrected, according to the shape of the cut face of the tree left by the previous stroke. The self-corrective . . . process is brought about by a total system, tree-eyes-brain-muscles-axe-stroke-tree; and it is this total system that has the characteristics of . . . mind." Delgado's apt observation on the social sphere of man supports these views in more concrete terms: "We cannot be free of parents, teachers, and society, because they are the extracerebral sources of our mind."

Freud's basic concepts are similar in some ways, because his belief that "the child is the father of the man," adapted from Wordsworth, tells us that we became the kinds of adults we are as a result of our past experiences with parents, siblings, relatives, teachers, and significant others. We are, in sum, the product of our ancestors (the environment of origin), of our upbringing and life experiences (the environment that surrounds, accompanies, and interacts with us throughout our existence), and even of the goals, ideals, and expectations for which we are preparing ourselves (the environment of the anticipated future).

Nevertheless, humans are not puppets, robots, programmed computers, or simple pawns of circumstances. A human being is an active agent, an interactor, a modifier of environment, a conqueror and master of obstacles and difficulties, a chooser among alternatives. Humans learn from the past, adapt to or alter their present circumstances, and prepare for the future. Man inherits not only his biological qualities through the reproduction of the species, but also the accumulated knowledge, wisdom, and progress of countless generations throughout history. A child born today in a civilized nation inherits, besides his physical characteristics, myriad other things. A world of wheels, steel, plastic, cement, printing presses, telephones, scientific agriculture, television, radios, automobiles, airplanes, vaccines, asepsis, anesthesia, blood transfusions, and antibiotics, for example, represents an accumulated body of human information and technology which affects the nature of the organism as profoundly as its biological determinants.

It is difficult to maintain at all times a balanced, longitudinal, dynamic perspective of the constant interaction between man and his circumstances. The fact that there is constant interaction between each of us and the environment (physical, familial, and social) has tremendous significance to the practice of medicine generally and psychiatry in particular. There have been narrow, reductionistic tendencies in many quarters concerning the study of human beings which emphasize unduly "man" alone (hero; earthgod; measure of all things; unique combination of chemical substance, cells, tissues and organs; reason incarnate), or "environment" alone (a construct in which man is seen as the fully determined, predictable and inevitable product of his biological inheritance; of his parents, times, and societies; or of the economic, political, social, and religious concepts to which he is committed). Some firmly believe that the only genuinely important thing is the individual and whatever is inside him: organs, hormones, intelligence, emotions, intrapsychic life. Others believe that families, societies, religions, and social-economic-political systems constitute the core of human experience. Therefore, a comprehensive view of man as an individual organism as well as man as a socially and environmentally affected creature is necessary for an accurate sense of the human condition.

## ON DISEASES AND PSYCHIATRIC CONDITIONS AS REACTIONS

Symptoms and signs of disease can be viewed as pathological entities that come from sources inside us, totally independent of the environment, or as reactions of the body and the mind to external, injurious agents or forces. Simple observation tells us that, in the substantial majority of cases, diseases fall into the second category.

Accidents and traumas of all kind are produced in and by the environment. Infections are caused by pathological, invasive agents which attack other organisms. The infections can be acute or chronic, of abrupt onset or of insidious development, but nevertheless pneumonia and tuberculosis, appendicitis and leprosy, enteritis and malaria all are associated with elements external to the afflicted organism. If we eliminate known invasive pathological entities, we are left with an obvious minority of disease types (degenerative, metabolic, and psychogenic) for which either no cause is yet known, or which appear to be engendered within the organism. Again, this is a matter of controversy. Some forms of diabetes are now seen as probably caused by mumps epidemics which once damaged the pancreas; the lesion was not perceptible at the time, but nevertheless eventually rendered the pancreas unable to perform properly. Cancer, multiple sclerosis, and several medical mysteries seem perhaps related to slow-growing viruses. For many years, beriberi, rickets, scurvy, and pellagra were considered legitimate "process" diseases, until the investigators realized that they were carential disease, associated with inadequate diet. General paresis was universally misunderstood as a paranoid psychosis with "degenerative" effects in some parts of the body, until the *Spirochaeta pallidam* of syphilis was found in the cerebral tissues. Some of those plausible "process" diseases ended, after all, as "social" diseases: mumps epidemics could be eradicated by vaccines, carential diseases by abundant and proper diet, general paresis by treatment and control of syphilis. How many other medical mysteries will be similarly solved?

The etiology of most psychogenic diseases is still obscure, but we can speculate and hypothesize using certain guidelines and known facts. Psychoanalysis has defined the dynamics of numerous mechanisms and the pathogenesis of a good number of emotional disorders. Furthermore, our knowledge of the normal mechanisms of emotions is broadening. If a man sees a menacing lion, a very attractive woman, a despised enemy, or the corpse of a beloved relative, he will normally feel fear, sexual attraction, anger, or grief. These emotions are experienced by the entire body: chemical substances enter the blood stream and prepare our body for flight, sex, combat, weeping, or whatever *reaction* we have to a particular stimulus. But we do not become frightened, amorous, hostile, or sad because of our hormones; on the contrary, we secrete the associated hormones because we react with fear, sexual arousal, anger, or sadness to our initial perceptions. First is the perception, followed by the physiological response. Nobody is seriously looking for the bacteria, the hormone, or the enzyme of fear, love, rage, or mourning as the "cause" of our basic emotions. Sometimes, however, we look for the chemical causes of emotional illness with more enthusiasm than for the circumstances that can trigger profound and lasting (though perhaps masked) emotions within us.

Enough is known about stress and the mental causes of somatic illnesses to affirm that psychophysiological disorders are originated at the level of our emotions and thoughts, and eventually suffered at the level of our organs and systems. The notion of stress, so brilliantly developed by Selye, and its relationship to illness have been concretely investigated by Holmes and Rahe, who concluded that a cluster of social events requiring change in ongoing life adjustment is significantly associated with onset of illness. The magnitude and implications of these changes can be measured on their Social Readjustment Rating Scale (3). The SRRS consists of 43 life events empirically derived from clinical experience in the United States. In terms of the scale, social readjustment measures the intensity and length of time necessary to accommodate to a life event, regardless of the desirability of the event. The "events" are given "values" measured in "points." Before the scale was published, fifteen years of research was conducted, investigating the potential relationship between change and ill health (physical or mental). The respondent checks the events listed that have occurred in his life during the past twelve months, and adds the corresponding points. The total score measures the amount of stress one has been subjected to in the one-year period. It can be used to predict one's chances of suffering serious physical or psychiatric illness during the next two years. If the score is more than 300 points in a year, one is facing odds of 80 per cent of becoming ill, and as the score increases, so do the odds that the illness will be of a serious nature.

Holmes and Rahe based their research on ideas evolving from Adolph Meyer's theories of psychobiology, from his invention of the "life chart," and from his concept of psychiatric disorders as "reactions." This latter concept has been, and still is, a pivotal one in American psychiatry.

Harold G. Wolff—as Holmes and Rahe mentioned—subsequently incorporated concepts "of Pavlov, Freud, Cannon and Skinner in the Meyerian schema . . . adducing . . . powerful evidence that stressful life events, by evoking psychophysiological reactions, play an important causative role in the natural history of many diseases" (3).

The proponents of the theory of certain pathological disorders being purely generated from within ("endogenous," "process," "nuclear," "organic," "essential") often argue that no clear primary cause, or even a precipitating event, can be found in those disorders. The fact remains, however, that in accord with the views of Holmes-Rahe and others, no clear-cut, specific event causes the disease, but rather the cumulative effect of stresses of all kinds suffered in too short a time, before the organism has had the chance to assimilate and to recover from them. As in the prize-fighting ring, it is seldom the sudden, isolated, surprising punch that disposes of the opponent, but a series of punches that weaken and predispose the victim to the effect of a final blow. It is as if, in real life, a series of blows to the abdomen, the thorax, the arms and the head, as well as a number of knockdowns, precede the knock-out punch, the serious illness for which hospitalization is indicated. Applying their research only to depression, Thompson and Kendrie in Canada studied "Environmental Stress in Primary Depressive Illness" (4). They found that depressed patients (as compared with two other groups, one of polyarthritic patients and one of staff controls) had a significantly higher score of life stress than the other two groups. Nevertheless, they did not find any significant differences, with respect to life stresses, between onset of "endogenous" and "exogenous" depressions. They stated that their findings were similar to those published by Leff, Roatch, and Bunney in 1970 (5). They ended their paper affirming that "our findings of a significantly higher mean life-change score in the total depressed population as compared to control groups is strikingly similar to the study reported by Payhel et al., who used an essentially similar scale. This would appear to support the concept of life-change playing a role as a precipitant in most depressive disorders irrespective of diagnosis."

The paper by Payhel et al. (6) is one of the most interesting in relation to the theme of "Life Events and Depression." In a carefully controlled study of 185 depressed patients and 938 healthy subjects of the same community, the investigators examined two questions: Are life events most frequent just prior to the onset of depression and, if so, are all life events more frequent, or only certain types? They found first two discernible patterns in the categorization of events: (a) Changes in the social field can be considered *entrances* (birth of a child, marriage, engagement, a person moving in, and the like) or *exits* (death, divorce, separation, a child moving out, and so forth). (b) Certain events are perceived in general by American society as *undesirable* and others as *desirable*, although both clearly constitute change. Their final results indicated: A general *excess* of life events prior to the onset of depression, with those events regarded as *undesirable* and those involving *exits* particularly distinguishing the depressed patients from the controls.

Therefore, it seems that negative life events involving *loss*, or *social undesirability* (which can represent *loss* of reputation, status, fortune, and good will), when falling upon one person too rapidly, preceded depression. Perhaps this is not an earthshaking finding; perhaps it is not even surprising. But it seems to indicate that depression (as a symptom, a syndrome, or a disease) does not necessarily come out of the blue sky or from inaccessible, dark corners of our brain, but from the manner, degree, and speed with which certain negative events accumulate in the life of an individual. A combination of "points" of stress involving losses, rather than a specific trauma, added to the degree of genetic predisposition, emotional vulnerability, and psychological scars of past depressive episodes in a given individual, might ultimately explain depressions as reactions to the vicissitudes of life.

## ON MIGRATION AND DEPRESSION

Migration is movement from one place, locality, or country to another. Etymologically, the term "migrate" comes from the Latin *migratus*, meaning to change. Migration is the epitome of change. It encompasses at once many items of the SRRS. There are types and degrees of migration, of course. A migrant worker, for instance, is a person who moves regularly in order to find work, especially in the harvesting of crops. An emigrant is a person who, for nonpolitical and voluntary reasons, leaves his country of origin with the intention of establishing permanent residence in another country. A refugee is a reluctant emigrant, a person who goes into forced exile, often with bridges literally burned behind him. The 1951 U.N. Convention defines a refugee as "a person who, owing to a well-founded fear of being persecuted for reasons of race, religion, nationality, membership in a particular social group or political opinion, is outside the country of his nationality and is unable, or owing to such fear unwilling, to avail himself of the protection of that country."

There are now about fifteen million refugees in the world, according to the World Refugee Report. The United States, "a nation of immigrants," is celebrating its Bicentennial Year with almost 220 million inhabitants. During those two hundred years, the nation received nearly sixty million people from abroad, including legal and illegal immigrants, men and women brought as slaves, refugees, and Americans born outside the United States territory. Immigrant descent is the rule and not the exception here.

Physical illness, poverty, poor nutrition, longing for familiar ways, inability to communicate in an unknown language, and difficulty in adapting to entirely new customs and values have initially characterized almost every immigrant group to reach these shores. Immigrants have been well represented in mental hospital populations. The causes which bring so many immigrants to psychiatric care are, above all, the number, the intensity, and the speed of their life events; the radical changes; the incessant struggles; the anguish of the uprootedness and the losses; the difficulty in adapting to demands, criticisms, indifference or sheer rejection; the barriers to communication, and the increasing despair before odds deemed too many and too much. Only in the last decades have these factors been given their due weight by investigators. The pioneer works of anthropologists Ruth Benedict, Margaret Mead and the psychiatrist Karen Horney, among many others, directed attention to the enormous importance of cultural conditions as formative and decisive factors in an individual's life history. Opler (7) writes that "while it was common, not too long ago, to speak of the 'Melting Pot in America,' the last decade, which produced some of the publications of the Midtown Manhattan research, has dignified such terms as 'Beyond the Melting Pot,' and 'ethnicity,' standing for ethnic group subcultures, and the myriad of terms alluding to such ethnic groups in our midst as 'Black Pride,' the dignity and respect (*dignidad y respeto*) required by Puerto Ricans for their self-esteem and group identification, and 'Red Power' for the resurgent feeling among American Indians of their historic rights and Pan-Indian aspirations."

The factors that can prevent mental illness, and especially depression, which in my experience is the most prevalent of the psychiatric disorders in immigrant and refugee populations, can be classified in three general dimensions: those elements referring to the migrating population, those elements referring to the host country or region, and those referring to the clash or the mixing of the two groups. For the migrating populations, their numbers, the characteristics of their original culture, their level of occupational and educational preparation, the causes and conditions under which they left their country or region, the precipitousness of the dislocation, the previous affinity or lack of it with the language, customs, values and socio-economic-political system of the new land, and the type and degree of community reception they encounter, are decisive factors. Dodge, writing from New Zealand (8) affirms that "probably the factor of greatest significance in the maintenance of personal and social mental health is the existence of community support for the newly arrived migrant. This support will usually be provided by fellow countrymen who have migrated previously and should be encouraged, as it is the migrant's own community which is generally the best fitted to render such support. Of equal importance is the acceptability of the migrant by the host community."

Even under the best circumstances, migration, acculturation, and assimilation are painful experiences. Wittkower and Dubreuil (9) state that "three aspects of social organization deserve special attention regarding their relevance to mental illness: anomie, rigidity and minority status." "*Anomie*," they continue, "refers to the lack of integration of social organization and is sometimes used synonymously with social disorganization. A relationship between anomie and increased frequency of mental disorders has been established. . . . There is plenty of evidence that low standards of education, poverty, ethnic diversity and migration tend to create anomie and stress because they uproot the individual from his accustomed environment, deprive him of significant statuses and gratifying roles, and produce value polymorphism. . . . Social rigidity is the reverse. . . . This means that the overall social structure of parts of a society has become so inflexible that individuals must conform to prescribed social norms with little or no personal choice." As for *minority status*, they wrote: "Lastly, social organizations can make social or cultural groups vulnerable to mental disease by reducing them to an inferior economic, social or cultural status." Therefore, immigrant populations can be handled by the host communities in negative or positive ways. The sociocultural changes could be noxious to mental health if they accumulate negative factors such as anomie, role deprivation, value polymorphism, social rigidity, inferior status, "exits" from the social field, socially undesirable events, lack of communication, or hostility from the established population. In those cases, most of the psychiatric casualties will be of a depressive nature. Prevention should be based on preparation of the would-be immigrant concerning what to expect realistically, and preparation of the host country or region concerning the best ways to receive and to help immigrants and refugees. In any case, two decisive factors about final outcome are similarity and flexibility: the more flexible and the more similar the arriving and the receiving cultures are, the better the adjustment of the immigrants.

In a Seminar on Depression held in Puerto Rico in 1973 (10), the participants made some excellent points of relevance to the United States. They began by quoting a study of the National Institute of Mental Health, which estimates that eight million Americans are depressed, 125,00 are hospitalized for depression every year, and perhaps an additional 200,000 should be hospitalized. We tend to think of migration only in terms of strangers from abroad coming here, but, as the participants astutely observed, "geographical mobility or migration always has been one of the fundamental characteristics of American society. For years the rule of thumb has been that one in five Americans moves each year. The latest figures show that it may be closer to 30 percent. . . . Industrialization has also led to much of our society's mobility. The big companies want mobile soldiers who can be moved at will throughout the U.S. or even throughout the world. . . . But what is good for the company is not necessarily good for the employee and his family. When individuals move geographically or socially, they unlink and lose contact with friends, neighbors and people they worked with. There is a sense of loss. The first one to feel this loss usually is the wife. . . . Social and geographical mobility also affects those who stay where they are. . . . There is a breaking of the old relationship and the formation of new relationships when someone leaves and someone arrives" (10) .

So migration can touch everybody's existence in our nation. There are the migrant employees of the government, the military, and the big companies, and those drawn by the lure of better employment, higher wages, and brighter opportunities in other regions; there are the migrant workers of the seasonal harvests; there are the thousands and thousands of children moving every year to colleges, universities, and work opportunities, and the large number of youthful runaways; there are the victims of massive urban renewals; there are the immigrants arriving in an uninterrupted flow, and then, in spasmodic spurts, waves of refugees every so often. And there are those who remain, but who are touched nevertheless by the successive tides of migration of the comers and the goers. "The whole history of man," writes Weidman, "has not prepared us to deal with this situation. Our history is based . . . on ethnocentrism, which is really the belief that my nationality and cultural background are the best and all else is inferior. . . . As developing countries become more industrialized, the people become more like westerners, and they show more depressive symptoms (10) ."

The refugee, the ultimate migrant, suffers more intensively all the experiences and stresses described. When psychopathology is present, depression is by far the predominant entity. In a paper about Cuban refugees in the United States, Azcárate (11) describes their psychiatric symptomatology as an expression of an overwhelming sense of anxiety, depression, and inability to cope with stress. In his view, it is primarily experienced as an attitude of helplessness, a feeling that nothing can be done. Everything is beyond control: separation from the family, length of exile, return to Cuba.

It is customary to describe the Cuban story in the United States as a "success story." Phrases like "golden exile," "those amazing people," "the ones who brought new life to Miami" and many other similar ones are used with frequency. "In Miami," Dr. Weidman points out, "the Anglos perceive the Cubans as doing very well—thriving, really taking over, and incorporating every good thing into themselves. . . . The Cubans . . . feel that they have moved into a minority-group situation, and that they have lost their families, their traditions, their social status, and their dominance. . . . They feel that they can not take care of their families the way they could in Cuba, that they have lost their status and prestige" (10). These opposing views are not necessarily contradictory. Success customarily derives from exemplary performance. Anxiety and depression derive from experience of loss, uprootedness, known and unknown dangers and obstacles, conflict of loyalties, uncertainty, and isolation. It is the silent inner price that has to be paid for the acclaimed, outer victory. Parallel to almost every public "success story" of a Cuban refugee, there is a private "banana-boat story" of escape, tears, blood, sweat, and toil which have left deep-seated psychological scars.

The recognition of the many problems associated with mobile societies, migrating populations, and swelling currents of exiles; the unbiased discussion of the causes, the prevention, and the treatment of psychiatric symptomatology—especially depression—generated by the movement of masses of individuals from one place to another; and the certainty that in modern times all of these phenomena are increasing imposes a moral obligation upon all of us. We should observe, study, talk, write, discuss, and alert the public about the magnitude of a state of affairs that involves all of us.

## SUMMARY

Human beings move through life like the planets around the sun, or the wind of the hurricanes, in two simultaneous ways; there is a movement of rotation, or constant interaction with the immediate environment, and there is a movement of translation, or continued displacement through time and space. The study of human beings, and therefore of their diseases, should be approached from those interactional and longitudinal points of view.

Depression, as one of the most prevalent forms of human suffering and ill health, will never be clearly understood if we conceptualize it as an exclusive product of either "something wrong with the patient" or "something wrong with the environment." The emotional *reaction* (that basic Adolph Meyer concept) of the patient to an accumulation of negative and rather precipitous life events conveying loss and social undesirability seems in essence to constitute what we call a clinical depression.

Migration is the epitome of change, and the refugee is the epitome of the migrant. The kinds of life events which accumulate the stresses of change, loss, and social undesirability weigh most heavily upon the person who moves from one stable cultural niche to another. In consequence, depression, open or masked, is the most prevalent psychiatric condition in migrants and others who are subjected to massive alteration of accustomed life circumstances.

## REFERENCES

1. Donne, John. "No Man Is an Island." Selected writings. Keith Fallon, ed., Stanyan Books, Random House: New York, 1970, p. 1.
2. Minuchin, J. "Families and Family Therapy." Cambridge, Mass.: Harvard University Press, 1974, pp. 4-6.
3. Holmes, T., and Rahe, R. H. "The Social Readjustment Rating Scale." *J. Psychosomatic Research* 11:213-218, 1967.
4. Thompson, K. C., and Kendrie, H. C. "Environmental Stress in Primary Depressive Illness." *Arch. Gen. Psychiat.* 26:130-132, February 1972.
5. Leff, M. J., Roatch, J. F., and Bunney, W. E. "Environmental Factors Preceeding the

Onset of Severe Depressions." *Psychiatry* 33:293, 1970.

6. Payhel, E. S., Myers, J. K., Dienelt, M. N., Klerman, G. L., Lindenthal, J. J., and Pepper, M. P. "Life Events and Depression." *Arch. Gen. Psychiat.* 21:757-760, December 1969.

7. Opler, M. K. "The Use of Culture in Psychiatry." *Am. J. Psychoanalysis* 33:120, 1973.

8. Dodge, J. S. "The Health and Welfare of Immigrants." *New Zealand Med. J.* 77:370, June 1973.

9. Wittkower, E. D., and Dubreuil, G. "Psychocultural Stress in Relation with Mental Illness," *Social Science and Medicine* 7:696-697, 1973.

10. Araneta, E., Schwab, J. J., Weidman, H., and Woodbury, M. "The Epidemiology of Depression: Causes and Manifestations with Special Transcultural Considerations." Proceedings of a seminar held in San Juan, Puerto Rico, p. 15 and others, July 27-28, 1973. Presented as a service to physicians by Merck, Sharp and Dohme.

11. Azcárate, E. "Influence of Exile in the Psychopathology of Cuban Patients in the U.S.A." Paper presented at the Annual Meeting of the American Psychological Association, Miami, Florida, 1970.

7

# Current Psychoanalytic Concepts of Depression

ROBERT B. WHITE

In the past ten to fifteen years there has been as much ferment among psychoanalysts regarding the depressive disorders as there has been among our psychiatric colleagues who have a chemotherapeutic and biologic orientation to mental illness. Anthony and Benedek (1), Mendelson (2), Bowlby (3,4), Jacobson (5), Gaylin (6), Beck (7), Rochlin (8) and others have provided extensive discussions of the psychoanalytic concepts regarding depression as well as extensive reviews of the psychoanalytic literature and the literature from other fields relevant to the psychoanalytic concepts of the depressive disorders. There is almost as much disagreement among psychoanalysts regarding the psychopathology of depression as Goodwin and Bunney (9) have noted among the biological psychiatrists regarding the biochemical aspects of the etiology of the affective disturbances. Being, therefore, unable to present a resumé of "the" psychoanalytic theory of depression, I will limit my remarks to those themes in the psychoanalytic and related literature on depressive disorders which seem to me to be the most significant. The themes I will emphasize first are:

1. The affect of depression is a response to the loss (or the threat of loss) of someone, something, or some physical or psychological function which is an important source of security and satisfaction. As Gaylin (6) has noted: "What is important to realize is that depression can be precipitated by the loss or removal of anything that the individual over-values in terms of his security. To the extent that one's sense of well-being, safety, or security is dependent on love, money, social position, power, drugs, or obsessional defenses—to that extent one will be threatened by its loss." He goes on to note that when a person loses his crucially important sources of security, he will develop a depressed condition characterized by a sense of helplessness and hopelessness. It is this affective state which typifies depressive illness.

Gaylin comments further: "When the adult gives up hope in his ability to cope and sees himself incapable of either fleeing or fighting, he is 'reduced' to a state of depression. This very reduction, with its parallel to the helplessness of infancy becomes, ironically, one last unconscious cry for help, a plea for a solution to the problem of survival via dependency. The very stripping of one's defenses becomes a form of defensive maneuver." The importance of the state of helplessness and hopelessness in the etiology of depressions was first emphasized by Bibring (10) and has been elaborated on by Engel (11) and Schmale (12).

2. The loss which evokes the affect of depression may be *real, fantasied,* or *symbolic,* a distinction which will be discussed at length later in this paper.

3. The affect of depression derives from the biologically innate responses of the infant to the loss of the physical and/or emotional contact with the mother in the age period of approximately six months to thirty-six months, a period during which the mother is the child's primary, perhaps sole, source of security.

4. Loss of contact with the mother in infancy and early childhood may result from either the physical absence of the mother or her emotional absence (that is, her lack of adequate affective responsiveness to the infant). Either type of loss disrupts the normal development of the child and creates a greater than ordinary vulnerability later in life to loss of people, capacities, possessions, or circumstances which provide security. This vulnerability stemming from loss in infancy sensitizes the individual to loss in later childhood, adolescence, or adulthood.

From the age of approximately twelve months on, the father and other parental or family figures progressively share the function of providing the child with a fundamental sense of security, or sense of basic trust, as Erikson (13) has aptly termed it. From about age twelve months on, loss of any parental figures will come to have a traumatic effect similar to that of loss of the mother in the first year or two of life. Here we touch upon the family dynamics of depression, an important topic that cannot be pursued further on this occasion.

5. This sensitizing effect of early parental loss predisposes the person who experiences it to respond to later losses with a greater degree of depression than a person who has not suffered early childhood loss. The relationship between loss of a parent in childhood and the later incidence and severity of depressive illness has been noted by numerous investigators—Beck (7), Winnicott (14), Bowlby (15,3,4) and others. The importance of both loss in childhood and loss in later life to the onset of depressive illness has been clearly demonstrated in the elegant and systematic study of depressed patients by Leff, Roatch, and Bunney (16).

## THE AFFECT OF DEPRESSION AS A RESPONSE TO LOSS

René Spitz (17,18) first systematically studied the response of infants to loss of contact with the mother. Bowlby (3,4) has recently reported on his own long-term study of the impact on children of parental loss, and has provided an extensive survey of the literature on the subject. Bowlby describes three phases in the response of the small child (between the ages of approximately six and thirty-six months) to physical separation from the mother.

1. *The phase of protest.* This phase involves weeping, wailing, and anxious, agitated, angry searching or calling for the mother. Anger is prominent, and the child may turn this upon himself in such activities as head-banging or he may turn it toward others in temper outbursts. He looks eagerly toward any sight or sound that suggests his mother might be returning. This phase may last hours or days, rarely longer than a week. This is, of course, very reminiscent of the first phase of grief in the adult which has been so admirably studied by Gorer (19) and Parkes (20). After some hours or days of this painful, agitated state of protest, the child enters the second stage, that of despair.

2. *The stage of despair.* This stage may last days or weeks and is characterized by symptoms which are very similar to those exhibited by adults in the second stage of grief. The child ceases his agitated protesting behavior and becomes quieter and withdrawn. He now looks and acts dejected, depressed, and despairing. He eats poorly, often loses weight, and has little interest in toys or people. When his mother returns, this disturbance subsides. If she does not, this depressed state often changes into the third stage of detachment.

3. *The stage of detachment.* The severity and length of this final stage

depend on a variety of factors, most important of which is the length of time the mother is absent, although other factors such as the quality of the prior mother-infant relationship are also of significance. However, beyond a certain time, return of the mother often fails to reverse the child's detachment, and then he usually becomes incapable of forming an emotionally close or meaningful, lasting relationship with her or anyone else. How long is too long for the mother to be absent is debatable, and depends on a variety of factors such as the child's inborn temperament, the adequacy of the relationship to the mother prior to the separation, the preceding emotional climate in the family, the child's age at the time the separation occurs, the availability of an adequate substitute mothering person, and so on. Once he has entered this phase of detachment, the child shows no joy when reunited with his mother, and for hours, days, or longer he will act as if she were no more important than anyone else. Once the stage of detachment has begun, the child no longer appears sad or depressed, and may on the surface seem to have become better adjusted to the separation from the mother. But such a child has relinquished his intense emotional investment not only in his mother, but in people generally. His seemingly improved behavior is not evidence of a healthier mental state; on the contrary, it is a symptom of his inability to form emotional attachment with anyone. In short, it is a symptom of his inability to care. From this matrix comes the detached schizoid person and the emotionally empty psychopath who is incapable of loyalty or love.

## EXPERIMENTAL AND CLINICAL STUDIES OF LOSS IN CHILDREN

Numerous studies (21,22,23,24) of the effect of separation in infancy on behavior in later life make clear the extreme importance of loss in the first few years of life. Ainsworth's unpublished study that is cited by Bowlby (4) is especially instructive. Normal infants were subjected at the age of twelve months to experimental separation from the mother for two periods of three minutes each. The experiment was conducted in a bland, non-threatening atmosphere. All of the infants exhibited various degrees of distress which quickly abated after reunion with the mother. However, when the experiment was repeated two weeks later, the infants were significantly more distressed by the mother's brief absences on this second occasion than they had been on the first occasion. Obviously the few minutes of separation from the mother two weeks earlier had made the children more vulnerable to loss of contact with her than they had originally been—they had been sensitized, so to speak.

If a very few minutes of separation from the mother affects a twelve-month-old infant so profoundly that the separation can produce symptoms of distress two weeks later, it is not difficult to imagine the greater degree of vulnerability to loss that occurs when separation from the mother occurs repeatedly or lasts for weeks or months. Winnicott (13) has described one such instance in the case of a little boy separated from his mother for six weeks when he was eighteen months old. The separation was due to an illness in the mother. At age eleven years he witnessed his father's accidental death by drowning. This previously normal youngster developed a near psychotic depressive reaction some months after the father's death. Psychoanalytically oriented treatment demonstrated that the boy's extreme response to the father's death was a result of his special sensitivity to loss. This special sensitivity to loss was in large measure a consequence of the separation from his mother when he was eighteen months old. This type of gross disruption of the relation between child and parent produces obvious disturbances in the development of the child. But the more subtle disturbances in what Erikson (13) has termed mutuality in the parent-child interaction are probably of greater clinical significance than these dramatic and conspicuous pathogenic conditions. Ainsworth, Bell, and Stayton (25) have provided a most persuasive summary of their studies which demonstrate the importance of the subtle and more common aspects of the mother-infant interactions, a study worthy of the attention of all psychiatrists.

## LOSS IN THE ETIOLOGY OF EXPERIMENTALLY INDUCED DEPRESSIONS IN PRIMATES

The profound long-term impact on various nonhuman primates of loss of contact with the mother or other important sources of security has been experimentally demonstrated by Harlow (26) and his co-workers (27) as well as by Kaufman (28), Spencer-Booth and Hinde (29), and others. For our purposes the most instructive of these various experiments is the one performed by Spencer-Booth and Hinde on rhesus monkeys at the age of approximately eight months. The monkeys were separated from their mothers for one or two periods of six days each. During the separation the babies demonstrated the phases of protest and despair similar to that shown by human infants at age eighteen to twenty-four months under similar circumstances. All of the baby monkeys tended to cling more or to stay closer to their mothers for up to three months after reunion, as compared to controls. Even more interesting was the long-range effect of such brief separations. At the age of twelve months and at the age of thirty months the experimental monkeys continued to show a markedly greater needful attachment to their mothers than did controls. In addition, they still showed behavioral manifestations of the depression which were so grossly obvious during the period of experimental separation. The twice-separated monkeys showed more marked effects than the monkeys separated only once. Similar results were noted by McKinney, Suomi, and Harlow (30) in a series of somewhat different experiments. They showed that repeated short-term separations of infant rhesus monkeys from either the mother or agemates to whom the babies had become attached produced "a striking arrest of social development." They comment: "By the techniques of repetitive short-term separations, we have produced monkeys 9 months old that behaved like monkeys 3 months old or younger."

## LOSS IN THE ETIOLOGY OF DEPRESSION IN HUMAN ADULTS

The data I have cited thus far have been obtained mostly from experimental and clinical studies on children and laboratory experiments on primates. I wish now to turn to the matter of the clinically manifest depressive disorders seen in adults and to set forth some views which are widely shared among psychoanalysts and which have been recently summarized by Gilliland and me (31).

Originating from a childhood response to loss of parental love, the affect of depression in later life may be evoked by a variety of losses—*real*, *fantasied*, or *symbolic*. The types of losses which are of greatest clinical importance include:

1. Loss of a relationship with an emotionally important person due to death, divorce, the waning of affection, geographical separation, and the like.

2. Loss of health, important body functions, physical attractiveness, or physical or mental capacities due to disease, injury, or aging.

3. Loss of status or prestige (that is, loss of esteem in the eyes of others).

4. Loss of self-esteem (that is, loss of esteem in one's own eyes).

5. Loss of occupational or financial security.

6. Loss of a fantasy or, more precisely, the loss of hope of fulfillment of an important fantasy.

7. Loss of a symbol, usually referred to as a symbolic loss.

The first five of these categories of loss are easily understood and involve losses that are obvious and real.

Category 6, loss of hope of fulfillment of an important fantasy, usually accompanies a real loss, but the loss of the fantasy may be more devastating than the real loss itself. The case of a ski instructor who sustained a fracture of his leg which was so severe that it would prevent him from ever again jumping in competition illustrates a devastating loss of a fantasy which accompanies a moderate real loss. Although his fracture would not prevent him from working in the future as a ski instructor, it did put an end to any hope of his realizing his fantasy of winning a gold medal as a ski jumper in the Olympics, a secret fantasy which had been an important sustaining factor in the young man's psychological integration for some years. Although his injury was not extremely serious by ordinary standards, and by those standards did not impose serious loss, it did produce a severe depressive reaction because it involved the loss of hope of ever attaining an important fantasy. Another example of this type of loss of a fantasy is a person who overidealizes a friend, lover, or mate, and then becomes depressed when the other person proves incapable of living up to the fantasied expectations.

Category 7, the loss of a symbol (usually referred to as a symbolic loss), is exemplified by the case of a sports car enthusiast. This man, age forty-nine, had for years been an avid competitor in sports car rallies in his area. For several years he had regularly won most events, a feat he largely attributed to the outstanding performance of his sleek, immaculately cared for, crimson Ferrari. Despite the fact that the automobile was fully covered by insurance and could be replaced, he became significantly depressed when his beloved Ferrari burned up. To this man there could never be another Ferrari such as the one he had lost. Obviously his sports car was an important symbol of something he valued highly and was desperately afraid of losing. Psychoanalytic treatment revealed that this man's Ferrari symbolically represented several things which he felt he was in the process of losing—youth, agility, physical attractiveness, and sexual potency, to name a few.

In summary, losses which evoke depression may be *real, symbolic,* or *the loss of an important fantasy.* Most commonly, losses which are sufficiently painful to produce a significant degree of depression involve all or some combinations of these three types of loss. The case of the bereaved mother cited in a subsequent part of this paper demonstrates how a real loss by death of a son also involved both the loss of a fantasy and of a symbol. However, it should be noted that any significant changes in a person's life circumstances, even changes which he desires, involve a loss of the prior circumstances on which his sense of security was dependent to some degree. As Marris (32) has recently noted, any change in a person's life situation produces a grief-like longing for the way things used to be.

## REACTIVE AND ENDOGENOUS DEPRESSIONS

When a persistent mood of morbid depression is the principal symptom of a psychiatric illness, the diagnosis of depressive illness is warranted. In this paper I will not explore in depth the controversial question of whether there is any fundamental difference, except of degree, between a neurotic depression and a psychotic depression. It is my view that there is no difference except of degree.

However, the earlier comments on the role of loss in the etiology of depressive illness force me to discuss the distinction between reactive and endogenous depressions. I grant that there may be instances of depressive illness that arise more or less independently of any life stress or psychological conflict. I grant that biochemical abnormalities, probably genetic in origin, may play a significant role in the etiology of some depressions. But I contend that truly endogenous depressions occur extremely rarely, if at all. I have never seen one—that is, I have never seen a depression of psychotic or of neurotic degree in which some significant loss (real, fantasied, or symbolic) was not a demonstrably significant etiologic factor—if sufficient time and attention was devoted to obtaining a detailed history.

In this regard I share the views of Leff, Roatch, and Bunney (16). They studied forty consecutive inpatients at the National Institute of Mental Health who had unequivocal depressive disorders of sufficient severity to require hospitalization. During treatment these patients had an average of sixty semiweekly psychotherapy sessions of one hour's duration each. The families of the patients were also intensively interviewed.

Thirteen of the forty patients strictly fulfilled the following criteria for endogenous depression—at least they did so during the first week or so of their hospital stay.

1. Absence of any discernible precipitating event.
2. Severe degree of depression.
3. Psychomotor retardation or agitation.
4. Diurnal variation of mood with worsening in the morning.
5. Insomnia with early awakening.
6. Weight loss.
7. Self-reproach and guilt.
8. Lack of reactivity to the environment.

Data collected during the first week of hospitalization failed to reveal any precipitating stress in these "endogenous" depressions. However, after several weeks of hospitalization, all of the patients with "endogenous" depressions gave more information than they had during the first week of their hospital stay. In the year prior to the onset of symptoms, all had suffered clear-cut stressful precipitating events. All of these precipitating events involved loss and tended to cluster in the month prior to onset. For example, one female patient found that her boyfriend was going to marry someone else within a few weeks; a male patient who very much wanted children learned that his marriage was barren because of his low sperm count; another suffered the loss of a close family member by death. Furthermore, in addition to these recent losses, a great majority of the forty patients had suffered some significant childhood loss.

It was only after many intensive interviews that these childhood losses and recent precipitating events were disclosed by many of these "endogenously" depressed patients. As they gave more data about themselves, it became clear that the same number and type of precipitating events had occurred in the lives of the patients with endogenous as with the patients with reactive depressions. These findings by Leff et al. are similar to those reported by Paykel (33,34,35) and his co-workers, although they found that approximately 15 per cent of depressive illnesses may be "endogenous."

Goodwin and Bunney (9) found a similar relation between precipitating events and the tendency of depressed patients to enter into a manic phase. They state, and I would agree with them, that the etiological implications in the dichotomy of reactive and endogenous depressions may be misleading. They note: "If precipitating events are important in the onset of depression, they must be considered to be important in the more severe 'endogenous' depression as well as in the milder 'reactive' depression. An exception to this may be the patient with frequent and regular cycles of mania and depression. In a preliminary study of four (such) cases we were unable to identify precipitating stresses that preceded the regular onset of depressive or manic episodes."

In my own experience, when depressive episodes are carefully studied, they are always found to occur in response to some type of significant loss, although I readily grant that some biologic factor, perhaps genetic in origin, may predispose some people to become depressed in response to losses which other persons might bear with little or no difficulty. Traumatic events in childhood, which involve loss of or separation from parents, also create a predisposition to respond with depression to events involving loss in later life as Heinicke (36), Beck (7), Bowlby (3,4) and others have suggested. Whatever may be the interplay of genetic, biochemical, and experimental factors in the production of depression, experiences of loss are important, probably essential, etiologic factors, whether the depressed state takes the form of a suicidal psychosis or a period of low mood in a relatively normal person.

## THE PSYCHODYNAMICS OF DEPRESSION

Characteristically, but not invariably, severe depressive disorders tend to occur in very compulsive people who are conscientious to a fault. Never having been able to live up to the dictates of an excessively harsh and vindictive Superego, the depressed person falls victim to the unrealistic criticisms and insatiable demands of his own conscience.

Such a conscience (and the ambivalence that is inherent in the obsessive-compulsive person with such a conscience) is the seedbed from which most severe depressions spring. The person who is always under criticism from a relentlessly harsh conscience tends to be overly dependent on love, good will, and praise from others to counteract his constant inner sense of worthlessness. Consequently, he is especially vulnerable to loss of love and the loss of relationships with people from whom he seeks to obtain reassurance of his worth. His relationship to such people is analogous to that which a starving man has to a person who possesses ample food. The starving man is at the mercy of the other, who may, if he chooses, tyrannize the hungry man by withholding food. This childlike dependence on others for emotional support makes for relationships which are inherently ambivalent; that is, because the person feels tyrannized by those on whose approval his self-esteem so desperately depends, he is prone to hate the very people he loves and needs. Whenever his expectations and need for love are not fulfilled, underlying rage erupts. His harsh conscience and perfectionistic obsessive-compulsive defenses make his own hostility difficult for him to accept or even acknowledge, and he frequently turns it back on himself.

The relationship of morbid depression to loss, ambivalence, and the way in which loss unleashes the hostile component of an ambivalent relationship is exemplified in the case of a patient whose son unexpectedly died. The mother of a handsome, bright, and very promising teenage boy was devastated by his death from acute leukemia, a fact which first became manifest only two weeks prior to his death. Initially she refused to believe that the diagnosis was correct. When chemotherapy of the leukemia was ineffective, she became enraged at the very competent physician who was treating her son. Being a religious person, when the son's death was imminent she began to pray, bargaining with God by promising to do various acts of religious devotion and sacrifice if her son was spared. When her son died, she flew into a rage, first at the doctor, then at the God whom she loved and revered, and finally at the son she adored. She grabbed a knife and made wild threats to kill the physician; she cursed God and vowed never to go to church again; finally she screamed and pounded on the body of her son, wailing, "Don't do this to me—you're not being fair. Come back, come back."

This unfortunate woman suffered a variety of losses, real, symbolic, and fantasied. She sustained a real loss in the death of her very attractive son whose bright future was an important sustaining factor to her life. She also sustained a severe symbolic loss in that her son was an important symbol of the mother's sense of worth and accomplishment, especially so because she had two other children with serious congenital defects. Finally, because of the boy's death she suffered the loss of a very important fantasy, the fantasy that she who was so devout would be magically protected by God. This fantasy was smashed when first the doctor failed to bring about a miraculous cure, and next the God she had worshiped faithfully failed to spare her son from death. This combination of real loss, symbolic loss, and loss of a fantasy left her temporarily disorganized, frightened, hurt, and angry, much as a small child feels when deserted by his parents. Next, she identified with her son and refused to eat or move from the bed because, she stated, since he could no longer move or eat, neither could she. Finally she became depressed, threatened suicide, and berated herself for not having fed her son properly and not having made him obtain more rest, failings on her part which she insisted were responsible for his leukemia.

In these observations on grief, a naturally occurring experiment on the effect of loss, we can see the causes and the defenses involved in a case of depression of extreme degree. The mother's relationship with her son was ambivalent, as is apparent in the personal gain which she demanded from the promise of her son's future. He was unduly regarded as a supplier of esteem and support, and her love for him was tinged with these selfish needs. His impending loss badly disrupted the organizing, controlling, and defensive functions of her Ego. She regressed, looking in a childlike fashion to the doctor to perform a godlike miracle. When he could not do this, her rage at him erupted. Then she turned to God. When He performed no miracle in response to her prayers, she became enraged at Him. When all hope was lost, she turned her anger on her dead son. Her anger subsided when she resorted to identification with the lost son, becoming like him in her inability to eat or move from her bed. Finally she turned her anger on herself in the depressive, self-accusatory idea that she was somehow responsible for causing her son's fatal illness. Her self-accusations were intoned in a manner very reminiscent of her earlier complaints at her son for deserting her. Here, we can see that her identification with the dead boy allowed her symbolically to maintain the relationship with him, and that some of her self-accusations were accusations directed toward him who was now psychologically located within herself as a result of her identification with him.

## SUMMARY

Loss results in depression. The affect of depression signals that a loss has occurred or is anticipated. When depression does not reach a clearly morbid degree, the affect and its physiologic concomitants probably represent nothing more than the biologically innate response to loss. In less severe but nonetheless pathologic forms of depression—that is, depression out of proportion to the reality of the loss—the loss produces regression and revives the intense sense of hopelessness and despair that the small child experiences when the parents are absent for an extended time. In the most extreme types of depression, in which morbid guilt, self-accusations, feelings of worthlessness, and extreme hopelessness occur, we can see the effect of identification with the person whom the patient feels he has lost and the use of the mechanism of turning aggression against the self. Because of regression, the hostile component of the ambivalent relationship to the lost person is primitive and destructive. In turning such infantile aggression against the self, much of the hostility intended for the lost person is turned against the lost person who now, through the process of identification, is symbolically within the depressed person.

## SOME SUGGESTIONS FOR THE FURTHER STUDY OF DEPRESSIONS

In closing, I would note that in my view depressive illnesses are truly psychosomatic disturbances. I would conjecture that inborn temperamental-biochemical differences may make some people innately more vulnerable than others to the effect of emotional loss and that some significant alterations of brain chemistry occur in the course of severe depressions, as the effectiveness of lithium carbonate and antidepressant medications would suggest. To what degree these possible biochemical changes represent a physiological concomitant of the psychological state of depressed affect rather than a cause of the depressed mental state is open to debate. As I will note later, the study of grief is a potentially valuable approach to this problem.

Regarding the disturbances of brain function that may predispose to depression, we know of some perinatal difficulties that increase vulnerability to separation from the mother. As Ucko (37) has shown, infants who suffer significant degrees of anoxia at birth, but who have no obvious intellectual or neurological defects, are at age two and three years more sensitive to change in their environment generally, and are more disturbed by separation from their mother than are children who are not anoxic at birth. The genetic factors that may be involved in depressive disorders have recently been summarized by Winokur (38).

We know that emotional deprivation in the first year or two of life can disturb such basic biologic functions as the excretion of growth stimulating hormone from the pituitary, as documented in the syndrome of emotional dwarfism. We know that a particular type of disturbed mother-infant relationship in early childhood, probably by age two or three, can produce irreversible transsexualism. We know that infants deprived of adequate maternal care in the first year or two of life can be permanently and seriously impaired in their capacity to develop properly.

There is now overwhelming evidence that experiences in the first year or two of life can create irreversible reaction patterns and personality traits, a process similar to imprinting in lower species. It seems feasible that experiences in early infancy can permanently skew or distort neurophysiological-hormonal-enzyme systems and produce a physiologic as well as a psychologic vulnerability to loss in later life, and hence to depressive illness. As Harlow and his co-workers (30,39), as well as Reite, Kaufman, Pauley et al. (40) and others have noted, experimentally induced depressions in monkeys offer a promising but as yet inadequately explored method for studying the relationship between the psychological and the neurochemical factors in the etiology of depression.

Grief in humans is another potentially fruitful field for a combined psychoanalytic, biochemical, and neurophysiological study of depression. For example, the study of grief in the spouses or parents of fatally ill patients would allow us to take advantage of a naturally occurring experiment on the psychological and physiological impact of loss. Such a study might clarify the chicken-egg aspect of the biochemical correlates of depression. Grief-striken people often show all of the psychological, behavioral, and vegetative disturbances that characterize severely depressed patients. Serial studies of such people from the moment they learn that a loved one has a fatal illness until the loved one dies and the symptoms of grief have abated might settle the question of whether the various biochemical alterations reported in depressed patients are the result of depression or its cause. Such studies raise obvious ethical and humanitarian problems. However, properly done, such studies could not only avoid harm to the bereaved subjects, but could be of benefit to them. All who have suffered the pain of harsh grief seek to find some sense or meaning in the experience. Putting the painful experience to some use that might be beneficial to others lessens the sting of loss.

## REFERENCES

1. Anthony, E. J., and Benedek, T., eds. *Depression and Human Existence*. Boston: Little, Brown, 1975.
2. Mendelson, M., *Psychoanalytic Concepts of Depression*, 2nd ed. New York: Spectrum, 1974.

3. Bowlby, J. *Attachment* (Vol. 1 of *Attachment and Loss*). New York: Basic Books, 1969.
4. Bowlby, J. *Separation* (Vol. 2 of *Attachment and Loss*). New York: Basic Books, 1969.
5. Jacobson, E. *Depression.* New York: International Universities Press, 1971.
6. Gaylin, W., ed. *The Meaning of Despair.* New York: Science House, 1968.
7. Beck, A. T. *Depression: Causes and Treatment.* Philadelphia: University of Pennsylvania Press, 1967.
8. Rochlin, G. *Griefs and Discontents.* Boston: Little, Brown, 1965.
9. Goodwin, F. K., and Bunney, W. E. Psychobiological aspects of stress and affective illness, in J. P. Scott and E. C. Senay, eds., *Separation and Depression.* Washington, D. C.: American Association for the Advancement of Science, 1973.
10. Bibring, E. The mechanism of depression, in P. Greenacre, ed., *Affective Disorders: Psychoanalytic Contribution to Their Study.* New York: International Universities Press, 1953.
11. Engel, G. L. *Psychological Development in Health and Disease.* Philadelphia: Saunders, 1962.
12. Schmale, A. H. Adaptive role of depression in health and disease, in J. P. Scott and E. C. Senay, eds., *Separation and Depression.* Washington, D. C.: American Association for the Advancement of Science, 1973.
13. Erikson, E. H. *Childhood and Society.* New York: Norton, 1950.
14. Winnicott, D. W. A child psychiatry case illustrating delayed reaction to loss, in M. Schur, ed., *Drives, Affects, Behavior.* New York: International Universities Press, 1965.
15. Bowlby, J. Effects on behavior of disruption of an affectional bond, in J. M. Thoday and A. S. Parkes, eds., *Genetic and Environmental Influences on Behavior.* Edinburgh: Oliver and Boyd, 1968.
16. Leff, M. J., Roatch, J. F., and Bunney, W. E. Environmental factors preceding the onset of severe depressions. *Psychiatry* 33:293-311, 1970.
17. Spitz, R. A. Hospitalism. An inquiry into the genesis of psychiatric conditions in early childhood. *Psychoanal. Study Child* 1:53-74, 1945.
18. Spitz, R. A. *The First Year of Life.* New York: International Universities Press, 1965.
19. Gorer, G. *Death, Grief, and Mourning.* Garden City, N. Y.: Doubleday, 1965.
20. Parkes, C. M. *Bereavement: Studies of Grief in Adult Life.* New York: International Universities Press, 1972.
21. Heinicke, C. M., and Westheimer, I. J. *Brief Separations.* New York: International Universities Press, 1965.
22. Bergmann, T., and Freud, A. *Children in the Hospital.* New York: International Universities Press, 1965.
23. Provence, S., and Lipton, R. C. *Infants in Institutions.* New York: International Universities Press, 1962.
24. Heinicke, C. Some effects of separating two-year-old children from their parents: A comparative study. *Hum. Relat.* 9:105-176, 1956.
25. Ainsworth, M. D. S., Bell, S. M., and Stayton, D. J. Infant-mother attachment and social development, in M. P. M. Richards, ed., *The Integration of a Child Into a Social World.* New York: Cambridge University Press, 1974.
26. Harlow, H. F. *Learning to Love.* New York: Jason Aronson ,1974.
27. Harlow, H. F., and Suomi, S. J. Induced depression in monkeys. *Behav. Biol.* 12:273-296, 1974.

28. Kaufman, I. C. Mother-infant separation in monkeys, in J. P. Scott and E. C. Senay, eds. *Separation and Depression*. Washington, D. C.: American Association for the Advancement of Science, 1973.

29. Spencer-Booth, Y., and Hinde, R. A. Effects of brief separations from mothers during infancy on behavior of rhesus monkeys 6-24 months later. *J. Child Psychol. Psychiatry* 12:157-172, 1971.

30. McKinney, W. T., Suomi, S. J., and Harlow, H. F. New models of separation and depression in rhesus monkeys, in J. P. Scott and E. C. Senay, eds., *Separation and Depression*. Washington, D. C.: American Association for the Advancement of Science, 1973.

31. White, R. B., and Gilliland, R. M. *Elements of Psychopathology: The Mechanisms of Defense*. New York: Grune & Stratton, 1975.

32. Marris, P. *Loss and Change*. Garden City, N. Y.: Anchor Press, 1975.

33. Paykel, E. S. Life events and depression: a controlled study. *Arch. Gen. Psychiat.* 2: 753-760, 1969.

34. Paykel, E. S., Prusoff, B. A., and Klerman, G. L. The endogenous-neurotic continuum in depression: rater independence and factor distributions. *J. Psychiatr. Res.* 8:73-90, 1971.

35. Paykel, E. S. Life events and acute depressions, in J. P. Scott and E. C. Senay, eds., *Separation and Depression*. Washington, D. C.: American Association for the Advancement of Science, 1973.

36. Heinicke, C. M. Parental deprivation in early childhood: a predisposition to later depression? in J. P. Scott and E. C. Senay, eds., *Separation and Depression*. Washington, D. C.: American Association for the Advancement of Science, 1973.

37. Ucko, L. E. A comparative study of asphyxiated and non-asphyxiated boys from birth to five years. *Dev. Med. Child. Neurol.* 7:643-657, 1965.

38. Winokur, G. Genetic aspects of depression, in J. P. Scott and E. C. Senay, eds., *Separation and Depression*. Washington, D. C.: American Association for the Advancement of Science, 1973.

39. Harlow, H. F., and Suomi, S. J. Induced depression in monkeys. *Behav. Biol.* 12:273-396, 1974.

40. Reite, M., Kaufman, I. C., Pauley, J. D., et al. Depression in infant monkeys: physiological correlates. *Psychosom Med.* 36:363-367, 1974.

**8**

# Depressive Factors in Adolescent Eating Disorders

## HILDE BRUCH

The traditional picture of depression is that of a sad person, guilt-ridden and isolated, with poor appetite and emaciated features. Psychodynamic explanations of depression have focused on the unconscious fear of starvation as holding a central position in the motivational organization of the depressive spell. Though related to experiences of deprivation early in life, the reappearance of this fear is precipitated by some current emotional upheaval—in particular, the loss of a loved one, or other situations that precipitate the sense of isolation. When the loss is experienced as irreparable, the person may become depressed and then is unable to take proper steps to regain his psychic balance. Such a person will exhaust his energy in self-reproaches, and although he suffers from fear of starvation, he may lose his appetite in a self-punishing way and will show a characteristic weight loss.

It is less commonly known that the opposite may occur. Though caught in a similar pattern of despair some people react differently: they alleviate this fear of starvation by eating. Like people who have been exposed to true starvation, their desire and need for food may become insatiable. The weight gain may represent an attempt to repair a basic depressive situation. It is important to recognize the deeper significance of the overeating and other symptoms of reactive obesity, because such people are apt to become depressed when reducing is attempted without the psychic problems having been resolved (2).

A description of this type of obesity—as far as I know the oldest one on record—was given by David Hume in his *Letter to a Physician*. In 1729, when he was 18 years old, Hume suffered from a severe depression. He had given up the law as a career and decided to push his fortune in the world as a scholar and philosopher. At first he was happy with this course but then —I quote from the letter—"all my ardor seemed in a moment to be extinguished, and I could no longer raise my mind to that pitch which formerly gave me such excessive pleasure. . . . In this condition I remained for nine months, very uneasy to myself." He gradually recovered his spirits but became suddenly obese. "There grew upon me a very ravenous appetite. . . . This appetite had an effect very unusual, which was to nourish me extremely; so that in six weeks time I passed from one extreme to another, and being before tall, lean, and raw-boned, became a sudden the most sturdy, robust, healthful-like fellow you have seen, with a ruddy complexion and a cheerful countenance."

Hume remained fat for the rest of his life, and he is always included in the list of Englishmen who achieved greatness in spite of their corpulence. An interesting difference in the cultural attitude toward obesity is expressed in his speaking with pride of this change and of his friends congratulating him on his recovery. In our own time everybody would have been acutely concerned about this sudden obesity.

A modern adolescent will invariably blame his feelings of depression on his being too fat. It is sometimes only in retrospect that an individual will acknowledge that depressive feelings had been the cause of overeating. Take the case of a woman in her late thirties who had been a fat child and who in her adolescence had established a fairly good control over her weight after overcoming, with psychiatric help, her tendency to depression. She functioned well as a wife and mother of three children. She maintained her weight at about 140 pounds, which was slightly plump for her short figure.

Then she found herself unexpectedly pregnant, and after some hesitation she and her husband felt that they were fortunate to have another child. When the baby was born it was defective, with a severe Down's syndrome. To protect her feelings, the obstetrician and husband decided that she should not even see this deformed baby. It was a traumatic decision to leave the baby in a home specializing in the care of such defective children. The woman suffered from nightmares of having deserted a lovely child and of having rejected motherhood, constantly blaming herself, until her husband took her to see the child. When she saw how seriously deformed the baby was, her anxiety and guilt subsided. A few weeks later it died of a malformation of the heart. This she could accept with sadness but without guilt.

During these months of acute distress she found herself continuously eating. Though she hated becoming fat again, she was also fully aware that the alternative was to slip into such a severe depression that she would be nonfunctioning. In retrospect she recognized more clearly than she had ever admitted to herself that depressive and angry feelings had played a role in her adolescent obesity. Once she had recognized that she had not neglected or abandoned her child but that it had been the victim of a genetic misfortune, her despair gradually lifted and she began a successful reducing regimen.

The possibility of obesity being the symptom of an emotional upheaval was first discussed in the French literature in the late nineteenth century. One example was the case of a father who began to put on weight immediately after the death of his son, and who was embarrassed about this and could not understand how he could become fat in view of his grief and bereavement. Throughout his life he had never weighed more than 130 pounds, but within a few months after his son's death his weight rose to 200 pounds, and within a year to 235 pounds.

In the more recent literature, there are many references to the development of obesity after upsetting events and periods of great emotional stress. German authors noted after World War I that women who had lived for a long time in uncertainty or who were grieving over the loss of their loved ones had a tendency to put on weight. The German vernacular word for this condition is *Kummerspeck* (fat of sorrow). During World War II, reports from France described a "paradoxical" form of obesity, chiefly in young women, who had been exposed to bombing or other hardships, and who also were amenorrheic. The characteristic aspect of this type of obesity was the rapid development and spongy character of the fat tissue. This was explained as due to the influence of traumatic experiences on the hypothalamic regulatory mechanisms.

It is now generally recognized that obesity develops not infrequently after the death of a family member, or after separation from home, or when a love affair breaks up, or in other situations evoking the fear of desertion and loneliness, or when the fear of death or injury is aroused. I have called this type of obesity "reactive obesity." It is a form more commonly observed in adults, but such sudden increases in weight are also observed in children and adolescents. Overeating and obesity appear to serve the function of warding off anxiety of depressive reactions.

To give one example: a very bright 12-year-old boy gained forty pounds during the six months following the death by accident of an older brother who had been the mother's confidant and favorite. The mother admitted having felt closer to this son than to her husband, and that she had become completely wrapped up in her grief, feeling guilty if she did not remember him every minute. She lived in constant fear of losing her younger son too and would not permit him to engage in former activities or even let him continue his old friendships. It was in this setting that the sudden gain in weight occurred. As the mother faced her own problems, she was able to let her son become more independent and self-reliant and thus capable of establishing control over his eating. This boy did outgrow his obesity.

People with a tendency toward this form of obesity are often aware that they eat more when they are worried or tense and they feel less effective and competent when they try to control their food intake. They are often referred to as compulsive eaters, and they are aware of the difference between real hunger and this neurotic need for food. They may use expressions like "I get mad in my stomach," or "I get this gnawing feeling and nothing can change it but a luscious meal," or "It's my mouth that wants it; I know that *I* have had enough."

Quite often emotional problems are hidden under a complacent façade. The people do not get angry and thus contribute to the misconception that fat people are good-natured, jolly, and cheerful. Instead of expressing anger, or even experiencing it, they become mildly depressed, and the overeating thus serves as a defense against becoming more severely depressed. It is in this group that the supportive and comforting value of overeating can be clearly recognized, in spite of the long-range handicaps of the ensuing obesity.

Such defensive overeating takes the place at times of such severe emotional stress that the question is not so much "Why overeating?" but "What would be the alternative?" All statistics agree that obese people have a high morbidity and mortality rate for most diseases—with one exception: their suicide rate is significantly lower. In evaluating the life history of such people I have often been impressed that the situations in reaction to which obesity develops are of a nature that might have provoked despair in other persons. However undesirable obesity may be rated, as a defensive reaction it is less destructive than suicide or paralyzing deep depression.

In extensive psychosomatic studies Crisp in England observed that "detectable neuroticism or severe depression might not be recognized as long as the obese state is maintained" (3). On the basis of my own experience with numerous patients, I have come to the conclusion that for many fat people, obesity has an important positive function; it is a compensatory mechanism in a frustrating and stressful life situation.

People who use food to combat anxiety and loneliness are apt to become depressed when dieting is enforced. Even without marked obesity, the secure knowledge that one's appetite and needs will be fulfilled is necessary for one's sense of well-being. Mildly depressed patients are often concerned about the loss of satisfaction from ordinary activities. They often complain of having lost all interest, of not finding anything worthwhile. The immediate enjoyment of food serves as reassurance that life still holds some satisfaction. During such a depressive spell they are apt to eat quite impulsively, as soon as the idea strikes them that something might be tasty or enjoyable.

Insoluble life situations making for continued frustration, rage, and anxiety may provoke overeating. A young girl who lived an unhappy and unappreciated life in a home that was dominated by a stepmother described her irrational use of food: "Sometimes I think I am not hungry at all. It is just that I am unhappy in certain things—things I cannot get. Food is the easiest thing to get, that makes me feel nice and comfortable. I try to reason with myself and tell myself that these problems cannot be solved by eating."

She was one of the many fat people who succeeded in showing a fairly complacent attitude toward the world during the daytime and was quite efficient in her work. When she was alone at night, the tension and anxiety became unbearable. "I think then that I am ravenously hungry and I do my utmost not to eat. My body becomes stiff in my effort to control my hunger. If I want to have any rest at all I have to get up and eat; then I go to sleep like a newborn baby."

Patients with this type of eating pattern, which Stunkard has labeled Night-Eating Syndrome, are unable to adhere to any dietary regime as long as their problems and conflicts are unresolved, or as long as they remain in the frustrating environment (4). Some can reduce without difficulty in a hospital, but they will regain this weight as soon as they return to the old setting. Not uncommonly, enforced reducing precipitates panic states and depression.

An 18-year-old girl who had been slightly plump as an adolescent gained a considerable amount of weight when she went away to college. Her parents reacted to this as if it were a great tragedy and pressured her into spending two months of the next summer in a hospital reducing center. Under the strict regime of the medically supervised diet, she lost 33 pounds, bringing her weight down to the normal range. Her parents were so delighted with the result that they sent her off to college with a glamorous new wardrobe, which had been practically forced upon the girl.

In spite of all the praise and enthusiasm she was painfully unhappy and became acutely depressed on return to college, and had to leave after a month. She represents one of the numerous unfortunate cases where the whole family pressure goes in the direction of enforced reducing, with complete neglect of the underlying personality problems.

When she was seen in consultation she was not only severely depressed but also confused about who she was and what to do. She described the whole reducing experience as a terrible psychological shock. She felt watched all the time, constantly in danger of being punished or humiliated for deviating from any prescription or doing something wrong. The feeling of being watched persisted after she left the reducing program and became even stronger after she returned to college. Everybody made such a fuss about her being so glamorous and slim that she felt she owed it to her friends to stay on a diet, though she knew she could not do it. Her only defense against becoming unable to function and breaking down completely was to go on enormous eating sprees. She would order large amounts of ice cream and have packages of cookies and hamburgers sent up to her room; in her anxiety about losing control she ate nearly constantly. Within a month she regained the weight she had so painfully lost.

The review of her development revealed that she had had many depressive reactions before the enforced diet and that she used eating as a defense against this miserable feeling. As the panic-like tension diminished, her eating habits returned to normal and the weight gain stopped. However, she advisably postponed efforts at reducing until she felt more secure about herself and her life plans.

Abnormal weight increases occur not only as a reaction to situational stress but may also be observed in manic-depressive illness. Weight increase may actually be the first sign of the beginning of this illness. I offer as an example the history of a 15-year-old girl, the oldest child in a middle-class family, where the father was considered a failure because his moderate success did not compare to the great wealth which the mother's brothers had acquired. Thanks to gifts from the wealthy relatives, the children enjoyed many privileges, at the price of always doing their best to please the rich uncles. The girl was given many educational and material advantages and she felt obliged to live up to "their" expectations. Though slightly plump, she was considered a pretty girl. Until she was 15 years old, she was praised by the whole family for being so well behaved. Then came a period of undefined illness and her behavior suddenly changed. She became loud, overactive, and promiscuous, "throwing all propriety to the wind," and gained 50 pounds within three or four months. This was followed by a period of her being quiet, "maddeningly proper," and looking desperate and sad; during this phase she lost most of the excess weight. Then she appeared normal for a short time, and from then on would go through definite cycles of manic behavior with enormous gain in weight, and a depressive episode with weight loss. She never lost all the excess weight, however, and by the time she was seen in consultation she was definitely obese. The family was particularly concerned about the weight increases, and tended to disregard the other behavior changes. They wanted a formula to make the girl reduce and stay reduced.

The relation between weight changes and depressive reaction is entirely different in anorexia nervosa. Until recently, all cases of severe weight loss for psychologoical reasons were lumped together under this diagnostic label. Anorexia nervosa is now recognized as a distinct syndrome in which *relentless pursuit of thinness* is the leading motive, in the absence of other psychiatric illness. Characteristically, the illness develops during the adolescent years, mainly in young girls. In the older literature one may find severe weight loss in depression incorrectly reported as examples of anorexia nervosa. Many of the somewhat older patients supposedly suffering from anorexia nervosa fall in this misdiagnosed class.

In the true anorexia nervosa, the patient attempts to establish control over her body and to attain the ultimate in thinness by deliberately restricting what she eats and actively refusing food, though there is no true loss of appetite. There is enormous pride in attaining and maintaining the ultimate in thinness, and in spite of their cachectic appearance, these girls live in constant fear of losing control and getting fat. Any weight gain, even of a mild degree may precipitate a depressive reaction. Many of the secondary symptoms of anorexia nervosa, vomiting and the use of laxatives and diuretics, have the function of preventing this worst of all fates.

A depressive tone is frequently encountered in anorexia nervosa after it has existed for some time. In retrospect, certain behavior changes may be identified that had occurred before the onset of the bizarre dieting, but rarely are they severe enough for the family to have recognized them or to have caused the patient to complain.

Occasionally, however, the picture of anorexia nervosa may develop during an adolescent depression. I have observed only two such patients. The weight loss is then not a symptom of the depression but an effort to combat it. One girl was the oldest in a family plagued by many illnesses of an unusual nature. There were repeated hospitalizations of the parents or the children, each suffering at one time or another from a life-threatening disease. The patient responded to these repeated separations by becoming quiet and withdrawn, and somewhat hypochondriacal. When she was 8, both parents developed serious, potentially fatal illnesses with lengthy hospitalization. Though the children were told, there was an atmosphere of secrecy about all this illness.

This girl did quite well in school and was popular in a superficial way. Menarche occurred at 12½, and she would become depressed with every period. A year later her mother nearly died from a hemorrhage after a biopsy. The girl responded by becoming indifferent, had frequent crying spells, and felt guilty because she did not love her parents enough; she became preoccupied with the possibility of their death.

When she was 14 she suddenly became concerned about becoming too fat and developing a pot belly. At that time her weight was 110 pounds, appropriate for her height, but she decided to lose weight. She was exhilarated when she lost five pounds during the first month, and she continued to diet, though her parents argued with her. She became more isolated and had trouble falling asleep, but she stuck to the restricted diet. Within six months her weight dropped to 68 pounds.

She was hospitalized and met some other patients with anorexia nervosa. She imitated some of their symptoms but soon regained her appetite and her weight rose to 90 pounds. After discharge she felt she could not enjoy life, felt under terrific pressure, but instead of starving herself, she began to gorge. One day after stuffing herself with food she took pills from her mother's cabinet in a suicide attempt. She was readmitted to the hospital and only at this point talked about the long-standing depressive feelings, her despair about not being in touch with her feelings, how she had never been able to let herself go, never even permitting herself to feel or express anger.

In this case the depressive feelings and social withdrawal preceded the onset of the anorexic behavior. Missing are the defiant pride in being thin which is characteristic of primary anorexia nervosa, and the hyperactivity and perfectionism. This girl's good school performance had been an effort to please her parents, not an urgent desire for her own accomplishment.

The true anorexic is satisfied with herself, cheerful, and overactive, as long as she controls her weight. If the controls break down and there is a real increase in weight, severe depression, anxiety, guilt, and shame develop. This is what happened to a 19-year-old girl who had been anorexic for over two years. She was very tall (nearly 5'9"), and her weight had fluctuated during these two years between 85 and 100 pounds. She had become anorexic while at a prestigious boarding school where she felt she was a failure because her grades were not as high as she had anticipated. In her local high school she had been outstanding, and she had taken it for granted that as the perfect daughter of perfect parents she would always be the best in everything. She returned to her local high school, where she graduated with honors.

Her weight was about 100 pounds when she enrolled in a college of high standing. From the beginning there were difficulties, such as her parents not only accompanying her but staying for a week, and she felt reduced to the status of a small child by their solicitude. It so happened that her roommate was also exceedingly dependent on her mother, and they both were a few days late in coming to the dormitory. As it turned out, the roommate was completely disinterested in her studies, was preoccupied with a boyfriend, and the anorectic girl felt excluded. She consulted with a nutritionist in an effort to follow a reasonable diet and was told that she was well informed about her nutritional needs.

Within a few weeks it became apparent that things were not going well. She was continuously preoccupied with food, gave up regular meals, and went on enormous eating sprees. The first weight gain appeared desirable and she received many compliments about her beautiful figure, but she became alarmed when her weight reached 112 pounds.

She spent the midterm break with her family, and they admired her for looking so well. After that, things began to deteriorate. She suddenly felt more and more isolated. Her eating became entirely out of control. She would go to several restaurants or delicatessens in a row, buy large amounts of candy bars, and eat continuously. Within one month her weight increased from 115 to 135 pounds. In view of her height she was still well proportioned, though her face showed the rapid weight increase. She became acutely depressed about her appearance, unable to concentrate on her studies, and preoccupied with suicidal thoughts. She had had a previous depressive episode and took some of the medication prescribed at that time, which made her even more depressed. On her own request she was hospitalized, while attending classes. Within a few days the depression subsided because she now felt protected against her uncontrollable candy spree. She did not stop eating but was moderate in what she took and felt reassured when she lost weight during the hospitalization. Though frantic with fear of getting fat she was determined not to go back to her old starvation regime and set herself the goal of maintaining her weight at 115.

## CONCLUSION

I have presented here several cases illustrating various pictures of the interaction between depression and weight fluctuations in young people. The examples varied from weight gain during a depressive spell, when food is used to alleviate the depressive feelings and to counteract the fear of impoverishment or starvation, to abandonment of all controls during the manic phase, and to the diametric opposite in anorexia nervosa, excessive control and restriction in an effort to combat the sense of helplessness and lack of identity. They represent only a few of the manifold possibilities of such interaction.

Both eating disorder and depressive reactions are descriptive terms for a variety of conditions whose clinical manifestations show different faces. It is not possible to give a general formulation, but for effective treatment it is important to recognize the pattern of interaction in each individual case.

## REFERENCES

1. Bruch, H. *Eating Disorders: Obesity, Anorexia Nervosa and the Person Within*, New York: Basic Books, 1973; London: Routledge & Kegan Paul Ltd., 1974.
2. Bruch, H. Reactive obesity, Chapter 12, pp. 244-266, in *The Importance of Overweight* by Hilde Bruch, New York: W. W. Norton & Company, 1957.
3. Crisp, A. H., and Stonehill, E. Treatment of obesity with special references to seven severely obese patients. *J. Psychosom. Res.*, 14:327-345, 1970.
4. Stunkard, A. J. Eating patterns and obesity. *Psychiat. Quart.* 33:283-292, 1959.

9

# Depression in the Elderly

CHARLES M. GAITZ

Depression as an affect, a mood, or a syndrome may occur at any age, and it is frequently observed among elderly persons. Some consider depression to be the most frequently occurring psychiatric illness in old age. Elderly persons may manifest depression as a reaction to stresses that are characteristic of late life, or they may have an almost lifelong history of depressive episodes.

Although the literature dealing with diagnosis and treatment of elderly persons with depression is quite extensive, relatively few empirical data are presented. Even a brief review, however, reveals that the concepts are varied, that the term "depression" is used rather loosely, and that the factor of age probably deserves more attention in both diagnosis and treatment than it has received.

We will here be concerned primarily with diagnosis, especially with differentiating depression from normal aging processes. I shall review some of the recent literature on this question and then present some empirical data on aging that reveal why the diagnosis of depression in elderly persons may be difficult. It is of course difficult to define "normal aging" and to agree on measures or vantage points for determining abnormality or pathology. It seems likely, however, that depression may be confused with changes experienced by a large proportion of elderly persons, leading physicians to diagnose depression more frequently than warranted.

Diagnosing depression in elderly persons—regardless of whether we are concerned with depression as an affect, a symptom, or a syndrome—is complicated, because social and health factors are especially likely to affect the old. For example, physiologic changes occur with aging, but attitudes and behavior determine, to some extent, the resultant degree of impairment. Alterations in social roles also affect mood.

The physician's own concepts of aging also influence their diagnosis and treatment. To illustrate, Lippincott (1) points out that an examiner, believing that decreasing sexual drive is a natural consequence of aging, may overlook this cue to depressive illness, just as one may disregard suicidal ideation, believing that the elderly persons are not inclined to take their own lives. Pfeiffer and Busse (2) report on studies showing that in 1966, 28 per cent of all persons who committed suicide were over 60 years old. Among white men there is an almost linear increase in suicide rates with advancing age, and a similar trend is beginning to appear among black men. The suicide rate for women is much lower, even though depression is at least as common among women as men. The significance of this finding is not clear.

Commenting on the problems of identifying and diagnosing depression in the elderly, Lippincott (1) calls attention to several other characteristic differences. Since elderly patients often recognize the decrease in their mental capacity, depression may be a reaction to, or a factor in, their decline in mental function. Physical diseases may also affect cerebral function, or they may produce symptoms such as pain and fatigue, which then may be confused with somatic complaints associated with depression. Many elderly persons who have lost a spouse or a friend, whose children have moved away, or who have suffered physical illness feel alien and isolated. Close examination, however, may reveal underlying depressive illness. Some elderly persons feel that life is over and that they are a burden to family members and society. These attitudes may explain why elderly persons tend to react so strongly to fluctuations in health and why they often experience postoperative depressions and respond severely to other illnesses.

There is some disagreement in the current literature about the symptomatology of depression, but Neumann (3) offers some hints for the diagnostician, noting that many patients first present themselves to family physicians with "vague new symptoms." The patient's effort to solicit interest and concern should alert the physician to the possibility of depression. If he listens to his patient, he begins to hear about loneliness, sadness, lack of purpose. Further inquiry brings forth more typical symptoms. Neumann and others emphasize the need to evaluate the patient's physical condition, to differentiate grief reactions from depression, and to distinguish, to the extent possible, depressive from organic brain syndromes. Compared to the depressed person, the patient with organic brain syndrome is more likely to be confused and to show decreased intellectual function, markedly impaired memory, and deteriorated personal appearance and hygiene. A depressed patient is likely to use his intact memory to explain his depression, comparing his present with his early life. Pointing out differences between depressions of early and of late life. Neumann believes that in younger persons depression is likely to be a distortion of reality, whereas in aged persons depression is usually a reaction to reality, a recognition of the limitations and liabilities associated with advanced age.

A study comparing elderly patients admitted to hospitals in New York City and London found that the diagnosis of organic brain disease is made much more frequently in the United States than in England (4). It is conceivable that many elderly patients in the United States who are being diagnosed as having organic brain syndrome would, upon closer examination, be diagnosed as having a functional disorder, probably a depression. This has some important implications. If psychiatrists are inclined to show less therapeutic enthusiasm for elderly patients with organic diagnosis than for those with a functional illness, treatment opportunities may be missed because of the too-frequent diagnosis of organic disease.

Fann and Wheless (5) call attention to the similarity of symptoms of depression and "senility." An elderly depressed patient may be incontinent, confused, and disoriented; a patient who is both senile and depressed may seem apathetic and have little interest in surroundings or activities. Slowing of intellectual processes, psychomotor retardation, symptoms of sadness and dejection, with loss of appetite, insomnia, and fatigue, are observed in both depressed patients and those with organic brain disease. Summarizing the impressions of others, these authors conclude that elderly persons are confronted with many changes and losses that may precipitate depression. These include the social pressures of forced retirement, lowered financial resources and status, physical incapacity, and loss of friends and intimates through death. Adaptation to new and often adverse conditions is demanded at the time when these aged persons' ability to cope and adapt is diminished. Thus the stresses that occur late in life have a greater impact than those that occur earlier because of this declined capacity to adapt to change. These and other factors tending to produce feelings of inferiority and loss of self-esteem may lead to depression.

As Renshaw (6) reminds us, normal mourning, appropriate sorrow and sadness, demoralization, dejection, defeat, and frustration all need to be differentiated from clinical depression. Unlike depression, these feelings are usually closely related in time to environmental stress, they are transient, and the patient accepts them as normal discomfort. They rarely produce physiological signs and symptoms. Loss of appetite, weight loss, insomnia, and self-blame are rarely part of the clinical picture. Renshaw points out that losses of family, of friends, of meaningful work, of looks, of sense perception, of sexual attractiveness, and of prestige accumulate. Losses suffered by the elderly are predictable, steady, and often numerous.

Hall (7) calls attention to the intimate relationship between physical and depressive illness in the aged, pointing out that aged depressive patients may neglect their health to the point of developing such physical complications as avitaminosis, anemia, or dehydration, and then present to the physician what appears to be an organic confusional state. A variety of unrelated physical illnesses may coexist. Some of the earliest symptoms of such organic diseases as myxedema, malignancy, uremia, or cerebral arteriosclerosis may resemble depressive symptoms. To further complicate diagnosis, severe depression may be a side effect of drugs used in the treatment of other physical or psychiatric problems.

Discussing geriatric psychopathology and the low utilization of psychiatric services by the aged, Feigenbaum (8) suggests that older persons are more likely to experience unhappiness than younger persons but are less likely to define their discomfort as psychologic. They tend to accept pain as a natural part of life; it has occurred to them and to their friends before and is a familiar and socially accepted phenomenon. Younger persons, on the other hand, are surprised, even enraged, at the unfairness of fate having chosen them to suffer. Feigenbaum believes that these differences are a pure developmental effect, independent of maturation during different economic or social periods. Moreover, he believes that the communications media, as well as personal acquaintances, lead old people to expect to be unhappy, while the young expect to be happy. Thus elderly persons are less likely to perceive themselves in psychologic disequilibrium; they are also less likely to believe that help is available to reduce psychologic discomfort, primarily because of their negative conceptions about psychiatrists and mental institutions. These factors may explain why elderly persons with underlying psychological problems first present themselves with physical complaints.

Goldfarb (9) discusses the possibility of depressive disorders in the chronologically old as a style of adaptation. "Depressed" ways of life may thus be considered as complex adaptational efforts in the face of special stresses. A full explication of his view of depressive disorders is not possible here, but Goldfarb believes these are "attempts to circumvent defects or failures in the individual's culturally acceptable dependency striving adapting mechanisms." A state of helplessness is central to the subjective distress and adaptive maneuvers of these patients. They often have lost a conviction of personal adequacy that, for others, derives from a satisfactory supportive relationship with one or more protective persons simultaneously or separately. Goldfarb views the purposeful search for a parental figure by a helpless patient as a problem-solving maneuver. If a psychiatrist then regards an elderly depressed patient in this way—as a person caught up in searching for aid and support—and responds to the search by permitting the patient to regard him as the sought-for surrogate parent, the patient feels successful. Although essentially an illusory fulfillment, the patient's satisfaction yields increased self-esteem and improved functioning. With such small successes, the patient may relinquish dependence on the psychiatrist in exchange for more realistic and gratifying patterns of behavior. Goldfarb's formulation of depressive disorders provides a rationale for one kind of effective doctor-patient relationship.

Goldfarb's formulations about depressive disorders do not emphasize the classic psychoanalytic concepts of raising the patient's awareness of hostile and aggressive feelings and redirecting these toward appropriate objects. Mendelson (10), reviewing the evolution of psychoanalytic thinking about intrapersonal aspects of depression, also takes issue with this tradition. He points out that there are many kinds of depression "in which the pathology has more to do with low self-respect, loneliness, intense needs for affection, acceptance and intimacy, or with feelings of inadequacy and ineffectiveness, in which the element of hostility is either absent or secondary in nature." Emphasis on hostility and aggression, rather than on the patient's poor self-image, may deepen the depression of the patient who is made to feel that he is not only lonely and inadequate but also hostile, aggressive, unlikable, and bad. Mendelson's comments seem especially applicable to the depressed elderly.

Zung (11) has emphasized the need for a physician to know the "baseline" of depressive complaints for the normal aged before he can properly assess those of his patient. Zung examined a group of elderly persons living in a home for the aged and another group attending a senior citizens center and found that the baseline of depressive complaints in the normal aged is higher than those for a normal younger population. The rank order of mean responses showed that the subjects rated themselves as worst on the predominantly biological symptoms such as decreased libido, decreased appetite, and the presence of diurnal variation, and least on those items which measured mood disturbances. Zung concluded that the major cause of feelings of depression in the aged is often related to apathy, disinterest, feelings of inferiority, and loss of self-esteem.

I have attempted here to point out some of the problems in differentially classifying and diagnosing depression in elderly persons. Physical health, social status, and the processes associated with normal aging are but some of the factors to be considered. The results of a study conducted in our laboratory provide further support to the belief that the conceptualization and diagnosis of depression are extremely complex matters. Unfortunately, the data do not provide clear-cut answers, but they do confirm my opinion that the "state of the art" does not enable us to distinguish clearly between normal aging and what we label clinically as depression. This is one aspect of the still broader problem of establishing distinctions between mental health and mental illness.

## NORMAL AGING PATTERNS VS. DEPRESSION

The signs and symptoms observed and labeled depression and those regarded as concomitants of aging are much alike. Whether this should lead us to conclude that "depression" is part of a normal aging pattern is not clear, but possibly the question is addressed by one of the theories of aging—namely, the disengagement theory. The disengagement theory does not describe affective components as much as it emphasizes a lifestyle of diminished activity and social withdrawal, and reduced involvement with things and people. This pattern, to those who ascribe to it, is a successful, not a pathological, process of aging.

Relatively few empirical data are available to answer some of the questions that follow from these considerations. We offer the following data to suggest that in a "normal" community-dwelling sample of elderly persons are characteristics that seem quite similar to or suggestive of what one might, in a different context, label depression. These data are not conclusive, but they emphasize the importance of caution before concluding that a client is depressed, especially when the client's symptomatology has appeared for the first time in old age. The data suggest that "depression" may be diagnosed too often or in error.

The data are from a community survey of nearly 1,500 residents of Houston; our goal was to study the relationship of leisure and mental health, with particular attention to age and ethnic differences. The mental health measures used were the Twenty-two Item Screening Scale, and self-reports regarding health status, self-satisfaction, and happiness. For leisure measures, we have a score of total participation, and also the activities were dichotomized into three alternatives.

## Instruments Used

*Twenty-two Item Screening Scale.* The Twenty-two Item Screening Scale of psychiatric symptoms was developed by Langner (12) and has been used by other researchers. In this instrument a score is obtained by asking the respondent which of twenty-two symptoms are characteristic of him. Thus if a respondent answers that three symptoms of the twenty-two are typical of him, his score would be three. In general, respondents with high scores reported more distress, unhappiness, anxiety, and despair than did those with low scores. This symptom scale is not intended to cover the whole range of psychopathology. According to Langner (12), the screening score "does, however, provide a rough indication of where people lie on a continuum of impairment in life functioning due to very common types of psychiatric symptoms." It is a short, easily administered series of questions developed as a screening instrument for general populations.

Since we thought that factor analysis might uncover some stronger relationships to age and ethnicity than would the total score, we studied the twenty-two items by a factor analysis procedure (Verimax rotation) to discover whether any statistically independent, underlying dimensions existed among the twenty-two symptoms (13). The factor analysis indicated three major factors which we arbitrarily named "anxiety," "depression," and "somatic complaints." Three additional scores for each respondent were computed based on the factor loadings of the symptoms important to each factor.

The important items on each of the three factors are:
*Anxiety*

Would you say that you sometimes can't help wondering if anything is worthwhile any more?

Are you the worrying type?

Do you feel somewhat apart even among friends?

Do your personal worries get you down physically?

Do you feel that nothing ever turns out the way you want it to?

Do you have periods of such restlessness that you cannot sit long in a chair?

Are you often bothered by nervousness?

Do you often have any trouble getting to sleep or staying asleep?
*Depression*

Are you most of the time in low or very low spirits?

Do you feel weak all over much of the time?

Do you have periods when you can't take care of things because you can't "get going"?

Would you say that your appetite is poor?

*Somatic*

Have you ever had any fainting spells?

Do your hands often tremble enough to bother you?

Are you often bothered by your heart beating hard?

*Affective Balance Scale.* Norman Bradburn (14) developed a measure of psychological well-being for general populations. He hypothesized that a person's psychological well-being consists of a balance between a positive-affect dimension and an unrelated negative-affect dimension. To measure each dimension, respondents were asked to reply to ten items tapping five positive and five negative feelings. To reflect positive affect, a respondent was asked whether, in the preceding few weeks, he felt pleased with accomplishments, pleased that things are going his way, proud over a compliment, particularly excited or interested in something, or on top of the world. Summing a point for each reported feeling gives a score range for positive affect from 0 to 5. Similarly, the negative feelings are summed in answers to feeling bored, upset over a criticism, depressed or very unhappy, lonely or remote from other people, or feelings of great restlessness (an overlap with one of the twenty-two symptom items).

*Self-appraisal items.* In order to measure self-appraisal of health, self-esteem, and happiness, three general questions were included in our questionnaire to obtain global appraisals of a respondent's opinion of his physical health status and of feelings he has about himself. The three questions are: (1) How is your health, in general—very good, pretty good, not so good, or poor? (2) How do you feel about yourself as a person—pretty good, just okay, could be better, or not so good? (3) All things considered, how happy would you say you are right now—very happy, pretty happy, or not too happy?

*Leisure participation measures.* We asked each respondent about the frequency of participation in 17 categories of leisure activities. Participation was scored in two ways: (1) Frequency of participation in each of the 17 individual leisure categories was obtained and then scored with a range of 0 to 2 reflecting the level of participation. Adding these scores provided a summary participation score ranging from 0 (for low participation in all activities) to 34 (for frequently doing all 17 activities). (2) The leisure activities were grouped according to three dichotomies: (*a*) *active* versus *passive* participation, (*b*) *social* versus *individual* types of leisure participation, and (*c*) *external* activities participated in away from home versus *home-based* activities. Within each dichotomy the frequency of participation in the various leisure categories was summed, giving every respondent six scores, which indicated his frequency of participation in each grouping.

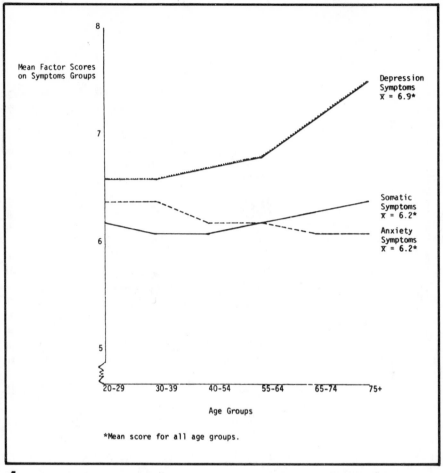

**1**   Mean Factor Scores on Three Symptom Groups By Age Cohort.

## Results

*Twenty-two Item Screening Scale.* Examination of the average scores revealed no significant difference between age cohorts. When the data are further examined, however, using the scores on the three factors—depression, anxiety and somatic complaints—a statistically significant age-related pattern becomes apparent. This is shown in Figure 1.

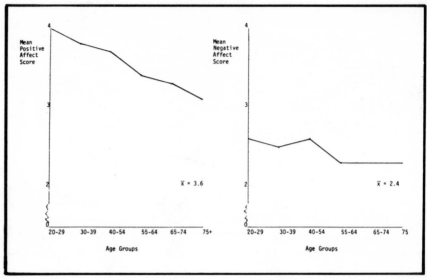

**2**    Mean Positive and Negative Affect Scores Reported By Age Cohort.

The factor incorporating symptoms suggesting depression shows a rise in the older age groups, whereas the report of somatic and anxiety symptoms is rather constant in all of the age cohorts.

*Affect Balance Scale.* No differences between age cohorts were found when affect balance scores were compared, but there were differences in total affect expressed (as measured by a sum of the positive and negative experiences reported). Younger groups consistently report more of both positive and negative affect than do middle-aged and older age groups. This age-related pattern of older persons expressing *less* affective experiences has also been reported by Bengston (15). The restrictive affect expressed by older age groups suggests a possible restriction of life experiences from which to draw satisfactions or dissatisfactions (16).

The mean positive and negative affect scores also show an age-related pattern (Figure 2). The scores, more so for the report of positive than negative affect, show a decline with age. Although the explanation or implications are not clear, the data suggest another reason to be cautious before labeling an elderly person as depressed.

*Self-appraisal of happiness.* The distribution of responses for the total sample regarding present degree of happiness is skewed toward the happier end of the scale. However, the percentage of responses of "not too happy" increases as age increases (16 per cent of the persons aged 75 and older responding "not too happy"), although the decreasing pattern with increasing age is weak.

*Self-appraisal of health.* A large majority of the sample report being in "pretty good" or "very good" health. Only 16 per cent of the respondents say that their health is "not good" or "poor," and these responses were given more frequently by the middle and older age groups than the younger age groups. The fewest of "not good" and "poor" health status ratings were in the 20-to-29-year-old group, and the number increased in each successive age group, with the highest number in the 75 and older age group.

*Total leisure participation.* Our data reveal that the summary leisure participation score declines sharply with age, when the age cohorts are compared. Dividing leisure activities into types, however, showed that the level of participation declined with age for active, social, and external types of leisure but not for passive, individual, and home-based activities.

It is also important to note that these trends were not affected by the self-reported health status. This suggests that the declines were primarily age, not health, related.

For this analysis (17), we grouped together respondents who rated their health as "poor" and "not so good" (N = 230) for comparison with the group who rated their health as very good (N = 479). We excluded the more than 700 respondents who reported "pretty good" health. It should be borne in mind that, regardless of how a subject rated his health status, all respondents in the study were well enough to participate in an interview lasting 1½ to 2 hours, including the very old respondents.

Figure 3 shows the summary leisure participation score plotted with age by each of these low/high self-rated health groups. The pattern is a decreasing level of leisure participation from the 20-to-29-year old group to the 75 and older group, the low-rated health group participating less at each age level than did the high health-status group.

*Self-appraisal of satisfaction.* The distribution of data of the question of satisfaction with oneself as a person showed a significant positive association between good feelings about oneself and increasing age. Again, the association is weak, but the improvement with older age in self-satisfaction continues into the very old age group. Interpretation of this finding is also difficult. This is the only score that suggests that a "positive" mental health dimension increases with age. Possibly this can be understood as reflecting more acceptance of negative experiences or diminished expectations of self and others by persons as they age.

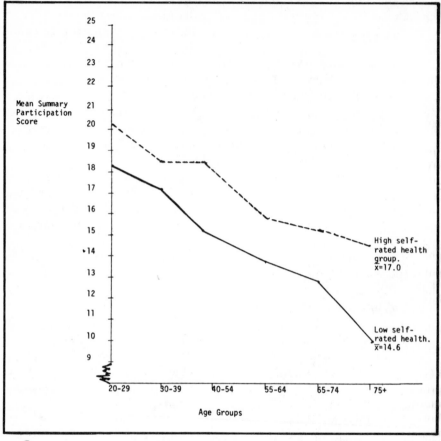

**3**    Mean Summary Leisure Participation Score By Age Cohort.

## SUMMARY

To diagnose a patient as depressed when his or her symptoms are severe and associated with a profound impairment of function is no problem. To determine the significance of relatively mild to moderate symptomatology is another matter. This seems to be especially difficult for elderly persons when one has to take into account that certain changes occur with aging and that these changes resemble depression. Yet it is desirable to attempt a differentiation because of implications for management. A person experiencing changes associated with "normal aging" probably will not respond to the same treatment modalities as would a person who manifests symptoms of depression. From a somewhat different point of view, improving the quality of life and satisfaction does not necessarily derive only from treatment in a medical setting. Nor is it likely that providing better housing, a more stable income, and opportunities for more activity and social interaction in the community will represent adequate management of a severely depressed person. These steps may relieve a person's despair and frustration associated with aging, but such approaches may have no effect on a person with a profound psychotic depression.

Persons as they age have manifestations which seem to fall on a continuum of depression-like behavior and symptomatology, and at some point such changes constitute psychopathology. To distinguish between normal aging and pathology demands a comprehension of the relationship of the symptomatology and behavior with cultural, social, and physical health factors.

Empirical data obtained from a sample of persons living in the community have been reported in this paper. These persons were not identified as psychiatric patients, nor was there any reason to suspect that they were depressed. Nevertheless, a number of them, especially the elderly respondents, have signs and symptoms and other characteristics suggestive of depression.

Compared to groups of younger persons, the elderly persons in our sample tended to report more frequently symptoms and complaints characteristic of depression. Their self-reports indicated that they saw themselves as physically impaired, and a larger percentage reported themselves to be "not too happy." In reporting recent affective experiences, they tended to report fewer positive and negative experiences, possibly suggesting apathy. A measure of total leisure participation revealed that the elderly group had lower participation scores and that the decline with age was especially related to participation in active, social, and external types of leisure. These differences apparently are independent of health status.

These data are by no means conclusive; they are not offered to prove that depression is an inevitable concomitant of chronological aging. These phenomena do emphasize, however, the need to be cautious in diagnosing depression in the elderly. A more precise definition and classification of depression is required before we can distinguish depression from changes more properly associated with aging.

## REFERENCES

1. Lippincott, R. C. Depressive illness: identification and treatment in the elderly. *Geriatrics* 23:149-152, 1968.
2. Pfeiffer, E., and Busse, E. W. Mental disorders in later life—affective disorders; para-

# 166 GAITZ

noid, neurotic, and situational reactions. Chap. 7 in E. W. Busse and E. Pfeiffer, eds. *Mental Illness in Late Life.* Washington, D. C.: American Psychiatric Association, 1973.

3. Neumann, C. P. Depression in the aged: its diagnosis and treatment. *Community Medicine* 38:403-406, 1974.
4. Copeland, J. R. M., Kelleher, M. J., Kellett, J. M., Gourlay, A. J., Cowan, D. W., Barron, G., and DeGruchy, J.—U. K. Team; Burland, B. J., Sharpe, L., Simon, R., Druiansky, J., Stiller, P.—U. S. Team. Cross-national study of diagnostic of the mental disorders: a comparison of the diagnoses of elderly psychiatric patients admitted to mental hospitals serving Queens County, New York, and the former borough of Camberwell, London. *Brit. J. Psychiat.* 126:11-20, 1975.
5. Fann, W. E., and Wheless, J. C. Depression in elderly patients. *Southern Med. J.* 68: 468-473, 1975.
6. Renshaw, D. C. Depression in the 1970's. *Dis. Nerv. Sys.* 34:241-245. 1973.
7. Hall, P. Differential diagnosis and treatment of depression in the elderly. *Gerontologia Clin.* 16:126-136, 1974.
8. Feigenbaum, E. Geriatric psychopathology—internal or external? *J. Amer. Geriatrics Society* 22:49-55, 1974.
9. Goldfarb, A. I. Depression in the old and aged. Chap. 8 in F. F. Flach and S. C. Draghi, eds. *The Nature and Treatment of Depression.* New York: Wiley, 1975.
10. Mendelson, M. Intrapersonal psychodynamics of depression. Chap. 3 in F. F. Flach and S. C. Draghi, eds. *The Nature and Treatment of Depression.* New York: Wiley, 1975.
11. Zung, W. W. K. Depression in the normal aged. *Psychosomatics* 8:287-292, 1967.
12. Langner, T. S. A twenty-two item screening score of psychiatric symptoms indicating impairment. *J. Health and Human Behavior* 3 (Winter) : 269-276, 1962.
13. Armor, D. J. and Couch, A. S. *Data-text Primer.* New York: The Free Press, 1972.
14. Bradburn, N. *The Structure of Psychological Well-Being.* Chicago: Aldine, 1969.
15. Bengston, V. Family solidarity and psychological well-being in three generations. Presented to the American Psychological Association, Honolulu, Hawaii, 1972.
16. Scott, J. and Gaitz, C. M. Ethnic and age differences in mental health measurements. *Dis. Nerv. Syst.* 36, 7 (July) : 389-393, 1975.
17. Gaitz, C. M. and Scott, J. Age and the measurement of mental health. *J. Health and Social Behavior* 13 March: 55-67, 1972.

10

# Sleep and Sleep Abnormalities in Depression

ISMET KARACAN
ROBERT L. WILLIAMS
PATRICIA J. SALIS

## SLEEP AND DEPRESSION

Every physician who deals with depressed patients is aware that sleep disturbance of one sort or another is often a part of the symptom picture in depression. In many patients the complaints are of inadequate and generally unsatisfactory sleep. In some others the problem is too much sleep. This fact led rather naturally to an early study of depressed patients by sleep researchers. Indeed, one of the earliest studies of a psychiatric research group using electroencephalographic (EEG) sleep monitoring techniques was an evaluation of manic-depressive patients by Diaz-Guerrero and his colleagues in 1946 (1).

As with many other diseases, the implicit assumption of most investigators studying depression has probably been that the sleep EEG is a unique

Some of the work described here was supported in part by a grant from Pfizer Laboratories and by Houston Veterans Administration Hospital research funds.

objective method both of describing and quantifying the specific sleep disturbances of depressed patients and of exploring more general questions concerning the neurophysiological functioning of the patients. Since sleep normally occupies at least one-third of an individual's life, complete understanding of a mental illness which involves central-nervous-system function requires assessment of cerebral activity during sleep as well as during wakefulness. The EEG is one of the few nonintrusive methods of monitoring brain activity in humans. Furthermore, the quality and quantity of data derived from the sleep EEG is superior to that from the waking EEG because there are at least two distinct states of consciousness during sleep—rapid-eye-movement or REM sleep and non-REM (NREM) sleep. REM sleep is a state of intense autonomic activity which resembles wakefulness in many respects and which takes its name from the characteristic rapid conjugate eye movements. It is also the state of sleep most commonly associated with dreaming. The eye movements are monitored by electro-oculographic (EOG) recordings. NREM sleep is characterized by more synchronized brain activity, specifically in the form of sleep spindles and slow delta activity. Physiologically it conforms more closely to the conventional view of sleep as a state of quiescence.

A second major advantage of the sleep EEG over the waking EEG is the considerably more favorable signal-to-noise ratio. Brain-wave patterns during sleep are sufficiently organized to allow reliable visual scoring of six stages—NREM stages 1, 2, 3, and 4; the REM stage; and waking stage 0. In addition, specific phasic events, such as sleep spindles, K-complexes, beta activity bursts, alpha activity bursts, delta waves, and eye movements, are clearly visible and can be detected and described in detail, especially by automated systems. Many researchers believe that analyses of the characteristics of these waveforms may prove more fruitful than analyses of the sleep stage data, since the waveforms represent, in a sense, the raw data in the EEG-EOG, whereas the sleep stages are somewhat arbitrary summary classifications of complex and dynamic events.

The early description of depressed patients by Diaz-Guerrero et al. (1) has generally been confirmed by later studies (2-7). In particular, in comparison to healthy individuals, many depressed patients sleep less, take longer to fall asleep, awaken more frequently and/or for longer periods during the night, exhibit greater amounts of light stages 1 and 2 sleep and smaller amounts of deep stages 3 and 4, and shift from stage to stage more frequently. This characterization must, however, be immediately qualified, because one of the most consistent findings has been great variability, both among patients in a study sample and from night to night in a given patient. One source of this variability, suggested by longitudinal studies (3,6,8-10), is probably the clinical status of the patients. The severest phase of illness is usually characterized by low sleep times and stage 4 amounts. Clinical improvement is generally associated with improvements in sleep patterns, although certain disturbances, such as the stage 4 deficits, may persist in spite of clinical improvement.

Variability of results is most characteristic of REM sleep parameters. Reduced REM sleep amounts and latencies to the first REM period have characterized findings in some, but certainly not all, patients. Various other REM sleep anomalies, such as unusually long first REM periods, unusually short NREM intervals between REM periods, elevated numbers of REM periods, abnormally frequent eye movements, unusually abrupt transitions between waking and REM sleep, and elevated numbers of awakenings from REM sleep, have been reported for some patients, but these findings are by no means universal. The longitudinal studies of depressed patients have revealed significant night-to-night variations in REM sleep characteristics. In spite of this, several researchers (3,6,10) interpret their findings as indicating that during the severest phase of illness depressed patients exhibit signs of prior or coexisting REM deprivation—erratically reduced REM sleep amount and REM latency and elevated number of eye movements. These investigators also report that clinical improvement is accompanied by increased amounts of REM sleep.

It is obvious from the foregoing that it has not been possible to establish a clear description of sleep EEG-EOG patterns in depression. Certainly some of the inconsistencies in the results are due strictly to methodological factors. For example, many study patients have been medicated in some fashion or another, and, as we shall discuss below, psychotropic medications very definitely affect EEG-EOG sleep patterns. Another reason for the lack of meaningful consistent results may be that the most informative parameters have not been examined. This assumption has recently led to evaluations of various different types of parameters. For example, some of the interpatient variability may derive from the fact that sleep patterns are less disturbed in neurotic than in psychotic depressives (11-13), and that differences in severity of illness may determine differences in sleep patterns (11,14). Among other things, it appears that there is a negative relationship between rated degree of depression and both amount of eye movement activity (15, 16) and REM latency (17). Another potentially fruitful line of research would seem to involve more detailed analyses of the EEG-EOG waveform characteristics. EEG-EOG abnormalities of various sorts have been described in a number of studies (6,8,13,18-20). It may be that subtle differences in waveform characteristics would provide the basis for more meaningful descriptions of sleep in depression.

## SLEEP AND ANTIDEPRESSANT DRUGS

The same characteristics of sleep EEG-EOG data which make sleep laboratory studies attractive in the search for understanding of brain function and mental illness also make them logical in the evaluation of drugs affecting the central nervous system. In addition, it is becoming increasingly clear that the sleep EEG-EOG is supremely sensitive to drug effects, and we might even go so far as to propose that classification of drugs on the basis of sleep EEG-EOG effects may constitute the most rational method of classification. The sensitivity of the sleep EEG-EOG is apparent in both gross and refined parameters. For example, a patient's report of sleep disturbance is obviously confined to aspects of sleep quantity that he may perceive, such as the amount of sleep, the time to fall asleep, the time awake during the night, and the number of awakenings. The patient's estimate of these quantities may or may not be accurate. Qualitative descriptions of the soundness or restfulness of sleep are not presently relatable to any objective measures. On the other hand, the sleep EEG-EOG can provide exact values for the various quantitative aspects of sleep duration and fragmentation. It can also provide values concerning the qualitatively different stages of sleep and waveforms of sleep. This information is totally unavailable to the patient, and therefore a diagnosis of sleep disturbance based solely on a patient report neglects crucial aspects of the sleep process.

The same is true of evaluations of drug effects which rely exclusively on patient reports. Of course, one primary aim of treatment is to relieve the patient of his perceived sleep disturbances. But a more general goal should be to normalize all aspects of sleep, both the perceived and the nonperceived. This goal follows directly from the assumption that normal sleep has a certain configuration for a reason, and that even if we do not yet understand that reason, there is clear risk in tampering with the normal configuration without sufficient justification.

These remarks are intended to set the proper framework for a brief review of the effects of several major antidepressants on sleep patterns. In addition, it should be remembered that though the existing data are highly suggestive, the pharmacology of sleep is generally still in a very primitive state, and the sleep pharmacology of antidepressants is no exception. We have recently completed a critical review of the major sleep studies of psychoactive drugs. Careful examination of over 50 studies of antidepressants in terms of the adequacy of the study design, the number of subjects, and the statistical procedures indicated that only five could be considered "definitive." And finally, one should only very cautiously generalize results obtained from study of normal subjects to patient populations. With our present knowledge we do not know whether such generalization is valid or not.

Amitriptyline is the most carefully examined of the antidepressants. It has been studied principally in healthy subjects, in doses ranging from 25 to 75 mg (21-24). In both acute and chronic studies it has consistently been shown to reduce REM sleep. It has usually been found to increase sleep time. In at least two of the studies it increased REM latency and amounts of stages 2 and 3 sleep. In the chronic (28 drug days) study by Hartmann and Cravens (22), drug discontinuation was accompanied by increases in amounts of REM and stages 0 and 1, and by decreases in amounts of stages 2 and 4 and in REM latency.

Desipramine, studied in healthy subjects and six depressed patients, has been evaluated during both short- and long-term administration (25-28). The doses have ranged from 75 to 100 mg. The drug has generally been found to reduce REM sleep amount, at least initially. It may also elevate stage 4 sleep amount and reduce the numbers of awakenings and stage changes and the amount of stage 0.

Imipramine has been studied primarily in healthy subjects (24,25, 29-33), although some psychiatric patients and endogenous depressives have been evaluated (29,33). The doses have ranged from 25 to 150 mg, and both short-term and long-term effects have been assessed. In all studies the amount of REM sleep was reduced. Several investigators observed increased amounts of stage 2 sleep, decreased amounts of stage 4 sleep, and increased REM latency.

Lithium, in doses ranging from 300 to 2400 mg/day, has generally been found to reduce the amount of REM sleep, increase REM latency, and increase the amount of stage 4 sleep in depressed, manic, and hypomanic patients (34-37). All the studies have involved observations over a long drug administration period.

In depressed or anxious-depressed patients, the monoamine oxidase inhibitor phenelzine has been shown to reduce the amount of REM sleep and possibly increase the amount of stage 2 sleep; withdrawal of the drug may be associated with increases in REM sleep amounts (38-40). The doses have ranged from 45 to 90 mg/day and the studies have been both short- and long-term.

These data clearly suggest that a major effect of antidepressants is a reduction in the amount of REM sleep. This finding is somewhat paradoxical, in view of the fact that many depressed patients exhibit reduced REM sleep amounts during the most serious phase of their illness. An interesting aspect of this complex problem has been investigated by Vogel and his colleagues (41). They have found that experimental suppression of REM sleep is effective in facilitating clinical improvement, especially in endogenous depressives.

## SLEEP, NEUROTIC DEPRESSION, AND DOXEPIN

In the remainder of this report we will present some data from a recently completed study of doxepin, a tricyclic agent. A complete report of the results appears elsewhere (42). This discussion should serve to describe the methodology of a sleep laboratory study and the sleep patterns of a rather strictly defined group of neurotic depressives, as well as to present evidence of doxepin's effectiveness in alleviating many of the sleep disturbances of such patients.

In our study we evaluated 11 neurotic depressive outpatients. A prestudy selection phase allowed the selection of patients who met the following criteria: a primarily diagnosis of clinical depression according to DSM-II criteria; a minimum Total Score of 20 on the Hamilton Psychiatric Rating Scale for Depression (43), and a minimum score of 3 on the three items (nos. 4, 5, and 6) concerning sleep; from the Profile of Mood States (POMS) (44), minimum scores of 16 on the Tension-Anxiety factor and 28 on the Depression-Dejection factor; complaints of insomnia symptoms to the interviewing physician; good health, determined by a physical examination; absence of reports of acute or chronic health problems or medical treatment on the Cornell Medical Index Health Questionnaire (45); and, from EEG-EOG recordings made on the first four laboratory nights, an average latency to stage 2 onset from "lights out" of 30 minutes or more and/or an average total time awake during the night of 30 minutes or more. None of the patients was taking concurrent psychotropic medications and none had taken any such medication for more than a day or so within four weeks of entering the study.

Eight of the eleven patients were females and three were males. The average age was 40 years (range 23-51 years). The patients' illnesses had lasted from two months to 14 years. A Global Evaluation of each patient's clinical status on the fourth study night indicated that two patients were markedly ill, eight were moderately ill, and one was mildly ill. Six of the patients had undergone previous drug treatment with mixed success.

Table 1 illustrates the study treatment and evaluation schedule. The study proper consisted of 40 consecutive days and 16 laboratory sleep recordings for each patient. The first four days constituted a baseline placebo period (PI) and sleep was monitored on all four nights. The drug treatment pe-

# Table 1. Treatment and Evaluation Schedule for Study of Effects of Doxepin HCl in 11 Neurotic Depressed Patients

## STUDY PERIODS, LOCALES, AND NIGHTS

| Procedure | Baseline Placebo Period (P1)* Lab. | | | | Drug Period 1 (D1) Lab. | | | Home | Drug Period 2 (D2) Lab. | | | Home | Drug Period 3 (D3) Lab. | | | Final Placebo Period (P2)* Lab. | | |
|---|---|---|---|---|---|---|---|---|---|---|---|---|---|---|---|---|---|---|
| **Night:** | 1 | 2 | 3 | 4 | 5 | 6 | 7 | 8.....16 | 17 | 18 | 19 | 20.....34 | 35 | 36 | 37 | 38 | 39 | 40 |
| EEG-EOG Recordings | X | X | X | X | X | X | X | | X | X | X | | X | X | X | X | X | X |
| Presleep Questionnaire | X | X | X | X | X | X | X | X......X | X | X | X | X......X | X | X | X | X | X | X |
| Postsleep Questionnaire | X | X | X | X | X | X | X | X......X | X | X | X | X......X | X | X | X | X | X | X |
| Hamilton Depression Scale | | | | X | | | X | | X | | | | X | | | X | | |
| Profile of Mood States | | | | X | | | X | | X | | X | | X | | X | X | | X |
| Global Evaluation | | | | X | | | | | | | X | | | | X | | | |

*Placebo = 2 black and white placebo capsules at bedtime

**Drug = 2 50mg black and white doxepin capsules at bedtime

173

riod was 33 days in length, and sleep recordings were made on initial [drug period 1 (D1): nights 5-7], intermediate [drug period 2 (D2): nights 17-19], and final [drug period 3 (D3): nights 35-37] drug nights. On remaining nights (8-16 and 20-34) during the drug treatment period the patients slept at home. The last three study nights constituted a final placebo period (P2, nights 38-40). On drug nights two 50 mg black-and-white doxepin capsules were administered at bedtime; on placebo nights two black-and-white placebo capsules were administered. On home sleep nights, patients administered the medication to themselves. All capsule administration was double-blind.

The physician-rated Hamilton Depression Scale and 5-point Global Evaluation of clinical status and the patient-rated POMS were completed periodically during each study phase. The Global Evaluation consisted of ratings of change in patient status from the baseline (night 4) rating; the five rating categories were "marked," "moderate," and "slight" improvement; "no change"; and "worse." The Hamilton and Global Evaluation ratings were single-blind.

Our sleep EEG-EOG recording procedures have been described elsewhere (46). Each night, following the electrode attachment procedure, patients completed a 22-item Presleep Questionnaire concerning their daytime activities and feelings. Prior to the first laboratory night each patient was allowed to select his preferred retiring and arising times and these times were held reasonably constant for each laboratory night. If the patient awoke before his scheduled arising time and wished to get up for the day, he was allowed to do so. Otherwise, he was awakened and/or arose at the scheduled time. EEG-EOG recordings began at "lights out" and were continuous throughout each night. Soon after arising, patients completed a 31-item Postsleep Questionnaire concerning the quality and quantity of the completed night of sleep and feelings on awakening. They then left the laboratory to conduct their normal daily activities.

Patients were instructed not to take naps or drink alcoholic beverages, especially on days preceding laboratory nights, and not to take any other psychotropic medication. These instructions were generally followed, but there were several deviations. A total of six daytime naps exceeding 30 minutes in length occurred on days before laboratory nights. One patient took naps on the second and third days of the initial drug period (D1); four other patients took one nap each during four different study periods (P1; first day of D1; D2; and P2). We know from previous work (47) that morning naps have little or no effect on subsequent nighttime sleep, but that afternoon naps may reduce the amount of stage 4 sleep that night. Three of the patients' naps occurred after noon. One short (35 minutes) afternoon nap occurred during the initial placebo period and appeared to have no effect on nighttime sleep. The other two afternoon naps occurred during the drug treatment period (days 7 and 18). If these two naps affected nighttime stage 4 amounts, it was in a direction opposite to the observed effect of doxepin.

Three drugs affecting the central nervous system were taken on days preceding laboratory nights: one patient took a beta blocker on day 7 (D1), one took a muscle relaxant with sedative properties on days 18 and 19 (D2), and one took an oral contraceptive on days 35-40 (D3 and P2). Two patients rather consistently drank a beer, a cocktail, or a glass of wine at dinnertime. Four other patients reported dinnertime drinks on one or two study nights. One patient reported drinking two glasses of wine at 10:30 P.M. on night 7. The days on which these drugs and alcohol were consumed were rather evenly spread throughout the study and thus the effects on sleep parameters were not confined to a particular study condition. The amounts of alcohol consumed by a given patient never exceeded two highballs, and in all but one case the drinks were taken before or at dinnertime. For these reasons it is unlikely that the alcohol significantly affected any nighttime sleep measures. Common effects of alcohol are reduced amounts of stages 1 REM and 4 sleep and increased fragmentation of sleep. Only the first effect would possibly be parallel to the observed effects of doxepin, and in any case the group values for Percent Stage 1 REM were within the normal range for our laboratory at all study phases.

Each sleep EEG-EOG recording was scored randomly and blindly for the five sleep stages and waking stage 0 (46). These basic data were summarized for the total night in terms of 26 sleep EEG-EOG parameters. For each parameter, data from all nonadaptation nights within a study condition were averaged and the average formed the patient observation for that condition. (Nights 1, 17, and 35 were treated as laboratory adaptation nights for analyses of all parameters.) Following coding, Presleep and Postsleep Questionnaire data for laboratory nights were treated in a similar fashion. The POMS data consisted of scores on the Tension-Anxiety and the Depression-Dejection factors. The Hamilton Depression Scale data consisted of a Total Score and individual scores on the items concerning sleep. Again, for these two instruments only data from nonadaptation nights are presented. Global Evaluation data for nights 19 (D2) and 37 (D3) consisted of assessments of change from the original baseline (night 4) ratings.

Paired t-tests were used to evaluate the significance of differences among the five study conditions for all except the Global Evaluation data. For these data analysis of covariance was used, with independent variables consisting of an overall mean and the effects of baseline ratings of clinical status, and dependent variables consisting of the ratings of change at the two later study periods.

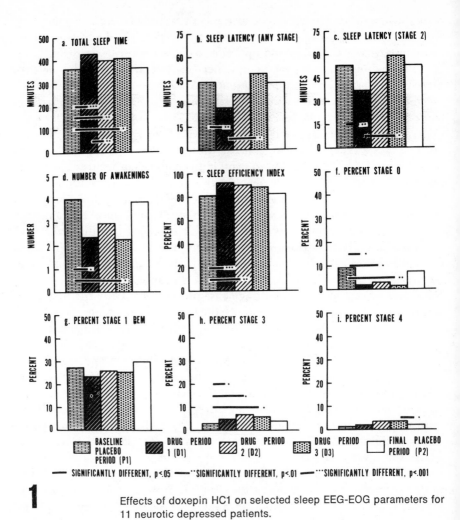

**1**    Effects of doxepin HC1 on selected sleep EEG-EOG parameters for 11 neurotic depressed patients.

For this report we have selected the most interesting results for discussion. The study showed clearly that the sleep EEG-EOG patterns, subjective ratings of sleep quality and quantity, and patient and physician ratings of mood and clinical status were improved by doxepin therapy. The most dramatic changes in sleep patterns occurred in the parameters relating to the amount of sleep and wakefulness and to the amount of stages 3 and 4 slow-wave sleep. Figure 1a shows the changes in Total Sleep Time (time from sleep onset to morning awakening, less intermittent waking time) during each of the five study periods. The improvement in Total Sleep Time was sustained at a significant level throughout the drug treatment period, although the greatest improvement occurred during the first days of drug administration. For the group, Total Sleep Time returned to baseline levels when doxepin was discontinued, but the change was not consistent enough to reach statistical significance.

Especially during the initial drug period, the improvement in Total Sleep Time was partially due to reductions in time to fall asleep. Figures 1b and 1c show data for two measures of this time—the latency from "lights out" to the first sleep stage, whatever its nature [Sleep Latency (Any Stage)]; and the latency from "lights out" to stage 2 onset [Sleep Latency (Stage 2)]. During the second drug period these latencies were still below baseline levels, but not significantly so. By the final drug period, the improvement had disappeared. Thus doxepin had only a transitory effect on EEG-EOG measures of time to fall asleep.

The improvement in Total Sleep Time was primarily due to reductions in wakefulness after sleep onset. Figure 1d shows the changes in the Number of Awakenings. In general there were fewer awakenings throughout the drug treatment period than at baseline, but the change was not significant at the middle drug period. During the final placebo period the Number of Awakenings generally returned to baseline levels.

Figure 1f shows the data for Percent Stage 0, or the amount of nocturnal wakefulness after sleep onset relative to the Sleep Period Time (minutes of all six stages between sleep onset and final awakening). As with Total Sleep Time, the changes in this parameter were sustained at a significant level throughout the drug treatment period and disappeared with drug discontinuation.

The Sleep Efficiency Index is the best overall measure of the quantity of sleep. It is the ratio of Total Sleep Time to total Time In Bed (time from "lights out" to arising). Figure 1e shows that Sleep Efficiency was significantly improved during the initial and middle drug periods, and was still above baseline levels at the final drug period (though not significantly).

Figure 1g shows that there were no significant changes in Percent Stage 1 REM throughout the study, although there was some suggestion of slight, transitory REM suppression during the early days of drug administration. The lack of significant changes in amount of REM sleep is in marked contrast to the effects of most other tricyclic agents.

Amounts of slow-wave sleep were elevated during doxepin therapy in comparison to baseline. Figure 1h shows that the elevation in Percent Stage 3 was sustained at a significant level throughout the drug treatment period.

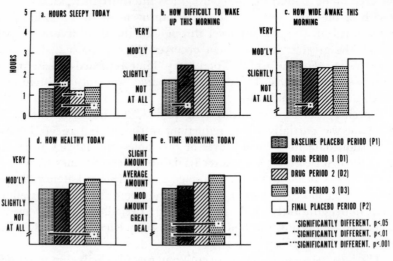

**2**    Effects of doxepin HC1 on selected Presleep and Postsleep Questionnaire responses of 11 neurotic depressed patients.

The gradual increases in Percent Stage 4 (Figure 1i) during the drug treatment period were not statistically significant, but the significant change between the final drug and final placebo periods suggests that the drug was affecting this parameter. It may be that with longer-term administration of doxepin the amount of stage 4 sleep would be found to increase significantly.

The distinction between stages 3 and 4 sleep is somewhat arbitrary and depends upon the percentage of each minute containing delta activity. For this reason it is common to combine these two stages to obtain an overall measure of slow-wave sleep. In this study we found that combined Percent Stages 3 and 4 was significantly elevated, in comparison to baseline levels, at all three drug periods (D1: $p < .05$; D2: $p < .001$; D3: $p < .001$). In addition, there were significant increases over early drug values at both the middle ($p < .01$) and final ($p < .05$) drug periods. On drug discontinuation, values dropped significantly ($p < .01$) from final drug levels. This is dramatic evidence of the effectiveness of doxepin in combating the patients' slow-wave sleep deficits.

We now turn to data derived from the Presleep and Postsleep Questionnaires. One cluster of items indicated the occurrence of a transitory drug hangover effect on early drug days. On the Presleep Questionnaire, patients reported being sleepy during the day (Figure 2a) significantly more during the first drug period than at baseline. This effect disappeared in the later

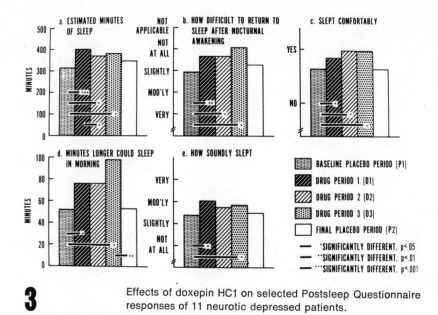

**3**    Effects of doxepin HC1 on selected Postsleep Questionnaire responses of 11 neurotic depressed patients.

drug periods. On the Postsleep Questionnaires, during the first drug period the patients described themselves as having more difficulty waking in the morning (Figure 2b) and as being less wide awake after waking (Figure 2c) than at baseline. These reports were no longer different from baseline at later drug periods. These data support the patients' verbal reports of increased daytime drowsiness on early drug days. It will be recalled that one patient was so sleepy on the second and third drug days that she took daytime naps.

Two other items on the Presleep Questionnaire are of interest. The patients generally reported feeling healthier (Figure 2d) and worrying less about personal problems (Figure 2e) during the drug treatment period than at baseline. These changes became significant by the final drug period, and persisted through the final placebo period. In the case of daytime worry, this carry-over effect was significant. These results are typical of several other Presleep Questionnaire items. They suggest that certain subjective daytime improvements were not experienced by the patients until drug therapy had progressed a number of days, but that the effects outlasted the drug therapy for at least a short period.

Figures 3a-3c show data for three items on the Postsleep Questionnaire. Significant positive changes in all three items—estimated minutes of sleep, difficulty returning to sleep after awaking during the night, and comfort of sleep—were sustained throughout the drug treatment period. As we saw earlier, the EEG-EOG parameters related to the first two items, Total Sleep Time (Figure 1a) and Percent Stage 0 (Figure 1f), were also significantly improved at all drug periods, so our patients did perceive these changes quite reliably.

As the data on Figures 3d and 3e indicate, for ratings of ability to sleep longer in the morning and of soundness of sleep there were general positive changes throughout the drug treatment period, but the changes at the middle drug period were not statistically significant. Results for the first item indicate that patients troubled by early morning awakening felt improved in this respect.

Results of another Postsleep Questionnaire item corresponding to an EEG-EOG parameter are shown on Figure 4a. The estimated time to fall asleep was significantly reduced at the first drug period in comparison to baseline, and it later returned to baseline levels. It will be recalled that this same pattern of significant changes occurred in the two measures of Sleep Latency (Figures 1b and 1c). Thus the transitory effect of doxepin on time to fall asleep was verified on both subjective and objective measures.

The overall rating of sleep (Figure 4c) was also significantly improved at the initial drug period but not at later ones. This is a rather interesting finding in view of the sustained positive changes in subjective ratings of several specific aspects of sleep (hours slept, difficulty returning to sleep, comfort of sleep, soundness of sleep, ability to sleep longer in the morning). It suggests that some aspects of sleep may be given more weight than others in a patient's rating of his sleep quality. In these patients, the pattern of significant changes in the overall rating of sleep was parallel to that for estimated time to fall asleep (Figure 4a), the difficulty in waking in the morning (Figure 2b), and the feeling of being wide awake after arising (Figure 2c). Figure 4b shows the identical pattern for ratings of tension or anxiety on waking. It may be that one or more of these items are key factors in a patient's rating of his overall sleep quality.

Figure 4d shows that there were significant changes in ratings of restlessness. Significant positive changes were reported at early and middle drug periods, but not at the final drug period. The sleep EEG-EOG parameter most often related to reports of restlessness is the Number of Stage Changes. In this group of patients there were no significant changes in values for this parameter at any point in the study.

Several Postsleep Questionnaire items underwent delayed effects. The estimated number of awakenings (Figure 4e) was generally reduced throughout the drug treatment period, but the change on early drug days was not significant. We saw earlier that the EEG-EOG parameter Number of Awak-

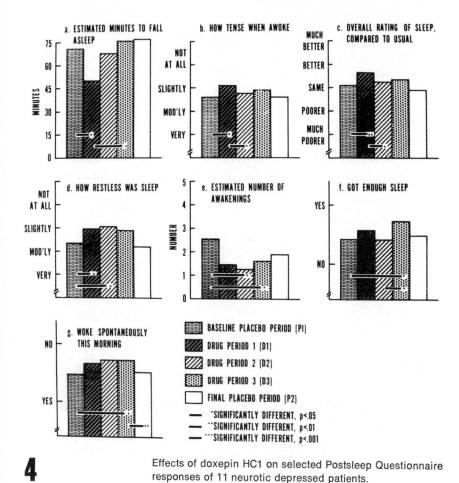

**4**  Effects of doxepin HC1 on selected Postsleep Questionnaire responses of 11 neurotic depressed patients.

enings (Figure 1d) was also reduced at all drug periods, but not significantly at the middle drug period. Thus the patterns of significant changes in the subjective and objective measures were not quite identical, but they were in general agreement. In contrast to estimates by many individuals studied in sleep laboratories, our patients' estimated number of awakenings was consistently lower than the number scored from EEG-EOG tracings.

The remaining two Postsleep Questionnaire items were not significantly changed until the final drug period. At that time the patients began reporting that they had obtained enough sleep (Figure 4f) and that they did not

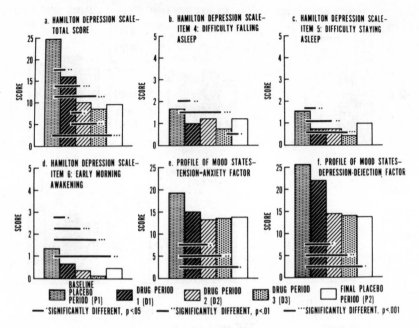

**5** Effects of doxepin HC1 on Hamilton Depression Scale and Profile of Mood States scores for 11 neurotic depressed patients.

wake spontaneously in the morning (Figure 4g). The latter result means that the patients had to be awakened at their scheduled arising times by the technician. An immediate effect of drug discontinuation was a return to baseline ratings for this parameter, indicating that the patients again began to awaken before their scheduled arising times.

Our final results concern the physician and patient ratings of mood and clinical symptoms. All four measures taken from the physician-rated Hamilton Depression Scale—the Total Score (Figure 5a) and the scores for three items related to sleep (Figures 5b-5d)—showed significant improvement during the drug treatment period. For the Total Score and for the items concerning difficulty staying asleep and early morning awakening, the improvements were significant at all drug periods. The Total Score and the Item 6 score remained significantly different from baseline after drug discontinuation. The physician's Global Evaluations were significantly improved at the middle and final drug periods (no rating was made at the initial drug period) and there was no evidence that degree of improvement was related to baseline ratings of severity of illness.

Figures 5e and 5f show the results for the Tension-Anxiety and the Depression-Dejection factors of the patient-rated POMS. On both factors significant improvement did not occur until the middle drug period, but it was then sustained throughout the remainder of the study, even after drug discontinuation.

For EEG-EOG and Postsleep Questionnaire items there were no significant differences between baseline and final placebo values, suggesting that most improvements in subjective and objective measures of sleep were directly dependent on the presence of drug. On the other hand, the persistence during the final placebo period of significant improvements in mood (ratings on the POMS and ratings on the "time worrying today" item of the Presleep Questionnaire) and in clinical symptoms rated on the Hamilton Depression Scale suggest a carry-over effectiveness of doxepin, at least for a three-day period. It might be of interest to determine the limits of this carry-over effectiveness. In any case, these results demonstrate the greater sensitivity of sleep EEG-EOG patterns to actual drug administration than ratings of clinical symptoms and moods.

Before concluding, we should discuss briefly the baseline sleep patterns of our patients. Their sleep was clearly disturbed in a number of respects. As required by the selection criteria, values for Sleep Latency and total minutes awake after sleep onset were abnormally large. On nights 1-4, ten of the eleven patients exhibited an average Sleep Latency (Stage 2) of 30 minutes or greater. On the same nights six of the patients were awake during the night in excess of 30 minutes. Comparisons with normal subjects of similar ages (46) revealed that the patients experienced slightly reduced Total Sleep Time; reduced Sleep Efficiency Index; greatly lengthened Sleep Latency (Any Stage) and increased Percent Stage 0; reduced Percent Stages 3 and 4; earlier first nocturnal awakening; and later onset of stages 3 and 4 sleep. In the low-normal range were group averages for Number of Stages and REM Interval Length (NREM time between REM periods). In the high-normal range were Number of Awakenings, Percent Stage 1, and Latency to Stage 1 REM and Stage 2 from sleep onset. Most values were in general agreement with data derived from other studies of neurotic depressives (11,12,17). However, in our patients Percent Stage 1 REM was somewhat higher than previously reported values (27% vs. 20-21%), Percent Stages 3 (3% vs. 16%) and 4 (2% vs. 6%) were lower and Latency to Stage 1 REM (97 minutes vs. 50-55 minutes) was longer. Some of these discrepancies may be due to differences in scoring procedures. On the other hand, our patient sample was possibly more strictly defined in terms of presenting symptoms and characteristics, and the differences may in part reflect this fact.

This brief review of sleep EEG-EOG studies in depressed patients and of antidepressant effects on sleep patterns, and the presentation of the results of one study in our laboratory, should illustrate the nature of sleep research in this area. We feel certain that use of sleep EEG-EOG techniques can answer many questions concerning brain function in humans. We believe that the sleep EEG-EOG is the method of choice for accurate diagnosis of sleep disturbances. We also believe that it is a uniquely sensitive tool for the evaluation and study of drugs affecting the central nervous system, and especially of sleep medications. Once accurate diagnosis and sufficient description and classification of drug effects have been achieved, then rational treatment of sleep disturbances will become possible. In the realm of mental illness, there can be no doubt that the understanding of brain function available through sleep EEG-EOG studies will eventually contribute greatly to the understanding of the disease processes themselves.

## REFERENCES

1. Diaz-Guerrero, R., Gottlieb, J. S., and Knott, J. R. The sleep of patients with manic-depressive psychosis, depressive type. An electroencephalographic study. *Psychosom. Med.* 8:399-404, 1946.
2. Gresham, S. C., Agnew, H. W., Jr., and Williams, R. L. The sleep of depressed patients. An EEG and eye movement study. *Arch. Gen. Psychiatry* 13:503-507, 1965.
3. Hartmann, E. Longitudinal studies of sleep and dream patterns in manic-depressive patients. *Arch. Gen. Psychiatry* 19:312-329, 1968.
4. Mendels, J., and Hawkins, D. R. Sleep studies in depression. In T. A. Williams, M. M. Katz, and J. A. Shield, Jr., eds., *Recent Advances in the Psychobiology of the Depressive Illnesses.* D.H.E.W. Publication No. (HSM) 70-9053. Washington, D. C.: U. S. Government Printing Office, 1972, pp. 147-170.
5. Oswald, I., Berger, R. J., Jaramillo, R. A., Keddie. K. M. G., Olley, P. C., and Plunkett, G. B. Melancholia and barbiturates: A controlled EEG, body and eye movement study of sleep. *Br. J. Psychiatry* 109:66-78, 1963.
6. Snyder, F. NIH studies of EEG sleep in affective illness. In T. A. Williams, M. M. Katz, and J. A. Shield, Jr., eds., *Recent Advances in the Psychobiology of the Depressive Illnesses.* D.H.E.W. Publication No. (HSM) 70-9053. Washington, D. C.: U. S. Government Printing Office, 1972, pp. 171-192.
7. Zung, W. W. K., Wilson, W. P., and Dodson, W. E. Effect of depressive disorders on sleep EEG responses. *Arch. Gen. Psychiatry* 10:439-445, 1964.
8. Green, W. J., and Stajduhar, P. P. The effect of ECT on the sleep-dream cycle in a psychotic depression. *J. Nerv. Ment. Dis.* 143:123-134, 1966.
9. Lowy, F. H., Cleghorn, J. M., and McClure, D. J. Sleep patterns in depression. Longitudinal study of six patients and brief review of literature. *J. Nerv. Ment. Dis.* 153:10-26, 1971.
10. Mendels, J., and Hawkins, D. R. Sleep and depression. IV. Longitudinal studies. *J. Nerv. Ment. Dis.* 153:251-272, 1971.

11. Mendels, J., and Hawkins, D. R. Sleep and depression. Further considerations. *Arch. Gen. Psychiatry* 19:445-452, 1968.

12. Snyder, F. Sleep disturbance in relation to acute psychosis. In A. Kales, ed., *Sleep. Physiology and Pathology. A Symposium.* Philadelphia: J. B. Lippincott, 1969, pp. 170-182.

13. Hauri, P., and Hawkins, D. R. Individual differences in the sleep of depression. In U. J. Jovanovic, ed., *The Nature of Sleep.* Stuttgart: Gustav Fischer Verlag, 1973, pp. 193-197.

14. Snyder, F. Electrographic studies of sleep in depression. In N. S. Kline, and E. Laska, eds., *Computers and Electronic Devices in Psychiatry.* New York: Grune & Stratton, 1968, pp. 272-303.

15. Hauri, P., and Hawkins, D. R. Phasic REM, depression, and the relationship between sleeping and waking. *Arch. Gen. Psychiatry* 25:56-63, 1971.

16. Kupfer, D. J., and Heninger, G. R. REM activity as a correlate of mood changes throughout the night. Electroencephalographic sleep patterns in a patient with a 48-hour cyclic mood disorder. *Arch. Gen. Psychiatry* 27:368-373, 1972.

17. Kupfer, D. J., and Foster, F. G. Interval between onset of sleep and rapid-eye-movement sleep as an indicator of depression. *Lancet* 2:684-686, 1972.

18. Hawkins, D. R., Mendels, J., Scott, J., Bensch, G., and Teachey, W. The psychophysiology of sleep in psychotic depression: A longitudinal study. *Psychosom. Med.* 29:329-344, 1967.

19. Mendels, J., and Hawkins, D. R. Sleep and depression. A controlled EEG study. *Arch. Gen. Psychiatry* 16:344-354, 1967.

20. Hawkins, D. R. Sleep research and depression. In T. A. Williams, M. M. Katz, and J. A. Shield, Jr., eds., *Recent Advances in the Psychobiology of the Depressive Illnesses.* D.H.E.W. Publication No. (HSM) 70-9053. Washington, D. C.: U. S. Government Printing Office, 1972, pp. 141-146.

21. Hartmann, E. Amitriptyline and imipramine: Effects on human sleep. *Psychophysiology* 5:207, 1968 (abstract).

22. Hartmann, E., and Cravens, J. The effects of long term administration of psychotropic drugs on human sleep: III. The effects of amitriptyline. *Psychopharmacologia* 33: 185-202, 1973.

23. Nakazawa, Y., Kotorii, T., Kotorii, M., Horikawa, S., and Ohshima, M. Effects of amitriptyline on human REM sleep as evaluated by using partial differential REM sleep deprivation (PDRD). *Electroencephalogr. Clin. Neurophysiol.* 38:513-520, 1975.

24. Saletu, B., Allen, M., and Itil, T. M. The effect of Coca-Cola, caffeine, antidepressants, and C chlorpromazine on objective and subjective sleep parameters. *Pharmakopsychiatr. Neuropsychopharmakol.* 7:307-321, 1974.

25. Dunleavy, D. L. F., Brezinova, V., Oswald, I., MacLean, A. W., and Tinker, M. Changes during weeks in effects of tricyclic drugs on the human sleeping brain. *Br. J. Psychiatry* 120:663-672, 1972.

26. Zung, W. W. K. Effect of antidepressant drugs on sleeping and dreaming. II. On the adult male. Excerpta Medica Int. Cong. Series No. 150, 1968, pp. 1824-1826.

27. Zung, W. W. K. Antidepressant drugs and sleep. *Exp. Med. Surg.* 27:124-137, 1969.

28. Zung, W. W. K. Effect of antidepressant drugs on sleeping and dreaming. III. On the depressed patient. *Biol. Psychiatry* 1:283-287, 1969.

29. Durrigl, V. Some problems of the therapy of sleep disturbances in depressed patients. In W. B. Koella, and P. Levin, eds., *Sleep, Physiology, Biochemistry, Psychology,*

*Pharmacology, Clinical Implications.* Basel: S. Karger, 1973, pp. 132-139.
30. Fujii, S. Effects of some psychotropic and hypnotic drugs on the human nocturnal sleep. *Psychiatr. Neurol. Jap.* 75:651-673, 1973.
31. Hata, H. Effects of some neuro-active drugs on REM sleep and rapid eye movements during REM sleep in man. *Psychiatr. Neurol. Jap.* 77:52, 1975 (abstract).
32. Takahashi, Y., Kipnis, D. M., and Daughaday, W. H. Growth hormone secretion during sleep. *J. Clin. Invest.* 47:2079-2090, 1968.
33. Toyoda, J. The effects of chlorpromazine and imipramine on the human nocturnal sleep electroencephalogram. *Folia Psychiatr. Neurol. Jap.* 18:198-221, 1964.
34. Chernik, D. A., and Mendels, J. Longitudinal study of the effects of lithium carbonate on the sleep of hospitalized depressed patients. *Biol. Psychiatry* 9:117-123, 1974.
35. Kupfer, D. J., Wyatt, R. J., Greenspan, K., Scott, J., and Snyder, F. Lithium carbonate and sleep in affective illness. *Arch. Gen. Psychiatry* 23:35-40, 1970.
36. Kupfer, D. J., Reynolds, C. F., III, Weiss, B. L., and Foster, F. G. Lithium carbonate and sleep in affective disorders: Further considerations. *Arch. Gen. Psychiatry* 30:79-84, 1974.
37. Mendels, J., and Chernik, D. A. The effect of lithium carbonate on the sleep of depressed patients. *Int. Pharmacopsychiatry* 8:184-192, 1973.
38. Bowers, M., Jr., and Kupfer, D. J. Central monoamine oxidase inhibition and REM sleep. *Brain Res.* 35:561-564, 1971.
39. Kupfer, D. J., and Bowers, M. B., Jr. REM sleep and central monoamine oxidase inhibition. *Psychopharmacologia* 27:183-190, 1972.
40. Wyatt, R. J., Fram, D. H., Kupfer, D. J., and Snyder, F. Total prolonged drug-induced REM sleep suppression in anxious-depressed patients. *Arch. Gen. Psychiatry* 24:145-155, 1971.
41. Vogel, G. W., Thurmond, A., Gibbons, P., Sloan, K., Boyd, M., and Walker, M. REM sleep reduction effects on depression syndromes. *Arch. Gen. Psychiatry* 32:765-777, 1975.
42. Karacan, I., Blackburn, A. B., Thornby, J. I., Okawa, M., Salis, P. J., and Williams, R. L. The effect of doxepin HCl (Sinequan) on sleep patterns and clinical symptomatology of neurotic depressed patients with sleep disturbance. In J. Mendels, ed., *Sinequan® (Doxepin HCl): A Monograph of Recent Clinical Studies.* Princeton: Excerpta Medica, 1975, pp. 4-22.
43. Hamilton, M. A rating scale for depression. *J. Neurol. Neurosurg. Psychiatry* 23:56-62, 1960.
44. McNair, D. M., Lorr, M., and Droppleman, L. F. *EITS Manual for the Profile of Mood States.* San Diego: Educational and Industrial Testing Service, 1971.
45. Brodman, K., Erdmann, A. J., Jr., and Wolff, H. G. *Cornell Medical Index Health Questionnaire Manual.* Los Angeles: Western Psychological Services, 1949.
46. Williams, R. L., Karacan, I., and Hursch, C. J. *Electroencephalography (EEG) of Human Sleep: Clinical Applications.* New York: Wiley, 1974.
47. Karacan, I., Williams, R. L., Finley, W. W., and Hursch, C. J. The effects of naps on nocturnal sleep: Influence on the need for stage 1 REM and stage 4 sleep. *Biol. Psychiatry* 2:391-399, 1970.

11

# The Wish to Die: Pathological Depression or Rational Decision

NORMAN DECKER

## INTRODUCTION

Death is a subject of great concern, anxiety, and fascination to all physicians. The care and management of the dying patient is perhaps the most emotionally demanding task a physician will meet in his career. Facing the dying patient, the physician must empathetically confront the issues of mortality and separation from loved ones. More directly, he must face feelings of helplessness, impotence, and guilt. There are very few sources of human anxiety that are untapped in this encounter.

The psychiatrist who is consulted in the care of terminally ill patients is confronted with issues which in other contexts would be unambiguous, but which become highly complex when the patient is aware that survival and a return to health are virtually impossible. The most difficult of these issues is the case of the patient who knows his prognosis and wishes to end his life without enduring the heroic attempts of physicians who are dedicated to prolonging it.

187

When I first encountered patients who wished to die, I thought in terms of a traditional psychiatric frame of reference. In this context, suicide is a pathological state, the product of irrational mental processes. I was soon forced to modify that belief. There are times when wanting to die seems an overwhelmingly rational thought. The notion of a "rational suicide" intrigued me. I felt it needed further thought and clarification. Put otherwise, the question was—when did a suicidal wish denote a pathological state of depression requiring treatment and when was it a reasonable solution to a life problem?

Suicide is a term so cloaked in emotion and controversy that I will henceforth rely largely upon what I intend to be a more dispassionate phrase, "the decision for death." I believe that the decision for death is a multifaceted problem which deserves careful thought and exploration. Many questions of medical management, decision-making, ethics, legality, humanism, and compassion are involved. I have few, if any, answers, but I hope that what follows will provoke some further thought on this issue and help to clarify further discussion.

## BACKGROUND

Willing oneself to die is considered unacceptable in our society, but attitudes toward suicide have varied from culture to culture and from period to period. The repugnance with which modern Western society views suicide is well summarized by the poet Alvarez (1). Until very recent times suicide has been viewed as a criminal act, and in many localities suicidal threats or unsuccessful attempts still carry certain criminal consequences.

Some historical examples illustrate that the decision to end one's life is often the product of contending imperatives. The ancient Jewish defenders of Masada, when finally faced with Roman conquest, committed mass suicide rather than allow themselves to be tortured, maimed, killed, or taken into slavery. The inmates of concentration camps during World War II frequently died, as Viktor Frankl describes (2). Because of a loss of will to live under intolerable circumstances, they simply gave up hope, withdrew, and died rapidly thereafter. This might be considered a passive decision for death. In similar fashion, servicemen taken prisoner during the Korean conflict were often subjected to horrifying conditions of imprisonment. As has been amply documented (3), many also "gave up," made a passive decision for death, and rapidly perished.

Terminal patients will occasionally perform an overt suicide, but the frequency of this phenomenon is not great. It is my contention, however, that the passive form of decision for death is far more common.

## QUALITY OF LIFE

When discussing the decision for death and trying to make a distinction between rational or irrational forms, the criteria for decision-making must be considered. The "quality of the individual's life" is a primary considera- tion. The phrase is here used as a measure of the rationality of a death choice. If the quality of life is so dismal that all the patient can look for- ward to is further pain and suffering, then dying might be a rational choice. A rational decision—either for life or death—is predominantly reality-based. An irrational decision is significantly divorced from realistic standards and is not based upon full consideration of alternatives. By this definition, ra- tional decisions tend to be closer to the patient's best interests and irrational decisions further away. Thus, using "quality of life" as a standard, the deci- sion of the Jews to die at Masada, and of the concentration camp victims to die during World War II, can be seen as rational choices. Similarly, perhaps there are advanced cancer patients who might rationally wish to die. We have observed that no one can choose his own death without some com- ponent of irrational fantasy. How these balance against objective factors will determine the rationality of a death decision, but all death decisions are not necessarily associated with clinical depression or other disturbed thought processes.

## CLASSIFICATION SCHEME

There is an extensive literature on a patient's right to die (4,5). There is even a literature on one's right to suicide (6). What will be proposed here is a simple classification scheme attempting to categorize, as dispassionately as possible, the many situational varieties of the decision for death. Those decisions which are based primarily in the symptoms of clinical depression will be distinguished from those which follow a clear and accurate realiza- tion that there are no prospects for relief from anguish other than death. It is hoped that by making these distinctions, we will be able to talk more clearly about decisions to die and the decision-making process. Ultimately, we hope to suggest treatment of that which should be treated, and to make the patient's terminal days less agonizing. The classification scheme will be followed by several case histories which will illustrate some of the categories proposed.

The patient's decision for death can be subclassified into active (overt suicide) and passive forms. Each, in turn, can be classified into conscious or unconscious forms, although it does not seem possible to conceptualize an active-unconscious decision. Finally, and most important, each can be classified into rational or irrational forms. It should be noted that the mirror image of each of these forms is the decision for life. I feel that the decision for life can be classified and divided in much the same fashion and that, for example, an actively positive decision for death is identical with an actively negative decision for life. It is a medical presumption that in the vast majority of cases both patient and physician will make a decision for life and that the decision for death is a less common phenomenon.

In times past it was considered that someone died a natural death if his illness killed him, and this was clearly distinguished from suicide. As medical procedures evolved, however, it became possible to alter the progression of an illness and to save an otherwise doomed life. Penicillin in pneumonia and insulin in diabetes have become routine life-saving measures. A patient's voluntary choice not to accept a life-saving measure constitutes a decision for death. In most routine medical matters, this is a relatively clear and simple situation. In the care of the terminally ill, however, it becomes far more complex. A life-saving measure may only sustain life for a few months, and any life-saving measure only preserves life for a limited period of time. As Kubler-Ross (7) has stated, the difference between the terminally ill and the rest of us does not have to do with the imminence of death but only with the time span involved. In that sense all life-saving medical treatments only prolong life. It becomes increasingly difficult to judge the quality of a decision, whether it is for life or death, or whether it is rational or irrational, when factors such as inconstant cure rates, short duration of cure, and heavy treatment morbidity are considered. Again, the vague but inescapable question of quality of life has to arise. Penicillin is relatively innocuous, but the possibility of morbidity and mortality secondary to administration of anti-neoplastic drugs and life-saving surgical procedures is considerable. It must finally be pointed out that the categories suggested, the active and passive choices, the conscious and unconscious choices, and the rational and irrational choices, exist along several continuums. They are not neatly bounded and discrete. They intrude upon one another and occasionally overlap.

## CASE HISTORIES

In the following case histories I will attempt to illustrate the various categories proposed as useful in approaching the patient who has made a decision for death.

### Case 1

For a reference point let me first briefly present a suicidal, nonterminally ill patient whose decision for death might be classified as active, irrational, and conscious. A 32-year-old single woman with a lifelong history of extreme attachment to and overdominance by extremely protective parents completed graduate school and moved to another city. She saw this as a belated attempt to free herself from her parents' grasp and establish some independence. She was soon consumed by feelings of guilt, worthlessness, depression, and despair, and a wish to end her life. Her depression could be seen as resulting from the emotional separation from her parents and its continual worsening secondary to the liberation of angry feelings and wishes toward them. Feelings of loss, helplessness, isolation, and despair became prominent, and her anger, through various complex mechanisms, turned on herself in the form of guilt and self-destructive impulses (8). Her self-evaluation had little in common with a realistic assessment of her assets and liabilities. Her view of her future bore little relationship to the realistic possibilities that lay before her. In short, she was in a psychotic depressive state which required active psychiatric intervention.

## Case 2

A 45-year-old man suffered from widespread metastatic adenocarcinoma of the lung. He had been told in another hospital that nothing could be done for him. He came to the Veterans Hospital, where a course of chemotherapy was elected. He was quite depressed and voiced suicidal wishes to his wife. He and his wife separated during the course of his therapy. Her active involvement with another man was known to the patient. She came to visit him rarely during his hospitalization. The patient eloped from the hospital, drove to the seashore approximately fifty miles away, and drowned himself. I consider this an irrational suicide based largely on the dynamics of loss, rage, and internalization of anger. The patient was clearly depressed, and a psychiatric intervention could have prevented his suicide and provided the oncologist with time to work, perhaps successfully.

## Case 3

A 17-year-old boy suffered a traumatic quadriplegia following an accidental gunshot wound while cleaning a rifle. After his initial state of shock wore off, he cooperated actively in his treatment until he was informed by his physicians of the full nature of his injury and the prognosis for permanent quadriplegia. He then became extremely depressed and refused to cooperate in his treatment. Although his state of cooperation waxed and waned during the months that followed, he remained essentially depressed and uncooperative. At one point he begged his mother to kill him with a pistol. He continued throughout his illness to wish for death. He was fully aware that refusal to cooperate in his own care would insure his early demise. He developed numerous infections and intestinal obstruction, underwent multiple surgical procedures, and ultimately died nine months after his initial injury.

I consider this case a clear example of a passive, conscious, probably irrational, decision for death on the part of the patient. Although many might claim that quadriplegia is an untenable lifestyle, with an inadequate "quality of life," in point of fact most quadriplegics are able to make some adaptation to their disorder. It is clear that this patient was unable to tolerate the narcissistic injury involved in his clinical situation. He was athletic and physically oriented prior to the injury and found the loss of these capacities more than he could bear. My feelings would be that in such a case every effort toward treatment of depression and psychological rehabilitation is in order.

## Case 4

A 63-year-old man was admitted with inoperable carcinoma of the esophagus with mediastinal extension. At the time of his admission he was in a catabolic state, markedly malnourished because of his virtually negligible capacity for oral intake. This was all secondary to his esophageal stenosis. It was felt that the patient was not far from death by starvation and any active treatment modality would have to follow a better state of nutrition. It was also felt that the patient might benefit from a course of chemotherapy. A nasogastric tube was accordingly passed with the hope that several weeks of tube feeding might be followed by a course of chemotherapy. The patient repeatedly pulled out the nasogastric tube, stating that it was uncomfortable. He insisted that he was able to eat and urged the physicians to simply leave his tray at his bedside and he would eat something. When house staff or nursing staff returned to find the tray untouched he always insisted that he had already eaten. He was otherwise quite peaceful and content. His only request was for a Bible. We decided to confront the patient with his denial and with the immediacy of his death by starvation if he continued to refuse nutrition. This seemed to startle him and he consented to the nasogastric tube. Nevertheless, he died within the next 12 hours secondary to a hypokalemic state associated with his starvation.

This case illustrates the blurring of clear distinctions to which I alluded earlier. The patient was clearly making a passive decision for death, but was this on rational or irrational grounds? Believing that his decision was based largely on a pathological state of denial, we felt that it was irrational and that an active step toward interrupting the state of denial was in order. The physicians, making a decision for life, felt that theirs was a rational decision based on a strong hope for a remission of his disease following chemotherapy. It is of note, parenthetically, that it is extremely difficult for the oncology staff to tolerate a death by starvation. The feelings of helplessness, inadequacy, and severe anxiety seem more prominent in this and similar cases than in most other clinical situations. Perhaps the request for a Bible indicated that the patient expected his rapid demise and, putting himself in God's hands, had made an at least partially rational decision for death based on a peaceful acceptance of what he believed to be the inevitable. If that were indeed the case, then the physicians' decision for life could be seen as an irrational one based more upon their own needs than upon those of the patient. A decision for death on the part of both patient and physician may be rational, acceptable, and humane.

## Case 5

A 55-year-old man was treated for carcinoma of the pyriform sinus with esophageal obstruction. His wife was estranged and in prison; his sons were in the military. Whenever he was home on pass, the family would steal hospital equipment that was sent home with him and sell it. There was continual squabbling over who would get his Social Security check. One son was clearly trying to utilize the father's illness to get out of a difficult military assignment. The patient was beyond treatment by conventional modalities and was usually quite depressed. Nevertheless, he continued to manage his own nasogastric tube and his own feedings and to do a great deal in caring for himself. As the family situation became increasingly stormy and it became apparent to him that he no longer was able to go home, he became extremely depressed and pulled out his tube. No effort was made by the staff to have him return the tube. He soon suffered an aspiration pneumonia which was not treated actively by the staff, and he died shortly thereafter.

The last stage of this man's illness illustrates a decision for death on the part of both patient and physicians. In both cases it was both passive and conscious. Whether or not it was rational can be debated, illustrating once again the difficult distinctions in some of these clinical situations. The patient's severe depression was related to his intense feelings of isolation and rejection by his highly pathological family. Closeness and warmth were what he needed most and got least from his family. Whether a more active supportive role by the staff would have made his life a little longer and his dying a little easier is difficult to determine.

## Case 6

A 75-year-old man was the victim of several painful losses during the last decade of his life. Two wives and several siblings succumbed. During the three years prior to his hospitalization he lived with his one remaining brother, who then died. He had operated a small business in an office building which he had owned for many years. Some years prior to his hospitalization he closed the business and, following the death of his brother, elected to enter a nursing home. He was hospitalized for a relatively minor medical illness. During his hospitalization the house staff learned that he was going to sign over the office building to a bank to clear a large debt. The building was worth a great deal more than the debt, however, and a psychiatrist was called to determine his mental competency. There was no doubt as to his competency. He was completely alert. Similarly, there were no signs or symptoms of significant depression. Having lost all the major libidinal attachments in his life and being too old to work, the patient had simply decided to relinquish all further earthly possessions and wait to die.

I would consider this to be a conscious, passive, rational decision for death; the only difference between this case and some of those discussed previously is that the time span between the decision and the death was somewhat different.

## DISCUSSION

A clear view of the process by which a decision for death is made by severely or terminally ill patients can help to dispel the attitudes of rationalization and projection which are generally prominent among attending staff. When the patient in Case 4, the man with inoperable cancer of the esophagus, claimed that he was getting adequate nutrition, what was his motive? Was he terrified to face the truth and engaged in a desperate attempt at self-deception to his own detriment? Or was he attempting to prepare for his inevitable demise by detaching himself from the world in a quiet way, realizing somewhere inside that he had nothing to look forward to other than additional pain and suffering? A clear sense of motivations is necessary to a proper evaluation of the decision-making process.

The crux of the classification scheme I suggest involves a distinction between rationality and irrationality. The case of the elderly man giving away his building might be seen as a pathological depression rather than a rational decision for death. I feel it is extremely important to make a determination of the rationality of decision for death. If it is rational—i.e., seems to be predominantly determined by objective criteria, a clear and realistic sense of the prospects and alternatives ahead—then I feel it is justified. If the decision is irrational, if it does not represent an accurate assessment of prospects for the quality of life, then it is not justified and psychiatric intervention is appropriate and necessary. Practically, this means whether or not the physicians will attempt to interfere with the patient's decision. If the decisions are unclear, I think our mandate is watchful, humble waiting—with an attempt to understand empathetically. The very act of trying to empathize sufficiently with our patients to know their motives cannot fail to increase the frequency of accurate judgments.

It must be considered that no patient's decision for his own death can ever be totally rational. Fantasies of revenge, reunion, and fusion invariably play a role. Many authors have emphasized this point (8,9,10,11). To this I would reply that few, if any, human actions are ever totally rational in motivation (12). If the objective criteria for a patient choosing death seem valid and no significant psychopathological state can be discerned, I feel that the notion of a *relatively* rational decision for death can be entertained. As we all age and our energies decline, we normally gradually withdraw interest from our activities and environment. As Kubler-Ross (7) has noted, this process of decathexis can, in the terminal state, progress to a normal, even healthy process of acceptance of death.

## REFERENCES

1. Alvarez, A. *The Savage God: A Study of Suicide.* New York: Bantam Books, 1973.
2. Frankl, V. E. *Man's Search for Meaning: An Introduction to Logotherapy.* New York: Washington Square Press, 1963.
3. Kinkeade, E. The Study of Something New in History. *The New Yorker* magazine, October 26, 1957.
4. Group for the Advancement of Psychiatry. *The Right to Die: Decision and Decision Makers.* Vol. VIII, Symposium No. 12, New York Mental Health Materials, Inc., November, 1973.
5. Russell, O. R., Ph.D. *Freedom to Die: Moral and Legal Aspects of Euthanasia.* New York: Behavioral Publications, 1975.
6. Szasz, T. *The Myth of Mental Illness.* New York: Hoeber Medical Division, Harper & Row, 1964.
7. Kubler-Ross, E. *On Death and Dying.* New York: Macmillan, 1969.
8. Freud, S. Mourning and Melancholia, in The Standard Edition of the Complete Psychological Works of Sigmund Freud. London: The Hogarth Press, 1917, Vol. XIV, p. 237.
9. Freud, S. The Psychogenesis of a Case of Homosexuality in a Woman, in The Standard Edition of the Complete Psychological Works of Sigmund Freud. London: The Hogarth Press, 1920, Vol. XVIII, p. 145.
10. Menninger, K. Psychoanalytic Aspects of Suicide. *Int. J. of Psychoanalysis* 14:376, 1933.
11. Stengel, E. Complexity of Motivation to Suicidal Attempts. *J. of Mental Science* 106: 445, 1960.
12. Waelder, R. The Principle of Multiple Function. Observations on Overdetermination. *The Psychoanalytic Quarterly* 5:45, 1936.

12

# Suicide in Depression

## ALEX D. POKORNY

## I. GENERAL RELATIONSHIPS

Suicide and depression are closely related. In fact, we sometimes talk
as if suicide occurs only in depression and depression always includes suicidal
behavior. I do not agree with either one of these oversimplifications, though
I agree there is a strong relationship. In any consideration of depression we
therefore need to focus on how this relates to completed suicide and to
suicide risk. This is what I propose to do here.

I will first take up some general relationships of suicidal behavior to
depression. I will next describe findings from a series of studies in which I
have personally been involved relating to this relationship. I will then take
up the prediction of suicide—that is, the identification of persons at suicidal
risk and the quantitative estimation of that risk. Finally, I will discuss the
issue of prevention of suicide.

I first want to define some terms. The term "suicide" by itself is unfortunately vague unless one is reading it from vital statistics documents, lists

of causes of death, or in the general context of deaths, as in "suicide rates." The word "suicide" has been applied to completed suicide, to attempted suicide, suicidal preoccupation, "suicide equivalents," "unconscious self-destructive urges," etc., often without making it clear which is intended (1). I will use the following terminology: 1. Completed Suicide (CS). 2. Suicide Attempt (SA). 3. Suicidal Ideation (SI). The term "Suicidal Behavior" will be used to include all of the above. I believe that Completed Suicide and Suicide Attempt are largely self-explanatory, except to specify that Suicide Attempt involves an event in which a potentially lethal act has been performed. The category of Suicidal Ideation includes all related behavior short of actually performing a potentially lethal act, and includes behavior elsewhere classified as suicidal preoccupation, suicidal rumination, suicide threats, etc. Regarding the term depression, I use it throughout in the sense of a diagnosable psychiatric disorder unless otherwise specified.

Suicide rates in depressive disorders are high. Likewise, suicidal ideation is typically associated with a depressed state (2). Three-fourths of severely depressed patients report suicidal wishes (2). In fact, this is often used in the identification of depression and estimation of its intensity. Suicide is practically the only feature of depression that poses a reasonably high probability of fatal outcome (2). In virtually all studies which follow up psychiatric patients by diagnostic category, the affective disorders have shown the highest completed suicide rate (3). Robins and his associates (4,5) investigated 134 consecutive cases of completed suicide by interviewing relatives shortly after the event and also by looking up medical records and other available information, on the basis of which they attempted to make or obtain psychiatric diagnoses. It was found that 45% of the 134 subjects appeared to have an affective disorder.

There are even higher suicide rates in those persons, regardless of psychiatric diagnosis, who have a history of suicide attempts. I will return to these two topics—high suicide rates in affective disorder and even higher rates in previously suicidal patients—later in presenting some of my own work. Suicide has been described as the mortality component in the spectrum of depressive illness. It has been found that with surprising regularity 1/6 of persons with affective disorder end their lives by suicide, or very close to 15%. Sainsbury (6) has listed six studies which have followed large numbers of affective disorders and has found that in all six the percentage of deaths due to suicide comes very close to 15%. Guze and Robins (7) have done an elegant review of 17 separate studies with various sample sizes and various durations of follow-up. They found that the percentage of deaths due to suicide ranges from 60% down to 12%. However, when they graphed these rates against the percent of the total sample that had died from any cause, they found a striking relationship: in the earlier years of follow-up the percent of deaths due to suicide would typically be much higher, and it was only when 40% or more of the total group of subjects were dead that the percent of death by suicide leveled off at 15%. It thus appears that deaths by suicide typically occur earlier than deaths from other causes. This parallels the usual finding, to be touched upon again later, that risk of completed suicide is greatest immediately after psychiatric hospitalization or immediately after a suicide attempt.

There is generally believed to be some overlap between the categories of depressive disorder and alcoholism. There are high completed suicide rates in both groups.

An important feature about affective disorders is that they have a good prognosis; therefore, if we can identify and successfully treat an affective disorder, this may prevent a suicide. We need to keep this hopeful note in mind when discussing statistics, rates, and outcomes, all of which may leave a sense of inevitability about all of this.

## II. FINDINGS FROM STUDIES IN THIS CENTER

During the past 20 years I have conducted a series of investigations on completed suicide, using as the study population the present and former patients of the Houston VA Hospital. I will summarize and present aspects of these studies dealing with suicide in depression.

In one study of 44 subjects who had previously been patients and who subsequently completed suicide (8), it was found that 12 of the 44 subjects had had a diagnosis of depression. An even larger number, 13, had been diagnosed as schizophrenic, but this is misleading because schizophrenia is a more common diagnosis in this patient group. This same study showed that 31 of these 44 subjects had some previous suicidal history, with 14 having had suicide attempts. We also studied the issue of which patients had been placed on suicidal precautions during any previous hospitalization. Twenty percent of the suicide group had had such an order on their charts, whereas only 2% of the controls had been so identified.

In another study (9), I derived suicide rates in relation to previous psychiatric diagnosis. There are many studies showing that series of individuals who have committed suicide have had pre-existing psychiatric disorders, but it is much rarer to find studies which are prospective in nature: that is, starting with groups of patients who have been given one or another psychiatric diagnosis and following them up to see what suicide rates will be. In this study, over 11,000 patients were followed up in terms of whether they were living or dead and whether they had died by suicide. This information was then converted, through computations involving number of cases involved and time at risk for each case, into suicide rates (rates are expressed as number of instances per 100,000 persons per year). 116 instances of completed suicide were identified. Again, the number of schizophrenic subjects equaled the number of depressive subjects (31 cases each). However, when this was converted to rates, it was found that depressive disorders had by far the greatest rate, namely 566, as compared to 167 in schizophrenics, 119 in neurosis, 130 in personality disorders, 133 in alcoholics, and 78 in organic patients. These rates should be compared with the U.S. national rate in recent years of about 11 per 100,000 per year. Since military veterans are mostly males and are all age 17 and older, a more appropriate rate, adjusted for age and sex, is about 23. You will note that these diagnostic group rates are all higher. In the case of depressives, the rate is about 25 times the expected rate. For all psychiatric cases taken together, the rate was 165, which is more than 7 times the expected rate. Since there is no certainty that all cases of suicide were uncovered, these rates are probably underestimates. It is evident that depressive cases are strikingly more prone to suicide than other psychiatric syndromes.

In another study (10), I followed up a group of 618 patients who had been referred for psychiatric consultation because of suicidal behavior. This entire group of patients was followed up to see which ones subsequently completed suicide. With this information, suicide rates and sample percentages could be derived through various groupings of the original series of patients. It was found that the suicide rate for the entire group was 740, which is even higher than the rate for depressive disorders shown in the previous study. Another finding of interest was that the rate was highest in the recently suicidal subjects. This again indicates that the risk seems to be greatest in the period immediately after an earlier attempt. The period of greatest risk of suicide was found to be during the first two years following the initial suicidal behavior. In fact, during the first three months the incidence of suicide was almost 1% of the entire group.

In another study (11) I explored the question of whether suicide in war veteran patients might be different from suicide in the general population. This is important since all of the studies reported here have been done with this particular group. I explored these questions: (1) Is the suicide rate in veterans different from general population rates for that age group and sex? (2) Is the distribution among the various age periods different from that in the general population? (3) Are the methods used by veterans different? and (4) How much are the suicide rates in veterans affected by the presence of a psychiatric illness? These questions were explored by comparing data on the psychiatric patient and ex-patient group of the Houston VA Hospital with population data about veterans in the State of Texas, and with death rates by suicide in veterans in the State of Texas. It was found that suicide rates in veterans do not differ from those in the general population of the same age and sex; however, suicides in male veterans tended to occur at an earlier age than in males in general. The presence of a psychiatric illness led to a ninefold increase in suicide rate. The method of suicide was not different in male veterans than in males generally, but male veteran psychiatric cases differed in that they had a higher percentage of poisoning and a lower percentage of firearms deaths.

In another study (12), this time not involving veterans, we investigated 28 consecutive single-driver auto crash fatalities from the standpoint of the possible role of emotional disturbance, alcoholism, and suicidal trends in these fatalities. From a detailed review of very extensive data obtained about each case, we concluded that 4 of the 28 crash deaths were probably suicides. We found that 12 of the 28 clearly showed depression just prior to the fatal crash (intoxication was even more common, being present in 18 of the 28 cases). We concluded that a substantial proportion of automobile driver fatalities are suicides, and this of course has significant implications with respect to corrective and control measures.

My associates and I (13) are currently involved in a major prospective study of 4,800 consecutive psychiatric admissions to the Houston VA Hospital. These are being followed up for a period of three or four years, and we are identifying all possible cases of completed suicide, along with suicide attempts, suicide ideation, hospital readmission, deaths from other causes, and other behaviors which might be viewed as "self-destructive." To date, our subject group of 4,800 veterans has been followed for an average of two and a half years.

Table 1 gives the diagnostic breakdown of our patient group. There are several items of interest in this table. First, the general death rates are high for the organic and alcohol group. When you look at completed suicide, the *numbers* are larger for the schizophrenic and alcohol groups, but the *rate* is highest for the affective disorder group, though also fairly high for the schizophrenic group. 1.4% of the affective disorders have died by suicide after an average follow-up of two and a half years. Also, the last column indicates that completed suicides account for 25% of the deaths in the affective disorder group, a finding which is consistent with the Guze-Robins finding mentioned earlier.

Table 2 shows the diagnostic breakdown of the total patient group and the completed suicide group. It turned out that 14 of our suicide subjects were in the young "Vietnam veteran" group, and therefore in the last two

Table 1. Numbers of Total Deaths and Suicide Deaths
by Diagnostic Category

| Diagnosis | No. of Cases | Total Deaths | | Completed Suicides | | % of Deaths Which Were CS |
|---|---|---|---|---|---|---|
| | | Number | Rate | Number | Rate | |
| Affective | 516 | 28 | 2171 | 7 | 543 | 25.0 |
| Schizophrenic | 836 | 26 | 1244 | 9 | 431 | 34.6 |
| Alcoholism | 1618 | 172 | 4252 | 8 | 198 | 4.7 |
| Drug Abuse | 720 | 22 | 1222 | 2 | 111 | 9.1 |
| Neurotic | 401 | 15 | 1496 | 3 | 299 | 20.0 |
| Pers. Disorder | 428 | 10 | 935 | 3 | 280 | 30.0 |
| Organic | 281 | 50 | 7117 | 0 | 0 | 0.0 |
| TOTAL | 4800 | 323 | 2692 | 32 | 267 | 9.9 |

columns these are shown separately. One striking difference is that the alcoholic suicides are all in the older age group whereas the two drug abuse suicides are in the younger age group. You will see in the top row that the percentage of affective disorders is about the same in both age groups.

Table 3 shows the age breakdown, this time comparing the completed suicides with the total group in terms of age distribution by decades. The one striking difference is the greater than expected number of completed suicides in the age group from 20-29.

Table 4 shows the suicide rates to date by various groups within our study. The group of interest is the one labeled "B," which is our high-risk group selected by a priori criteria at the beginning of our study using conventional guides such as age, severity of depression, being widowed or divorced, etc. This group certainly has a higher suicide rate than Group C, which is our control group, or Group A, which is the remainder. Of particular interest is the "BSA" group, which are those in our high-risk group placed there by virtue of having attempted suicide. This group has by far the largest rate, and in fact to date nearly 5% of this group have completed suicide. When the same data is converted to rates, it will be shown that the BSA, or suicide-attempt group, has a rate of 1915, a rate far higher than obtained even in the studies of follow-up of suicide attempts I cited earlier.

Table 5 shows the distribution of groups in two items from the expanded Brief Psychiatric Rating Scale. With respect to depressive mood, the

## Table 2. Diagnosis

| | All 4800 Subjects | Total | CS | Young (<a. 40) | CS | Old (>a. 40) | CS |
|---|---|---|---|---|---|---|---|
| Affective | 11% | 7 | 22% | 3 | 21% | 4 | 22% |
| Schizophrenic | 17% | 9 | 28% | 5 | 36% | 4 | 22% |
| Alcoholic | 34% | 8 | 25% | 0 | 0% | 8 | 44% |
| Drug Abuse | 15% | 2 | 6% | 2 | 14% | 0 | 0% |
| Neurosis | 8% | 3 | 9% | 2 | 14% | 1 | 6% |
| Pers. Disorder | 9% | 3 | 9% | 2 | 14% | 1 | 6% |
| Organic | 6% | 0 | 0% | 0 | 0% | 0 | 0% |
| TOTAL | — | 32 | | 14 | | 18 | |

completed suicide group showed a somewhat higher rating than the total group, but the differences are not very striking. In terms of suicidal ideation there is some increase in the percentage of the completed suicide group rated as having higher degrees of this.

Table 6 explores the question asked of the examining physician: "Regardless of the diagnosis, is there evidence of depression?" It can be seen that there is a somewhat greater incidence of slight, moderate, or severe depression in the group which later completed suicide.

Table 7 shows that far more of the completed suicides than of the general group had been previously placed on a suicidal precaution list. Part 2 of this table shows that a far greater proportion had shown a suicide-attempt history at time of the index admission. The bottom of the table shows the methods of suicide in our 32 subjects.

With respect to the point that 25% of our subject's deaths were completed suicide (rather than the traditional 15%), we need to note the finding of Pitts and Winokur (14), based on suicide rates in relatives of subjects of affective disorder who themselves appear to have had an affective disorder. Although they found a total of 16% of deaths by suicide, when this was split by sex it was found that the incidence of suicide in the deceased fathers who had suffered from an affective disorder was 28%, whereas in corresponding mothers it was 6%. Therefore, if we keep in mind that our VA subjects are virtually all males, then our 25% of suicide deaths corresponds closely to Pitts and Winokur's male rates.

One note should be added about diagnosis. In contrast to many studies

Table 3.  Age

| Age | C | S | All 4800 |
|---|---|---|---|
| | Number | Percentage | |
| 10 - 19 | 1 | 3% | 2% |
| 20 - 29 | 12 | 38% | 28% |
| 30 - 39 | 1 | 3% | 15% |
| 40 - 49 | 10 | 31% | 29% |
| 50 - 59 | 7 | 22% | 21% |
| 60 - 69 | 1 | 3% | 4% |
| 70 - 79 | 0 | 0% | 1% |
| TOTAL | 32 | | |

done by such researchers as Robins, Guze, and Murphy and associates (15) who use explicit research criteria for making diagnoses of affective disorder, schizophrenia, etc., our studies have been more naturalistic. In an attempt to see if we can predict suicide with ordinary clinical interviews and methods, we have chosen to go with the standard hospital diagnosis made by the assigned physician and his staff, and have followed the diagnostic criteria listed in DSM-II and conventional textbooks. It may be that this means we tend to underdiagnose affective disorders and overdiagnose schizophrenia, alcoholism, and neurosis, in relation to what would be diagnosed by the Washington University group. This is one of the several technical problems which plague this type of research. We have recently completed a study (16) of the first 20 subjects in this project who completed suicide following release from the hospital, matched with 20 control subjects on age, race, and time at risk in the community; we studied the effects of defenselessness ( the incapacity to defend against distressful negative self-feelings) and of stressful life events, each separately and then in interaction. The measure of defenselessness had a lot in common with measures of depression, and in fact this might have been labeled as depression. We found that neither defenselessness alone nor experience of adverse life events alone were predictive of completed suicide, but that the two in combination were significantly related to higher rates of completed suicide. We concluded that suicide is a response to experiences with self-threatening effects, in persons "predisposed" by inability to cope with such experiences.

Table 4.  Suicide Proportions and Rates (After 2.5 Years)

| | | | |
|---|---|---|---|
| A | 16/3152 | = | .0051 |
| B | 5/431 | = | .0128 |
| C | 2/805 | = | .0025 |
| BSA | 9/188 | = | .0479 |
| TOTAL B | 14/803 | = | .0174 |
| GRAND TOTAL | 32/4800 | = | .0067 |

RATES/100,000/YR

| | | | |
|---|---|---|---|
| A | ONLY | = | 203 |
| B | (TOTAL) | = | 697 |
| C | ONLY | = | 99 |
| BSA | | = | 1915 |

## III. PREDICTION OF SUICIDE

If we are to make best use of scarce resources in trying to prevent suicide, we must know where to focus our efforts. More specifically, we need to know which individuals, out of the large group of persons with some degree of depression or alcoholism or other mental disturbance, are the ones who unless stopped or helped will complete suicide.

This unfortunately is no easy matter. In fact, we can say that given present knowledge, it is not possible. It may be that the best we can do is to identify higher and higher degrees of risk, but that we will still be unable to say which individuals within this high-risk group are the particular ones who may complete suicide. This whole issue represents a high priority area for study, and I will try to summarize some of the relevant work.

There are certain inherent difficulties in the prediction of suicide. To begin with, this is a rare behavior. In the general population approximately 1 in 10,000 persons dies by suicide each year, and it would obviously strain the limits of any prediction system, even if it were highly reliable and valid, to identify this one individual. We must recognize that what indicators we now have are far cruder and are therefore simply not equal to this task. The job of prediction becomes slightly easier as one moves into higher-risk groups, but even in groups of persons previously treated for affective disorder or for suicide attempt, where the subsequent suicide rate may be in the order of 600-800, this still means only 6-8 per 1,000 each year. In other words, the overwhelming majority of persons who have been treated for affective disorder or who have been treated in connection with a suicide attempt do not commit suicide. It is of course possible to improve the odds

**Table 5. BPRS Items**

| | | Depressive Mood | | | S. Ideation | |
|---|---|---|---|---|---|---|
| | | CS | 4800 | | CS | 4800 |
| 0 | 3 | 9% | 29% | 22 | 69% | 77% |
| 1 | 2 | 6% | 11% | 2 | 6% | 5% |
| 2 | 6 | 19% | 15% | 1 | 3% | 7% |
| 3 | 11 | 34% | 21% | 3 | 9% | 7% |
| 4 | 8 | 25% | 18% | 2 | 6% | 3% |
| 5 | 1 | 3% | 5% | 0 | 0% | 2% |
| 6 | 1 | 3% | 1% | 2 | 6% | 1% |
| | 32 | | | 32 | | |

by including other contributing factors, but one quickly reaches limits of even multivariate prediction.

A useful terminology relating to degree of suicide risk has been proposed by Litman, Farberow, and the Los Angeles group (17). This classifies the degree of suicide risk according to the probability of future suicide, expressed as rates (suicide deaths per 100,000/yr):

Non risk = 0 to 5
Normal (minimal risk) = 5 to 50
Suicidal with low risk = 50 to 500
Suicidal with moderate risk = 500 to 5,000
Suicidal with high risk = over 5,000

Those classified as suicidal with high risk are up to 1,000 times as likely to die by suicide as the average citizen. The high-risk state is usually transient, and I know of no identified group with such a high rate on a long-term basis.

Another problem (8) in suicide prediction is a kind of paradox: If we could identify with certainty the one individual who is destined to commit suicide, we would be professionally and ethically bound to do everything in our power to stop it and thereby to "spoil" the prediction. What I am saying is that this may become an unresearchable question if we approach the point where identification of specific individuals becomes a possibility. The fact that in our previously reported studies a definite though small propor-

**Table 6. Regardless of Diagnosis, Is There Evidence of Depression?**

|  | 4800 | CS | |
|---|---|---|---|
| No | 45% | 9 | 28% |
| Slight or Moderate | 49% | 19 | 59% |
| Severe | 6% | 4 | 13% |
|  |  | 32 | |

tion of the subjects have gone on to complete suicide is therefore an indirect indicator that up to now individual prediction has not been possible.

There are other technical difficulties in study of completed suicide, such as the fact that known positive cases are no longer available for study; also, data obtained after a suicide from relatives, former physicians, and significant others may tend to be colored by knowledge of the unfortunate outcome; since suicide is typically a tragic and traumatic event for family and associates, it is difficult to move in right away and obtain full data, particularly since the very individual being questioned may feel responsible or may feel he is being criticized. One general adaptation to this problem has been to use data which is already in the records, and this is the approach my associates and I have used. This has the advantage of not having the data colored by knowledge of the subsequent suicide, and of not disturbing the bereaved. It also has the advantage that the subject himself has been available for study. The big disadvantage is that, since suicide is such a rare event, such data has to be available on large numbers of subjects. This usually cuts down on the volume and accuracy and even the type of data which may have been obtained and is thus available for study.

Prediction of suicide may be thought of in terms of long-range prediction and short-range prediction. It may even be feasible to split it into long-, medium-, and short-range prediction in the sense of: (1) Will this person ever commit suicide? (2) Is this person apt to commit suicide in the next one to three months? (3) Is this person apt to commit suicide in the next few minutes, hours, or days?

Under long-range prediction, we would include studies such as those summarized by Sainsbury and by Guze and Robins, in which about 15% of affective disorder subjects ultimately die as suicides. Under midrange prediction, we would include issues such as that rates of completed suicide are highest within a few weeks or months after discharge from a hospital. A

## Table 7.

**Ever on S. List?**

7/32 YES (22%)
  7% of 4800

| SA History | 4800 | Total | CS | Young (<a. 40) | CS | Old (>a. 40) | CS |
|---|---|---|---|---|---|---|---|
| Yes, Present Adm | 4% | 9 | 28% | 5 | 36% | 4 | 22% |
| Yes, earlier only | 13% | 2 | 6% | 1 | 7% | 1 | 6% |
| No | 83% | 21 | 66% | 8 | 57% | 13 | 72% |
| TOTAL | | 32 | | 14 | | 18 | |

| Method | |
|---|---|
| Firearms & Explosives | 19 |
| Overdose | 6 |
| Gases | 3 |
| Hanging | 2 |
| Cutting | 1 |
| Jumping | 1 |
| | 32 |

great deal of the work I will summarize here has to deal with long-range or medium-range prediction, and the findings, although of interest, are of limited use for the individual. I suspect that much of our clinical "suicide prediction" is of the short-range variety, and my belief is that this is much more valid but unresearchable because of the urgency of the situation, and the ethical requirements, and because the general complexity of crisis situations makes it impossible to apply any kind of standard or controlled methods of study.

We need to distinguish sharply between completed suicide and suicide attempts. Many of the published studies confound these two, which seem to be different although overlapping behaviors. Presumably some proportion, probably a small proportion, of suicide attempts represent the same behavior as completed suicide except that the outcome was not fatal. Presumably the same influences and relationships would apply to these "serious suicide attempts" as apply to completed suicide. The preferred terminology here is "high intent suicide attempts," referring to the motivation of the subject involved. This should be distinguished from the "high lethality suicide attempts," which refers to the medical dangerousness of the act. Although high intentionality and high lethality tend to be correlated, there is no necessary relationship. Suicide attempts (all kinds lumped together) are common in depressed patients as well as completed suicides, but it has been established that depressives seen after suicide attempts are as a group somewhat more like the group of personality or character disorders (18).

One of the interesting although perhaps impractical leads during the past few years has been the observation that an association may exist between increased suicide risk and high or increasing 17-hydroxycorticosteroid excretion (19,20). There have also been negative reports about this (21). It is of course not practical to do continual 24-hour urine samples on large numbers of persons, looking for this type of clue. Furthermore, it seems likely that such elevations in steroid excretions are secondary effects of psychic distress or suffering rather than being in some way causative of the suicidal urge. Nevertheless, these workers are to be commended for raising the possibility of a new kind of predictor in the form of a lab test or physiological measure. If a practical test with this capacity were to be developed, it would revolutionize the field.

An interesting new proposition has been advanced by Aaron Beck and associates (22) to the effect that negative expectations about the future— that is, hopelessness—may be a better predictor of suicide than depression. This group has developed standardized rating instruments for assessing the state of hopelessness and has shown in several studies that this instrument correlates well with high intentionality in suicide attempts. Our laboratory has confirmed that hopelessness is highly correlated with intentionality, but with our different type of sample, hopelessness was not as closely correlated as depression (13).

Akiskal and McKinney (23,24) have pointed out that there is much similarity between the "learned helplessness" behavior pattern and depression. This may be related to Beck's ideas about the perception of oneself as being hopeless and helpless and having no control over one's state.

One of the directions which efforts at prediction of suicide has taken is the development of suicide prediction instruments. I will mention only a few. Tuckman and Youngman (25) developed a scale for use with persons who had attempted suicide, consisting of 14 items. This included age, sex, race, marital status, whether or not employed, living arrangements, general health, and other factors generally regarded as predictive of suicide. They found that each of these items separately, and especially the scale as a whole, discriminated well between those who later did and did not complete suicide. Cohen and associates (26) added 8 items to the Tuckman-Youngman Scale and tried it on a different population. In their hands some of the original items did not predict successfully, whereas some of the new ones did, so that they also wound up with a 14-item checklist. This was found to identify reasonably well those among a group of 193 suicide attempters who would in the future either commit suicide or make a subsequent suicide attempt. More recently, Poldinger (27) has developed a weighted scale of 13 items which discriminated well between groups of patients who subsequently completed suicide or made a suicidal attempt and those who showed no suicidal behavior.

In addition to these more formalized scales, there are innumerable articles and studies which offer guidance in a more clinical, practical, and informal way about identifying those who are seriously suicidal. One of the more common "tips" which deserves repeating is that in depressed patients, suicide tends to occur when the depression is lifting. This may be partly due to the fact that the severely depressed person does not have the "energy" or executive capacity required to carry out a successful suicidal act, whereas this inertia decreases as the depression lifts. Another probable mechanism is that a firm decision to commit suicide may actually lessen agitation and misery, and often seems to result in a state of peaceful serenity that may be seen as lifting of depression.

Suicide is most frequent soon after discharge from the hospital (8). Suicide typically occurs in patients who have communicated their intentions either directly or indirectly (8). It is simply not true that people who talk about suicide won't commit suicide (28). Not only is the risk of suicide high immediately after discharge from the hospital, but it is high during weekend leaves from the hospital (2). It has been estimated that the suicide risk in the first six months after discharge is 34 times greater than the general population (29). Sainsbury (6) summarizes the characteristics of the depressed person who is a high risk for suicide as follows: (1) endogenous type of depression; (2) aged over 40; (3) will have lost one of his parents in childhood by suicide; (4) will have himself threatened suicide; (5) his illness will have been of short duration, or he may have recently been discharged from the hospital; (6) will be living alone; (7) will be likely to harp on his feelings of hopelessness and worthlessness and loss of energy; (8) may also be drinking heavily .

To this one might add: some recent crisis in one's personal life, work life, in health, etc. Furthermore, we might add the presence of symptoms such as persistent insomnia, anorexia, agitation, and various somatic and vegetative symptoms of depression. Farberow and McEvoy (30), in speaking of patients with anxiety and depressive reactions, stressed the importance of poor prognosis, suicidal history, sleeplessness, and marked anxiety as positive clues.

One approach to better recognition and diagnosis of depression is to use some form of screening test or instrument routinely, such as the Zung Depression Inventory (31). This does not provide the breadth of information which is provided by the longer, more cumbersome inventories such as the Minnesota Multiphasic Personality Inventory, but if we are focusing particularly on identification of depression, this should suffice.

Beck and associates (32) have developed a Suicide Intent Scale or SIS for subjects who have attempted suicide. This takes into account all of the relevant aspects of the suicide attempter's behavior, including the time before, during, and after the suicidal act. The scale is a 15-item schedule with 8 items covering the objective circumstances of the attempt, including items on the preparation for and manner of execution of the attempt, the setting, clues given to others which might favor or disfavor discovery, etc. The second part of this scale reflects the suicide attempter's conception of the method, lethality, or danger to life, the degree of premeditation, the alleged purpose of the attempt, etc. This scale has turned out to be very promising in correlations with other measures of suicidal behavior.

To get around some of the technical difficulties, we need to predict, rather than completed suicides, the state just preceding this, something like (1) a firm decision to commit suicide, or (2) a balance toward suicide, in considering the forces for and against, or (3) a state of very high suicidal risk, of overwhelming "suicidality." Beck is approaching this goal in focusing on high intentionality and its measurement. The shift of interest to this "presuicidal" state would eliminate many of the technical problems in study of suicide, in that subjects would still be available for study, the rarity of the phenomenon would not be a problem, and the ethical and therapeutic need to intervene would not conflict with the research goals.

Finally, we need to recall a sobering note from George Murphy (33) in which he raises some question about the push to identify the specific individuals who seem "destined" to commit suicide out of the total high-risk group. He points out that from a clinical standpoint all persons in the high-risk group, who are chiefly depressives, alcoholics, or suicide attempters, and who present themselves for treatment, need to be treated, so that identification of the specific individual may not be all-important. This makes sense if we are thinking of outpatient treatment and follow up, but the argument breaks down if appropriate treatment includes hospitalization and security measures.

## IV. PREVENTION OF SUICIDE

If we can identify the specific individuals at certain or at least very high risk of suicide, what can we do to prevent it? Having made the diagnosis, how satisfactory is the treatment? Unfortunately, the answer is that it is less than perfect. In the present state of knowledge we cannot always prevent or avert a suicide even in persons known to be moderately or even highly suicidal.

One first thinks of direct interference—that is, directly stopping or inhibiting the person bent on suicide. While this is usually possible and appropriate for the acute situation and for the short run, this has important limitations when considered as a long-term or permanent measure. The same argument might be applied to the role of the psychiatric hospital with closed wards and to commitment laws and related procedures. Incidentally, in the current climate of growing emphasis on consumerism, patients' rights, informed consent, etc., even the use of commitment, closed wards, and other physical restraints is becoming increasingly limited. But even in the years before this was true, these were still imperfect and less than fully satisfactory techniques. The number of spaces in closed wards in psychiatric hospitals is limited, and these are simply not adequate to house all the people who seem at moderate to high risk of suicide. Furthermore, on a humanitarian basis, one cannot or should not restrain or lock up persons indefinitely. Also, such measures often conflict with therapeutic goals, where we may want to give a patient freedom to try out new attitudes or take on additional responsibilities.

There has arisen in our country during the past fifteen years or so the suicide prevention center movement. If one could trust a name, this sounds like the solution to our problem. In fact, there is some question as to whether such centers prevent suicide at all (33). Callers to such services seem to differ from the typical person who commits suicide. There is evidence that persons thinking seriously of suicide rarely call a suicide prevention center even when this is available (33). Such centers have not shown any appreciable influence on suicide in their communities, with the single exception of the Samaritans Group in Britain. On the other hand, it may be demanding too much of the suicide prevention centers that they be expected to lower the general suicide rate, since none of our other measures seem to have this effect. Litman and associates (17) have shown convincingly that callers to a suicide prevention center are a high-risk group. Suicide prevention centers also appear to perform other useful functions, and are perhaps better considered as crisis intervention centers.

It may be that other community measures could be taken to reduce the risk of suicide, such as increased attention to persons living alone (6).

In large part, the approach to prevention of suicide which seems to me practical and has some chance of succeeding consists of those measures which constitute the diagnosis and treatment of depression, and to a lesser extent of alcoholism and schizophrenia. This will require: (1) a high index of suspicion for depression and affective disorder; (2) an active inquiry into suicidal ideation or planning; (3) an active pursuit of persons who seem to be at high risk; (4) an intensive and effective treatment program for depression, alcoholism, schizophrenia, etc.; (5) steps to insure patient compliance and continued participation in treatment programs.

From the standpoint of practicing physicians, we must be alert to the possibility of suicide. Where there is evidence of suicidal risk and there is doubt about the degree of this, we might want to hospitalize such patients for detailed evaluation. We should think of thorough and continuing treatment for depressives and should provide for follow-up and after-care (6).

It is important to recognize that few patients have a single-minded, unwavering resolve to commit suicide. More typically, patients are wavering and indecisive, although the balance of tendencies may vary. The doctor should always look for these balancing forces and should throw his weight on the side of the life-sustaining trends.

It does not appear possible, in my opinion, to eliminate suicide completely at the present time, even among the group of patients with depressive disorders. But with special attention to this vital area we should be able to make a conspicuous improvement.

We must be realistic and acknowledge that virtually nothing so far has influenced the suicide rate, referring to diagnostic and treatment measures. The introduction of ECT and the later introduction of antidepressant and other effective psychoactive medications have failed to make a noticeable change in national suicide rates. Neither has the steady increase in numbers of psychiatrists, the open-door policy, community psychiatry, the suicide prevention movement, etc. Only economic depression and war appear to influence the national rates, presumably because they affect *everyone*, whereas our efforts invariably affect only a fraction of the population. If we hope to make any significant impact on the national (or world) suicide rate through medical measures, we would need to make depression as rare as polio.

One of the newer therapeutic measures which might prevent individual suicides is the method of maintenance treatment of affective disorders, the "prophylactic" use of medications in the intervals between episodes of affective disorder. It has been shown (34) that maintenance use of lithium significantly reduces the number of recurrences of affective disorder in bipolar patients, and that both lithium and imipramine reduce the number of recurrences in unipolar affective disorders. It may be that other medications will have the same effect. Although no one has yet demonstrated any affect of such regimes on suicide rates, it seems plausible that anything which eliminates episodes of depression would prevent some suicide.

## SUMMARY

Suicide and depression are closely linked. About one-sixth of the deaths in persons with affective disorders are by completed suicide. To date, this rate and the general suicide rates have been resistant to the effects of treatment advances. There is much interesting and productive research in this area, but because of the relative rarity of suicide and the lack of precision in our predictors it seems unlikely that we will ever be able to identify the specific individuals who will complete suicide; it does seem feasible to identify a smaller group at such high risk that it should be possible to protect and treat them all. The prevention of suicide may rest largely on the recognition and treatment of depression. In addition to other treatment measures, maintenance or prophylactic use of lithium and other medications may offer new promise.

## REFERENCES

1. Pokorny, A. A scheme for classifying suicidal behaviors, Chapter 2 in *The Prediction of Suicide*, A. Beck, H. Resnik, and D. Lettieri, eds. Bowie, Md.: Charles Press, 1974.
2. Beck, A. *Depression: Causes and Treatment*. Philadelphia: U. of Pennsylvania Press, 1967.
3. Gardner, E., Bahn, A., and Mack, M. Suicide and psychiatric care in the aging. *Arch. Gen. Psychiat.* 10:547-553, 1964.
4. Robins, E., Gassner, S., Kayes, J., Wilkinson, R., and Murphy, G. The communication of suicidal intent: A study of 134 consecutive cases of successful (completed) suicide. *Am. J. Psychiat.* 115:724-733, 1959.
5. Robins, E., Murphy, G., Wilkinson, R., Gassner, S., and Kayes, J. Some clinical considerations in the prevention of suicide based on a study of 134 successful suicides. *Am. J. Public Health* 49:888-899, 1959.
6. Sainsbury, P. Suicide and depression, Chapter 1 in *Recent Developments in Affective Disorders*, A. Coppen and H. Welk, eds. Ashford, Kent: Headley Bros., Ltd., 1968.
7. Guze, S., and Robins, E. Suicide and primary affective disorders. *Br. J. Psychiat.* 117:437-438, 1970.
8. Pokorny, A. Characteristics of forty-four patients who subsequently committed suicide. *AMA Arch. Gen. Psychiat.* 2:314-323, 1960.
9. Pokorny, A. Suicide rates in various psychiatric disorders. *J. Nerv. Ment. Dis.* 139:499-506, 1964.
10. Pokorny, A. A follow-up study of 618 suicidal patients. *Am. J. Psychiat.* 122:1109-1116, 1966.

11. Pokorny, A. Suicide in war veterans: Rates and methods. *J. Nerv. Ment. Dis.* 144:224-229, 1967.
12. Pokorny, A., Smith, J., and Finch, J. Vehicular suicides. *Life-Threatening Behavior* 2:105-118, 1972.
13. Pokorny, A., Kaplan, H., and Tsai, S. Hopelessness and attempted suicide: A reconsideration. *Am. J. Psychiat.* 132:954-956, 1975.
14. Pitts, F., and Winokur, G. Affective disorder. III. Diagnostic correlates and incidence of suicide. *J. Nerv. Ment. Dis.* 139:176-181, 1964.
15. Murphy, G., Woodruff, R., Herjanic, M., and Fischer, J. Validity of the diagnosis of primary affective disorder. *Arch. Gen. Psychiat.* 30:751-756, 1974.
16. Pokorny, A., and Kaplan, H. Suicide following psychiatric hospitalization: The interaction effects of defenselessness and adverse life events. *J. Nerv. Ment. Dis.* 162:119-125, 1976.
17. Litman, R., Wold, C., Farberow, N., and Brown, T. Prediction models of suicidal behaviors, Chapter 10 in *The Prediction of Suicide*, A. Beck, H. Resnik, and D. Lettieri, eds. Bowie, Md.: Charles Press, 1974.
18. Paykel, E., and Dienelt, M. Suicide attempts following acute depression. *J. Nerv. Ment. Dis.* 153:234-243, 1971.
19. Bunney, W., and Fawcett, J. Biochemical research in depression and suicide, Chapter 10 in *Suicidal Behaviors: Diagnosis and Management*, H. Resnik, ed. Boston: Little, Brown, 1968.
20. Bunney, W., Fawcett, J., Davis, J., and Gifford, S. Further evaluation of urinary 17-hydroxycorticosteroids in suicidal patients. *Arch. Gen. Psychiat.* 21:138-150, 1969.
21. Levy, B., and Hansen, E. Failure of the urinary test for suicide potential. *Arch. Gen. Psychiat.* 20:415-418, 1969.
22. Minkoff, K., Bergman, E., Beck, A., et al. Hopelessness, depression, and attempted suicide. *Am. J. Psychiat.* 130:455-459, 1973.
23. Akiskal, H., and McKinney, W. Depressive disorders: Toward a unified hypothesis. *Science* 182:20-29, 1973.
24. Akiskal, H., and McKinney, W. Overview of recent research in depression. *Arch. Gen. Psychiat.* 32:285-305, 1975.
25. Tuckman, J., and Youngman, W. Assessment of suicide risk in attempted suicides, Chapter 13 in *Suicidal Behaviors: Diagnosis and Management*, H. Resnik, ed. Boston: Little, Brown, 1968.
26. Cohen, E., Motto, J., and Seiden, R. An instrument for evaluating suicide potential: A preliminary study. *Am. J. Psychiat.* 122:886-897, 1966.
27. Poldinger, W. Drug therapy in depressive states with special reference to suicide prevention, in *Suicide and Attempted Suicide*, J. Waldenstrom, T. Larsson, and N. Wungstedt, eds. Stockholm: Nordiska Bokhandelns Forlag, 1972.
28. Pokorny, A. Myths about suicide, Chapter 4 in *Suicidal Behaviors*, H. Resnik, ed. Boston: Little, Brown, 1968.
29. Temoche, A., Pugh, T., and MacMahon, B. Suicide rates among current and former mental institution patients. *J. Nerv. Ment. Dis.* 138:124-130, 1964.
30. Farberow, N., and McEvoy, T. Suicide among patients with anxiety or depressive reactions, Chapter 20 in *The Psychology of Suicide*, E. Shneidman, N. Farberow, and R. Litman, eds. New York: Science House, 1970.
31. Zung, W. A self-rating depression scale. *Arch. Gen. Psychiat.* 12:63-10, 1965.
32. Beck, A., Beck, R., and Kovacs, M. Classification of suicidal behavior: I. Quantifying intent and medical lethality. *Am. J. Psychiat.* 132:285-287, 1975.

33. Murphy, G. The clinical identification of suicidal risk, Chapter 8 in *The Prediction of Suicide*, A. Beck, H. Resnik, and D. Lettieri, eds. Bowie, Md.: Charles Press, 1974.
34. Pokorny, A., and Prien, R. Lithium in treatment and prevention of affective disorder. *Dis. of Nerv. Sys.* 35:327-333, 1974.

Phenomenology and Treatment of Depression

13

# Operational Diagnosis and Diagnostic Categories of Depressive Disorders

WILLIAM W. K. ZUNG

*Nomina si nescis perit cognitio rerum.*
(Knowledge of things depends upon the knowledge of their names.)

In a continuing effort toward understanding the clinical entity which we call depressive disorders, I have previously examined the diagnosis of depression using an epistemological approach by reviewing the past and current literature on the classification of depression as a psychiatric disorder (1). In that historical review I emphasized that there is a wide divergence in the names we give to this clinical entity, and that diagnosis and treatment must go hand in hand. In a subsequent publication, I attempted to demonstrate the convergence of the diagnostic process and stressed the point that the present state of confusion referable to the names by which depressive disorders are designated is more of a dialectical dilemma, and therefore more apparent than real (2). In that review, I summarized the most-often-used psychiatric diagnostic categories in present-day practice for depressive disorders, and showed that there exists a common data base which the various nosological systems draw upon. This data base was summarized into the Affective Disorder Diagnostic Sheet, and its method of application was demonstrated in that publication.

The following figure shows in a flow diagram the relationship of these two previous efforts to the total picture with respect to the diagnosis of depressive disorders.

In the cells numbered 8, 10, 12 and 14, we have the various diagnostic categories which are used today, diagnostic categories being those depressions that have been given names as a disorder, illness, syndrome or symptom complex, and which have been perpetuated because they continue to have some value. Cell 8 represents the American Psychiatric Association Diagnostic and Statistical Manual (DSM) nomenclature, which in its present DSM-II form will be replaced by DSM-III. This revision of classification by the APA of its DSM within the space of less than a decade does not reflect progress in psychiatry as much as dissatisfaction with this classification.

Cell 10 represents those diagnostic categories which have some presumed etiological basis for their labels, such as the endogenous-reactive depressions.

Cell 12, called clinical typology, are those diagnostic categories whose labels reflect the clinical profile of the patient as he or she is perceived by the clinician. These include the agitated-retarded depressions.

Cell 14 includes what I call the statistical typology of diagnostic category of depressive disorders. Under this would be included such types as those generated by multivariate analysis of multiple-item rating scales, such as the hostile depression.

I have added an additional diagnostic category of depressive disorders to the schema and have called it biological (16). In this method of categorizing subgroups of patients with depressive disorders, biological measurements are made and patients are classified according to the results on these variables. The newer biological subgroups include those most recently proposed by Maas by the use of biochemical and pharmacological variables (3). The two groups A and B are based upon urinary levels of 3-methoxy-4-hydroxy-phenyl glycol (MHPG), and clinical response to psychotropic drugs. Group A depressed patients show: (1) low pretreatment urinary MHPG; (2) favorable response to treatment with imipramine or desipramine; (3) elevation of mood following dextroamphetamine; and (4) modest or no increment in urinary MHPG level following treatment with imipramine, desipramine, or dextroamphetamine. Group B depressed patients are characterized by: (1) normal or high urinary MHPG at pretreatment; (2) failure to respond to imipramine, but response to amitriptyline; (3) no mood change following

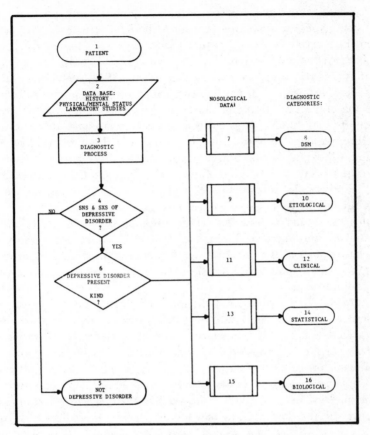

**1**   Flow chart of the diagnostic process for depressive disorders.

dextroamphetamine; and (4) decrease in urinary MHPG following treatment with imipramine, desipramine, or dextroamphetamine.

Older uses of pharmacological methods to categorize diagnostic groups include the works of Shagas (4) in his work with sedation thresholds using barbiturates, while Gellhorn and Loofbourrow (5) have summarized the work using mecholyl and noradrenaline tests.

Meldman has attempted to bring the findings of many investigators in the field of attention and arousal to bear on clinical psychiatry, with an attempt to categorize disorders as "attentional diseases" (6). Emotional disorders then, including depression, are categorized by the biological phenomena of activation, arousal, and selective attention. Affective disorders, for example, show emotional hyperattentionism, cognitive hypoattentionism, and actional hyper- or hypoattentionism. Although decrease in arousal seems apparent in severely depressed patients with associated loss of interest and decreased psychomotor activity, neurophysiological studies using electromyography (EMG) and electroencephalography (EEG) indicate the presence of increased arousal in depression. It may be that the clinically apparent slowing and retardation is a function of increase in arousal beyond the point of optimal functioning. Specific studies to support this method of categorizing patients using the attention model are those reported by Whatmore and Ellis (7,8) using EMG measures; by Wilson and Wilson (9), Paulson and Gottlieb (10), and Zung (11) using photically elicited EEG arousal responses; by Zung, Wilson, and Dodson (12) using auditory responses during all-night sleep EEG recordings.

Using the results of these tests as the nosological data base (No. 15), the diagnostic category labeled biological (No. 16) could conceivably have nomenclature such as hypothalamosis, or diencephalic diatheses. More specifically, the subcategories could reflect dysfunctions of the arousalstat, appestat, or libidostat.

Returning to the dialectical dilemma of sorting out diagnostic categories, we can see from the figure that each category requires a nosological data base (cells 7, 9, 11, 13). The construction of the Affective Disorder Diagnostic Sheet or ADDS provided a systematic method of recording the necessary data which is common to all the categories. Table 1 summarizes the use of the ADDS as a nosological data base for categorizing depressive disorders.

The question now is this: If we can define the diagnostic categories and systematize the nosological data base upon which the diagnoses are made, can we agree on what is the core psychopathology found in depression in the first place? This takes us to Cell 4 in the figure. If we can standardize the operational definition for this decision process, then we are much closer to understanding what depression is.

Operational definitions are derived from a systematic study of the signs and symptoms of depression. The contents of an operational definition should reflect both the author's intent and reason as to what he included and excluded, and the purpose to which the definition might be appropriately used. Thus an operational definition may be formulated as a method of including or excluding subjects for a study in the genetics of depression (13). Another operational definition might be formulated in order to test the validity of a specific hypothesis about depression, such as certain psychoanalytic formulations of depression (14). In this latter case, the author had converted his operational definition into a rating scale, and the items contained would reflect the psychoanalytic orientation of its author.

Hamilton published his operational definition of depression—in the form of an interviewer rating scale with 21 items and variable scoring—as a method of recording the total clinical picture of the depressed patient, reflecting the quality, quantity and clinical course of the patient's illness in its totality (15). An attempt to improve the Hamilton scale was made, and resulted in a 23-item, 4-point scoring modification called the Physician Depression Scale (16). The intent of the modification was to improve the rating scale, but not the operational definition.

The effort of the U.S.-U.K. Bilateral Diagnostic Project has largely been to investigate possible differences in the diagnostic process for schizophrenia and depressive disorders in the United States and United Kingdom. For their purposes, an operational definition of depressive disorders incorporating both U.S. and U.K. viewpoints was formulated into a rating scale called the Mental State Interview Schedule. The U.S. concept of depression was formulated into a rating scale by Spitzer, Fleiss, Burdock, and Hardesty as the Mental State Schedule (17), and the U.K. concept of depression was formulated into a rating scale by Wing, Birley, Cooper, Graham, and Isaacs as the Present State Examination (18).

In the course of developing an operational definition for depressive disorders, I had performed a literature search, summarized the most commonly found characteristics, and formulated a definition (19).

Tables 2-5 compare the operational definition which is the basis for my Self-rating Depression Scale or SDS with the operational definitions proposed by Hamilton (Table 2), Beck (Table 3), and the U.S.-U.K. Mental State Interview Schedule (Table 4), all of which are in the form of rating scales. Table 5 compares the SDS items with the Feighner definition for primary affective disorders.

In these tables, I have attempted to match the items which measure the same sign or symptom in the respective scales, with the identifying number or letter as they appear in the original works of the various authors. We can see from these tables that there are items in one operational definition that are not in another, and that the closest matching of items is between the Zung and the U.S.-U.K. definitions. Here, there is only one item which is different, that of the feeling of emptiness, which is not present in the U.S.-U.K. schedule. In addition, the one item that is present in the Hamilton, Beck, and Feighner but which is not present in the Zung definition of depression is feelings of guilt. I had purposely not included this in my operational definition because it represented a culture-bound symptom, and was rooted in a particular school of psychiatric thinking. Studies had been published which reported that African natives did not experience depression, the implication being that they were incapable of experiencing guilt (20). When

## Table 1. Diagnosis of Depressive Disorders by Typology Using the Affective Disorder Diagnostic Sheet

| Affective Disorder Diagnostic Sheet | APA DSM II | Etiological typology | | Clinical typology | | Statistical typology |
|---|---|---|---|---|---|---|
| | | Endogenous-Reactive | Unipolar-Bipolar | Psychotic-Neurotic | Primary-Secondary | |
| **A. DEMOGRAPHIC** | | | | | | |
| 1. Age | X | X | X | | | X |
| 2. Sex | | | | | | X |
| 3. Race | | | | | | X |
| 4. Marital status | | | | | | X |
| 5. Education | | | | | | X |
| 6. Occupation | | | | | | X |
| **B. PRESENT ILLNESS** | | | | | | |
| 1. Precipitating factor? | X | X | | | | X |
| 2. Sxs of depression? | X | X | X | X | X | X |
| 3. Sxs of mania? | X | | X | | X | X |
| 4. Psychotic? | X | X | | X | | X |
| 5. Duration of P.I.? | | | | | | X |
| 6. Previous tx for P.I.? | | | | | | X |

C. PAST MEDICAL
   HISTORY
   1. Premorbid
      personality
   2. Previous
      psychiatry hx?
      a. Depression?
      b. Mania?
      c. Other dx?
      d. Hospitalization?
      e. Previous tx?
      f. Age initial onset?
D. FAMILY HISTORY
   1. Depression-Mania?
   2. Other?

223

Table 2.  Comparison of the Zung and Hamilton Operational Definitions
for Depressive Disorders

| Scale Item | Zung | Hamilton | Scale Item |
|---|---|---|---|
| | I. PERVASIVE PSYCHIC DISTURBANCE | | |
| 1. | Depressed mood | Depressed mood | (1) |
| 2. | Crying spells | Depressed mood | (1) |
| | II. PHYSIOLOGICAL DISTURBANCE | | |
| 3. | Diurnal variation | Diurnal variation | (18) |
| 4. | Sleep disturbance | Insomnia early, middle, late | (4, 5, 6) |
| 5. | Decreased appetite | Somatic symptoms gastro-intestinal | (12) |
| 6. | Decreased weight | Loss of weight | (16) |
| 7. | Decreased libido | Genital symptoms | (14) |
| 8. | Constipation | Somatic symptoms, GI | (12) |
| 9. | Tachycardia | Anxiety somatic | (11) |
| 10. | Increased fatigue | Work and activities | (7) |
| | | Somatic Sxs general | (13) |
| | III. PSYCHOMOTOR DISTURBANCE | | |
| 11. | Psychomotor agitation | Agitation | (9) |
| 12. | Psychomotor retardation | Retardation | (8) |
| | IV. PSYCHOLOGICAL DISTURBANCE | | |
| 13. | Confusion | Retardation | (8) |
| 14. | Emptiness | | |
| 15. | Hopelessness | | |
| 16. | Indecisiveness | Work and activities | (7) |
| 17. | Irritability | | |
| 18. | Dissatisfaction | Work and activities | (7) |
| 19. | Personal devaluation | | |
| 20. | Suicidal rumination | Suicide | (3) |
| | | ITEMS NOT IN ZUNG | |
| | | Feelings of guilt | (2) |
| | | Anxiety Psychic | (10) |
| | | Hypochondriasis | (15) |
| | | Insight | (17) |
| | | Depersonalization and derealization | (19) |
| | | Paranoid symptoms | (20) |
| | | Obsessional and compulsive symptoms | (21) |

**Table 3.  Comparison of the Zung and Beck Operational Definitions
for Depressive Disorders**

| Scale Item | Zung | Beck | Scale Item |
|---|---|---|---|
| I. PERVASIVE PSYCHIC DISTURBANCE | | | |
| 1. Depressed mood | | Sadness | (A) |
| 2. Crying spells | | Crying | (J) |
| II. PHYSIOLOGICAL DISTURBANCE | | | |
| 3. Diurnal variation | | | |
| 4. Sleep disturbance | | Insomnia | (P) |
| 5. Decreased appetite | | Anorexia | (R) |
| 6. Decreased weight | | Weight loss | (S) |
| 7. Decreased libido | | Loss of libido | (U) |
| 8. Constipation | | Somatic preoccupation | (T) |
| 9. Tachycardia | | Somatic preoccupation | (T) |
| 10. Increased fatigue | | Fatigability | (Q) |
| III. PSYCHOMOTOR DISTURBANCE | | | |
| 11. Psychomotor agitation | | | |
| 12. Psychomotor retardation | | Work retardation | (O) |
| IV. PSYCHOLOGICAL DISTURBANCE | | | |
| 13. Confusion | | | |
| 14. Emptiness | | | |
| 15. Hopelessness | | Pessimism | (B) |
| 16. Indecisiveness | | Indecisiveness | (M) |
| 17. Irritability | | Irritability | (K) |
| 18. Dissatisfaction | | Dissatisfaction | (D) |
| | | Social withdrawal | (L) |
| 19. Personal devaluation | | Sense of failure | (C) |
| 20. Suicidal rumination | | Suicidal ideas | (I) |
| | | ITEMS NOT IN ZUNG | |
| | | Guilt | (E) |
| | | Expectation of punishment | (F) |
| | | Self-dislike | (G) |
| | | Self-accusations | (H) |
| | | Body image change | (N) |

guilt as a condition of depression was removed from the operational definition, it was found that Africans did have depressive disorders like anyone
else (21).

When a rating scale is based upon a systematic approach using an operational definition, then any change in the rating scale could constitute a

Table 4. Comparison of the Zung and Wing-Spitzer Operational
Definitions for Depressive Disorders

| Scale Item | Zung | U.S.-U.K. Mental State Interview Schedule (1968) | Items: |
|---|---|---|---|
| I. PERVASIVE PSYCHIC DISTURBANCE | | | |
| 1. Depressed mood | | Feel sad, depressed | 76:1, 77:1/33.2 |
| 2. Crying spells | | Crying | 78:1/34:2, 35:2 |
| II. PHYSIOLOGICAL DISTURBANCE | | | |
| 3. Diurnal variation | | Time feel worst | /45:2, 46:2 |
| 4. Sleep disturbance | | Sleep soundly | 24:2/50:2-56:2 |
| 5. Decreased appetite | | Appetite | 22:2/47:2 |
| 6. Decreased weight | | Lost weight | /48:2, 49:2 |
| 7. Decreased libido | | Sex life | 26:2/60:2-62:2 |
| 8. Constipation | | Bowels regular | /57:2, 58:2 |
| 9. Tachycardia | | Heart pounded | /42:1 |
| 10. Increased fatigue | | Easily tired | 32:1/33:1 |
| III. PSYCHOMOTOR DISTURBANCE | | | |
| 11. Psychomotor agitation | | Restless | 33:1/37:1, 38:1 |
| 12. Psychomotor retardation | | Slowed down | 47:1, 48:1/18:2 |
| IV. PSYCHOLOGICAL DISTURBANCE | | | |
| 13. Confusion | | Thinking impaired | 46:1/38:3, 77:1 |
| 14. Emptiness | | | |
| 15. Hopelessness | | See future | 41:3-44:3/36:2 |
| 16. Indecisiveness | | Making decisions | 45:1/78:1 |
| 17. Irritability | | Easily irritated | 27:2/64:2 |
| 18. Dissatisfaction | | Stay interested | 40:2-45:2/27:3-33:3 |
| 19. Personal devaluation | | Like yourself | 70:1-71:1/28:2 |
| 20. Suicidal rumination | | Think about dying | 16:2-21:2, 79:1/37:2 |

redefinition of the depressive disorder itself. For various reasons of their own, several authors have made attempts to improve the Self-rating Depression Scale. In one attempt, the author in his comment section stated that "devising a self-administered scale that will differentiate statistically between groups of depressed and non-depressed subjects is a ridiculously easy matter" (22). He then proceeds to use the "seven items of the SDS which showed good separation of scores between normals and depressives" as demonstrated by my work, and then added additional items (see Table 6). In this particular effort, the omission of the original items changes the operational definition of depression as a psychiatric disorder, and the addition of what

Table 5. Comparison of the Zung and Feighner Operational Definitions
for Depressive Disorders

| Scale Item | Zung | Feighner Primary Affective Disorders | Scale Item |
|---|---|---|---|
| I. PERVASIVE PSYCHIC DISTURBANCE | | | |
| 1. Depressed mood | | Depressed, sad, blue | (A) |
| 2. Crying spells | | | |
| II. PHYSIOLOGICAL DISTURBANCE | | | |
| 3. Diurnal variation | | | |
| 4. Sleep disturbance | | Sleep difficulty | (B.2) |
| 5. Decreased appetite | | Poor appetite | (B.1) |
| 6. Decreased weight | | Weight loss | (B.1) |
| 7. Decreased libido | | Decreased sexual drive | (B.5) |
| 8. Constipation | | | |
| 9. Tachycardia | | | |
| 10. Increased fatigue | | Loss of energy | (B.3) |
| III. PSYCHOMOTOR DISTURBANCE | | | |
| 11. Psychomotor agitation | | Agitation | (B.4) |
| 12. Psychomotor retardation | | Retardation | (B.4) |
| IV. PSYCHOLOGICAL DISTURBANCE | | | |
| 13. Confusion | | Diminished thinking | (B.7) |
| 14. Emptiness | | | |
| 15. Hopelessness | | Hopeless | (A) |
| 16. Indecisiveness | | | |
| 17. Irritability | | Irritable | (A) |
| 18. Dissatisfaction | | Loss of interest | (B.5) |
| 19. Personal devaluation | | | |
| 20. Suicidal rumination | | Thoughts of death | (B.8) |
| | | ITEMS NOT IN ZUNG | |
| | | Self-reproach or guilt | (B.6) |

he considered nonrelevant items is open to question. It was an unfortunate choice of items which were called control questions and which are not scored. In point of fact, all six of these items can reflect the absence or presence of a depressive disorder, and are therefore not nonrelevant.

Snaith, Ahmed, Mehta, and Hamilton published the Wakefield Self-Assessment Depression Inventory which "is therefore largely a modification and shortening of Zung's Self-rating Depression Scale" (23). Their rationale for changing the SDS was as follows: (1) Zinkin and Birtchnell (24) pointed

### Table 6. The Zung SDS Modified by Rockliff into the Self-Rating Questionnaire for Depression (SRQ-D)

| Scale Item | Zung | Rockliff | Scale Item |
|---|---|---|---|
| **I. PERVASIVE PSYCHIC DISTURBANCE** | | | |
| 1. | Depressed mood | Feel blue | (3) |
| 2. | Crying spells | Crying spells | (7) |
| **II. PHYSIOLOGICAL DISTURBANCE** | | | |
| 3. | Diurnal variation | Discouraged in A.M. | (5) |
| 4. | Sleep disturbance | Difficulty sleeping | (9) |
| 5. | Decreased appetite | Poor appetite | (11) |
| 6. | Decreased weight | | |
| 7. | Decreased libido | | |
| 8. | Constipation | | |
| 9. | Tachycardia | | |
| 10. | Increased fatigue | Tired | (1) |
| **III. PSYCHOMOTOR DISTURBANCE** | | | |
| 11. | Psychomotor agitation | | |
| 12. | Psychomotor retardation | Slowed down | |
| **IV. PSYCHOLOGICAL DISTURBANCE** | | | |
| 13. | Confusion | Think clearly | (14) |
| 14. | Emptiness | Life empty | (13) |
| 15. | Hopelessness | | |
| 16. | Indecisiveness | | |
| 17. | Irritability | | |
| 18. | Dissatisfaction | Avoid social activities | (15) |
| | | Enjoy things | (17) |
| 19. | Personal devaluation | Personal worth | (18) |
| 20. | Suicidal rumination | Better dead | (16) |
| | | **NONRELEVANT ITEMS NOT IN ZUNG:** | |
| | | Annoyed by noise? | (2) |
| | | Enjoy music? | (4) |
| | | Involved in arguments? | (6) |
| | | Headaches? | (8) |
| | | Have accidents, injuries? | (10) |
| | | Enjoy TV? | (12) |

out that 10 of the 20 items in the Zung scale occurred more frequently than others when the test was administered to depressed patients, and (2) a notable omission from both Beck's and Zung's scales are statements dealing with anxiety as a symptom. With respect to the first point, we have to keep in mind that admittedly there is a difference in the frequency with which certain signs and symptoms will occur in a population of patients with depressive disorders. But in point of fact, for any single given patient, the most important core symptom(s) for him or her may be those that have been deleted. In addition, clinical profiles of patients with respect to their symptomatology change over time, and what might be "frequent" at the first testing might not be the predominant psychopathology at a later testing. Thus, if we look at their attempt to modify the SDS, we notice missing such items as indecisiveness, suicidal ruminations, disturbances in appetite, weight and libido (see Table 7). With respect to the second point, items pertaining to anxiety were purposely not included in my scale, since I had conceptually separated depression and anxiety into two distinct disorders and formulated an operational definition for anxiety as a disorder (25-27).

A third attempt to improve the SDS was published by Wang, Treul, and Alverno, and was called the Self-Assuring Depression Scale or SADS (see Table 8). In this publication, the authors said the SADS "was constructed for the purpose of establishing a reliable and less complex self report which could be completed by most depressed patients with a minimal amount of assistance" (28). This modification has the same effect as the Wakefield in terms of modifying a rating scale and thereby altering the operational definition of depression by both errors of omission and errors of commission.

A logical step in testing the validity of the operational definition used in the SDS is to apply it in cross-cultural or cross-national studies. In the first study we reported, collaborators from Japan, Australia, Czechoslovakia, England, Germany, and Switzerland provided SDS data on populations of psychiatric patients (29). Results indicated that patients diagnosed as having depressive disorders in the countries studied had values comparable to one another and to those previously reported in U.S. studies and were significantly higher than for nondepressed patients (P = < .01). Correlations between SDS indices obtained from patients and global ratings made by clinicians showed a significantly high correlation (r = .53) for depressed patients. The ability to predict therapeutic intervention by using the SDS index alone was 87%, and 89% when the global rating was used. This is based upon an SDS index of 60 and a global rating of 3 (out of 5) as points at which intervention is indicated.

As a further step towards establishing the efficacy of the operational definition set out in the SDS, a cross cultural study of normal subjects was carried out (30). Collaborators from Czechoslovakia, England, Germany, Spain, and Sweden collected data from normal subjects. The criteria for normalcy used were that the subjects were capable of carrying out age-appropriate activities (attending school, working at a job, keeping house) and were in good physical health. The occupational distribution of the subjects ranged from professional, semiprofessional, skilled, and unskilled work-

**Table 7. The Zung SDS Modified by Snaith et al. into the Wakefield Self-Assessment Depression Inventory**

| Scale Item | Zung | Wakefield Self-Assessment Depression Inventory | Scale Item |
|---|---|---|---|
| **I. PERVASIVE PSYCHIC DISTURBANCE** | | | |
| 1. | Depressed mood | Feel sad | (1) |
| 2. | Crying spells | Weeping spells | (4) |
| **II. PHYSIOLOGICAL DISTURBANCE** | | | |
| 3. | Diurnal variation | | |
| 4. | Sleep disturbance | Sleep easily | (7) |
| | | Sleep badly | (12) |
| 5. | Decreased appetite | | |
| 6. | Decreased weight | | |
| 7. | Decreased libido | | |
| 8. | Constipation | | |
| 9. | Tachycardia | | |
| 10. | Increased fatigue | Tired no reason | (10) |
| **III. PSYCHOMOTOR DISTURBANCE** | | | |
| 11. | Psychomotor agitation | Restless | (6) |
| 12. | Psychomotor retardation | Easy do things | (2) |
| **IV. PSYCHOLOGICAL DISTURBANCE** | | | |
| 13. | Confusion | | |
| 14. | Emptiness | | |
| 15. | Hopelessness | | |
| 16. | Indecisiveness | | |
| 17. | Irritability | Irritable | (11) |
| 18. | Dissatisfaction | Enjoy things | (5) |
| | | Lost interest | (9) |
| 19. | Personal devaluation | | |
| 20. | Suicidal rumination | | |
| | | **ITEMS NOT IN ZUNG** | |
| | | Panic | (3) |
| | | Feel anxious | (8) |

ers, to students and housewives. Results of the study showed that the mean SDS indices of all subjects tested was below the 50 morbidity index. However, mean SDS indices of Czechoslovakia and Sweden were higher than the mean for all countries combined, and the mean SDS indices for England and the United States were significantly lower, thus demonstrating some differences in depressive symptomatology in normal adults among the countries studied.

Table 8.  The Zung SDS Modified by Wang, Treul, and Alverno into the
Self-Assessing Depression Scale (SADS)

| Scale Item | Zung | Wang | Scale Item |
|---|---|---|---|
| **I. PERVASIVE PSYCHIC DISTURBANCE** | | | |
| 1. | Depressed mood | Feel sad | (1) |
| 2. | Crying spells | Crying spells | (3) |
| **II. PHYSIOLOGICAL DISTURBANCE** | | | |
| 3. | Diurnal variation | | |
| 4. | Sleep disturbance | Trouble sleeping | (4) |
| 5. | Decreased appetite | Good appetite | (2) |
| 6. | Decreased weight | | |
| 7. | Decreased libido | | |
| 8. | Constipation | | |
| 9. | Tachycardia | | |
| 10. | Increased fatigue | Feel tired | (10) |
| **III. PSYCHOMOTOR DISTURBANCE** | | | |
| 11. | Psychomotor agitation | | |
| 12. | Psychomotor retardation | | |
| **IV. PSYCHOLOGICAL DISTURBANCE** | | | |
| 13. | Confusion | | |
| 14. | Emptiness | | |
| 15. | Hopelessness | Hopeful future | (8) |
| 16. | Indecisiveness | | |
| 17. | Irritability | Irritable | (7) |
| 18. | Dissatisfaction | Interest in doing things | (6) |
| 19. | Personal devaluation | Confidence | (5) |
| 20. | Suicidal rumination | | |
| | | **ITEM NOT IN ZUNG** | |
| | | Feel anxious | (9) |

Further studies using the SDS in cross-national investigations to survey symptoms in depressed and normal adults were conducted in the Netherlands (31) and in India (32). Results of both of these studies demonstrated that depressed patients scored similarly in the Netherlands and India as compared to those results previously obtained from the United States, Japan, Czechoslovakia, England, Germany, and Spain. In addition, the normal subjects scored in these two countries similarly as did normal subjects surveyed and reported in the other countries. Those results as well as those reported by others (21) indicate that there is a basic core of depressive symptoms which exhibits itself in all cultures and nations.

Attempting a definition of depressive disorder provokes a plethora of answers and questions, and we are not at the point where we can answer them with finality. We can ask questions like "What do we mean when we say somebody has a depressive disorder?" or "What are the core signs and symptoms of depression?"

Heuristically, using Occam's razor, we can reduce the observed signs and symptoms of a depressive disorder and correlate these to the most basic core functions we know, that of life itself. Life functions can be listed as:

1. Behavior
2. Growth
3. Metabolism
4. Reproduction
5. Movement
6. Responsiveness
7. Adaptation

If we use as a basic working hypothesis that every activity of a human being is the result of understandable psychic, physiological, psychomotor, and psychological processes, then we could postulate and view that disorder called depression as involving a dysfunction of life's processes. Depression as a disorder may be a syndrome of general withdrawal of the functions of life. What is this General Withdrawal Syndrome? Specifically, in the *psychic* sphere, it is a disturbance of *behavior*—of man's ability to think, feel, experience emotions, and express them. In a depressive disorder, there is a loss of these capacities. Feelings are withdrawn, and the person seems apathetic, down, disinterested in the world around him, and void of the joie de vivre. In the *physiologic* sphere, there are disturbances of *growth, metabolism,* and *reproduction.* There is decreased appetite and food intake, weight loss, impaired sleep, dysautonomias, decreased energy level, and decreased libido. In the *psychomotor* sphere, *movement* is disturbed, as expressed by agitation, restlessness, and aimless wandering. More frequent movement disturbances are those of retardation, inhibition, and slowing down of body movements and thought processes. In the *psychologic* sphere, there are disturbances in *responsiveness* and *adaptation.* The person has a loss of the sense of well-being, is confused, irritable, and unable to make decisions. Adaptation is disturbed and the person becomes less capable of coping or evolving methods of dealing with himself and the environment, and suicide becomes the only way out.

If depressive disorders are manifestations of a General Withdrawal Syndrome, then what I have just described is the "What is it?" part of the disorder. The "How is it?" aspect of the disorder is a question that is difficult to answer at this time. The "Why is it?" may be easier to answer. We know that depressive disorders are self-limiting illness, and that the patient at the end of his or her depression will achieve *restitutio ad integrum*. The variable time period during which a person is depressed may be used by the organism as a time for the processes of restoration, replacement, reconstitution, renovation, reintegration, repair, reorganization, and recovery to health.

An operational definition of a depressive disorder, if ever standardized and agreed upon, should spur us on to further studies of etiology, treatment, prognosis, and prevention. I feel certain that these altered functions of life will become generally recognized as the basis for the core signs and symptoms of depressive disorder.

## REFERENCES

1. Zung, W. W. K. From art to science: The diagnosis and treatment of depression. *Arch. Gen. Psychiat.* 29:328-337, 1973.
2. Zung, W. W. K. The diagnosis of depression—A dialectical dilemma, in Sudilovsky, Gershon and Beer, eds. *Predictiveness in Psychopharmacology: Preclinical and Clinical Aspects.* New York: Raven Press, 1975.
3. Maas, J. Biogenic amines and depression. *Arch. Gen. Psychiat.* 32:1357-1361, 1975.
4. Shagas, C., and Jones, A. A neurophysiologic test for psychiatric diagnosis: Results in 750 patients. *Am. J. Psychiat.* 114:1002-1009, 1958.
5. Gellhorn, E., and Loofbourrow, G. *Emotions and Emotional Disorders.* New York: Harper & Row, 1963.
6. Meldman, M. *Diseases of Attention and Perception.* Oxford: Pergamon Press, 1970.
7. Whatmore, G., and Ellis, R. Some neurophysiologic aspects of depressed states: An electromyographic study. *Arch. Gen. Psychiat.* 1:70-80, 1959.
8. Whatmore, G., and Ellis, R. Further neurophysiologic aspects of depressed states: An electromyographic study. *Arch. Gen. Psychiat.* 6:243-253, 1962.
9. Wilson, W., and Wilson, N. Observations on the duration of photically elicited arousal responses in depressive psychoses. *J. Nerv. Ment. Dis.* 133:438-440, 1961.
10. Paulson, G., and Gottlieb, G. A longitudinal study of the electroencephalographic arousal response in depressed patients. *J. Nerv. Ment. Dis.* 133:524-528, 1961.
11. Zung, W. W. K. Photic arousal response in depressed patients during ECT. *Acta Psychiat. Scand.* 45:295-302, 1969.
12. Zung, W. W. K., Wilson, W. P., and Dodson, W. E. Effect of depressive disorders on sleep EEG responses. *Arch. Gen. Psychiat.* 10:439-445, 1964.
13. Feighner, J. P., Robins, E., Guze, S., Woodruff, R., Winokur, G., and Munoz, R. Diagnostic criteria for use in psychiatric research. *Arch. Gen. Psychiat.* 26:57-63, 1972.
14. Beck, A. T., Ward, C. H., Mendelson, M., Mock, J., and Erbaugh, J. An inventory for measuring depression. *Arch. Gen. Psychiat.* 4:561-571, 1961.
15. Hamilton, M. A rating scale for depression. *J. Neurol. Neurosurg. Psychiat.* 23:56-62, 1960.
16. Rickels, K., Jenkins, B. W., Zamostien, B., Raab, E., and Kanther, M. Pharmaco-

therapy in neurotic depression: Differential population responses. *J. Nerv. Ment. Dis.* 145:475-485, 1968.

17. Spitzer, R. L., Fleiss, J. L., Burdock, E. I., and Hardesty, A. S. The Mental Status Schedule: rationale, reliability and validity. *Comp. Psychiat.* 5:384-395, 1964.

18. Wing, J. K., Birley, J. L. T., Cooper, J. E., Graham, P., and Isaasc, A. D. Reliability of a procedure for measuring present psychiatric state. *Br. J. Psychiat.* 112:499-515, 1967.

19. Zung, W. W. K. A Self-rating Depression Scale. *Arch. Gen. Psychiat.* 12:63-70, 1965.

20. Asuni, T. Suicide in Western Nigeria. *Br. Med. J.* 2:1091-1097, 1962.

21. Murphy, H., Wittkower, E., and Chance, N. Crosscultural inquiry into the symptomatology of depression: A preliminary report. *Transcult. Psychiat. Res.* 1:5-21, 1964.

22. Rockliff, B. W. A brief Self-rating Questionnaire for Depression (SRQ-D). *Psychosom.* 10:236-243, 1969.

23. Smith, R. P., Ahmed, S. N., Mehta, S., and Hamilton, M. Assessment of the severity of primary depressive illness—Wakefield self-assessment depression inventory. *Psychol. Med.* 1:143-149, 1971.

24. Zinkin, S., and Birtchnell, J. Unilateral electroconvulsive therapy; Its effects on memory and its therapeutic efficacy. *Br. J. Psychiat.* 144:973-988, 1968.

25. Zung, W. W. K. A rating instrument for anxiety disorders. *Psychosom.* 12:371-379, 1971.

26. Zung, W. W. K. The differentiation of anxiety and depressive disorders: A biometric approach. *Psychosom.* 12:380-384, 1971.

27. Zung, W. W. K. The differentiation of anxiety and depressive disorders: A psychopharmacological approach. *Psychosom.* 24:362-366, 1973.

28. Wang, R. I. H., Treul, S., and Alverno, L. A brief Self-Assessing Depression Scale. *J. Clin. Pharmacol.* February-March, 1975.

29. Zung, W. W. K. A cross-cultural survey of symptoms in depression. *Am. J. Psychiat.* 126:116-121, 1969.

30. Zung, W. W. K. A cross-cultural survey of depressive symptomatology in normal adults. *J. Cross-Cult. Psychol.* 3:177-183, 1972.

31. Zung, W. W. K., van Praag, H. M., Dijkstra, P., and van Winzum, C. Cross-cultural survey of symptoms in depressed and normal adults, in T. Itil, ed., *Transcultural Neuropsychopharmacology.* Bozak, Istanbul, Turkey, 1975.

32. Master, R., and Zung, W. Cross-national survey of symptoms in depressed and normal adults in India, *Arch. Gen. Psychiat.*, in press.

14

# Psychological Correlates Of Severity of Depression

GEORGE M. FAIBISH
ISHAM KIMBELL

A number of investigators have stressed the heterogeneous nature of depressive disorders (1,2). Factor analytic studies have isolated various subtypes of depression, and such subtypes frequently differ with respect to severity of the depressive illness (2,3). Although depression is generally considered a self-limiting disorder, there is significant variety in its duration and course. Despite limited modern data on duration, outcome, and relapses in neurotic and psychotic depressions other than manic-depressive conditions, a review of studies by Beck (4) revealed findings of average duration ranging from three months to one and a half years, and in older patients, up to three to five years. Yet there have been relatively few studies specifically directed at investigating factors that might be related to severity and prognosis in depression.

The present study represents an attempt to discover psychological characteristics associated with severity and outcome in depressed patients. The characteristics chosen for study were cognitive ability; psychomotor speed and skill; organization, productivity, and reality of thought; and quality of emotional expression. Measurement of these functions was obtained by means of objective and projective psychological tests. The investigation undertook to explore relationships rather than to test specific hypotheses. However, there was a general expectation that level and quality of cognitive activity would prove more predictive of severity than would emotional state or psychomotor response. It was also anticipated that, rather than a simple relationship, a patterning of relationships between psychological functions and various dimensions of depression might be found.

## METHOD

The subjects of the study were 42 male veteran recent admissions to the Psychiatric Service of the Veterans Administration Hospital, Houston. All patients were subjects in a series of investigations of drug treatment for depression, and were treated with one of several antidepressant, stimulant, or antipsychotic medications for a period of four weeks. Patients who responded well initially to a placebo trial were excluded. All patients in the present study were diagnosed depressive reaction, and any receiving some other primary diagnosis were excluded from the analysis. Patients 65 years or older were also excluded. The mean age of subjects was 45 years, with a range of 29 to 62. Average education was 9.5 years and ranged from no formal schooling to graduate study.

At the time of entry into the drug research project, patients were administered a battery of tests consisting of seven subtests from the Wechsler intelligence scales, 25 cards of the Holtzman Inkblot Technique (5), seven cards selected from the Thematic Apperception Test, 30 words of the Kent-Rosanoff word-association list, the Purdue Pegboard, Moran-Mefferd speed of closure (6), and a brief test of speed in reading and naming colors. Except for vocabulary, the Wechsler subtests were chosen for their sensitivity to depressive conditions as reported by Rapaport et al. (7). Alternate or matched forms of the Wechsler test (WAIS and Wechsler-Bellevue II), the Holtzman Inkblot Technique, the Thematic Apperception Test, Speed of Closure, and Word Association were used, and the subjects were divided into two groups, designated A and B, on the basis of the set of tests administered. The TAT stories were scored for emotional tone (8), total number of words produced, and the number produced per minute. Word-association responses were scored for reaction time and commonality of associations according to the Minnesota norms (9). Speed of closure, the Purdue Pegboard, and color reading and naming were scored for speed of response. The Wechsler tests and the Holtzman test were scored according to standard procedures.

Just prior to beginning of drug treatment, patients were interviewed and independently rated on the Inpatient Multidimensional Psychiatric Scale (IMPS) by two raters. They were similarly rated on the IMPS at the end of the treatment trial. The ratings were scored for five depressive factors and their total, and the scores of the two raters combined. The factors were based in somewhat modified form on those found by Overall (10) in a factor analysis of the IMPS; they are designated here as depressed mood, guilt, psychomotor retardation, anxiety, and physical symptoms. Subsequently, the patients' records were inspected to determine the number of weeks spent in the hospital for psychiatric reasons within the year following the study admission. The pre-treatment IMPS factor scores, the post-treatment IMPS factor scores, and the time spent in the hospital respectively constituted criterion measures of initial severity, short-term prognosis, and longer-term prognosis.

## RESULTS

Criterion ratings had high reliability, as indicated by inter-rater correlations of .95 for pre-treatment IMPS total score and .98 for post-treatment IMPS total score. Product-moment correlations were computed between the 30 individual test variables and three criterion measures; pre-treatment IMPS total, post-treatment IMPS total, and time in hospital, and the resulting correlations for groups A and B were averaged. The correlations obtained were generally of a low magnitude and failed to reach statistical significance. Correlations of age and education with the criteria were also very low, and partial correlations revealed that neither age nor education had any substantial effect on the correlations between test variables and criterion measures.

A cluster analysis of test variables was performed on the basis of hypothesized categories verified by inspection of intercorrelations. Twenty-eight of the 20 test scores were grouped into six categories, as presented in Table 1.

The category designated intellectual functioning essentially represents level of ability on the Wechsler intelligence scales. Psychomotor performance was found to split into two categories. One represented sustained activity on tasks involving activity of persistent and generally rapid type. The other, designated psychomotor reaction, appears to measure rapidity and adequacy of response to changing stimuli. Ideational activity represents organized, imaginative ideation, well-defined ego boundaries, and awareness of convention; it corresponds to Holtzman's Factor I. Mental control represents well-

**Table 1. Psychological Test Categories and
Component Variables**

| Psychological Category | Component Test Variables |
| --- | --- |
| Intellectual Functioning | Wechsler Arithmetic, Similarities, Digit Span, Vocabulary, Digit Symbol, Picture Completion, Block Design. |
| Psychomotor Sustained | Wechsler Digit Symbol; TAT Total Words; Purdue Pegboard; Speed of Closure; Color Naming and Reading. |
| Psychomotor Reaction | TAT Words per minute; Holtzman Inkblot Responses, Reaction Time; Word-Association Reaction Time, Commonality. |
| Ideational Activity | Holtzman Inkblot Movement, Integration, Barrier, Popular. |
| Mental Control | Holtzman Inkblot Form Definiteness, Form Appropriateness, Pathognomic Verbalization, Penetration, Color. |
| Emotional Control | TAT Emotional Tone; Holtzman Inkblot Anxiety, Hostility. |

defined, realistic, controlled perceptions, and is consistent with Holtzman's Factor IV. Emotional control reflects the absence of disturbed emotional reactions expressed in fantasy activity; it bears some relationship to Factor III found by Holtzman (5).

To estimate the correlations of the test categories with severity of pretreatment depression, the correlation of variables within a given category with each of the IMPS factors and their total was averaged. The resulting matrix of average correlations is presented in Table 2. Since the test categories are scored in a positive—i.e., "good" direction—whereas the IMPS is scored in the direction of pathology, a negative correlation means that high psychological performance is associated with a low degree of pathology.

The average correlations between psychological functioning and clinical severity are of a low order. Averaging of the correlations tends to minimize the multivariate regression and is therefore a very conservative and undervalued estimate of the true relationship. Table 3 presents the highest correlations found for each psychological category with a given criterion factor. Such a correlation is also a conservative estimate, and represents the minimum possible value of the best fit between weighted variables of a test category and a criterion.

Table 2. Average Correlations between Psychological Test Categories and Pre-Treatment Clinical Ratings

| Psychological Test Category | Pre-Treatment IMPS Factor | | | | | |
|---|---|---|---|---|---|---|
| | Depressed Mood | Guilt | Psychomotor Retardation | Anxiety | Physical Symptoms | Total Factors |
| Intellectual Functioning | 02 | 05 | -10 | 06 | -02 | 01 |
| Psychomotor Sustained | -08 | 11 | -15 | -13 | -04 | -06 |
| Psychomotor Reaction | 09 | -04 | -07 | 01 | -05 | -04 |
| Ideational Activity | -04 | -13 | -02 | -08 | -19 | -16 |
| Mental Control | -04 | -10 | -01 | 01 | 10 | -05 |
| Emotional Control | 01 | 05 | 14 | -01 | 11 | 07 |

Interpreting Tables 2 and 3 together, a pattern of relationships between psychological functions and severity of clinical factors is discernible. First, level of intellectual functioning shows only a limited relation to clinical severity; a low level of intellectual ability is mildy related to greater psychomotor retardation. The next category, sustained psychomotor skill, shows a similar relationship to clinical retardation and apparently is also disturbed by depressed or anxious affect. It bears a modest relationship to general severity of symptoms. Psychomotor reactivity also tends to be negatively related to clinical severity, but the magnitude of the relationships tends to be less than for sustained activity, and its relationship to affect—i.e., depression and anxiety—is ambiguous. Ideational activity shows the greatest and most consistent relationship to symptom severity. Patients whose level of active, articulated perception is diminished generally show greater pathology, whether mental, affective, or physical. The relationships for controlled mental functions tend to be negative, although they are low; affective expression of guilt appears related to poor mental control, whereas physical symptomatology is related·to high control of thought processes; this suggests the possibility of some inhibitory factor at work. Emotional control has a similar relationship to degree of physical symptomatology and also shows a mild relationship to psychomotor retardation. Like mental control, emotional control is associated with less disturbed affect, as reflected in lower expression of depressed or anxious mood. Emotional inhibition also appears related to interference with psychomotor and biological functions.

The same statistical procedure was followed to analyze the relationship of pre-treatment psychological measures to post-treatment IMPS ratings as for the pre-treatment ratings. The results for average test correlations are presented in Table 4 and the results for maximum correlations within each test category in Table 5.

The average correlations between test clusters and post-treatment factor ratings are quite low, but the maximum correlations are more substantial. A high level of ideational activity tends to be predictive of low residual pathology, except for the clinical retardation factor. In a number of instances, a higher level of functioning predicts relatively high subsequent pathology— i.e., poorer treatment outcome. This relationship applies particularly to intellectual and sustained psychomotor function, and to some extent to control of affectively disturbing fantasies. Patients initially displaying better cognitive and psychomotor functioning tend particularly to show residual affective symptoms of depression, guilt, and anxiety. Two of the psychological categories, psychomotor reaction and mental control, failed to show any substantial relationship to post-treatment levels of pathology.

**Table 3. Maximum Correlations between Psychological Test Category Variables and Pre-Treatment Clinical Ratings**

| Psychological Test Category | Pre-Treatment IMPS Factors | | | | | |
| --- | --- | --- | --- | --- | --- | --- |
| | Depressed Mood | Guilt | Psychomotor Retardation | Anxiety | Physical Symptoms | Total Factors |
| Intellectual Functioning | 12 | 18 | −22 | 12 | −14 | 07 |
| Psychomotor Sustained | −23 | 18 | −25 | −31 | −12 | −25 |
| Psychomotor Reaction | 28 | −19 | −12 | −14 | −16 | −18 |
| Ideational Activity | −14 | −24 | −14 | −27 | −30 | −28 |
| Mental Control | −15 | −24 | −19 | −10 | 20 | −19 |
| Emotional Control | −23 | 16 | 15 | −26 | 40 | 19 |

Table 4. Average Correlations between Psychological Test Categories and Post-Treatment Clinical Variables

| Psychological Test Category | Post-Treatment IMPS Factor | | | | | | | Weeks in Hospital |
|---|---|---|---|---|---|---|---|---|
| | Depressed Mood | Guilt | Psychomotor Retardation | Anxiety | Physical Symptoms | Total Factors | | |
| Intellectual Functioning | 07 | 21 | -07 | 12 | 07 | 11 | | -01 |
| Psychomotor Sustained | 08 | 27 | -02 | 16 | 05 | 15 | | -19 |
| Psychomotor Reaction | -03 | 01 | -07 | 09 | -05 | -01 | | 00 |
| Ideational Activity | -10 | -03 | 13 | 00 | -05 | -02 | | -14 |
| Mental Control | -04 | -02 | 10 | -03 | -02 | 00 | | 00 |
| Emotional Control | 08 | -06 | -03 | 09 | 01 | 02 | | 06 |

Table 5. Maximum Correlations between Psychological Test Category Variables and Post-Treatment Clinical Variables

| Psychological Test Category | Post-Treatment IMPS Factors | | | | | | |
|---|---|---|---|---|---|---|---|
| | Depressed Mood | Guilt | Psychomotor Retardation | Anxiety | Physical Symptoms | Total Factors | Weeks in Hospital |
| Intellectual Functioning | 22 | 32 | −23 | 26 | 29 | 29 | 25 |
| Psychomotor Sustained | 27 | 46 | 25 | 39 | 19 | 40 | −28 |
| Psychomotor Reaction | −15 | −11 | −15 | 26 | −12 | −14 | 21 |
| ideational Activity | −29 | −24 | 39 | −23 | −28 | −29 | −20 |
| Mental Control | −16 | −11 | 23 | −26 | 19 | −18 | −14 |
| Emotional Control | 35 | −17 | −18 | 14 | 24 | 20 | 15 |

### Table 6. Average Intercorrelations of IMPS Factors

| | Pre-Treatment IMPS | | | | |
|---|---|---|---|---|---|
| Factor | Depressed Mood | Guilt | Psychomotor Retardation | Anxiety | Physical Symptoms |
| Depressed Mood | | 33 | 26 | 71 | 09 |
| Guilt | | | 27 | 17 | 02 |
| Psychomotor Retardation | | | | 21 | 38 |
| Anxiety | | | | | 17 |
| | Post-Treatment IMPS | | | | |
| Depressed Mood | | 75 | 34 | 72 | 77 |
| Guilt | | | 44 | 69 | 51 |
| Psychomotor Retardation | | | | 46 | 41 |
| Anxiety | | | | | 44 |

With regard to prediction of longer-term prognosis in terms of amount of hospitalization, sustained psychomotor activity and ideational activity are the only pre-treatment psychological factors related to prognosis to any appreciable degree. In both cases, a high level of cognitive activity tends to predict less need for continued or repeated hospitalization. It should be noted that psychomotor activity of a sustained type shows a different direction of prediction for short-term and longer-term prognosis.

Of some interest are the relationships found within the set of criteria used in the study. Product-moment correlations among the pre-treatment IMPS factors and among the post-treatment IMPS factors are presented in Table 6. The pre-treatment ratings generally show low intercorrelations, confirming the relative independence of the factors originally extracted by Overall (10). The single exception is the fairly high correlation between depressed mood and anxiety. The intercorrelations are much higher for the post-treatment ratings. This would indicate that depressive manifestations are more global following treatment than before.

The relationship between pre-treatment and post-treatment ratings is presented in Table 7. They indicate the extent to which pre-treatment levels of severity predict residual levels of pathology. The correlations in general tend to be positive but low. The correlations in the diagonal of the matrix, underlined in the table, represent the relationship between pre- and post-levels for the same factor. They are higher than the others, but still of a low order. The ability of pre-treatment symptoms, including global sympto-matology, to predict overall residual pathology is also very limited, as indicated by their low correlations with the total post-rating. A degree of relationship is present for initial emotional disturbances involving depressed, guilty, and anxious feelings, while earlier psychomotor and physical disorder bear a negligible relationship, if any, to post-treatment general pathology.

Initial severity of symptomatology does even more poorly in predicting subsequent duration of the depressive illness, as estimated by hospitalization over a period of a year. Table 8 presents the correlations between pre-treatment factors and length of hospitalization. The relationships between symptomatology following four weeks of treatment and length of hospitalization, also presented in Table 8, are a little greater but still of low degree and variable. Affective symptoms of depression or anxiety tend to predict longer hospitalization.

## DISCUSSION

The low order and uncertain significance of the relationships found between psychological functioning and severity or prognosis in depression make any conclusions very tentative indeed. The use of a variety of medications likely attenuated correlations between psychological functioning and the measures of outcome because of varying treatment effects, although such heterogeneity would render the results more generalizable. Moreover, causal relationships cannot be inferred, particularly with regard to the measures taken at the same time.

If any interpretation of the results can be made, it is that the relationship between psychological variables and clinical status is patterned and complex rather than simple, the relationship varying according to the particular psychological factor, the particular clinical factor, and the course of disorder. Perhaps a few tentative generalizations can be made. Trends in the data suggest that depressed patients who manifest a more active, productive, organized mental life will show less pathology initially and following treatment and have a better prognosis with respect to subsequent hospitalization.

**Table 7. Average Correlations between Pre-Treatment IMPS Factors and Post-Treatment IMPS-Factors**

| Pre-Treatment IMPS Factors | Post-Treatment IMPS Factors | | | | | |
|---|---|---|---|---|---|---|
| | Depressed Mood | Guilt | Psychomotor Retardation | Anxiety | Physical Symptoms | Total Factors |
| Depressed Mood | 33 | 22 | −07 | 20 | 40 | 27 |
| Guilt | 17 | 38 | 21 | 18 | 19 | 29 |
| Psychomotor Retardation | 01 | −11 | 43 | −01 | 18 | 09 |
| Anxiety | 31 | 34 | 06 | 35 | 33 | 35 |
| Physical Symptoms | −09 | −14 | 26 | −06 | 09 | −02 |
| Total Factors | 22 | 27 | 25 | 23 | 34 | 31 |

Note: Underlined values represent pre- and post-rating of the same factor.

Table 8. Average Correlations between Pre- and Post-IMPS Factors
and Length of Time Hospitalized

| Factor | Pre-Treatment IMPS | Post-Treatment IMPS |
|---|---|---|
| Depressed Mood | 03 | 23 |
| Guilt | −12 | −09 |
| Psychomotor Retardation | −01 | −12 |
| Anxiety | 10 | 25 |
| Physical Symptoms | 06 | 13 |
| Total Factors | −01 | 11 |

Patients who have the ability to perform rapidly and continuously appear to manifest less severe initial pathology and better long-term prognosis, although short-term outcome may be rather poor. A high degree of control over emotionally disturbing fantasies in test productions is related to clinical inhibitory features involving a diminution in expression of emotional distress, psychomotor activity, and biological functions. To a less clear extent, strictly controlled mental processes may bear some relationship to an excessively inhibited clinical state. The converse of this, that deficits in mental and emotional control are associated with heightened symptoms of disturbed affect, is consistent with Beck's theories regarding the relationship between cognitive disturbances and negative emotional attitudes in depression (4). Taken together, all of the above findings suggest that the dynamic, participatory, drive-related aspects of cognition and emotion may be the most significant factors involved in the severity of depressive features.

If the psychological correlates are of a low order, so too are the relationships found among the clinical variables themselves, whether taken at the same or different times. The various symptom groups were moderately related only after treatment, perhaps indicating that patients improve or fail to improve in a generalized manner. Initial severity of depressive symptoms predicts short-term prognosis in either a rather specific or modest way, or both. Earlier levels of severity predict later hospitalization only to a limited extent, and initial severity does not do so to any significant degree at all.

The findings of other investigators indicate that composition, severity, and prognosis of depressive disorders have limited or complex relationships. Grinker et al. (11) extracted different factors in analyzing features of depression, depending on whether ratings were based on subjective concerns or observable behavior, with little relationship between the two sets of depressive manifestations. Bromet, Harrow, and Tucker (12) found little or no relationship of demographic characteristics, childhood events, or prior length of illness to length of hospitalization in depressives treated with antidepressant medication. More severe symptoms gave a worse prognosis, although the correlations on average were quite small. Other studies, however, have shown that endogenous depressions respond better than neurotic depressions to either ECT or antidepressant medication (13,14), although the neurotic or reactive depressions are typically considered to be less severe (2). Jacobs et al. (15) compared response to psychotherapy (with or without medication) of depressed patients who were either withdrawn and felt helpless and worthless or were impulsive and defensive. The withdrawn, helpless group manifested greater initial emotional distress and better outcome. Overall et al. (16) found a differential pattern of outcome, depending on type of depression and type of drug administered. Patients who were more depressed and retarded responded better to an antidepressant, whereas those who were more anxious showed more improvement with phenothiazine treatment. These studies as well as the present one attest to the complex, heterogeneous nature of depression with respect to symptomatology, severity, and prognostic features.

## REFERENCES

1. Blumenthal, M. D., Heterogeneity and research on depressive disorders. *Arch. Gen. Psychiat.* 24:524-531, 1971.
2. Klerman, G. L. Clinical research in depression. *Arch. Gen. Psychiat.* 24:305-319, 1971.
3. Hamilton, M., and White, J. M. Clinical syndromes in depressive states. *J. Ment. Sci.* 105:985-998, 1959.
4. Beck, A. T. *Depression: Clinical, Experimental and Theoretical Aspects.* New York: Harper & Row, 1967.
5. Holtzman, W. H., Thorpe, J. S., Swartz, J. D., et al. *Inkblot Perception and Personality.* Austin: University of Texas Press, 1961.
6. Moran, L. J., and Mefferd, R. B., Jr. Repetitive psychometric measures. *Psychol. Rep.* 5:269-275, 1959.
7. Rapaport, D., Gill, M., and Schafer, R. *Diagnostic Psychological Testing*, Vol. 1. Chicago: Year Book Publishers, 1945.
8. Zubin, J., Eron, L. D., and Schumer, F. *An Experimental Approach to Projective Techniques.* New York: Wiley, 1965.
9. Russell, W. A., and Jenkins, J. J. *The Complete Minnesota Norms for Responses to 100 Words from the Kent-Rosanoff Word Association Test.* Minneapolis: University of Minnesota Department of Psychology, 1954.
10. Overall, J. E. Dimensions of manifest depression. *J. Psychiat. Res.* 1:239-245, 1963.

11. Grinker, R. R., Miller, J., Sabshin, M., et al. *The Phenomena of Depressions.* New York: Hoeber, 1961.
12. Bromet, E., Harrow, M., and Tucker, G. J. Factors related to short-term prognosis in schizophrenia and depression. *Arch. Gen. Psychiat.* 25:148-154, 1971.
13. Carney, M. W. P., Roth, M., and Garside, R. F. The diagnosis of depressive syndromes and the prediction of E.C.T. response. *Br. J. Psychiat.* 111:659-674, 1965.
14. Kiloh, L. G., Ball, J. R. B., and Garside, R. F. Prognostic factors in treatment of depressive states with imipramine. *Br. Med. J.* 1:1225-1227, 1962.
15. Jacobs, M. A., Muller, J. J., Skinner, J. C., et al. Personality characteristics of depressive patients associated with improvement in an open-ward setting. *J. Nerv. Ment. Dis.* 153:126-132, 1971.
16. Overall, J. E., Hollister, L. E., Johnson, M., et al. Nosology of depression and differential response to drugs. *JAMA* 195:946-948, 1966.

15

# Mood-Active Agents
# In Depression

### JOSEPH C. SCHOOLAR

It has been said that depression is one of the commonest illnesses of mankind; certainly it is one of the commonest that a psychiatrist is called on to treat. It has been said further that depression is one of the diseases most often mistreated. Factors impinging on a patient that may eventuate in depression are multiple; they may be internal or external, and they may be broadly classified as psychological, social, and biological. Robert Burton was indeed prophetic in commenting on the multivaried approach necessary in the treatment of melancholy; ". . . him that shall take upon him to cure it . . . will have to be a magician, a chemist, a philosopher, an astrologer" (1).

In this paper I shall discuss briefly the psychotropic medications that may be used to treat depression, focusing, in Burton's schema, on the role of the psychopharmacologist.

Three pharmacological approaches to the treatment of depression are in current use: the tricyclic antidepressants, the monoamine oxidase inhibitors, and lithium.

## TRICYCLIC ANTIDEPRESSANTS

Although the tricyclic antidepressants (Figure 1) were not the first pharmacological agents to be used, they are the drugs most widely chosen, and statistically they are probably the most efficacious.

Tricyclics are structurally quite similar to the phenothiazines and the thioxanthenes, which helps to explain the similarity in side effects of the three classes of compounds.

The basic phenothiazine nucleus consists of three benzene rings (Figure 1, A, B and C), the B-ring containing sulfur and nitrogen. Significant changes in activity may be wrought by substitution: substitution at position 2 results in quantitative changes in drug action; qualitative changes result from substitution at position 10.

The thioxanthenes differ from the phenothiazines in that the B-ring nitrogen has been replaced with a carbon, and there is a double-bond linkage at position 10.

The first group of tricyclic antidepressants are represented by the third structure of Figure 1, the dibenzazepines, or iminodibenzyls. A seven-membered ring replaces the six-membered ring at B, with the nitrogen retained. Drugs in this class are the imipramines.

In the dibenzocycloheptenses (Figure 1), the structural change is the same as that of the thioxanthenes—namely, the nitrogen is replaced by a carbon, and a double bond connects the side chain. Antidepressants of this class are amitriptyline, nortriptyline, and protriptyline.

Finally, an oxygen may be included in the seven-membered B-ring to constitute the dibenzoxepins. The major drug of importance of this class is doxepin.

Table 1 shows the side chains of the different classes of tricyclics and their average daily dosage range. The drug tolerance of patients varies, and the rapidity with which the daily dosage is increased must be individualized for each patient depending on the appearance of side effects, especially orthostatic hypotension. A rule of thumb may be to begin with one-third of the projected therapeutic level and increase the dose stepwise until the full level is reached. Certainly the patient should be fully informed of both the therapeutic and undesirable actions of the drug.

An adequate therapeutic trial of any antidepressant compound requires three weeks at full therapeutic dosage before failure may be said to have occurred and treatment changed to an alternative drug or treatment modality. Attempts have been made to shorten the lag time between drug institution and the onset of beneficial effects by using side-chain demethylation (desipramine, nortriptyline), but these efforts have been disappointing.

Phenothiazine Nucleus

Thioxanthenes

Dibenzazepines

Dibenzocycloheptenes

Dibenzoxepins

**1**    Tricyclic antidepressants.

Efforts have long been made to define the clinical manifestations that would constitute a rational basis for selecting one antidepressant over another. At present, drug side effects are probably the basis for such selection as often as are primary therapeutic actions. Some agents have been said to be more "activating" than others, to increase motivation in the insufficiently

## Table 1. Tricyclic Antidepressants

| Substituent | Generic Name | Trade Name | Dosage (mgm/day) |
|---|---|---|---|
| *Iminodibenzyls* | | | |
| $CH_2CH_2CH_2N(CH_3)_2$ | Imipramine | Tofranil | 100-300 |
| $CH_2CH_2CH_2NHCH_3$ | Desipramine | Pertofrane Norpramin | 100-300 |
| *Dibenzocycloheptenes* | | | |
| $CHCH_2CH_2N(CH_3)_2$ | Amitriptyline | Elavil | 100-300 |
| $CHCH_2CH_2NHCH_3$ | Nortriptyline | Aventyl | 50-150 |
| $CH_2CH_2CH_2NHCH_3$ | Protriptyline | Vivactil | 15-60 |
| *Dibenzoxepins* | | | |
| $CHCH_2CH_2N(CH_3)_2$ | Doxepin | Sinequan Adapin | 50-300 |

motivated patient or to reduce withdrawal and the like, but in my view these finer distinctions have not been clinically impressive. Thus one is left with such generalizations as the sedating properties of amitriptyline and its consequent utility in treating the sleepless, depressed patient or the patient who manifests a significant anxiety component, and with the antianxiety properties of doxepin. Beyond this point target-symptom specificity is not well established.

A more rational approach to drug selection and dosage adjustment would be to correlate bioavailability and therapeutic efficacy, and recent work in this area is both exciting and promising. Asberg and co-workers (2), using nortriptyline, found that antidepressant action requires serum levels of 160 to 200 ng/ml. They further reported that adults need 150 mg/day of oral nortriptyline to achieve this serum level, and that higher doses actually decrease antidepressant action. These authors therefore describe a "therapeutic window" of effective dosage range, effectiveness decreasing on either side of the window. Their report has been substantiated by Kragh-Sorensen et al. (3).

Glassman (4) reported a different situation for amitriptyline. Agreeing that a range of 160 to 200 ng/ml is required for adequate therapeutic effect, he reported a different dose-response curve. At an oral dose of 3.5 mg/kg (240 mg/day), he found that only 60 percent of his patients reached a serum level of 170 ng/ml; he found no decrease in effectiveness at higher daily dosages. These reports, if substantiated, indicate that specific pharmacodynamics and dose-response relationship must be developed for each agent. The information might well be the first step toward developing methods for early prediction of an individual patient's response to a particular drug.

With respect to dosage schedule, there has been an increasing practice among clinicians to instruct patients, once their dosage is stabilized, to take all of their daily medication at bedtime. Patients seem to sleep better and to tolerate any remaining hypotensive effects better, without loss of therapeutic effect. One must remember, however, that the severity of certain side effects may be increased by flooding the system with a large amount of drug once a day. This observation applies particularly to the uncertain effects of the tricyclics on cardiac irregularities and repolarization. It would therefore seem much wiser to have stabilized patients follow an every-twelve-hours regimen until the nature and significance of these adverse effects are precisely determined for each patient individually.

Adverse effects have been thoroughly investigated by Cole and Davis (5). Generally, they indicate changes in the autonomic, cardiovascular, and central nervous systems, or are secondary to an allergic or idiosyncratic response to the drug. In my view, patients should be advised of possible side effects so that if they occur the patient may participate in their management. Patients should also be told that most, but not all, side effects occur early in treatment and are transitory.

The most common adverse effects of tricyclic antidepressants are summarized in Table 2. Whether their occurrence requires dosage reduction, with subsequent cautious attempts to increase the dose, or discontinuation of the drug and selection of another agent or modality, depends upon a careful consideration of the severity of the adverse effect relative to the clinical status of the patient and the urgency of treatment. Whether to continue the drug, reduce the dose, or discontinue the drug altogether are therefore matters of clinical judgment. Reinstitution of a discontinued drug after a particular side effect is cleared, usually, but not always, evokes the adverse effect again. Further, cross-sensitivity between classes of drugs (iminodibenzyls and dibenzocycloheptenes) is the rule, so that switching from one class to another is ordinarily to no avail. Less is known about cross-sensitivity between dibenzoxepin and the other classes.

## Table 2.  Tricyclic Antidepressants

---

Side effects

    Anticholinergic:  dry mouth, hypotension, constipation, edema, glaucoma

    Allergic & hypersensitivity:  skin rash, jaundice, agranulocytosis, leukopenia

    Cardiovascular:  QT, T, S-T changes

    CNS:  fine tremor, twitching, convulsions, ataxia, dysarthria

Overdosage

    CNS:  agitation, delirium, convulsions, bowel and bladder paralysis; shock

    Cardiac:  rhythm disturbances; A-V; I-V block

Treatment

    Lavage

    Anticonvulsants

    Respiratory support

---

Dryness of the mouth generally lessens with time, and the patient may find it reduced or at least more tolerable by using chewing gum or lozenges. Hypotension is orthostatic and may be particularly dangerous in the elderly. Depending on its degree, patients may be instructed to exercise their limbs before rising from a lying or sitting position and to get up slowly. Known or suspected glaucomatous patients should have tonometric examinations.

Development of a skin rash calls for drug discontinuation and antihistaminic or other therapy. Jaundice is the cholestatic, obstructive type, and it is rarer than was originally reported. In contrast to the hepatic dysfunction that may be caused by monoamine oxidase inhibitors (*v.i.*) , it is rarely life-threatening.

Adverse CNS effects are uncommon at therapeutic dosage levels. They are reported to reduce the convulsive threshold, however, which is significant for treating patients with known or suspected epileptogenic foci (5) .

Currently there is considerable interest in the cardiac effects of the tricyclics and the phenothiazines. Reported changes include T-wave depression, lengthening of the S-T segment, and widening of the QRS complex. Arrhythmias have been reported at high dosages, with atrioventricular or intraventricular block. Whether these changes occur, under what conditions, whether they are attributable to the tricyclics, and their significance to the clinical status of the patient are questions being actively investigated. Patients with preexisting cardiac disease may well be more susceptible to these effects. At this juncture it is important to recognize that cardiac changes may occur, and that a heightened index of suspicion is necessary for patients with known or suspected cardiac disease.

Instances of successful suicides through acute overdosage with tricyclics are relatively rare; suicidal patients seem to prefer barbiturates or other agents. When overdosage does occur, however, complications obviously depend on the amount of drug taken. Treatment includes gastric lavage, anticonvulsive therapy, and respiratory support.

A number of investigators, among them Cole and Davis (5), reported that imipramine and amitriptyline may precipitate episodes of confusion, schizophrenia, or manic excitement. The current belief is that such episodes occur in patients who are predisposed to the underlying disease and thus require a reevaluation of their clinical data. Organic disease such as a space-taking lesion must be ruled out. In my own experience, such episodes occur early in the treatment course if they occur at all.

## MONOAMINE OXIDASE INHIBITORS

The monoamine oxidase (MAO) inhibitors entered the psychiatric realm serendipitously, and although they preceded the tricyclics, their use is now generally reserved for patients refractory to the tricyclic group, not only on the basis of efficacy but, more importantly, because of the MAO inhibitors' potential toxicity and adverse side effects. In my view they have a definite place in the treatment of carefully selected patients who are capable of following the necessary dietary and other requirements; to ignore their role in the pharmacological armamentarium would be a therapeutic error.

Figure 2 shows the MAO inhibitors in common usage, their formulas, and an acceptable dosage range. Again, the drug should be introduced at a low level and the dose increased stepwise. For many clinicians, the non-hydrazine drug, tranylcypromine, is the most popular.

Adverse effects of the MAO inhibitors include a variety of reactions (Table 3). Autonomic side effects such as dry mouth, constipation, and hypotension usually occur early in the treatment course, if at all; urinary hesitation and impotence have been reported.

Liver dysfunction, which occurs only with the hydrazines and has not been reported in patients on tranylcypromine, is a serious possibility. In contradistinction to the obstructive jaundice sometimes seen from the tricyclics, the jaundice caused by MAO inhibitors is the parenchymatous type. Whether it is the result of allergy or another condition such as enzyme deficiency is unknown.

| | Generic Name | Trade Name | Dosage (mgm/day) |
|---|---|---|---|
| *Hydrazines* | | | |
| CONHNHCH(CH₃)₂ (pyridine ring) | Iproniazid | -- | |
| CONHNHCH₂CH₂CONHCH₂ (pyridine ring + benzene ring) | Nialamide | Niamid | 150-225 |
| CONHNHCH₂ (isoxazole ring with CH₃, benzene ring) | Isocarboxazid | Marplan | 20-60 |
| CH₂CH₂NHNH₂ (benzene ring) | Phenelzine | Nardil | 45-75 |
| *Nonhydrazines* | | | |
| CH—CH-NH₂ with CH₂ (cyclopropane, benzene ring) | Trancylcypromine | Parnate | 20-30 |

**2**    MAO inhibitors.

Patients who ingest foods high in tyramine may suffer a pressor reaction with increased blood pressure, nausea, vomiting, occipital headache, stiff neck, and intracranial bleeding. This phenomenon, at first not understood, resulted in several deaths in the early 1960s. Thus it is imperative that patients receiving MAO inhibitors exclude from their diet foods high in tyramine. The list given in the current *Physicians' Desk Reference* (6) includes cheese (especially strong or aged varieties), sour cream, Chianti, sherry, beer, pickled herring, liver, canned figs, raisins, chocolate, soy sauce, the pods of broad beans (fava beans), yeast extracts, or meat prepared with tenderizers. The pressor effect is also potentiated by sympathomimetic amines, histamine, and bee venom (5).

Adverse CNS effects of the MAOI's include agitation and confusion. Precipitation of frank schizophrenic episodes has been reported, again presumably in patients with an underlying susceptibility to the disorder. Other reports are that depressed patients may convert from a retarded to an agitated state, even to frank hypomania.

**Table 3. MAO Inhibitors**

Side effects

    Autonomic: dry mouth, dizziness, hypotension, constipation, hesitation, impotence

    Allergic: hepatocellular damage (hydrazines only)

    Pressor: w/tyramine. Stiff neck, occipital headache, nausea, vomiting, ↑ BP →intra-cranial bleeding

    Combination w/tricyclics: restlessness, dizziness, tremulousness, twitching, convulsions, hyperpyrexia →death

    CNS: mental clouding, confusion, agitation, ppt. schizophrenia

The ability of MAO components to potentiate the action of a variety of drugs—sympathomimetic amines, opiates (meperidine), barbiturates, methyldopa, ganglionic blocking agents, procaine, other anesthetic agents, and chloral hydrate—underscores the need for a careful drug history.

Of special significance is the ability of the tricyclics and the MAO inhibitors to potentiate one another. Patients who receive both classes of drugs, either concomitantly or in close temporal proximity, may experience hypertensive crises. It has therefore long been the rule to allow a two-week drug-free period for wash-out purposes before changing a patient's prescription from one of these classes of antidepressants to the other. Although there has been a recent reevaluation of the possibilities of mixing MAO inhibitors and tricyclics, using small doses and careful monitoring, the technique must be considered investigative and not for general clinical use.

Overdosage from the MAO inhibitors usually begins to be manifested by agitation, and it may proceed through tachycardia, hyperthermia, increased respiratory rate, hyperreflexia, and ultimately coma. Cole and Davis (5) point out that a lag period of one to six hours may occur between ingestion and manifestations of overdosage; clinicians should be aware of this lest they be lulled into a false sense of security. Chlorpromazine is reported as useful in treating overdosage, presumably because of its adrenergic blocking action.

## LITHIUM

Lithium has now been in general psychiatric use for a quarter of a century, and for five years in the United States. Part of the reason for the delayed introduction of lithium in this country is the fact that lithium salts initially were used as a salt substitute by patients on low-sodium diets. Since the monitoring of serum lithium levels was uncommon at that time, toxic manifestations were frequent. With more refined and precise measuring techniques, this difficulty has been overcome, so the lithium ion has become well established as uniquely effective in the treatment of affective illness.

The literature on lithium is voluminous. Excellent overviews and statements of clinical use include the reports of the Veterans Administration Cooperative Studies (7,8,9,10), the report of the American Psychiatric Association Task Force on the Current Status of Lithium Therapy (11), and the five-year review by Baldessarini and Lapinski (12). What follows has been taken largely from these sources.

There seems to be general agreement on several aspects of the current status of lithium, indications for its use, and its efficacy in manic-depressive illness. The APA task force was quite clear in its statement that "lithium is the treatment of first choice" in the acute *manic* episode. The group was pointedly cautious, however, in its conclusions and recommendations pertaining to the use of lithium in the acute depressive episode. The V.A. Cooperative Studies (8) compared the efficacy of lithium to that of imipramine in treatment of both bipolar and unipolar depressive patients. The investigators found lithium to be superior to imipramine in treatment of the depressive phase of bipolar illness, but found imipramine more useful for treating clearly unipolar disease.

Thus the current solid indication for lithium therapy is in the treatment of bipolar illness—that is, therapeutically in acute manic episodes and prophylactically for recurrent depressions.

Lithium has been given therapeutic trials for other disorders, particularly those with an affective component, such as schizo-affective schizophrenia, and those with significant cyclicity. In these cases the utility of lithium has been disappointing, but it should be recognized that active research is continuing and that definitive statements must be made with caution.

Proper patient selection is of paramount importance in lithium therapy. Patients who are impulsive, apt to comply poorly with dosage regimens, and especially suicidal patients are not good candidates for the use of lithium, particularly if they are outpatients.

Laboratory studies prior to the administration of lithium are dictated by the possible side effects of the drug. Lithium is excreted almost totally by the kidneys in rates related to age and dependent on the availability of sodium. That is, if sodium is unavailable, lithium is reabsorbed from the proximal tubules. Thus, as pointed out by the APA task force, "significant renal disorder that might impair adequate elimination of the lithium ion is an absolute contraindication" to the use of lithium. Any regimen that requires a diuretic or restricted dietary intake of sodium would therefore become a relative contraindication. Other relative contraindications named by the task force are significant cardiac disease and organic brain disease. In addition, lithium is known to affect both thyroid size and function in a few cases. Preparation for lithium usage would therefore routinely include urine analysis, blood urea nitrogen, and/or creatinine clearance, and thyroid studies. Other studies, such as electroencephalogram, echogram, skull x-rays, electrocardiogram, and electrolytes should be obtained as indicated by the patient's history and physical status.

The considerations that apply to lithium use in acute mania or hypomania obtain also for its prophylactic use in depression, the only difference being the desired serum level. The usual therapeutic range for mania is 1.0 to 1.6 mEq/l, whereas the prophylactic or maintenance level is 0.6 to 1.2 mEq/l. Typically this latter dose requires 600 to 1,500 mg of lithium carbonate per day. Usually treatment is initiated with 600 to 900 mg per day, and increased stepwise until the desired serum level is reached (12). On initiation of therapy the serum level must be monitored one to three times weekly. This may be decreased as the patient's ability to handle the lithium ion is assured, when dose plasma level ratios have become stable, and when close cooperation and communication between therapist and patient has been established.

It is important to take blood samples for lithium determination 10 to 12 hours after the last dose, so that blood levels may be compared from test to test.

The side effects of lithium arise from the accumulation of the lithium ion in the body. These effects may be divided into early and late phases. Early side effects generally affect the gastrointestinal, central nervous, or urinary systems. Gastrointestinal manifestations include nausea, which may be diminished by giving medication at mealtime, vomiting, abdominal pain, and diarrhea. CNS effects include a dazed feeling or complaints of "otherworldness." Patients sometimes complain of sleepiness. Among the neuromuscular manifestations, the commonest is a fine tremor of the hands, but sometimes patients complain of fatigue or frank muscular weakness. Additionally, patients may report polyurea with secondary thirst.

All of these early side effects seem to be totally reversible, and they usually disappear without reduction of drug dosage. They most often occur early in therapy, but patients should be monitored closely throughout drug therapy, and if the side effects persist, a dosage reduction may be required. It is especially important to recognize that the reoccurrence of side effects may herald increased lithium-ion concentration, and the cause should be determined. Vomiting, febrile illness with sweating, or other salt-losing episodes may be at the root of the problem. In such cases the dose should be reduced until the supervening condition has been corrected.

Late side effects consist mainly of edema and weight gain. Again, persistence of this side effect may indicate renal impairment and should be closely monitored. Elderly patients may be especially susceptible to adverse effects.

The APA task force reports that the occurrence of side effects is "not necessarily related to dosage." Intensity, however, once the side effect occurs, is dose-dependent.

Lithium intoxication is a serious manifestation that calls for immediate cessation of the drug and for supportive therapy, as well as the institution of measures designed to increase the excretion of the lithium ion from the body. Although intoxication has been said to be an extension and magnification of side effects, and almost never to occur precipitously, Glassman (13) recently reported that serum lithium levels may indeed increase abruptly, with sudden intoxication. Reportedly such an abrupt change in serum level involves the effect of lithium on aldosterone levels and therefore on renal function.

Signs of frank intoxication include increased tremor, dysarthria, ataxia, confusion, and lethargy. The patient may have nausea and vomiting. As the syndrome progresses, the picture includes muscular twitching and clonic contractions. The patient's confused state may progress to delirium, stupor and coma; seizures may occur.

Although one may expect intoxication at serum levels of 2.0 mEq/l or higher, patients are highly individual in their ability to handle the lithium ion. Some patients may develop severe adverse reactions at lower levels, while others may tolerate significantly higher levels without becoming intoxicated. As the task force stated, "the necessity for adequate clinical observation of the lithium patient cannot be overemphasized" (11).

Treatment approach to lithium intoxication lies in two areas, the first being the elimination of the lithium ion from the body and the second the maintenance of life-support systems while elimination proceeds. The biological half-life of the lithium ion is approximately 24 hours. Therefore, discontinuing the drug may often be the only necessary treatment, and it should result in the patient's rapid improvement. Renal impairment would obviously result in a more prolonged cure. Diuresis may be called for, but the diuretic employed should be an osmotic agent such as manitol or urea. Other diuretic agents may actually increase the selective reabsorption of lithium and are therefore contraindicated (12). Supportive therapy includes correction of fluid and electrolyte balance, the use of anticonvulsants, and pulmonary and cardiac support. The cause of death in fatal cases is said to be pulmonary complications.

# CONCLUSION

There is continuing controversy over the precise roles and value of therapy with pharmaceuticals in depression. The tricyclics have been shown in some studies to have little more therapeutic activity than placebo. Other studies have found them to be clearly superior, and most clinicians consider them to be the agents of choice in depression. There is at this time a rather vocal controversy, largely articulated in the nonprofessional press, concerning the use of lithium in unipolar depression and as a prophylactic agent in recurring depression. Although the MAO inhibitors have been abandoned by many clinicians because of their toxic properties, there are some, as Dr. Davis indicates elsewhere in this volume, who continue to find them useful and safe when properly administered. There is considerable research now underway which is attempting to identify antidepressant agents with fewer and less severe side effects than any of the currently available agents, with faster therapeutic uptake than the tricyclics, and, of course, with greater effectiveness in relieving the symptoms of depression. We have every reason to believe that some of this research will be fruitful, and that we will in the future be treating our patients with significantly improved pharmacological agents. As Burton indicated, however, pharmacology is only one of the components necessary to the successful treatment of depressive disorders. Pharmacological agents are included in most treatment programs for depression at this time, and it seems fair to say that our ability to relieve the distress of this disease is markedly enhanced by the availability of these compounds.

# REFERENCES

1. Burton, R. *The Anatomy of Melancholy*. London: John Dent & Sons, Ltd., 1932, Vol. 2, p. 15.
2. Asberg, M., Cronholm, B., Sjöqvist, F., et al. Relationship between plasma level and therapeutic effect of nortriptyline. *Br. Med. J.* 3:331-334, 1971.
3. Kragh-Sorensen, P., Asberg, M., and Eggert-Hansen, C. Plasma nortriptyline levels in endogenous depression. *Lancet* 1:113-115, 1973.
4. Glassman, A. H., Shostak, M., Kantor, S. J., et al. Plasma levels of imipramine and clinical outcome. *Psychopharmacol. Bull.* 11:27-28, October, 1975.
5. Cole, J. O., and Davis, J. M. Antidepressant drugs, in *Comprehensive Textbook of Psychiatry*. Edited by A. M. Freedman, H. I. Kaplan, and B. J. Sadock. Baltimore: Williams & Wilkins Co. 1975, pp. 1941-1956.
6. *Physicians' Desk Reference*. Oradell, N. J.: Medical Economics Co., 1975, p. 1389.
7. Prien, R. F., Caffey, E. M., Jr., and Klett, C. J. Factors associated with lithium response in the prophylactic treatment of bipolar manic-depressive illness. Veterans Administration Central Neuropsychiatric Research Laboratory Research Report No. 96.
8. Prien, R. F. The clinical effectiveness of lithium: comparisons with other drugs.

Veterans Administration Central Neuropsychiatric Research Laboratory Research Report No. 97.

9. Prien, R. F. Prophylactic treatment of recurrent depression: observations from a multihospital collaborative study. Veterans Administration Central Neuropsychiatric Research Laboratory Research Report No. 98.

10. Prien, R. F., and Caffey, E. M., Jr. Lithium prophylaxis—a critical review. Veterans Administration Central Neuropsychiatric Research Laboratory Research Report No. 99.

11. The current status of lithium therapy: report of the APA Task Force. *Am. J. Psychiat.* 132:997-1001, 1975.

12. Baldessarini, R. J., and Lapinski, J. F. Lithium salts: 1970-1975. *Ann. Intern Med.* 83:527-533, 1975.

13. Glassman, A. H. Personal communication. February 20, 1976.

14. Resource material prepared by Medical Education Services, Sandoz Laboratories, is acknowledged with appreciation.

16

# Antidepressant Plasma Levels

ALEXANDER H. GLASSMAN
MICHAEL SHOSTAK
SHEPARD J. KANTOR
JAMES M. PEREL

It has been almost nine years since Sjöqvist and Hammer demonstrated that individuals receiving the same oral dose of a tricyclic antidepressant developed markedly variable plasma steady-state levels (1). It is now clear that this marked variability is primarily the result of individual differences in the rate of drug metabolism (2). A major question persists, however, concerning what effect individual variability in the metabolism of antidepressant drugs has on clinical outcome.

While it has always seemed likely that the steady-state differences seen with tricyclic drugs would be clinically important, individual differences by themselves are not always clinically significant. Two conditions are required for blood level differences to be meaningful. The first condition is that the drug shows toxic effects at higher doses. Otherwise, ever-increasing doses can be given with little or no risk until even the most rapid metabolizer achieves

This work was supported in part by Public Health Service Grant MH-21133 from the National Institute of Mental Health.

adequate plasma levels. The second condition is that the metabolic pathway of the parent drug must be understood and the clinical activity of any metabolites identified and measured. Otherwise, plasma levels of the parent compound will only be measuring an unknown fraction of the biologically active compound present in the blood. Obviously the fewer the active metabolites, the more easily the system can be understood.

The tricyclic antidepressants meet both of these requirements, and it is likely that the observed differences in blood levels are clinically significant. In spite of this, few workers have attempted to study the relationship between blood level and clinical outcome because the actual measurement of plasma levels is technically difficult. Many of the early blood level studies reflect this difficulty.

The most sophisticated and persistent of the early workers has been Sjöqvist and his co-workers from Sweden and Denmark. They initially chose to study nortriptyline because reliable methods for its analysis were available and because it appears to have no active metabolites. Somewhat surprisingly, an inital study by Sjöqvist and Asberg revealed a curvilinear dose-response curve (3). That is, a poor clinical response was seen at both lower and higher blood levels while a good response was observed only in a middle plasma range.

This result has now been replicated in two subsequent studies (4,5). Asberg conducted a more careful replication in association with Kragh-Sorensen in Denmark, and later Kragh-Sorensen conducted a third, independent study. In each study the data reveals a curvilinear type of dose response curve. Drugs with this dose-response characteristic are frequently referred to as having a "therapeutic window"—that is, they have a dose range at which a maximum response is seen. The "therapeutic window" for nortriptyline appears to be a steady-state level of between 50-140 nanograms per ml, and levels either above or below that "window" show a lower response rate. It would now seem clear that on the usual therapeutic doses of nortriptyline the average plasma steady-state level will fall at the upper end of this "therapeutic window" (6). Because of this, patients who fail to respond at doses of 150 mg/day are more likely to be above that window than below it.

Four years ago our unit at the New York State Psychiatric Institute began to examine the relationship between plasma levels of imipramine and clinical outcome. Plasma analysis of imipramine is considerably more complex than nortriptyline measurement because imipramine is converted in man to a second active compound, desmethylimipramine. Both imipramine and desmethylimipramine are subject to the same large individual variability in their rates of metabolism as was seen with nortriptyline. In fact, the individual differences seen in steady-state plasma levels are probably slightly greater with imipramine than nortriptyline (7).

We have now studied response to imipramine in approximately sixty seriously depressed hospitalized patients. These patients averaged close to 60 years of age and women outnumbered men two to one. The sample included bipolar and unipolar depressives. Patients with delusions as part of their depressive symptomatology were included, but any patient felt to be schizophrenic or schizo-affective was excluded. Informed consent was obtained from all patients after the nature of the procedure had been fully explained.

The first observation was that delusional patients, as a group, tended not to respond (8), but male delusionals did somewhat better than female delusionals. Blood levels were examined and average levels were found to be the same in both delusional and nondelusional depressives. Thus drug noncompliance does not explain the response difference.

The literature does not supply adequate information to conclude with any certainty if this observation holds true for antidepressant drugs other than imipramine. Hordern and his co-workers have published data suggesting that amitriptyline is also less effective in delusional female depressives than it is in nondelusionals; however, the total number of delusionals studied was small (9). Nine out of ten of our delusional depressives who were unresponsive to imipramine responded dramatically to ECT. In our experience, this would be the treatment of choice for these patients.

The delusional depressives, because they were essentially unresponsive to imipramine, were excluded from the analysis when the relationship between plasma levels and outcome was examined. As a result, of the original sixty patients, forty-one nondelusional depressives were available for analysis. Because no prior information concerning imipramine plasma levels was available, the relationship of clinical outcome to the median plasma level was examined.

The median level resulting from an oral dose of 3.5 mg/kg was 180 nanograms per ml. Nineteen of twenty patients above the median plasma responded, while only six of twenty-one patients below the median responded. This difference is significant at the .01 level. The same data examined by means of a Pearson rather than a Chi square analysis reveals a correlation of .46, which is also significant at the .01 level. Thus it would appear that there is a strong association between the plasma level of imipramine and the antidepressant drug response.

Two conclusions can be drawn from these data. The first is that the association between blood levels and drug response is such that it will have a significant influence on clinical outcome. In theory there could exist a

PLASMA LEVEL  (NG/ML)

>180          <180

RESPONDERS          19          6

NON RESPONDERS      1           15

$$x^2 = 16.31$$
$$P < .0001$$

CLINICAL OUTCOME ABOVE AND BELOW
THE MEDIAN PLASMA LEVEL

**1**

relationship between plasma level and outcome such that 90% or 95% of the population on usual doses would attain adequate plasma levels, and although individual variability may be substantial, only a small percentage of the population would fail to reach therapeutic levels. Patients in this study were treated with doses ranging from 150 mgs in a 92-pound woman to 300 mgs in a 193-pound man. Although these are slightly higher than usual doses, there was a significant difference in response rates between those individuals who developed high and those who developed low plasma levels. Lower initial oral doses would only increase the percentage of patients not responding.

The second conclusion evident from these data is that, unlike nortriptyline, the dose response curve for imipramine is not curvilinear. With nineteen out of twenty patients responding above 180 ng, there can be no therapeutic window within the usually observed plasma level range. As a result, this means that the clinician is faced with a situation where two apparently similar tricyclic antidepressants call for entirely different clinical strategies. With nortriptyline (Aventyl®), unless there are extenuating circumstances, a patient who does not respond at the usual therapeutic doses should most

## DRUGS EFFECTING MICROSOMAL ENZYMES

| INHIBITOR (RAISE BLOOD LEVELS) | INDUCER (LOWER BLOOD LEVELS) |
|---|---|
| 1) RITALIN ® | 1) PHENOBARBITAL |
| 2) ANTABUSE ® | 2) BARBITURATE HYPNOTICS |
| 3) PHENOTHIAZINES | 3) SMOKING |
| 4) HALOPERIDOL | 4) ALCOHOLISM |
| 5) BIRTH CONTROL PILLS (ESTROGEN-CONTAINING) | 5) INSECTICIDES |
| | 6) DORIDEN |
| 6) MORPHINE | 7) ANTICONVULSANTS |
| 7) MEPERIDINE | 8) MEPROBAMATE |

**2**

likely have his oral dose decreased, while with imipramine (Tofranil®) a nonresponsive patient should most likely have his oral dose increased.

One might expect that amitriptyline, because its pharmacological action resembles imipramine more than nortriptyline, might also show a sigmoid rather than a curvilinear dose response relationship. However, in spite of the fact that amitriptyline is the most commonly used tricyclic antidepressant, there is no hard data available on whether the clinician should raise or lower the patient's oral dose when that patient is not responsive to usual doses of this drug.

Certain other pharmacological characteristics of the tricyclic drugs should also influence a physician's handling of these drugs (2). These characteristics include the unusual lipid solubility of these drugs and their propensity to be affected by either induction or inhibition of liver enzymes. All of the tricyclic antidepressants are highly lipid soluble compounds, and in practice this unusual lipid solubility would mean that an obese individual is very likely to have low plasma levels of any tricyclic. In a similar way, a patient exposed to any substance known to induce enzymes would again be likely to have low blood levels (see Figure 2). Thus, a patient who is a heavy smoker or who uses barbiturates at bedtime can usually be expected to have low blood levels. On the other hand, individuals exposed to enzyme inhibitors are likely to have higher than usual plasma levels. Thus, administration of disulfiram concomitant to a tricyclic can even be used deliberately as a means of raising plasma levels in patients with low blood levels. Methylphenidate has been used in just this way (12,13).

It is now clear that the large individual variability in plasma steady-state levels seen with the tricyclic atnidepressants does in fact affect the response rate. Certainly this is true with the two drugs that have been carefully studied—imipramine and nortriptyline—and it is probably true for amitriptyline and desmethylimipramine as well. Even though plasma level measurements are not readily available at this moment, the principles that have developed from these studies can be applied in such a way as to greatly increase our understanding of these drugs and to supply a far more rational basis for the drug treatment of depression.

## REFERENCES

1. Hammer, W., and Sjöqvist, F. Plasma levels of monomethylated tricyclic antidepressants during treatment with imipramine-like compounds. *Life Sci.* 6:1895-1903, 1967.
2. Glassman, A. H., and Perel, J. M. The clinical pharmacology of imipramine. *Arch. Gen. Psychiat.* 28:649-653, 1973.
3. Asberg, M., Cronholm, B., Sjöqvist, F., et al. Relationship between plasma level and therapeutic effect of nortriptyline. *Br. Med. J.* 3:331-334, 1971.
4. Kragh-Sorensen, P., Asberg, M., and Eggert-Hansen, C. Plasma nortriptyline levels in endogenous depression. *Lancet* 1:113-115, 1973.
5. Kragh-Sorensen, P. Antidepressant Blood Levels. Read at the 128th annual meeting of the American Psychiatric Association, Anaheim, Calif., May 5-9, 1975.
6. Alexanderson, B. Pharmacokinetics of desmethylimipramine and nortriptyline in man after single and multiple oral doses—a cross-over study. *Europ. J. Clin. Pharmacol.* 5:1-10, 1972.
7. Perel, J. M., Shostak, M., Gann, E., et al. Pharmacodynamics of imipramine and clinical outcome, in *Pharmacokinetics of Psychoactive Drugs: Blood Levels and Clinical Response.* L. Gottschalk and S. Merlis, eds. Spectrum, 1976, pp. 229-241.
8. Glassman, A., Kantor, S., and Shostak, M. Depression, delusions, and drug response. *Am. J. Psychiat.* 132:716-719, 1975.
9. Hordern, A., Holt, N. F., Burt, C. G., et al. Amitriptyline in depressive states: phenomenology and prognostic considerations. *Br. J. Psychiat.* 109:815-825, 1963.
10. Hordern, A., Burt, C. G., Gordon, W. F., et al. Amitriptyline in depressive states: six month treatment results. *Br. J. Psychiat.* 110:641-647, 1964.

11. Hordern, A., Burt, C. G., and Holt, N. F. *Depressive States.* Springfield, Ill.: Charles C. Thomas, 1965.
12. Wharton, R. N., et al. A potential clinical use for the interaction of methylphenidate (Ritalin) with tricyclic antidepressants. *Am. J. Psychiat.* 127:1619-1625, 1971.
13. Flemenbaum, A. Methylphenidate: A catalyst for the tricyclic antidepressants. *Am. J. Psychiat.* 128:239, 1971.

17

# Pharmacological Treatment of the Moderately Anxious and Depressed Patient

WILLIAM E. FANN
JEANINE C. WHELESS

The majority of depressed patients are ambulatory and nonpsychotic. Patients who present with neurotic depression often exhibit symptoms of anxiety, insomnia, restlessness, and tension—symptoms that also occur in anxiety neurosis (1). Roughly 60% of all depressed patients fall into the mixed anxiety-depression group (2,3,4,5). Thus, physicians in outpatient settings are frequently faced with the problem of differentiating among patients who suffer from predominantly depressive states, predominantly anxious states, or from a mixture of anxiety and depression in which one or the other symptomatology predominates. Discrimination of these subtypes of depressed patients has therapeutic significance, in that diagnosis generally influences the choice of pharmaceutical agents to be used in treatment. It is the purpose of this paper to review some of the available data regarding mixed anxiety-depression and to present it in a form which will be useful to clinicians who are faced with problems of differentiating diagnoses and prescribing proper pharmacotherapy to patients with this condition.

273

## THE ANXIOUS-DEPRESSED SUBTYPE

Although depressed patients differ from one another in numerous ways, it is possible to recognize that some profiles occur with greater frequency than others. Overall et al. developed a method for identifying modal profile types by correlational analysis techniques. The Brief Psychiatric Rating Scale (BPRS) was used to evaluate similarities and differences between patients in terms of relationships between their symptom profiles. Clinically depressed patients were subclassified empirically into three identifiable groups. The most frequently occurring group, "anxious-tense depression," had profile peaks on anxiety, tension, and depressive mood. Adjectives such as "agitated," "reactive," or "neurotic" are often applied to this group. This subtype is frequently diagnosed as "mixed anxiety with depression," "depressive reaction with anxiety," or "anxiety with depressive features." The other two subgroups of depression were "hostile depression" and "retarded depression."

After delineating the subtypes of depression Overall et al. studied the effects of two classes of drugs on patients in the different subtypes. Imipramine and thioridazine were the study drugs, and both were found to be active in reducing "depressive mood" in patients. Whether mood was elevated, however, depended upon the particular context—that is, which drug was prescribed for which subtype of patient. Thioridazine was superior in treating anxious depression, and imipramine was superior in managing retarded depression. The authors concluded that drugs appear to have specific antidepressant actions dependent upon the context of symptoms within which the depression appears (3).

Downing and Rickels (6) further studied the problem of differential response. The authors addressed themselves to the question of whether or not mixed anxious-depressed patients, assigned by their physicians to treatment with antianxiety agents, differed in target symptomatology from mixed anxious-depressed patients assigned to treatment with antidepressants. Furthermore, they wondered if treatment assignments reflected differences in relative or absolute levels of the patients' presenting anxiety and depression. Mean physician ratings for anxiety and depression for the two study groups reflected a number of anticipated differences. Presenting anxiety was significantly higher than presenting depression in the group assigned to treatment with antianxiety agents, and presenting depression was significantly higher than anxiety in the group treated with antidepressants. Anxiety was higher (although not significantly higher at conventional standards) in the anxiety rather than the depression group, and depression was significantly higher in the depression rather than the anxiety group. Although anxiety was predominant over depression in those patients treated with anxiolytics and depression predominant over anxiety in those patients treated with antidepressants, the amount by which anxiety exceeded depression in the anxiety group was about five times greater than the amount by which depression exceeded anxiety in the depression group. This finding would seem to indicate that those mixed anxious-depressed patients who are assigned to treatment with antianxiety agents are, on the average, persons in whom depression is distinctly secondary to anxiety. On the other hand, while depression tends to be the primary symptom in patients treated with antidepressants, concomitant anxiety contributes considerably to the patients' symptomatology.

Patient ratings of anxiety and depression produced some interesting findings. Similar to physician ratings, results indicated that anxiety was significantly higher than depression in the anxiety group patients and depression was significantly higher than anxiety in the depression group patients. While the anxiety of the anxiety group was significantly higher than that of the depression group, depression was also higher, although not significantly so, in the anxiety group patients. Additionally, the amount by which anxiety exceeded depression in the anxiety group was about the same as the amount by which depression exceeded anxiety in the depression group. Hence, the differences in relative saliency of the two symptoms across treatment groups seen in physician ratings did not emerge in patient ratings. Further study with multivariate analysis suggested that physicians were likely to assign patients to treatment with anxiolytics when they perceived the patients' anxiety as high relative to the level of presenting depression; but the decision to assign patients with severe depressive symptoms to treatment with antidepressants was but slightly affected by the patients' anxiety level (6). In another study, intake psychiatrist rating of depression reported that 67% of the sample of depressed patients was diagnosed as anxious-depressed. Results of the Brief Psychiatric Rating Scale (BPRS) indicated, however, that only 35% of the patients presented with mixed anxiety and depression (7).

Pursoff and Klerman studied mixed anxious-depressed patients divided into subgroups of those who were predominantly depressed and those who were predominantly anxious. Patients in the depressive group reported themselves to be more severely impaired than the anxious group on all factors of the Symptom Checklist (SCL) except somatization. It appears that depressed patients tended to exaggerate the nature of their complaints, a response tendency called "the sick set," perhaps as a way of communicating their helplessness, need for support, and desire for treatment. Thus the differences in level of symptomatology between anxious and depressed patients may not represent true differences.

When level of depression was held constant, anxious patients exhibited more somatization, probably indicative of the motor and autonomic concomitants of the anxious state. In depressed patients, mean ratings on depression items and on depressed factors were higher than on comparable anxiety ratings. Anxiety patients scored higher on anxiety items and factors than the depressed patients. Unlike the previous study, however, this study reported no tendency for patients in the anxious group to score higher on the anxiety factor than on the depressive factor (1).

## PLACEBO OR ACTIVE MEDICATION?

One of the first issues a physician must resolve in the treatment of a depressed patient is whether or not the patient needs medication. For many patients, depression tends to be a self-limiting illness, and the spontaneous recovery rate may be as high as 44% within the first year (2). Studies during the 1920's and 1930's indicated that over 40% of patients hospitalized for depression recovered within the first year and 60% within the second year without medication (8). Spontaneous recovery rates are particularly high for hospitalized patients; apparently removing the depressed patient from sources of conflict in his environment and the effects of the hospital milieu have a great impact on recovery.

Other considerations regarding depressed patients are that many show good response to placebo, and studies have indicated that the advantage of active medication over placebo is not very great. In two NIMH studies, patients with neurotic depression responded as well or better to placebo when compared to treatment with active medication. These patients also tolerated the adverse effects of the drugs less well than psychotic patients, a finding which supports the popular belief that the less sick the patient is, the less he will tolerate an active medication (2).

A seven-week study comparing chlorpromazine, imipramine, and placebo reported that during the first 4 weeks placebo, and to a lesser extent chlorpromazine, were more effective than imipramine in treating anxiety-depression. At weeks six and seven, when active medication was discontinued, however, patients on chlorpromazine showed less improvement than patients who had received placebo during the first five weeks. In one symptom area, loss of interest in activities, placebo was a better treatment during the entire seven-week course than either chlorpromazine or imipramine. Imipramine seemed to produce the best results overall; however, treatment differences between active medication and placebo accounted for only 10% of the predictable variance on outcome measures. The authors concluded that for patients suffering from neurotic depression, placebo is generally as effective as active medication, and that for many depressed patients, drugs play a minor role in treatment (5).

NIMH studies corroborated that the advantage of active medication over placebo for hospitalized depressed patients is not very great. After 3 weeks of treatment, patients receiving placebo averaged a 36% improvement rate compared to a 44% improvement rate for patients receiving drugs (2).

Other research, however, confirms the efficacy of drugs over placebo in the treatment of depression. In an extensive review of the literature on the efficacy of various antidepressant agents, Morris and Beck (9) indicated that tricyclic antidepressants were significantly more effective than placebo in 61 of 93 group comparisons (66%); amitriptyline produced successful results in 70% of the treatment comparisons, and imipramine was successful in 60% of the treatment comparisons. In no study was a placebo better than a tricyclic. Monoamine oxidase inhibitors (MAOI) did not show as strong a superiority over placebo as the tricyclics, and these drugs, including several which are not yet approved by the FDA, were more effective than placebo in 33% of the groups treated. When only MAO inhibitors which are marketed in the United States were included in the sample, 8 of 13 (62%) studies reported that MAO inhibitors were more effective than placebo. Tranylcypromine appeared to be the most effective monoamine oxidase inhibitor available and was more effective than placebo in 75% of the groups treated. In three studies comparing tranylcypromine and imipramine, the two drugs were reported to be equally effective.

Although the authors reported that drugs were superior to placebo in the treatment of depression, he commented that individualized treatment was necessary—a drug that was antidepressant in one individual might not produce the same results in another individual, and the same patient could respond differently to a medication at different times. The authors conceded that further research into differential response among the depressed subtypes was necessary.

## RATING SCALES FOR ANXIETY-DEPRESSION

Diagnostic assessment of anxious-depressed patients includes careful clinical history with attention to details of possible precipitating factors and a careful evaluation of the patients' phenomenology. Additionally, there are several rating scales—both physician-rating and self (patient)-rating—which have been shown to be useful in distinguishing depressed and anxious patients. Some of these include the Brief Psychiatric Rating Scale (BPRS), the Symptom Checklist (SCL), Hamilton Rating Scale, Raskin Rating Scale, Zung Self-rating Anxiety Scale (SAS), and Zung Self-rating Depression Scale (SDS). The Zung rating scales are converted to numerical values that have been standardized so that depression or anxiety is likely to be present in subjects scoring above fifty on the SDS or SAS. However, validity of the Zung scales is age-specific. Although only 12% of normal subjects aged 20 to 64 years scored above 50 in the SDS, 48% of normal subjects below 19 years of age and 44% of normal subjects above 65 years of age scored higher than fifty. In the SAS, all normal subjects between 20 and 64 years old scored below 50. However, 28% of normal subjects under 19 years of age and 19% of subjects over 65 years of age scored above fifty (10). When using the Zung scales, the physician should be aware of the age-related differences of response of very young and very old patients.

## PUBLISHED RESEARCH ON THE TREATMENT OF ANXIOUS-DEPRESSED PATIENTS

The term "depression" is used to refer to a symptom, a syndrome, or a diagnostic entity, and it is unclear whether antidepressant medications are effective for treating the symptom, the syndrome, or diagnostic entity. A current biochemical theory of depression, the norepinephrine hypothesis, postulates a deficiency of available norepinephrine at certain central synapses in patients who are depressed; this hypothesis explains the beneficial effects of some of the antidepressant agents. However, this hypothesis may be applicable only to special subclasses of depressed patients, specifically those labeled as "retarded depression," which is the smallest subtype. Evidence in the literature suggests that different subtypes of depressed patients respond differently to psychotropic medications and that each class of drugs may exhibit antidepressant properties for specific patients. Consequently, it may be a misnomer to label any drug or class of drugs as "antidepressants" (2).

Covi et al., however, reported little or no evidence for interaction between subtype of depression and medication. The authors also indicated that they had not been able to document the long-term effectiveness of treating anxious neurotic outpatients with the minor tranquilizers. This finding questioned the specificity and assumed therapeutic superiority of minor tranquilizers in treating anxiety, particularly since imipramine has been shown to have long-term antianxiety effects. The authors concluded that there was strong evidence for the use of imipramine in treating anxious or depressed outpatients (7).

In a placebo-controlled study assessing the symptomatic relief of depression and anxious-depression in outpatients prescribed amitriptyline or placebo, amitriptyline was consistently superior to placebo and drug-placebo differences increased over time. Amitriptyline was significantly more effective than placebo in reducing the symptoms of anxiety and depression; however, relief of somatic and anxious symptoms occurred more rapidly than relief of depressive symptoms. This indicated that although the lag time before antidepressant effect is established as long (2 to 4 weeks), antianxiety effects are discernible within hours of drug administration. Unfortunately, amitriptyline produced an unusually large number of side effects, particularly autonomic and sedative effects, and consequently was associated with more attrition and dose deviation than placebo. The majority of the subjects in the study were well-educated and employed. Previous studies have reported that this class of patients is most likely to be disturbed by the sedative effects of antidepressants (12).

Raskin et al. reported a great advantage of active medication over placebo in treating depressed patients with mixed symptoms of anxiety and depression and noted that the major and minor tranquilizers were the drugs of choice for this group. The authors found that anxious depressed patients were difficult to maintain on inert substances. Ten of thirteen placebo patients who were terminated during the first week of treatment were classified as anxious-depressed. Additionally, fourteen patients, twelve of whom were anxious-depressed, were maintained on diazepam but deteriorated rapidly when given placebo. A appreciable number of anxious-depressed patients appeared to be "true" diazepam responders. Those anxious-depressed patients who were maintained on placebo appeared to be "less sick" and consequently more prone to spontaneous remission (4).

Two NIMH studies were conducted comparing the efficacy of major and minor tranquilizers, tricyclics, and monoamine oxidase inhibitors in treating subtypes of depression. Subjects who were classified as mixed anxious-depressed had scored high on the BPRS factors of anxiety, tension, and depressive mood factors. In study one, both chlorpromazine and imipramine were effective in treating symptoms of anxiety; in study two, diazepam was more effective than either phenelzine or placebo for anxious-depressed patients (2).

Several VA studies have reported the beneficial effects of the major and minor tranquilizers for anxious-depressed patients. Thioridazine (Mellaril), Triavil [a combination of amitriptyline (Elavil) and perphenazine (Trilafon)], diazepam (Valium), and acetophenazine (Tindal) were all reported as being of value in the treatment of anxious-depressed patients (2).

In an early study, Hollister et al. (11), compared the effects of a phenothiazine, thioridazine, versus a tricyclic antidepressant, imipramine, in treating depressed patients. When the subjects were divided into three subtypes (anxious, hostile, retarded), the results indicated that thioridazine was superior in treating retarded depression. A later study compared the effectiveness of another phenothiazine, perphenazine, and a tricyclic, amitriptyline.

As was hypothesized, the phenothiazine proved to be more effective in treating anxious-depressed patients and the tricyclic in treating retarded depression.

The combination of phenothiazines and tricyclics did not appreciably enhance the therapeutic result from either type of single drug in properly selected subtype patients. Interestingly, however, the therapeutic potential of the combination appeared to depend on the most active drug for the subtype being treated. When the most effective single drug was perphenazine, the combination mimicked the action of the phenothiazine; when the most effective single drug was amitriptyline, the combination mimicked the action of the tricyclic.

As the prognosis for acute depressive episodes has improved, the focus of treatment has shifted toward prevention of relapse in the 40% to 50% of patients who experience recurrence of depression. Maintenance therapy has been shown to be both effective and relatively safe. Four studies comparing relapse rate of patients on tricyclics and placebo reported that the relapse rate is cut in half by tricyclic maintenance. Additionally, it appears that placebo relapse rate is directly proportional to severity of patients' illness prior to treatment (8).

Winstead et al. (13) reported on the drug-seeking behavior of patients admitted to a psychiatric ward. During a six-month period all patients were allowed to seek diazepam on demand (in addition to any regularly prescribed psychotropic medications). Details of 689 requests by 83 patients were recorded and drug-seeking behavior was expressed as a drug-seeking index (DSI) based on the ratio of requests to duration of stay. Although there was an increasing trend toward drug use, this appeared to be related to ward phenomenon and not to dependency, because the average DSI for individual patients was highest in the first quarter of hospitalization (when anxiety would have been highest) and least during the final quarter of hospitalization (when dependency would probably be most noticeable).

Twenty-seven percent of the patients never asked for drugs and requests were made on an average of only once every three days. The DSI was not related to either diagnosis or use of psychiatric drugs.

The results of this study suggest that when diazepam is made freely available, patients of all diagnoses seek it for the appropriate indication of anxiety, and most use it conservatively. Extensive use of antianxiety drugs might be reduced by prescribing them "as needed" rather than on fixed schedule (13).

The literature does not delineate clear-cut guidelines for the treatment of anxious-depressed patients. In fact, the data is often contradictory. The physician is again faced with the problem of prescribing medication to a heterogeneous group which responds differently to different agents. Generally, the best guidelines are those established by clinical experience.

The patient who is diagnosed as primarily anxious is likely to be prescribed a minor tranquilizer such as diazepam (Valium), chlordiazepoxide (Librium), or meprobamate (Miltown, Equanil). Many studies have shown these agents to be both effective in alleviating the symptoms of anxiety and relatively safe. However, tolerance develops to the effects of the antianxiety agents, and some patients will escalate the dose to continue achieving the pleasurable or distress-relieving effects of these drugs. After dependency is established, the patient would suffer from a withdrawal syndrome similar to delirium tremens if the intake of the medication were suddenly curtailed. Consequently, many physicians are reluctant to prescribe these drugs for an extended period of time. Instead, many clinicians prefer to start the anxious-depressed patient on a tricyclic antidepressant or low dose of neuroleptic. Such a regimen has become an accepted mode of therapy.

If the patient is primarily depressed with secondary symptoms of anxiety, most physicians agree that the proper therapeutic regimen would include beginning a tricyclic antidepressant. Not only do the tricyclics relieve the primary depression but their sedative properties are also efficacious in relieving symptoms of moderate anxiety.

For the group that is the locus of both anxiety and depression, it is probably the best strategy to begin either a tricyclic antidepressant or a low dose of a neuroleptic. Neuroleptics at low doses show pharmacological similarity to tricyclics. Such basic science findings support data from clinical experience, suggesting that this therapeutic approach is indeed valid (14). Thioridazine (Mellaril) has been shown to be effective in relieving moderate anxiety and depression and is usually the neuroleptic of choice for treating this group. The usual daily dose of thioridazine is from 40 to 200 mg.

The following guidelines may be beneficial for the clinician in outpatient practice treating patients with mixed anxiety-depression.

(1) Unless the patient is predominantly anxious with mild depression, then either a tricyclic antidepressant such as imipramine (Tofranil) or a neuroleptic such as thioridazine (Mellaril) could be prescribed. The patient should be advised of the possibility that these medications may make him feel worse; it is well known that neuroleptics and tricyclics make some nonpsychotic persons feel symptomatically worse, thereby aggravating their discomfort.

(2) If a trial on the neuroleptics and then the tricyclics (or the reverse) does not produce improvement, then the next therapeutic approach would be prescription of an antianxiety agent. Instructions to the patient should include a warning that tolerance and dependency on these medications can

develop and that the drugs should be taken only on an "as needed" basis and for the shortest time possible.

It is generally better to prescribe tricyclics and neuroleptics before antianxiety agents because experience has shown that the possibility of discomfort from or intolerance to the neuroleptic and antidepressant is increased in patients who change from antianxiety agents to tricyclics or neuroleptics. Although the reason for this reaction is not known, speculations include the fact that these classes of compounds are therapeutically opposite: the antianxiety agents are sedatives, anticonvulsants and muscle relaxants; the neuroleptics and tricyclics lower convulsive threshold and may increase muscle tone. Some individuals may experience the increased muscle tone and/or increased nervous system "irritability" as subjective, symptomatic intensification of the anxiety process. Another advantage of starting the neuroleptic or tricyclic first is that one avoids giving the patient a medication known to cause dependency and prescribes instead a medication that can be given over the long term, if necessary. The clinician must, however, be cautious about side effects, especially the cardiovascular and long-term neurotoxic effects associated with the neuroleptics and tricyclics, in planning the course for the chronic patient. As always, the risk-benefit ratio must be considered, with each patient's history reviewed to determine drug tolerances and sensitivities, contraindications, and expected degree of symptom relief compared to expected type and degree of nontherapeutic, unpleasant, or dangerous side effects.

## REFERENCES

1. Pursoff, B., and Klerman, G. Differentiating depressed from anxious neurotic outpatients. *Arch. Gen. Psych.* 30 (March 1974) : 302-309.
2. Raskin, A. A guide for drug use in depressive disorders. *Am. J. Psych.* 131:2 (February 1974) : 186-191.
3. Overall, J., Hollister, L., Johnson, M., and Pennington, V. Nosology of depression and differential response to drugs. *JAMA* 195:11 (March 14, 1966) : 946-948.
4. Raskin, A., Schulterbrandt, J., Reatig, N., Crook, T., and Odle, D. Depression subtypes and response to phenelzine, diazepam, and placebo. *Arch. Gen. Psych.* 30 (January 1974): 66-75.
5. Raskin, A., Schulterbrandt, J., Reatig, N., and McKeon, J. Differential response to chlorpromazine, imipramine and placebo: A study of subgroups of hospitalized depressed patients. *Arch. Gen. Psych.* 23 (August 1970) : 164-173.
6. Downing, R., and Rickels, K. Mixed anxiety-depression: Fact or myth? *Arch. Gen. Psych.* 30 (March 1974) : 312-317.
7. Covi, L., Lipman, R., Derogatis, L., Smith, J., and Pattison, J. Drugs and group psychotherapy in neurotic depression. *Am. J. Psych.* 131:2 (February 1974), 191-198.
8. Klerman, G., DiMascio, A., Weissman, M., Pursoff, B., and Payel, E. Treatment of

depression by drugs and psychotherapy. *Am. J. Psych.* 131:2 (February 1974) : 186-191.

9. Morris, J., and Beck, A. The efficacy of antidepressant drugs. *Arch. Gen. Psych.* 30 (5) : 667-674.
10. Zung, W., and Green, R. Detection of affective disorders in the aged. In *Psychopharmacology and Aging*, C. Eisdorfer and W. E. Fann, eds. Plenum Press, 1973, pp. 213-224.
11. Hollister, L., Overall, J., Shelton, J., Pennington, V., Kimball, I., and Johnson, M. Drug therapy of depression: amitriptyline, perpenazine, and their combination in different syndromes. *Arch. Gen. Psych.* 17 (October 1967) : 486-493.
12. Downing, R. Amitriptyline in anxious-depressed outpatients: a controlled study. *Am. J. Psych.* 131:1 (January 1974): 25-30.
13. Winstead, D., Anderson, A., Eilers, K., Blackwell, B., and Zarembra, L. Diazepam on demand. *Arch. Gen. Psych.* 30 (March 1974) : 349-351.
14. Fann, W. E., Lake, C. R., and Majors, L. F. Thioridazine in neurotic, anxious, and depressed patients. *Psychosomatics* 15:117-121, 1974.

Phenomenology and Treatment of Depression

**18**

# EST: A Special Case
# In Pharmacotherapy

MAX FINK

Induced seizures have been used in the treatment of the mentally ill for more than forty years, and despite much study there is considerable confusion concerning their mode of action. Some seek an explanation in the psychological factors of fear, expiation of guilt, or memory loss; some seek an explanation in electrophysiologic or pharmacologic mechanisms; some seek an explanation in biochemical changes. Others seek answers in combinations of these factors. Throughout, fashion dictates that the mode of action be described as unknown and the results as inexplicable.

But much is known of the process. The clinical efficacy is well defined, with most studies finding that the repeated induction of seizures relieves severe depression, and in comparative studies better results are reported for seizures than for other treatments. Seizure therapy is also useful in schizophrenic disorders and in acute mania. Much of the psychobiologic basis has been described, and the relationships between seizures and cerebral events, memory mechanisms, biochemical changes and electrophysiologic consequences have been studied in detail (1).

In this report, I should like to summarize our knowledge of the EST process,* and suggest that EST may be viewed as a special case of the pharmacotherapy of mental states.

## AXIOMS OF THE SEIZURE THERAPIES

One way of presenting what we know of this therapy process is a series of seven axioms—truths that are derived from the available data.

*1. Characteristic behavioral changes are the result of repeated cerebral seizures. Convulsions, apnea, hypoxia, and other peripheral events affect behavior secondarily.*

These conclusions are based on comparisons of seizure and subseizure treatments, the effects of modified seizures, and multiple monitored EST (2,3,4).

In some early comparative studies, patients referred for EST received currents that either elicited convulsions or failed to do so. Patients were assigned at random to either treatment regimen, and usually neither the patient, his therapist, nor the ward nurses knew which treatment the patient received. Patients were independently evaluated by clinicians, who did not know the type of treatment administered. In two published studies, the results were the same: patients receiving convulsive currents were rated as much improved or recovered more often and sooner than patients who received subconvulsive currents. In one study, the patients who were unimproved after 12 treatments with subconvulsive currents were continued in the same course, but received convulsive currents for the next four weeks. Almost all who had not improved in the first series did improve during this second course, indicating that the two treatments differed in efficacy (2).

With the introduction of curare, and later succinylcholine (Anectine) as part of the treatment regimen, it was possible to separate the effects of the convulsion—the motor effects on muscles and limbs—from the cerebral seizure. The clinical results of EST modified by succinylcholine and barbiturate are approximately equivalent to the results of unmodified EST. Some students found the unmodified seizures to have slightly better therapeutic results. This observation was unexplained until the cerebral events were recorded using EEG recording methods. Observers noted that not every administration of electric currents or flurothyl is accompanied by a cerebral seizure—many applications are followed by an incomplete or aborted seizure.

---

*Many euphemisms are used to describe the treatment process: shock therapy, convulsive therapy, ECT, EST, electroshock, electroplexy, electrotherapy and clonotherapy among the most frequent. After some reflection, I favor EST—electroseizure therapy—for reasons that are clarified in the text.

This is particularly true when succinylcholine hides the expression of the motor convulsion. These observations led Blachly to suggest that the proper treatment of patients by EST or flurothyl should be under EEG control— i.e., with monitoring of the seizure for duration and pattern—so that incomplete seizures can be repeated immediately.

In multiple monitored treatments, the clinical effects of EST are not related to oxygen deprivation, for when treatments are given under hyperoxygenation and the levels of blood gases maintained, the therapeutic efficacy is not reduced (3).

Finally, attempts to relate the therapeutic effects of seizure treatments to a blood constituent, to blood pressure, or to levels of metabolites or hormones in blood or CSF have not been successful (1,5,6). The best correlations of behavioral improvement are with a physiologic measure, that of persistent EEG slow wave activity. While some observers reported a direct relationship between the rate and degree of increased EEG slowing or the reduction in EEG fast activity, recent studies suggest the relationship not to be a causal one, but rather an expression of secondary effects, similar to memory loss.

2. *The characteristic clinical results are independent of the mode of induction of the seizure* [*i.e., seizures produced by electricity, by pentelenetetrazol (Metrazol), and by the inhalant, flurothyl (Indoklon) are equivalent*].

Studies comparing the clinical efficacy of flurothyl and electrical seizures, and of the various types of electrical inductions, find that the number of inductions necessary for a therapeutic effect are about equal. The principal difference among the inductions are in the secondary effects, particularly in memory, orientation, and confusion. While the different inductions usually produce seizures of equivalent length, there are differences in duration in some studies, and in these the behavioral changes are related more to seizure duration than to the mode of induction (1,9,10).

If these observations are true, we can expect that the treatment induction providing the least discomfort to the patient and accompanied by the least severe side effects should persist in clinical practice. Metrazol often elicited fear reactions and incomplete seizures. It was replaced by EST when electrical inductions were found easier and safer to administer. With flurothyl, the difficulty of a safe induction and a higher incidence of missed seizures also led to its discontinuation.

In electrical inductions, the type of current is less important than its intensity. Studies of square wave, unidirectional, and pulsed-wave currents find little relation between current characteristics and outcome, provided the current used is sufficient to induce a cerebral seizure (11).

As a corollary, the location of the EST electrodes affects the degree of changes in memory, orientation, and confusion, but not the clinical outcome.

Comparison of the effects of bitemporal, unilateral dominant, and unilateral nondominant hemisphere electrode placements show that the degree and type of clinical change are equivalent, but tests of memory and recall show significant differences. Patients treated through electrodes over the non-dominant hemisphere complain less of memory difficulties than patients treated through bitemporal electrodes (12,13). This observation is confirmed by psychological tests (14,15). The differences are most marked in tests of verbal memory, particularly using auditory tasks, and less so with visual and nonverbal memory tasks. These observations suggest that the electrical currents directly affect tissues that subserve such psychological processes as memory and orientation, but not those that subserve the therapeutic process. From these data, also, it is improbable that memory processes are central to the therapeutic process (1).

3. *The number of seizures required for a specific behavioral response varies with the psychopathology and age of the subjects, and not with factors in the induction of seizures.*

The target populations for convulsive therapy are the psychotic depressives, for whom therapeutic results can be achieved with 4 to 8 inductions. In other populations, such as schizophrenic patients, more seizures must be applied more frequently to elicit a behavioral change. The differential sensitivity to seizures is seen in the clinical behavioral measures and also in physiological (as EEG) and psychological tests (1,2).

Age affects outcome. Elderly patients require fewer inductions and exhibit more favorable clinical effects than younger patients.

Another factor, though less well defined, is that of personality type. Psychological tests evaluating the extent to which the subject uses explicit verbal denial as a defense mechanism, the degree of authoritarianism on the California F Scale, and the type of organization of the Rorschach protocol are reported to be related to the type of behavioral outcome and to the number of inductions necessary to achieve a favorable outcome. The studies do not separate clearly the interaction of personality and psychopathologic diagnosis, but personality measures remain useful predictors of clinical outcome.

4. *Time between seizure inductions affects the treatment process.*

When the impairment of memory and recall functions after EST could be reduced by changing the location of the electrodes and by hyperoxygenation, it was anticipated that multiple seizures within one or two days would reduce the duration of the treatment course (16). Multiple treatments in one day were tested, and only in rare instances was the course reduced from the usual 3 to 9 days, although multiple seizures occasionally enhanced the treatment response (4). These experiences suggest that the central therapeutic processes set in motion by a seizure require time to develop.

*5. Vegetative changes, as evidenced by changes in sleep, appetite, weight, menses, libido, and mood are significant accompaniments of the behavioral changes induced by repeated seizures.*

The physiological functions associated with the activity of the hypothalamus are frequently impaired in the depressive psychoses. These impairments improve early in treatment and remain improved following the treatment course. The persistence of improvement after EST may best be predicted by the degree and persistence of the changes in sleep, weight, and appetite, and impairment in these functions usually accompanies or precedes relapse. While these indices are less apparent in schizophrenic patients, the changes are frequently seen. The relation between the changes in these functions and clinical evaluations are more direct than the changes seen in memory tests or in the persistent electrical changes in the EEG, suggesting that the processes that underlie these functions may be central to the therapeutic process after repeated seizures (1,5,17).

*6. The effects of repeated seizures may be augmented or reduced by biochemical and pharmacologic interventions.*

The behavioral effects of repeated seizures may be enhanced by the administration of barbiturates. If patients are given an injection of pentothal after the first or second EST treatment, those patients who exhibit an increase in EEG slow wave activity or who show an improvement in their depressive symptoms are the patients who show the best outcome at the end of the treatment course. Patients who do not show this augmented response also show a poor therapeutic response. The same predictions can be made from the changes in language (defined as the expression of explicit verbal denial) following the administration of intravenous amobarbital. Sedation threshold studies also are useful physiologic predictors of the therapeutic response to EST.

The behavioral effects of repeated seizures may be reduced by the administration of anticholinergic drugs, such as Ditran, atropine or benactyzine, and by such hallucinogens as LSD. In experimental studies, the high voltage EEG slow wave activity and the denial language patterns after EST are temporarily reversed by these drugs. During these experiments the patients frequently exhibit their pretreatment behavioral patterns. These observations are part of the evidence for the suggestion that changes in cerebral cholinergic processes are central to the EST treatment process (1,2,18).

*7. The physiologic and psychologic effects of repeated seizures are reversible over a period of weeks; the behavioral and psychopathologic changes are more persistent, although they too are reversible.*

Measures of the effects of seizures, such as the increased slow wave activity of the EEG, redundancy of speech, changes in language patterns, and impairment of performance and memory tasks are reversed within two to three weeks after the last seizure. For psychologic tests, there may even be an improvement in performance over the initial measurements associated with the practice effect of repeated testing, particularly if the initial test results are impaired by the psychopathology (1,2,19). The behavioral changes do not persist beyond a few weeks, and are replaced either by behaviors that characterize the period of illness, or by those that characterize the pre-illness period. In the latter instance, the results may be said to have induced a favorable clinical result. The factors that influence this change are not well understood.

## THEORETIC MODELS

In another report, I summarized these observations by stating that

> From the clinical observations that are the basis for these "axioms," a viable theory of the mode of action of induced convulsions must not depend on a specific method of inducing seizures, nor on any single behavioral consequences (e.g., memory loss), nor on the peripheral systemic effects. The theory must incorporate the biochemical phenomena subsequent to seizures, with a rate of development in the order of days after seizures and additive for rates varying between 12 and 72 hours between seizures. The biochemical events must be enhanced by barbiturates, and reduced by anticholinergic, sympathomimetic, and antihistaminic agents. The theory must also make allowances for differences in the rate of response of different populations of the mentally ill and accommodate the differences in behaviors which are expressed, and which seem related not only to the type of symptoms manifested by patients, but their individual psychological organization (personality) as well [1].

No one of the many theories of the mode of action of the seizure therapies is acceptable. The psychologic theories that emphasize fear and repression fail to include the efficacy of seizures modified by barbiturates and succinylcholine. Dependence on memory mechanisms is unsatisfactory, since the modifications of seizures by unilateral nondominant placement of electrodes and by flurothyl provide dissociations between the therapeutic results and the degree of clinical confusion and memory deficit. The biochemical and physiologic theories lack relevance, since their formulation is based on the measurement of changes in peripheral systems. As with studies of catecholamines in depressive disorders, changes in blood and urine are heavily influenced by muscles and tissue outside the central nervous system. Their effects are substantial, overshadowing and masking the smaller, subtler, and perhaps more critical central changes. The biochemical and physiologic theories fail to account for differences in the individual response of patients and take insufficient cognizance of individual differences in experience and personality organization, or the role of psychologic factors in both short-term and persistent behavioral effects.

At the time of my earlier report, I supported a neurophysiologic-adaptive view of the seizure therapy process. In this view, the physiological effects of repeated seizures result in an increase in central neurohumoral activity, the expression of which varies with personality factors in the individual. Consistent with this view, I cited the data that catecholamines are materially reduced in patients with affective disorders, and increase with improvement. To encompass the psychologic observations, I concluded that those patients who conventionally use denial mechanisms used these mechanisms more often after repeated seizures (7,20,21).

These views, however, do not account for the variety of relations between psychologic variables and treatment outcome, nor the vegetative aspects; nor is there evidence that the denial process is directly related to clinical improvement. Denial appears to be a phenomenon which is associated with, but not central to, the EST process, similar to changes in memory (1) and in EEG slow wave activity (8).

If we cannot depend on psychologic, physiologic, or structural theories of the EST process, is there a more useful framework? In seeking complex explanations, perhaps we have been misled by overt aspects of the treatment process—the dramatic nature of the convulsion, our fear of electric currents, the discontinuity of the process (compared, for example, to drug therapies which are seen as providing a "steady state" blood level), and by our language (does the term "shock therapy" elicit thoughts of an eruptive and traumatic process, similar to a surgical procedure?). One can view seizure therapy as a complex process to elicit persistent biochemical changes in the brain, akin to the changes produced by chemicals in psychopharmacology. Changes in brain chemistry with seizures are dramatic; for example, levels of acetylcholine, cholinesterase, catecholamines, and monoamine oxidase are elevated in brain and spinal fluid. These neurohumoral changes must play some role in affecting behavior with EST in ways that are similar to the effects seen with drug therapy.

There are similarities in the treatment of depression with EST and with thymoleptic drugs. Clinical results vary with diagnosis; time for a treatment response is similar; dosage ranges are narrow; and maintenance treatments are needed to sustain a clinical response. Age is a factor in outcome, and the treatment response may be altered by adjunct drugs. There are differences as well as similarities, particularly in the known biochemical mechanisms, between pharmacological and seizure treatments. EST stimulates a central cholinergic response with characteristic increased high voltage delta wave activity and decreased fast frequencies in EEG measures. The thymoleptic drugs—imipramine and amitriptyline, for example—are defined as anticholinergic in their central effects. Their characteristic EEG patterns are increased theta activity with increased fast frequencies. Perhaps these differences are not critical to the therapeutic process.

The central biochemical processes underlying the vegetative changes are especially relevant to an understanding of EST. Evidence that the hypothalamus is both a source and a target for neuroendocrine substances suggests that these substances may serve to maintain behavioral homeostasis, particularly the aspects affected in disorders of mood. There is an appeal, for example, in the observation that the thyrotropin releasing factor (TRH) may have antidepressant effects when parenterally administered. There is an appeal in the actions of the hypothalamic releasing factors that have been identified, and in the separation of the peptide fragments of ACTH into CNS active and inactive fragments. One fragment of ACTH, that of the amino acids 4 to 10, has effects on learned responses in animals, and there are suggestions that this peptide fragment is active in man, affecting both electrophysiologic and behavioral measures (22) . Studies are now in progress to assess the usefulness of these fragments in reducing memory impairment after EST. To the extent that hypothalamic functions are reduced in depressive illness and increased by EST, these changes will have to be accounted for in any theory of the EST process.

At this juncture, it is difficult to characterize the manner in which biochemical mechanisms in EST affect behavior, just as it is difficult to define the mechanisms for the action of psychoactive drugs. Nevertheless, it is useful to seek understanding of EST with the same scrupulous methodology we utilize in seeking explanations for the drug therapies, without employing exclusively psychological, demonic, or physical constructs, as has thus far been customary in examining the EST process.

## CONCLUSION

Agreement upon a psychopharmacologic model for the study of EST will allow us to apply the principles of diagnosis, dosage, prognosis, maintenance therapy, predictors, and evaluation of efficacy and safety that have proven useful in clinical psychopharmacology. It will allow a more temperate evaluation of the processes than is provided by our present negative outlook. It will encourage more comparisons of the drug therapies with EST, culminating in clearer definition of their similarities and differences in terms of modes of action, efficacy, and time course. It will encourage objective evaluations of the special uses of EST, as in the prophylaxis of suicide and the relief of therapy-resistant psychoses. Additionally, viewing EST as a psychopharmacologic process may enlarge the small band of enthusiasts and pragmatists now assessing the treatment, and give some pause to those psychiatrists, antipsychiatrists, and political activists who wish to discard the treatment.

This review summarizes some of the extensive experience with seizure therapies and suggests that significant parameters of the treatment are well understood. The process is neither purely psychologic nor physiologic; neither convulsion nor shock are essential; the biochemical changes which are the basis for improvement are closely related to the changes induced by the drug therapies, and the modes of action appear to be likewise related. EST is a special psychopharmacologic intervention in which increases in central neurohumors and hypothalamic peptides augment the levels of these substances which occur in the pathologic process.

On a more clinical note, EST is a psychiatric and medical therapy, and nothing in the treatment process justifies its exclusion from acceptable clinical practice. Its use should not be arbitrarily limited by legal proscription. Its alleged use in coercion or in obtaining political compliance is to be deplored, as is the use of drugs under similar circumstances. It would be tragic for society to prematurely discontinue this useful treatment before a satisfactory substitute is available. The application of EST can be improved by more general use of modified seizures, selected electrode locations (i.e., unilateral nondominant electrode location should be considered routine), and monitoring of the cerebral seizure. More intensive research of EST should be encouraged both for its therapeutic outcome and for an understanding of brain functions, particularly the role of neurohumors and hypothalamic factors in human behavior.

## REFERENCES

1. Fink, M., Kety, S., McGaugh, J., and Williams, T., eds. *Psychobiology of Convulsive Therapy*. Washington: V. H. Winston, 1974.
2. Fink, M., ed. *Convulsive Therapy. Seminars in Psychiatry* 4:1-79, 1972.
3. Kalinowsky, L., and Hoch, P. *Somatic Treatments in Psychiatry*. New York: Grune & Stratton, 1961.
4. Abrams, R., and Fink, M. Clinical experience with multiple electroconvulsive treatments. *Comprehens. Psychiat.* 13:115-121, 1972.
5. Ottosson, J.-O. Psychological or physiological theories of ECT. *Internat. Jour. Psychiat.* 5:170-174, 1968.
6. Holberg, G. Biological aspects of electroconvulsive therapy. *Inter. Rev. Neurobiol.* 5: 389-412, 1963.
7. Fink, M., and Kahn, R. L. Relation of EEG delta activity to behavioral response in electroshock: Quantitative serial studies. *Arch. Neurol. Psychiat. (Chic.)* 78:516-525, 1956.

8. Volavka, J., Feldstein, S., Abrams, R., and Fink, M. EEG and clinical change after bilateral and unilateral convulsive therapy. *EEG Clin. Neurophysiol.* 32:631-639, 1972.

9. Fink, M., Kahn, R. L., et al. Inhalent induced convulsions: Significance for the theory of the convulsive therapy process. *Arch. Gen. Psychiat.* 4:259-266, 1961.

10. Laurell, B. Flurothyl Convulsive Therapy. *Acta Psychiat. Scand.*, Suppl. 213, Copenhagen: Munksgaard, 1970.

11. Green, M. A. Relation between threshold and duration of seizures and electrographic change during convulsive therapy. *J. Nerv. Ment. Dis.* 130:117-120, 1960.

12. d'Elia, G. Unilateral Electroconvulsive Therapy. *Acta Psychiat. Scand.*, Suppl. 215, Copenhagen: Munksgaard, 1970.

13. d'Elia, G., and Raotma, H. Is unilateral ECT less effective than bilateral ECT? *Br. J. Psychiat.* 126:83-89, 1975.

14. Dornbush, R., Abrams, R., and Fink, M. Memory changes after unilateral and bilateral convulsive therapy. *Br. J. Psychiat.* 119:75-78, 1971.

15. Berent, S., Cohen, B. D., and Silverman, A. Changes in verbal and nonverbal learning following a single left or right unilateral electroconvulsive treatment. *Biol. Psychiat.* 10:95-100, 1975.

16. Blachly, P., and Gowing, D. Multiple monitored electroconvulsive treatment. *Comprehens. Psychiat.* 7:100-109, 1966.

17. Ottosson, J.-O. Experimental Studies of the Mode of Action of Electroconvulsive Therapy. *Acta Psychiat. Scand.*, Suppl. 145, 35:1-141, 1960 .

18. Fink, M. Cholinergic aspects of convulsive therapy. *J. Nerv. Ment. Dis.* 142:475-484, 1966.

19. Squire, L., and Chace, P. M. Memory functions six to nine months after electroconvulsive therapy. *Arch. Gen. Psychiat.* 32:1557-1568, 1975.

20. Fink, M. A unified theory of the actions of physiodynamic therapies. *J. Hillside Hosp.* 6:197-206, 1957.

21. Fink, M. CNS effects of convulsive therapy. In J. Zubin and F. Freyhan, eds. *Disorders of Mood*, Johns Hopkins Press, Baltimore, Md.: 1972.

22. van Riezen, H., and Rigter, H. Possible significance of ACTH fragments for human mental performance. *Biol. Psychiat.* (in press) .

Phenomenology and Treatment of Depression

# 19

# The Antidepressant
# Regimen

## JAMES C. FOLSOM

Depression is a major health problem. Beck writes that "millions of patients suffering from some form of this disorder crowd the psychiatric and general hospitals, the outpatient clinics, and the offices of private practitioners. Depression may appear as a primary disorder, or it may accompany a wide variety of other psychiatric or medical disorders. Not only is depression a prominent cause of human misery, but its by-product, suicide, is a leading cause of death in certain age groups" (1).

Grinker, Miller, Sabshin, Nunn, and Nunnally add, "Despite its vagueness, depression is one of the most frequent diagnoses made on admission and at discharge, for patients in psychiatric units of general hospitals, and in private mental hospitals" (2).

Statistics published by the National Institute of Mental Health of the U.S. Department of Health, Education and Welfare, on patients in mental institutions during 1957, revealed that close to 15 percent of psychotic patients are classified under the headings of involutional psychoses, manic-depressive psychosis, and psychotic depressions. The ratio of females to males is almost two to one. In the private mental hospitals approximately 50 percent of the psychotic first admissions belong to the same three nosological entities, and the ratio of females is also about two to one. It is obvious that the admission rate of depression for psychiatric units in general hospitals and private mental institutions is over three times that of public mental hospitals, without including the vast number of neurotic depressions and other conditions overlying a depressive core [2].

According to Lehmann, "It is clear that depressions represent a serious public health problem. About two million persons, or about one percent of the population, are treated every year for depression in the United States. The suicide rate, which is one in ten thousand for the total population, is fifty times higher among depressed patients. And for each completed suicide there are almost certainly five to ten times as many attempted suicides. Approximately 50 percent of all general hospital patients referred for psychiatric consultations, and 25 percent of all patients admitted to mental hospitals, are depressed" (3).

Experience at our hospital for the 12-month period ending January 31, 1969, reveals that 21 percent of our admissions, or 401 cases, were treated on the Anti-Depression Program. The major diagnostic categories were: Anxiety Reaction with Depression (139 cases), Schizophrenia with Depression (127 cases), Depressive Reaction (68 cases). The other 67 cases were distributed among 15 diagnostic categories.

The problems of diagnosis of depression have caused much difficulty through the centuries. Grinker, Miller, Sabshin, Nunn, and Nunnally are of the opinion that from the time of the ancient physicians to the present there has been little or no improvement in the clinical observations and descriptions of the depressive syndromes. In their book *The Phenomena of Depression*, they state:

> In the nineteenth century, scientific medical developments overthrew the demonological approach to the etiology of mental disorders. Systems of classifications culminated in the work of Kraepelin, whose categories of depressions persist even today. The twentieth-century Freudian influence emphasized psychodynamics to the exclusion of clinical psychiatry and Kraepelinian clinical descriptive stereotypes were replaced by stereotyped psychodynamic formulations. Lately, an empiric behavioral approach has been revived, not in isolation, but in association with physiological, endocrinological and pharmacological methods [2].

There has long been much preoccupation with the endogenous-exogenous argument relative to the cause of depression. Mendels and Cochrane more recently concluded that "the so-called endogenous factor might represent the core of depressive symptomatology, whereas the clinical features of the reactive factor may represent phenomenological manifestations of psychiatric disorders other than depression, which 'contaminate' the depression syndrome. When depression is present in association with these other features, it might be regarded as just one of several symptoms" (4).

In Europe the concept of "vital depression" has been a primary concern. According to Lehmann, "This syndrome (vital depression) is characterized by a motiveless feeling of sadness and dejection, psychomotor disorders, a disordered sense of time, diurnal fluctuations, and various somatic disorders which are mainly localized in the chest and abdomen. Many European clinicians assume that anti-depressant drugs will not be effective unless a syndrome of 'vital depression' is present" (3).

Those of us who hold with psychodynamic models postulate the loss of an ambivalently held love object as the cause of depression. To protect against the loss there is an unconscious introjection of the object, which results in the unconscious turning of aggression against the self. This is an attempt to be rid of the hated part of the ambivalently held love object—even to the point of self-destruction, if necessary.

In describing the two other models of depression, Lehmann states: "The neurochemical model conceives of the physical substrate of depression as an imbalance of two biogenic amines in the central nervous system (CNS), i.e., norepinephrine and serotonin. The behavioral-neurophysiological model conceives of the functional substrate of depression as a particular state of the central nervous system, which is characterized by unresponsiveness to reinforcement because the depressed subject is incapable of experiencing a pleasurable reward from stimuli that ordinarily would be reinforcing" (3).

As has been previously suggested, we have not been concerned with diagnostic category or etiology of depression when prescribing the Anti-Depression Program. It has been sufficient that depression was one of the major presenting symptoms.

Lehmann gives this historical overview of the treatment of depression:

> In addition to simple, human assistance for a depressed person consisting of consolation, sympathy, and reassurance, only psychotherapy and a variety of relatively unsuccessful pharmacotherapeutic and physical treatment methods were available until the mid-1930s. There was a sophisticated dynamic background for psychotherapy in depressions, but the effectiveness of psychotherapy was very limited and almost entirely restricted to reactive and neurotic depressions. The numerous drug treatments proposed for depression were even less effective. They included tincture opii, which, for many years, was the treatment of choice for depression, photosensitizing agents, amphetamines, steroid hormones, nicotinic acid, and a host of other substances. Different physical

procedures—e.g., the artificial induction of anoxia, and x-ray irradiation—were also suggested and proved to be even less successful. Then, in brief succession between 1935 and 1940, hypoglycemic coma therapy, convulsive shock treatment, and prefrontal lobotomy were developed and proved to be potent therapeutic agents in schizophrenia and depression. Hypoglycemic coma therapy, which was mainly used for schizophrenic patients, has been almost entirely replaced by pharmacotherapy today, but electroconvulsive treatment and lobotomy have retained a place in the therapeutic program for depressions, particularly depressions of overwhelming severity or treatment-resistant chronicity [3].

It had been our experience, also, that none of the treatments for depression were completely satisfactory. Beginning in the fall of 1962 the attitude of Kind Firmness, combined with the Anti-Depression Program (which was based on an earlier "total-push" model), was introduced at the Tuscaloosa Veterans Administration Hospital (5). Continuing experience led to the belief that this therapeutic device was superior to anything else available for the treatment of depression. Whereas our staff had previously been observed to be quite upset when faced with a patient with depression, it was observed that after becoming experienced in the use of the new treatment approach, they welcomed the arrival of cases of depression and proceeded immediately with the treatment under the Anti-Depression Program. Experience had taught them that they would be successful in their therapeutic endeavors.

The Anti-Depression Program, using the attitude of Kind Firmness, has been used as our treatment of choice for depression since January 1963. No electroshock treatments have been used since that time. The average length of time on the Anti-Depression Program is five days—no matter how severe the depression, its diagnosis or etiology.

Research was undertaken to assess the effectiveness of the Anti-Depression Program, which our clinical judgment indicated was superior to ego supportive therapies widely in use. The study was designed to compare the effectiveness of the Anti-Depression Program, utilizing the attitude of Kind Firmness, with the effectiveness of Active Friendliness applied to depressed patients. In addition, since we had observed that many depressed patients responded to treatment prior to the time anti-depressant medications would have been effective, the additional contingencies of medication, placebo, and no anti-depressant medications were included in the design.

Descriptions of the contrasting attitudes follow:

## ANTI-DEPRESSION PROGRAM

The Anti-Depression Program provides the depressed patient with a highly structured environment in which every staff member coming in contact with him applies the attitude of Kind Firmness. The depressed patient is placed in a small, rather drab room, furnished with chairs, table, and a few shelves, where monotonous tasks are assigned to him. The tasks may consist of sanding a small block of wood, bouncing a ball, counting little seashells into a cigar box, mopping floors, making beds, and other such menial tasks. These assignments provide physical activity and a focus for his attention. He is never given anything to do which will bring him gratification. The Kind Firmness attitude indicates that all personnel working with the patient are to insist that he carry out all tasks assigned no matter how much he may complain. Staff are not to give in to his pleadings to be left alone to suffer. They are not to try to cheer him up nor to offer sympathy and encouragement. In fact, speech by the patient is discouraged. The patient is kept under close supervision at all times with a small group of other depressed patients. He is allowed no visitors, no mail, and no telephone calls. All tasks are assigned by nursing assistants, who assume a level of expectancy approaching perfection. Any shortcomings in the patient's performance are pointed out to him. In the case of the patient who is severely depressed, it may be necessary for a nursing assistant to take him by the hand and "assist" him to sand or mop. Patients on this program are kept busy during all their waking hours, except during meals and for very brief hourly breaks. If they do not sleep at night, the work program continues. It should be emphasized that while a patient's performance is criticized, he is never ridiculed or belittled. The purpose of this program is to provide an opportunity and cause for the expression of hostility. After there has been an appropriate externalization of his anger, the patient is taken off the program.

## ACTIVE FRIENDLINESS

The attitude of Active Friendliness is considered by the staff of the Tuscaloosa Veterans Administration Hospital to be at the other end of the continuum from the attitude of Kind Firmness. It requires that all staff members be actively friendly with the patient no matter how objectionable or distasteful he may be in his personal habits, in his language, his physical appearance, or other qualities. This requires that the staff move in and "take over" for the patient through total involvement. The staff is supportive and through assistance to the patient does not allow him to fail, thus building success for him. This approach provides the patient with a safe and friendly setting in which he receives praise as an immediate reward for his accomplishments. This approach has previously been known as "tender loving care" (TLC) or "giving love unsolicited." In such an environment, the patient can again become involved in activities and social interactions with a diminishing fear of the failure he has been so accustomed to experiencing.

This attitude is prescribed for apathetic, withdrawn, non-involved individuals—frequently regressed and deteriorated schizophrenics.

Subjects were selected for this study from those newly admitted patients who presented depression as a major symptom. The patients who could not complete the research battery of psychological tests were excluded. Patients were selected without regard to diagnosis or type of depression and were randomly assigned to one of six groups: (1) Kind Firmness only; (2) Kind Firmness with placebo; (3) Kind Firmness with antidepressant medication; (4) Active Friendliness only; (5) Active Friendliness with placebo; and (6) Active Friendliness with antidepressant medication.

The research battery of psychological tests consisted of the Minnesota Multiphasic Personality Inventory (MMPI), the Interpersonal Check List (ICL), and the Tennessee Department of Mental Health Self Concept Scale (TDMH). This battery was administered prior to commencing treatment, two weeks later, again six weeks following initial testing (or at time of discharge—whichever came sooner), and a follow-up administration six months from the date of commencing treatment.

Sixty-eight subjects (thirty-four treated with Kind Firmness, thirty-four with Active Friendliness) were included in the study. Twenty-four were treated with no medication, twenty-one with placebo, and twenty-three with medication. Review of the diagnoses carried by the Kind Firmness and Active Friendliness subjects revealed no significant differences. Approximately 40 percent of the subjects assigned to each attitude had clearly established psychotic conditions. There were two patients diagnosed as chronic brain syndrome with depression in each of these two attitudes. The remaining subjects were almost entirely diagnosed as having psychoneurotic conditions, usually anxiety reactions with severe depression.

The results obtained from the various tests included in the research battery were quite similar, and will be reported in detail elsewhere. The following comparisons of changes occurring during the six months of study, for each of the groups, are based upon inspection of mean MMPI profiles and statistical analyses of differences.

The groups treated by Kind Firmness and Active Friendliness without medication or placebo made comparable improvements by the time of the second testing. They maintained or slightly improved their gain by the third testing. The most significant difference was apparent at the time of the fourth testing when the group treated with the attitude of Kind Firmness showed continued improvement, whereas the group treated with the attitude of Active Friendliness tended to regress toward the starting point. The only group profile within "normal" limits was obtained on the fourth testing by the patients treated on the Anti-Depression Program with the attitude of Kind Firmness without medication or placebo. At the fourth testing, the differences between these groups on the D scale of the MMPI were highly significant $(p < .005)$.

Comparisons of the groups who received placebos revealed no significant statistical differences at any test period. Both groups showed a slight initial improvement but had regressed almost to their starting point by the time of the fourth testing.

The groups receiving medication showed improvement at the second testing, generally maintained the improvement through the third testing, but produced profiles at the fourth testing which were almost as elevated as those obtained at the initial testing.

The following section summarizes some of the conclusions that can be drawn from the consistent and statistically significant results of this study:

1. Depressed patients improved with both forms of attitude therapy investigated.

2. Patients treated on the Anti-Depression Program continued to improve or hold their gains through the research period of six months, while patients treated on the Active Friendliness Program tended to regress.

3. Following treatment on the Anti-Depression Program, patients were less depressed, less dependent upon physical complaints and symptoms, and less self-deceiving. In addition, they were less confused, anxious, ruminative, and repressed. They had a more positive self-concept and manifested improved interpersonal relationships with family members and others.

4. The group treated on the Anti-Depression Program without medication or placebos made greater gains than any other group. The mean test profile of this group was significantly more normal in appearance at the last evaluation.

5. The addition of placebos or anti-depressant medications as prescribed in this study did not improve the effectiveness of the two forms of Attitude Therapy in relieving depression.

6. The Anti-Depression Program utilizing the attitude of Kind Firmness is a safe and effective treatment technique.

A number of clinical observations also support the above conclusions. Patients on the Anti-Depression Program spent an average of 14 days less time in the hospital during this study than did the patients on the Active Friendliness Program. One patient on Active Friendliness remained depressed throughout the six months of the study but quickly responded to treatment on the Anti-Depression Program. Five patients assigned to Active Friendliness had to be removed because of a dangerous increase of psychological disturbances. These patients improved when treated with Kind Firmness. No patients required removal from the Anti-Depression Program because of increased disturbance. Many patients on the Anti-Depression Program spontaneously commented to the effect that the problems they had prior to hospitalization still existed, but that they had changed so that they were now able to face and deal with them.

## DISCUSSION

The results of this study support our position that depression, regardless of diagnostic category or etiology, can be treated more effectively with the Anti-Depression Program using the attitude of Kind Firmness than is possible with ego supportive techniques. The Anti-Depression Program is designed to assist the depressed patient to modify ineffective behavioral patterns and to adopt more adaptive ways of dealing with pressures, conflicts, and other stressful situations. The maintenance, or enhancement, of the improved level of functioning by the groups treated initially with Kind Firmness alone seems to indicate that such learning occurred.

It had been expected that there would be no differences between groups attributable to the medication contingencies. The obtained differences were surprising and warrant further study. It is suggested that patients receiving medication were depending upon the drugs rather than changed behavior for improvement and continued the previous patterns of behavior with the resulting return of depression.

The two groups receiving placebo—whether on Kind Firmness or Active Friendliness—showed no statistically significant differences. This was true at all four testing periods. We have no satisfactory explanation for these findings. It has been suggested that these patients were waiting for a drug effect which did not come.

Referring to the psychodynamic model, the Anti-Depression Program combined with the attitude of Kind Firmness can be conceptualized as the treatment team taking over part of the superego function of the depressed person. In essence, we say to him, "We do not approve of your decision to kill yourself. We do not approve of your directing anger toward yourself. We are taking over. The treatment for depression is work; therefore, we will see to it that you work during all of your waking hours."

Within the framework of the Anti-Depression Program, the patient uses the assigned tasks to symbolically punish himself. A gradual freeing of energy occurs as he proceeds with the tasks assigned. A point is reached at which the direction of the aggression is reversed. The patient is then able to appropriately externalize anger.

Within the overall Attitude Therapy Program, he is immediately rewarded for this adequate and appropriate expression of anger. The reward consists of social reinforcement of the behavior by staff members, who accept the expression of anger and interact with the patient in ways which provide gratification. In addition, more tangible rewards consist of changed activities and lifting of many of the restrictions which had been placed on the patient. The team approach, together with the use of Attitude Therapy, provides the patient with many additional opportunities to learn more realistic and effective behavior patterns during the remainder of his hospital treatment (5).

In closing, I wish to stress the fact that the Anti-Depression Program requires very little time on the part of the professional staff. Once the diagnosis has been made and the Anti-Depression Program has been prescribed by the treatment team, staff responsibility for the treatment process is assigned to Nursing Service. It is the Nursing Assistants who constantly supervise the patient on his work assignments. Other staff members serve mainly in a consulting role. However, when the depression is cured and a change is necessary in the treatment plan, the entire team meets together, and once a team decision has been made, the physician writes the necessary information for the treatment changes on the chart.

## REFERENCES

1. Beck, A. T. *Depression*. New York: Harper & Row, 1967, p. xiii.
2. Grinker, R. R., Miller, J., Sabshin, M., Nunn, R., and Nunnally, J. C. *The Phenomena of Depression*. New York: Paul B. Hoeber, Inc., 1961, pp. ix, x, 12, 23.
3. Lehmann, H. E. Clinical perspectives on antidepressant therapy. *Depression*, Supplement to *Am. J. Psychiat.* 124 (11) : 12, 13, 15.
4. Mendels, J., and Cochrane, C. The nosology of depression: The endogenous-reactive concept. *Depression,* Supplement to *Am. J. Psychiat.* 124 (11) :10.
5. The Treatment Team, VA Hospital, Tuscaloosa, Alabama. Attitude therapy and the team approach. *Ment. Hosp.* 16 (11) :307-323.

# 20

# The Crisis Management
# Of Depression

JUDITH M. SHERMAN

This paper will attempt to define a systematic practical approach to the acute management of depressed patients as they present to clinicians in emergency rooms, in late-night telephone calls, and in various consultative contexts. Following brief description of crisis intervention, clinical techniques and common clinical manifestations of depressed patients in crisis will be discussed in a problem-oriented format.

## CRISIS INTERVENTION

The definition of medical and psychiatric crisis must be made in the context of time and the individual patient. It has been described as "the turning point for better or worse in an acute disease or fever; a paroxysmal attack of pain, distress or disordered function; an emotionally significant event or radical change of status in a person's life; the decisive moment (as in a literary plot); an unstable or crucial time or state of affairs whose outcome will make a decisive difference for better or worse" (1). There is a general agreement that certain stages may be identified: (*1*) a pre-crisis state; (*2*) the crisis impact; (*3*) a period of disorganization or failure of habitual problem-solving responses; (*4*) trial and error disequilibrium responses or mobilization of external and internal resources in which the individual uses novel methods to attack the problem; and (*5*) post-crisis or resolution period (2,3).

The physician practicing crisis intervention assumes that individuals who have been experimenting with inadequate coping mechanisms in a crisis situation are particularly amenable to professional help during this period. The goal may be defined as restoration of an individual to his pre-traumatic level of overt functioning or utilization of the opportunity for psychiatric contact to raise the individual's level of function beyond that of the pre-crisis state.

A systematic approach by the therapist to the patient in crisis involves basically: (*1*) encountering the patient, (*2*) obtaining information, (*3*) making an assessment, (*4*) determining potentials for resolution.

Workers who deal routinely with crisis say that direct contact with the person in turmoil is the most important factor. Although this seems self-evident, most emergency consultations are ordered because of fear and unwillingness by inexperienced physicians to approach a patient with unusual or agitated behavior. It is imperative that the clinician convey an attitude of calmness and confidence. Harry Stack Sullivan has defined the therapist as "the individual in the room with the least anxiety."

After contact is established, the detective work begins. The question "Why now?" must be asked and asked again. "What happened in the patient's life prompting him to seek help?" "For whom does the crisis exist?" (4) Many patients present with no readily discernible precipitating event or crisis. These patients are difficult to assess. Patients are frequently able to describe turmoil occurring over a prolonged period of time without identifying the precipitating event which brought them to the emergency room. Clinicians commonly err in obtaining only that data sufficient to establish diagnosis without identifying the source of the acute crisis. This often results in premature plans for resolution which have little chance of success. Emphasis must be placed upon the time elements involved in the problem to establish indications for appropriate management. One problem-solving response to crisis is seeking help. Eliciting the context in which the decision for care was made often gives the clinician clues to determining a sense of the issues leading to the crisis. The precipitating event is often found in life events such as those described in Holmes and Rahe's Social Readjustment

Scale, discussed in greater detail in Dr. Rumbaut's paper. If the patient cannot identify what brought about his change of status, a detailed accounting of events occurring on the day he decided to seek help can be revealing. The interviewer should also ask whether the patient may be experiencing an "anniversary" response to former times of crisis. The nature of the stress which brings the patient to a crisis may range from death of a spouse or divorce to changes in work, a holiday such as Christmas, or school problems.

Evaluation of the patient in the social context of family, friends, colleagues, social agencies, and physicians should be conducted. It should be determined how significantly these parties are affected by the crisis, whether they augment or diminish the stress on the patient, and if they are potentially therapeutic allies in resolution. To accomplish this end the crisis worker must investigate the organization of the patient's resources and those of his community, often by searching out the information with aggressive use of the telephone. Initial expenditure of this time and energy will result in great savings later in making workable plans (2).

Another aid to developing a crisis history can be a defined check list covering basic areas of functioning which are possibly associated with the crisis. Such a list may include previous levels of functioning exhibited by the patient in school, work, military service; depression rating scales (Zung, Hamilton); and past records of psychiatric treatment. Items on the data base should be directed to functional problems rather than to development of the patient's entire history.

After sufficient relevant information has been gathered, the assessment should be made. The clinician should excuse the patient from the room and consider the problem at an appropriate distance: too often, confronted with a tearful, confused, agitated depressive, the therapist is drawn into the patient's view of the situation as hopeless. Although the final decision is the responsibility of the senior physician, a team approach to resolution is particularly valuable. Other clinic personnel contribute their findings and participate in a discussion of the patient's situation. Group discussion will reveal opinions of the patient's eye contact, body language, rapport with members of the team, or other subjective indicants. Varied areas of expertise or more extensive experience in dealing with different personality types may be possessed by individual staff members. Some patients presenting in crisis may be frightening or overwhelming for the clinician to deal with effectively on a one to one basis, and the support of another team worker may enable the therapist to relax and concentrate on the patient's problems. If a clearly defined psychiatric team is not available to the therapist, emergency room personnel can be taught to elicit information and serve as therapeutic allies (2).

## APPLICATION TO DEPRESSED PATIENTS

A variety of depressive pictures present in emergency rooms and private offices. Although we can say with some assurance that all depressed patients are in distress, not all are in an acute crisis at the time they are seen professionally. The following suggestions for management will not, therefore, be inclusive of all depressive types and situations, but only those involving immediate threats to the well-being of the patient. The focus of discussion will not be the diagnosis but rather the actual presenting behaviors, divided into subjective, objective, assessment, and plans for resolution of each problem.

## PROBLEM ONE: SUICIDAL PATIENTS

S: These patients may present as an unsuccessful suicide attempt or with active suicidal ideation. The most important piece of subjective information is whether or not the person genuinely intends to kill himself. The following questions can frequently be asked to elicit this information: (1) Are you still considering suicide? (2) How do you plan to do it? (3) Do you have the means? (4) Have you tried before and how? Demographic data may assist you in assessing risk. Risk is said to be increased with age, alcoholism, past history of impulse control problems, prior suicide attempt, family suicide, and among single men and married women. Questions designed to elicit the patient's fantasy perceptions of suicide, such as how he believes his death would affect others, and what he expects to happen after he dies, are significant. Investigate how the patient believes things must change for him to wish to live. Feelings of self-worth and motivation for change should be assessed, as well as type and degree of environmental support.

O: Objective data include the mental status exam, which should concentrate especially upon the patient's level of consciousness. It is extremely difficult to adequately assess a patient who is inebriated, who has ingested toxins, or who is recuperating from recent medical or surgical treatment of his suicide attempt. The patient's process of thinking, possibly disrupted by delirium, psychosis, or hallucinations, must be determined. The patient will respond to the therapist as a source of help or as an unwanted intruder, and his manner should be given careful attention. The patient's actual behavior in this regard should be weighed more heavily than verbalized statements such as "Leave me alone, I don't want help." Be particularly wary of patients who seem especially cheerful and calm; research verifies that these are the individuals who are most likely to be contemplating further self-destructive action.

A: The subjective and objective findings will usually answer the question of sincerity and currency of suicidal intent. Determining that the person remains actively suicidal does not automatically indicate whether hospitalization is required (5). Factors to consider are: (1) Is the patient capable of making rational decisions, or is he psychotically or organically impaired? (2) Are the factors which precipitated the crisis still present, and has the patient's response to the situation changed? (3) The opinions of the patient and his "interested others" concerning appropriate therapeutic action. (4) Can a nonsuicide contract be made? The issues involved in hospitalization can be summarized as follows: Institutionalization provides controls for a person who is not capable of providing himself with emotional support or who has impaired reality orientation. Hospitalization allows the patient time and space to change his mind, to begin psychotherapy or chemotherapy, and to remove himself from situational aspects of his crisis. Nevertheless, hospitalization relieves the patient of his responsibility for dealing with the crisis, and may be countertherapeutic. Additionally, the social stigma of a psychiatric hospitalization often reinforces the patient's feelings of self-depreciation, and can itself support further patterns of self-destructive behavior, abdicated responsibility, and chronic assumption of a sick role.

P: Plans should be clear to all parties involved, including the patient, family, and referring physician, and should be documented and explained on the record. Working with suicidally depressed patients involves risk-taking on the part of the physician, and the value of second opinions cannot be underestimated. The physician should carefully consider matters of legal liability in treating this population. Once the crisis is managed, these patients usually benefit from longer-term treatment to deal with problems of self-esteem (6).

## PROBLEM TWO: WITHDRAWN OR MUTE PATIENTS

S: There will obviously be little data available from the patient himself, and greater reliance upon other sources will be necessary. What happened immediately before the patient stopped talking? Is there a past history of similar events or significant psychiatric problems? The clinician's approach to these patients should be direct and firm.

O: There will invariably be a measure of nonverbal communication, and the therapist should be sensitive to it. Is the patient willing to make written notes or body movements in response to questions? Is the patient hallucinating? Has he had a vascular accident resulting in aphasia? On too many occasions, patients referred to psychiatrists as mute and withdrawn depressives or schizophrenics are in fact neurologically damaged aphasics. This should underscore the point in psychiatric crisis management that physical status should not be taken for granted. Similarly, the presence of physical illness does not rule out concomitant psychiatric illness.

A: Depression is an important part of the differential in mute and withdrawn patients. Retarded depression may present this way. The hostile, agitated, mute patient with suicidal ideation may be quite frustrating to work with, but will ultimately become more agitated and act out more aggressively if expeditious treatment is not instituted. The patient's immediate motive for silence should be determined. Is it a defense against an act, a fear of loss of control? Or a feeling that words can no longer reach the depth of his problem? Other differential points include hysteria, in which case one would investigate age of onset and previous occurrence, remembering that hysteria is a positive diagnosis and not one of exclusion. Voluntary mutism may occur in conjunction with depression, paranoia, or situational crisis, such as legal entanglement. Catatonic schizophrenia should be ruled out. Although these patients seem removed, they are usually acutely aware of their situation and will remember everything that is said to them.

P: Again, treatment should begin with development of as much information from other sources as possible. The clinician should continue to communicate verbally while observing nonverbal clues. The patient is in some sense taunting the therapist with his silence, and inviting a power struggle on a field of his choosing. The therapist should be prepared to deal with his own emerging frustrations and maintain a clinically positive attitude toward the patient. Time and observation will often clarify the problems and avoid useless confrontation.

Mute, withdrawn patients usually require hospitalization. If the cause of their withdrawal is fear of losing control, then offering them the structure and restraints of the hospital can be very helpful. Again, special care must be given to the retarded depressed patient who becomes too cheerful or acquires the sudden burst of energy with which to complete an act of self-destruction.

## PROBLEM THREE: AGITATED OR AGGRESSIVE BEHAVIOR

S: These patients usually present with frantic calls from emergency room staff, family, or the family physician. Police or other agencies may be involved. Ascertain for whom the crisis actually exists and what pressures are at work in the environment.

O: Alcohol or drug intake should be determined. Suicidal intent and the level of consciousness should be assessed immediately. Patients who are intoxicated are compromised in ability to make judgments and to participate in treatment contracts. Patients should also be evaluated in terms of the relationship to the therapist and to others in the environment. Do they become more or less agitated around family, for example?

A: The major task after calming the patient is to determine the etiology of his loss of control. Is this a psychotic process or a rage reaction? What is driving its continuation? Patients who have made abortive suicide attempts may present this way, as may psychotic depression, especially in the involutional stage.

P: To effectively deal with agitated patients, one member of the team should take information from accompanying individuals while another approaches the patient in separate quarters. The therapist must remain calm, firm, and in control. Shifting the attention, giving the agitated person a task to accomplish, and moving him to an area out of the battle zone will calm the patient to some degree. For psychotic patients, including psychotically depressed patients, emergency medication should be administered.

Many clinicians are currently using haloperidol injectable or concentrate 5 mg every 45 minutes to one hour until the patient is quiet. The advantage of haloperidol over chlorpromazine, which is also effective in calming agitated patients, is that less sedation and less hypotension are observed with haloperidol. Physical restraint of the patient may be necessary when agitation or impaired reality orientation impedes pacification by other means. Putting a patient in restraints should be planned and coordinated with adequate staff. However, restrained patients should not be left alone without human contact because this increases their rage and feelings of helplessness. Instituting needed controls for a patient lacking them and moving toward expectation of a self-control requires titration of the patient's anxiety and that of the therapist.

## PROBLEM FOUR: MULTIPLE SOMATIC COMPLAINTS

S: Patients present in psychiatric emergency centers because of increased somatic symptomatology or as referrals from stymied general practitioners. The patients often have little understanding of the reasons for the consultation or of what psychiatry is, or little awareness of psychological functioning. They are frustrated with their symptoms, and with medicine for its failure to improve their situation. Evaluation will often reveal many vegetative signs of depression: sleep loss, appetite changes, decreased libido, or general diminution of function. Life events and how the person perceives what is happening to him should be mutually investigated. A certain amount of crisis work has to be done, mitigating anger at the referring physician who "couldn't find anything wrong."

O: Patients must be observed for delusional components. Somatic symptoms should be scrupulously reviewed to rule out actual physical disease (myasthenia gravis, carcinoma of the pancreas, and Parkinson's disease, for example, may present as affective disorders).

A: The critical issue is to determine if depression exists and treat it appropriately. Other conditions such as psychotic delusions in schizophrenia and hysterical neurosis present with similar complaints but have very different past histories. Other assessment issues are the motivation and availability of treatment.

P: The focus of initial intervention is educational: the patient should be advised that he is not alone in his feelings, that his body expresses his emotions and serves a cathartic function in the absence of easy answers to his emotional upheavals. When possible, demonstrate the relationship of emotional feeling to somatic complaints such as muscle tension, headaches, and upset stomach. It should be determined whether and to what degree the patient is benefitting emotionally from his illness.

Tricyclic antidepressants are usually the best treatment for these patients. Side effects should be carefully explained, as this group is clearly one which will notice all bodily changes.

## PROBLEM FIVE: COMPLAINTS OF "DEPRESSION"

This problem is included because of problems in differential diagnosis. Things often aren't what they seem. Patients come into emergency centers stating that they are depressed, but not suicidal. Why did he pick this time? The problem may be a normal grief reaction or situational crisis. The problem may be loss of a place to live, legal issues, or a response to an abused drug. The word depression is widely and often imprecisely used in our culture, and clinicians must have the patience to determine whether they are facing clinical depression, or transitory unhappiness.

## PROBLEM SIX: COMPLAINTS OF "NERVOUSNESS"

Patients may occasionally present in emergency centers for lack of a primary physician with complaints of nervousness or shaking. Described as a physical complaint, it is important to define with the patient whether he is speaking of anxiety symptoms or a physical "nerve which runs down his arm making his hand shake." When questioned, these patients may give a history of many vegetative signs of depression and may be approached as patients with somatic complaints.

O: The shaking or nervousness the patient exhibits should be observed to rule out physical condition such as hyperthyroidism, parkinsonism, alcohol or drug withdrawal, or other neurological conditions.

A: Anxiety neuroses and alcoholism are differential points to consider, but it is depression that is frequently missed, leading to long-term and ineffective use of antianxiety agents.

P: Antidepressants, especially sedative tricyclics, may bring relief to this group of patients.

## RESOLUTION OF THE CRISIS

After the initial assessment and plans have been made, implementation of these plans must occur. What follows are three general resolutions to the emergency visit.

(1) No follow-up. Some patients are experiencing classic symptoms of a crisis without underlying significant pathology, and they benefit from crisis intervention technique with rapid solution of the disequilibrium phase. In these cases, no follow-up is indicated per se except for educating the person about alternatives available for treatment should they develop subsequent problems.

(2) Extended emergency care. For many of the problems listed above, a second or third visit with the therapist will clarify the nature and extent of the problems as well as the strengths of the patient. Time-specific contracts are important in this context because clinicians involved in emergency psychiatry can attest to the high "no show" rate for patients after the initial emergency visit. Another area of difficulty in this regard is the renegotiation of therapy contracts after resolution of the initial crisis.

(3) Referral to another physician or agency. The majority of cases seen in emergency centers have a past history of contact with other mental health practitioners (8). The relationship of the patient to his therapeutic situation is an important aspect of crisis evolution and resolution (9).

Psychodynamic implications of the visit to the emergency center and resistance to returning to the therapy setting should be explored before developing new treatment plans.

Appropriate referral to agencies or other physicians requires skill in matching patient needs to available clinicians or programs. Information about programs or interest changes and feedback about previous referrals can be useful in this regard. As with other plans discussed, the patient's expectations and wishes for further care should be understood. This critical step is occasionally overlooked in the pressured atmosphere of the emergency center, where plans are presented to a patient who remains passive and noninvolved, rather than within a therapeutic alliance.

## SUMMARY

In this chapter crisis intervention techniques have been discussed as they relate to the evaluation and management of patients with depression. The focus of evaluation has been on clinical observations in emergency settings rather than specific diagnostic categories. General management and specific treatment recommendations have been made.

## REFERENCES

1. *Webster's New Collegiate Dictionary*, 1975.
2. Bartolucci, G., and Drazer, C. An overview of crisis intervention in emergency rooms of general hospitals. *Am. J. Psychiat.* 130:953-960, 1973.
3. Rosebaum, C. P., and Beebee, J. *Psychiatric Treatment: Crisis, Clinic, and Consultation.* New York: McGraw-Hill, 1975, pp. 1-17.
4. Farberou, N. Crisis prevention. *Int. J. Psychiat.* 6:382-384, 1968.
5. Mendel, W., and Rapport, S. Determinants in the decision for psychiatric hospitalization. *Arch. Gen. Psychiat.* 20:321-328, 1969.
6. Rosenbaum, C. P., and Beebee, J. *Psychiatric Treatment: Crisis, Clinic, and Consultation.* New York: McGraw-Hill, 1975, pp. 19-39.
7. Comstock, B., and McDermott, M. Group therapy of patients who attempt suicide. *Int. J. Group Psychotherapy*, Vol. 25, No. 1, 1975.
8. Morrice, J. W. Emergency psychiatry. *Br. J. Psychiat.* 114:485-491, 1968.
9. Miller, W. B. A psychiatric emergency service and some treatment concepts. *Am. J. Psychiat.* 124:84-93, 1968.

21

# Outpatient Management
# Of Depressive Disorders

BETSY S. COMSTOCK

Sadness, a sense of personal ineffectiveness, fear of defeat, hopelessness, and loss of belief in a personal future are all familiar complaints to the psychiatrist who treats outpatients. Often these complaints are accompanied by failing physiologic processes. They stimulate suffering men and women (and some children) to seek help, while simultaneously diminishing their ability to cooperate in and to believe in the help that may be available. The doctor who attempts to provide treatment for these individuals in his or her office faces specific problems in evaluating patients, in engaging them in treatment, in monitoring the effects of treatment, and in accomplishing appropriate terminations. Everything depends upon the cooperation of the patient. Very little can be done for him against his will or if he is too indifferent, too passive, or simply too despondent to cooperate in his treatment. Treatment cannot be given and received, it must be participated in. Even the taking of medication supervised by a family member requires positive efforts on the part of the patient. The patient's efforts are derived from the will to live, the will to survive, to grow, and to recover. Psychiatric therapy must first culti-

315

vate this will for health. The various encumbrances which accompany depressive syndromes must be removed, in a progression whereupon improvement stimulates more improvement. When the sequence reverses, and failure seems to affirm the futility of any effort, the work must return to the primary task of developing willingness for success.

That is not to say that all treatment will succeed if the patient only wants to get well. Depressive symptoms are experienced by most people some of the time. Depression as a clinical disorder is of greater severity than what most people experience, it tends to be time-limited in any episode, and in many patients it may recur. In some it seems never to disappear. For some it is a fatal illness, leading to death by suicide. Those who do not accept its lethal potential do not understand the seriousness of the disorder.

This chapter deals with treatment of depressive episodes which can be managed without hospitalization. The chapter is the result of several hours of discussion by a group of psychiatrists with special interest in this aspect of treatment. The group included individuals in private practice, community clinics, and academic psychiatry. Members differed strongly on issues of evaluation and on initial treatment choices, but agreed upon the importance of early involvement in interpersonal terms, on the importance of understanding the interpersonal system in which depression arises, and on many aspects of therapy.

## PATIENT EVALUATION

There is general recognition that a subgroup of depressed patients can be identified by specific findings. These findings include sadness associated with self-blame, a sense of personal unworthiness, and physical manifestations of disordered function: agitation or psychomotor retardation, diminished appetite and libido, terminal sleep loss, and constipation. Such individuals are regarded by many as having endogenous depression, are thought to have associated biochemical defects, and are thought to be those most likely to respond to organic therapies. In contrast, exogenous or reactive depression is considered the functional or emotional response to environmental stresses which produce a sense of personal loss. These can be most appropriately dealt with through environmental interventions or through ego-strengthening techniques which help the patient tolerate his circumstances.

The validity of these distinctions has been challenged by many psychiatrists. It seems improbable that this volume can resolve the differences between two major schools of thought. No new evidence for either side emerged in the discussions reported in this chatper. What did emerge was a clear polarization of the group on this issue. One proponent of the "endogenous depression is a separate entity" viewpoint described an approach to treatment very specific for this group. Although the patients often presented with alarming symptoms, he felt confident that he could treat them successfully, and felt justified in providing assurances to that effect. He argued for the position that two to three weeks of supportive, protective care with use of antidepressant drugs can be expected to resolve most correctly diagnosed endogenous depressions. He stated that he does not use antidepressant drugs in cases where a precipitating stress can be identified. Cases of reactive depression seemed to him more difficult to treat than endogenous cases.

In contrast, other discussants were less sure of their ability to distinguish reactive from nonreactive or exogenous from endogenous states. They described marginal cases with mixed symptoms. Most agreed that thorough history-taking could produce evidence of significant stress in the life of almost anyone. Several psychiatrists reported cases in which antidepressant drugs had seemed effective in patients who appeared to have reactive depression.

The distinction between exogenous and endogenous depression seems to be conceptually attractive to most psychiatrists. In application, it is less attractive because of the difficulty many have in evaluating the importance of environmental factors. A further difficulty is that only very severely depressed patients show most of the diagnostic features of endogenous depression, even though less impaired patients may respond to the same treatment.

A final complication in assigning patients to endogenous vs. exogenous categories is encountered when psychodynamic ideas about depression are considered. Introjection of anger has been regarded as the mental mechanism most characteristic of depression. The theoretical formulation is that aggressive and hostile impulses are found unacceptable for some reason; the outward expression of these impulses, normally directed toward a specific important other person, is blocked by an unconscious mechanism; and the feelings of aggression and hostility are redirected back against the self, where they are expressed as self-blame and self-hatred. Clinicians discussing depression readily agreed that this mechanism often can be identified. The disconcerting aspect of this is that cases in which the mechanism is identified often present the stigmata of endogenous depression: low energy, weight loss, poor appetite, constipation, and sleep disturbance. Connecting links between psychodynamic shifts in depression and biochemical alterations in the central nervous system catecholamines have not been made. It is easy to believe that they exist. But the present state of incomplete knowledge leaves the clinician unable to distinguish cause and effect, and unsure of whether to attempt biochemical or psychoanalytically oriented treatment in such cases. Perhaps the expedient answer for the present should be to attempt both, simultaneously.

Evaluation of depressive presentations should go beyond examination for precipitating stress and identification of introjective mechanisms. The diagnostic process implicit in the DSM II classification, and outlined by Zung in this volume, suggests several specific questions. Determination of psychotic symptoms is critical, since treatment with antipsychotic drugs is indicated for management of the delusional aspects of the illness. It is important to resist the temptation to label any severe depression as "of psychotic proportions" solely because of the intensity of the patient's suffering. The designation of psychosis should be reserved for those cases in which judgment is impaired to a disabling degree, or where reality orientation and thought content has a clearly delusional quality. "I feel rotten" is a nonpsychotic statement. "I am rotting, see how my flesh is turning gray" is a psychotic statement. The latter, and not the former, provides an indication for antipsychotic medication.

When psychotic aspects of depressive illness have been identified, outpatient management may still be contemplated, although the majority of such patients are hospitalized, at least initially. In their long-term management, questions of the likelihood of recurrence and the appropriateness of lithium prophylaxis are encountered. A system of clinical care which received general endorsement from the group discussing outpatient management requires a careful development of history to determine if a psychotic depressive presentation is a first (and possibly only) episode. Lithium was considered justified if there was evidence of previous manic episodes, or if repeated cycles of depressive symptoms were associated with one or more psychotic intervals.

## TREATMENT MODALITIES

Four basic treatment approaches to depression were described by the psychiatrists in their discussions of outpatient management. These were
1. Pharmacotherapy coupled with supportive care.
2. Psychotherapy embodying verbal techniques aimed at uncovering psychodynamic antecedents of depression, enhancing self-understanding, and developing new personality strength.
3. Environmental alteration focusing on the crisis situation precipitating depression, or on longer-term situational factors predisposing to depression.
4. Systems treatment, in which the interpersonal field of the patient to some extent is engaged directly in the process of treatment.

Couples therapy and family therapy operate within this model. Each type of treatment was recognized as having specific indications, technical problems, and limitations. In practice, combinations of techniques were reported much more frequently than single modality approaches; and choice of techniques seemed to be more dependent on the therapist's training, skills, and theoretical orientation than on the patient's symptomatic presentations or on psychological data.

Pharmacotherapy was used by almost all psychiatrists present for this discussion. They agreed that it was considered indicated when patients presented with depressive affect coupled with somatic changes. Most agreed it should be used in any depression which was not obviously situationally derived. Some members of the group favored a trial with antidepressant drugs for all depressed patients and supported this choice with reports of good outcome in unlikely cases, such as those which were considered situational reactions and others in which chronic depressive expressions appeared to be characterologic.

Technical problems in using antidepressant drugs did not occupy a major place in the outpatient management discussion. Attention was focused on problems of terminating drug use. It was clear that current practice is quite varied, some discontinuing drugs soon after remission of symptoms and others continuing for long periods at a reduced dose, because of possible preventative value. Immediate relapse following discontinuation of antidepressant drugs was uncommon in the experience of the discussants. Most, however, had treated patients with cyclical depression whose recovery could only be considered an interval of remission. For these cases, treatment guidelines were not clear. Some therapists favored continued low-dose medication. Others felt their patients were better served by treatment-free intervals which emphasized the satisfactory nature of functioning during remission.

The limitations of pharmacotherapy center in its function as a symptom-reversing rather than as an illness-removing modality. Use of drugs does not alter susceptibility to depression beyond the time of drug use. It can only remove symptoms and prevent their recurrence for the duration of drug use. A substantial minority of patients fail to respond or are deprived of drug benefits because of inability to tolerate the drugs. And finally, some patients, who have excessive need for emotional support from others, experience the receiving of drugs from the doctor as the physical equivalent of receiving loving care and nurturance from the doctor. Use of drugs entrenches such patients in dependent relationships that promote either emotional regression or great dependency ambivalence. Patients who lack the necessary personality strengths to observe such attitudes in themselves and to reflect on their own dilemmas cannot use this experience in a way that promotes recovery.

Indeed, in some cases the relief brought about through symptom removal with drugs may be less important than the opportunity, without drugs, to maintain the patient's sense of autonomous functioning.

Psychotherapy for depression was considered by the discussants to be a highly relevant and important treatment modality. There was agreement that most patients who had a psychological orientation which made them thoughtful about themselves and who were able to cooperate with their therapist could benefit from verbal therapy. Goals of such therapy were described less in the realm of symptom removal and more in ego-development terms than was noted for drug therapy. They involved improving self-understanding and self-acceptance, developing new mechanisms for support of self-esteem, working through dependency conflicts, and giving up or maturing beyond emotional investment in unrealistic self-images. These could be undertaken either in group or in individual therapy. Transactional and behavior-modification techniques were considered useful, although most discussants presented a psychoanalytic viewpoint.

In the discussion of the psychodynamics of depression, comments were made on several important mechanisms. The defensive use of introjection as a means for converting unacceptable anger was acknowledged widely. This mechanism seems especially apt to be overlooked in instances of excessive or pathological grief. Sadness related to the loss of a loved person is generally viewed as healthy and may be discounted as an important part of a troublesome depressive illness. However, when it is associated with guilt and regret and undermines self-esteem, it provides a signal of introjection, of self-affliction with anger which more appropriately could have been directed toward the lost object. The therapeutic task in dealing with this kind of depression hinges on establishing a situation in which the forbidden anger can become acceptable, thereby relieving the introjective process. A therapist's accepting and encouraging attitude may be sufficient, or individualized work may be required to explore the specific nature of the prohibition.

A related mechanism of depression was identified by the participants as being the sadness of loss in a more general sense. In the absence of introjective phenomena, loss still was identified in case reports where a sense of being personally diminished was the response to loss. This can be conceptualized as the depression vulnerability occurring with ego mechanisms which are too rigidly fixed to external supports. When you take the stage away from an actor, depression follows. When you take approval away from a child, depression follows. Loss of acceptance, approval, reputation, social position, or of anything which enhances self-esteem is experienced by everyone as painful. By those who lack flexible compensating mechanisms, it is experienced as the onset of depression. The therapeutic task in such cases becomes examination of and rejection of the unreliable props, and increased reliance for self-esteem on personality aspects which are not so vulnerable to the whims of fortune.

Diminished self-esteem and consequent depression were discussed also in cases where no real loss was reported but rather where expected gains were not realized. In these cases self-esteem was sustained by fantasized and hoped-for success. When fantasy seriously outstripped reality, or when expectations ultimately were unmet, disappointment and the sense of being unappreciated and worthless were reported. A curious aspect of such depression is that it can occur in individuals who are high achievers and who might be expected to have high levels of self-satisfaction. Regrettably, they measure themselves by standards which forever advance before them and which reduce successive accomplishments to mere way-stations on the route to some further goal. Patients thus present with hopelessness and despair, fresh from exam periods in college when the grades were A but two papers were not perfect, or following the crowning success in a brilliant career when no further goal can be seized upon. In these cases, as in cases of more obvious loss, the task of psychotherapy is to allow the patient to shift to mechanisms of self-esteem which are consonant with the real life to be led. For some this may require substantial work to overcome early developmental deficiencies, but for others it may require only a brief period of self-assessment and reorientation.

Issues around patients' dependency-seeking are central in the dynamics of many cases of clinical depression. "Regression to the oral stage" refers to a condition in which emotional energy is excessively devoted to yearning for, and behavior is excessively devoted to seeking, nurturing care from specific others. The person thus seeking the pleasure expected from dependency gratification is apt to encounter disappointment and frustration, is apt to feel unloved and ill cared for, and ultimately may become fatigued and lose hope—in short, may be depressed. Even those who defend against such dependency yearning with strong reactions that produce self-sufficiency and ability to care for others experience disappointment, loss of hope, and depression. Choices in psychotherapy with such patients need to be made with some care. The therapist needs to know what the patient's best level of adjustment has been, and the reason that adjustment was lost, and the nature of the regression-producing experience. Supportive care may provide a hiatus which will allow the patient to regroup defenses to return to the former satisfactory level of adjustment. If this does not appear likely, or desirable, then therapy efforts need to be directed toward understanding and correction of the patient's vulnerability to dependency frustration; and this in turn will require exploration of its developmental antecedents. This involves a commitment for longer-term treatment than was necessarily implied in relation to any of the previously stated dynamics of depression. Nonetheless, some specific disability in the area of dependency gratification probably underlies dysfunctions of the types described above, and no therapy can be expected to proceed without some attention to these issues.

There are psychopathologic states in which depressive symptoms may be encountered, but which are not primarily depressive disorders and should not be treated as such. Borderline states and schizophreniform illness are frequently-encountered examples of this type of condition. In the long-term treatment of either, repeated episodes of depression can be expected. Management of these must be viewed in the perspective of the specific treatment. As the patient consolidates a firm sense of self and develops comfort in personal competence as well as ability to accept personal limitations, depression will recur with diminishing severity and present less of an impediment to progress.

Patients often view past psychiatric disturbances as blemishes which make them unattractive to themselves and others. However, progress toward recovery requires realistic self-assessment and self-acceptance. When these fail, depression-inducing dynamics are established: the patient contemplates his blemished self-image with despair, a sense of lost health, and with inability to progress beyond self-doubt and pity. Great effort may be required before the patient can develop the will to be well, and many fail to regain it.

The overall limitations on dynamically oriented psychotherapy for depression include these: (1) many patients cannot be motivated or do not have the requisite ego strengths to support such work; (2) some therapists do not believe that this work is indicated or do not find themselves sufficiently comfortable with depressive dynamics to tolerate the patient's self-exposure; and (3) the resources in terms of time, space, and professional therapists are nowhere sufficiently available to provide useful psychotherapy for all cases of depression.

Environmental alteration or crisis intervention is the third approach to management of depression. Whatever therapeutic response a psychiatrist makes, it remains true that the patient's environment is responding to him or her in modified ways when depression occurs. When the therapist becomes actively involved, some control can be exercised to assure that the modifications are in the best interest of the patient. Such modifications may take the form of a sick-leave extension rather than firing because of excessive absenteeism. Such active intervention to help prevent worsening of life-circumstances can aid recovery. Much of this effort falls within the professional discipline of social service. It requires careful judgment to decide what interventions are in the patient's interest, and which merely appear efficacious but will ultimately tend to infantilize the patient, diminishing his sense of competence and encouraging a nontherapeutic dependency. There are no hard-and-fast rules for making these judgments. The active interventionist thus steers a precarious course and needs close contact with the patient for obtaining clear data about the consequences of the interventions. Crisis intervention goes beyond social and environmental manipulation. It also involves specific types of interactions between the therapist and the patient, designed to temporarily provide the patient with certain strengths, extended from the therapist in an ego-lending fashion. These include techniques for reviewing decision-making processes, examining available alternatives at times of stress and anticipating their probable outcome, identifying types of transactions which characteristically have caused undesirable outcomes, etc. In short, the therapist allows the patient to benefit from the therapist's more objective viewpoint and greater command of rational process. This does not require making decisions for the patient nor giving him specific advice, but it does require more active participation in real-life decisions than occurs in traditional analytically oriented therapy.

Such participation may be indicated when a patient is unable, even with emotional support, to care for himself. An example of this occurs with acutely suicidal patients overwhelmed by depression. Convictions of hopelessness prevail, and available energy is directed toward escaping the painfulness of living. Crisis intervention then becomes imperative, for without it the patient will not survive to establish therapy goals that go beyond the question "to live or not to live." Intervention may take the form of exploring alternatives to ending life, identifying the immediate causes of giving up hope, and dealing directly with them. Establishment of a protective environment for the patient may be necessary, although it may at times be contraindicated.

Techniques of crisis management are detailed in a separate chapter of this volume. Limitations of crisis intervention are apparent from the time-limited nature of the techniques used. A few depressive presentations can receive definitive management through crisis techniques, but most require transfer of patients to a subsequent treatment setting, with some variable amount of work on longer-term goals. The crisis-team staff enjoys access to patients at times of minimal defensiveness, when resistance to therapy gives way because of the urgency of life's problems. This regularly is followed by restoration of customary defenses, producing surprisingly rapid changes in the direction of reduced motivation for treatment. If treatment planning has not included anticipatory work on resistance to therapy, referrals will be ineffective and the potential benefits of crisis approaches will be lost.

The fourth outpatient management modality found useful in treatment of depression involves systems approaches, the incorporation in the therapy process of a critical segment of the patient's interpersonal field. Since depression arises in patients in the context of their contacts with people who are emotionally important to them, treatment which includes the relevant others has logical appeal. This treatment approach is most indicated when depressed patients are recognized as the symptom-bearers of systems in which psychopathologic processes are displaced to them from others. Thus depressed adolescents treated alone have little chance for recovery while living in a family where a parent projects his or her own depression onto the child, who in turn is perceived and is responded to as inadequate and pitiable. Treatment in such a circumstance must involve the depressed parent in order to free the child from the covert assignment of expressing the family's discomfort. Similarly, couples may trade off symptom-bearing, such that one and then the other is depressed. Even in simultaneous individual therapy they may continue this pattern. Successful treatment requires direct identification of the trade-off in a setting where the couple's interactions are part of the therapy focus.

Technical problems associated with systems approaches are derived chiefly from the complexity of these therapies. Several individuals, rather than an identified patient, must be met, evaluated, worked with in terms of resistance to therapy, and finally contracted with before therapy can proceed. Concerns about confidentiality must be reviewed repeatedly. The vulnerabilities of stable, non-symptom-bearing participants must be considered. The therapist must be prepared to deal with shifts in family dynamics, to respond to heightened anxiety and to behavioral reflections of conflicts in participants other than the initially complaining patient.

Limitation of systems approaches also result from the complexity of these therapies. Only in selected cases and in favorable settings is it possible to acquire the cooperation of relevant individuals. The strong focus on interpersonal process may divert the initially identified patient from self-exploration at a level that could assure maximal personal growth. The emphasis on disordered process also may be interpreted as contradicting judgment about individual illness, and thus may discourage patients from taking medication which could be helpful.

## TREATMENT OUTCOME

Depression characteristically follows a time-limited course. For this reason, criteria of treatment success are difficult to establish. Any symptom duration which is less than the average-expected interval will suggest that benefit has been derived from the interventions undertaken. However, it is never possible to say how long the symptomatic episode would have lasted had it remained untreated. Research evaluations utilizing a large number of cases can reveal relative efficacy of various treatment modalities. For an individual case, however, precise evaluation is extremely difficult. Treatment must be continued to the point of symptom relief, or until the individual therapy objectives have been met. It will not be possible to say that a different treatment would or would not have worked faster or slower, or in the end would have been better or worse.

Gratification from the treatment of depression is available to therapists and to patients when both have a sense of relieved suffering and of personal growth which holds promise of protection from subsequent depression. Judgments about relieved suffering, and even objective measures demonstrating such relief, can be made. Judgments about ego strengthening as an outcome of therapy are subject to greater error, as is evident when a patient treated "successfully" returns with recurrence of a depressive syndrome. Asymptomatic patients look healthy, and a critical defect which leaves them vulnerable to clinical depression cannot always be identified.

## TERMINATION

Termination of treatment is indicated when treatment objectives have been met. Problems about termination may be encountered early when patients decide to stop treatment. Such interruption, of course, is a patient's privilege, but if possible it should be preceded by examination of the patient's motives and possible desire to maintain depressive symptoms for secondary gain. Pressure to change and the responsibility of good health may be intolerable to individuals with basically masochistic personalities or to patients who have accumulated so many emotional debts during their illness that a return to health represents a demand for massive repayment to family and friends.

Quite a different problem may be encountered when termination is approached by agreement between the therapist and patient. Separation anxieties inevitably are stimulated, and some degree of renewed dependence can be expected. The previous therapy work usually will have prepared the patient for dealing with this. However, depression-vulnerable patients may show alarming symptom recurrence as they approach termination, and repetitive attempts may be required before a satisfactory termination is completed.

The therapist also may contribute to a wavering, indecisive approach to termination. Knowledge that depression may recur inevitably detracts from the satisfaction felt in acknowledging that treatment is ended. Probably many psychiatrists are inwardly glad to note that their final bill has gone unpaid, signifying a persisting bond with the patient, promising resumption of therapy should it be needed. Unfortunately, such an attitude may be transmitted to the patient in the preparation for termination, with the undesirable result of retarding the work.

## SPECIAL PROBLEMS

Numerous problems are encountered by clinicians treating depressed patients in outpatient settings. The group of psychiatrists whose discussions are reported here devoted particular attention to three, reflecting perhaps the most serious challenges to professional abilities and also the most controversial special topics in this field of work. They included patients identified as treatment failures, those with recurrent illness, and those considered at risk for suicide.

Depressed patients who don't get well are not common. The maxim that depression is self-limiting fortunately is confirmed in the experience of most therapists. When treatment failure is encountered, it may relate to either of two treatment problems: either depression is secondary to a different and unrecognized psychopathologic state, or countertransference difficulties are interfering with the patient's recovery. Erroneous diagnosis of depression may lead to mismanagement of borderline states or of schizoaffective schizophrenia. Such cases cannot be expected to respond to antidepressant drugs nor to short-term exploratory psychotherapy. They are difficult and often show symptomatic worsening during crisis-intervention procedures. Although they can benefit after long-term work, both therapist and patient must have a realistic timetable in mind in order to avoid anxiety about treatment failure.

Therapist attitudes about a patient which interfere with the progress of therapy can be considered countertransference in a general sense. The more precise definitions which specify attitudes transferred from the therapist's past experience and those responsive to transference phenomena introduced by the patient seem too restrictive. What is intended here is the more general observation that therapists sometimes derive personal emotional benefit from the continuing illness of the patient. Or continuing illness may be produced by some disabling action by a therapist who harbors unrecognized hostility toward a patient. Therefore, when treatment failure is encountered and diagnostic errors have been looked for but not found, a therapist should examine personal attitudes toward the patient. Self-evaluation may enable the therapist to correct for previously unrecognized countertransference. If this fails, transfer of the patient to a different therapist should be considered.

A somewhat different problem is presented by a patient who gets well, but only for a brief time. Recurrent symptoms are to be expected in cycling affective illnesses. Repeated symptoms are indication for a careful search for overlooked psychodynamic issues. However, the cyclic nature of symptoms should focus attention on biochemical aspects of the illness. Repeated antidepressant therapy may be useful. Such cases also warrant a trial with lithium because of the possibility that it can have preventative value. These are difficult treatment cases because the recurrence of symptoms erodes any position of therapeutic optimism. Families, patients, and physicians need to establish realistic ideas about what treatment can accomplish. Long-term plans should accommodate a lifestyle marked by periods of illness, comparable to the lifestyle of individuals with other recurring physical or emotional disorders.

The problem of suicidal preoccupations should be dealt with in treatment of any depression, at least to the extent that it is necessary for the therapist to assure that suicide risk does not exist. Discussion of self-destructive impulses needs to be part of the evaluation phase and needs re-emphasis in any interval of affective change. Judgments about high risk traditionally have been related to demographic variables: male sex, old age, alcoholic, living alone, etc. However, these criteria have very limited predictive value. In an individual who is depressed, increased risk may be signaled by worsening depression, by loss of future orientation, by an attitude of resignation in a person previously filled with protest, or by direct statements about suicidal preoccupation. Errors in judgment occur in both of the two possible directions. Verbal complainers may be erroneously disregarded because they are judged hysterical or manipulative. On the other hand, patients seeking to dramatize their dysphoric state may be harmed by a therapist's overreaction, which may serve to reward self-destructive behavior and thereby may reinforce it. The most effective course to be taken with suicidal patients seems to be one of close attention and frank discussion of suicidal impulses coupled to the therapy position that each person individually has power over and responsibility for his or her life. This philosophic position, then, is opposed to hospitalization for most suicidal patients, since hospital care tends to foster dependency, to heighten separation anxieties at the time of discharge, and to reinforce self-destructive behavior. Hospitalization offers better protection from suicide than is otherwise available, although in-hospital suicide obviously can and does occur. Admission may therefore be indicated when a person's illness has removed his or her ability to attend to the choices favoring protection of life. This may occur in psychotic depression, or when any delusional process incorporates ideas about suicide. Hospital care also seems to be more efficacious in those cases where internalized hostility, indicated by self-blame and guilt, produces self-destructive impulses. Such patients are less prone to develop strong dependence on the hospital and are less likely than others to present with repetitive suicidal threats or gestures.

Suicidal patients managed on an outpatient basis benefit from frequent contacts, from knowing their despair is understood and accepted, and from an attitude of minimally demanding positive expectations on the part of their therapist. Too much ambition, or expectations raised too high, imposes a burden these patients will not accept. On the other hand, depressed and suicidal patients often are very sensitive to discouragement on the part of their therapist. The therapist therefore must monitor personal feelings in order to counteract the ill-effects of personal distress about patients.

## SUMMARY

Discussion of outpatient management of depression by a group of psychiatrists who work in varied settings yielded sharp differences as well as some shared convictions. The most controversy arose over the issue of the clinical usefullness of separating out reactive depression as a diagnostic entity, with the implication that reactive disorders don't respond to organic therapies. Many reported successful use of antidepressant drugs in cases where situational stress was conspicuous. In discussion on the psychodynamics of depression, primary emphasis was placed on the importance of recognizing and treating pathological grieving, and on the importance of recognizing dynamics approachable through short-term work as separate from those requiring long-term effort. Another area requiring sophisticated judgment was identified in discussions of crisis intervention efforts, in that it was recognized that short-term benefits may be too costly if they involve active interventions which infantilize patients and effectively diminish ego strengths.

The greatest agreement was reached in emphasis on the importance of interpersonal process, both in the genesis of depression and in its treatment. Enthusiasm for working in couples and in family therapy was reported by almost all discussants.

22

# The Relationship and Management of Depressive And Addictive Syndromes

JOHN R. STAFFORD

## HISTORY

Depression, as a mood, a symptom, a continuum of clinical syndromes, or a postulated disease entity, is among the most common complaints of human existence. Literary descriptions of melancholy and mourning can be found in the early recorded history of most civilizations.

Similarly, alcohol, opium, and cannabis have been known since antiquity, and disability resulting from their misuse has been described in ballad and biography. The current American estimates of ten million alcoholics, a half-million opiate addicts, and the indeterminate number of persons consuming billions of amphetamine, barbiturate, and sedative doses make substance abuse one of our major health problems.

## PSYCHOLOGICAL THEORIES

A relationship between depression and the addictions has been postulated for many years. Perhaps the earliest such association observed was the

329

use of alcohol or drugs to relieve melancholy with euphoria. Fenichel (1) notes that use of euphoric drugs for this purpose does not constitute addiction if terminated upon cessation of painful mental or physical states. However, as the propensity to classify mental disorders and seek their causes developed, patients were recognized to have continuing or recurrent symptoms of both depression and addiction. Kraepelin (2) described a form of alcohol excess (dipsomania) which exhibited an episodic course similar to his concept of manic-depressive illness.

In an 1897 letter to Fliess, Freud (3) suggested that masturbation was the primary addiction and that alcohol, tobacco, and morphine only enter into life as substitute and replacement.

Sachs (4) also postulated such a double function for the addictions, placing them midway between the neuroses (attempts to avoid psychic pain) and the perversions (attempts to obtain pleasure).

Abraham (5) was apparently the first to conceptualize addictions as a less painful alternative or equivalent to melancholia. This view is echoed in Fenichel's (1) characterization of addictions as impulse neuroses, sharing with perversions a common basis of predisposition described as "a fixation on the state where self-esteem is regulated by external supplies or where guilt motivates regression to this state."

Rado (6), in noting the satiation common to nursing infants and alcoholics, postulated an "alimentary orgasm," a state presumably not unlike the "total body orgasm" claimed by the "mainliner" of heroin, and indicative of regression to an oral stage.

In *Man Against Himself* (1938) (7) Menninger expands upon Freud's dualistic construct of life and death instincts. He concludes that alcoholism and morphinism represent "slow suicides," in which the person accepts responsibility for self-destruction only unwillingly and partially.

Later, in his 1963 volume, *The Vital Balance* (8), Menninger considers addictions as a manifestation of aggressive discharge displaced to one's own body, much in the manner of some depressions.

Blum (9), in a comprehensive review, linking traditional psychoanalysis, ego psychology, ethology, learning theory, anthropology, neurophysiology, and pharmacology, concludes that a single-causation model clearly is inapplicable to alcoholism. She notes that three distinct types of alcoholics can be delineated in terms of developmental stages:

Type I: "fixated at or regressed to oral stage, clinging passively to mothering persons, depressed when nurturant support not forthcoming, and narcissistic in choice of love objects."

Type II: "fixated at or regressed to anal stage, with capacity for sublimation, albeit with same-sex choice of love objects, capable of maintaining sense of self by helping others."

Type III: "fixated at or regressing to the phallic-Oedipal stage, unable to reconcile tenderness and sexuality toward same object, experiencing difficulty with authority figures."

Additionally, parallels are drawn to stereotypic behavior in animals and a treatment model aimed more at strengthening ego functions than resolving childhood conflicts.

Other writers assert with greater confidence the preponderant influence of one central conflict in the addictions. Salzman (10) notes that "the underlying personality type that lends itself to addictions is that of the obsessive-compulsive. The problem of control and the need to handle the anxieties that result from loss of control can be recognized as the overriding issue in people suffering from addictive disorders. While depression, anxiety, and a host of other psychological problems may be present, obsessional difficulties are omnipresent." Salzman sees the obsessive as *the* most prevalent characterological type, a universal and ubiquitous defense. Therein, omnipotent grandiosity or the "exemption from human consequences" are duplicated in the euphoriant drug experience, and depression or psychosis are seen as breakdowns of the more prevalent obsessional defense.

Popular influences in recent psychotherapeutic technique have been the reality therapy of William Glasser (11), and the "rational-emotive therapy" of Albert Ellis (12).

Glasser's theory, reduced to its simplest statements is that "people do not act irresponsibly because they are 'ill,' they are 'ill' because they act irresponsibly." Depression then occurs because of (1) the deficiency of enjoyable activity (e.g., loving and being loved, feeling worthwhile because of responsible productivity) or (2) a preponderance of irresponsible action (e.g., delinquent or addictive behavior).

Ellis focuses upon "irrational indoctrinating phrases" productive of dissonance between one's actual and idealized self and life situations.

Most explicit among theories of both depressive and addictive behaviors are those of the behavioral psychologists. Lewinsohn (13) summarizes the behavioral assumptions:

1. A low rate of response-contingent positive reinforcement acts as an eliciting (unconditioned) stimulus for some depressive behaviors (e.g., dysphoria, fatigue, somatic symptoms).

2. A low rate of response-contingent positive reinforcers is sufficient to explain the low rate of (operant) behaviors by the ("retarded") depressive.

3. The total amount of such response-contingent positive reinforcers received by an individual is presumed to be a function of three sets of variables:

    a. the number of events that are potentially reinforcing for the individual.

b. the availability of reinforcement in the environment.

c. the skill of the individual in possessing and emitting those behaviors which will elicit reinforcement from the environment.

Thus depression may arise when a social reinforcer (love, praise, companionship or pleasurable activity) is withdrawn. The absence of the availability of such reinforcers leads to a low or "retarded" rate of operant behavior. Finally, "depressed" behavior may serve to elicit *other* social reinforcers (e.g., sympathy, tender care, or even angry resentment) and the "depressed" behavior be perpetuated or maintained by this very attention. In other words, the increased availability of this new set of reinforcers serves to increase the rate of depressive behaviors, and additionally may diminish the trial of more adaptive activity.

Folsom's (15) success with the "antidepressant regimen," discussed in detail elsewhere in this volume, may be seen as a revision of contingency and reinforcement availabilities.

The concept of depressive equivalents which substitute for or "mask" depression—that is, behaviors such as addictions, psychosomatic symptoms, and "acting-out" behaviors—is seen as consistent with the behavioral formulation of depression (15). That is, such behaviors as intoxication, narcotic trafficking, and consumption rites secure attention and recognition from others. To the extent that the "post-dependent" environment is perceived as richer and more reinforcing than a depressed or impoverished "pre-dependent" environment, the rate of addictive behaviors can be expected to increase. This, in behavioral terms, is seen as one basis of securing "kicks," often offered as explanation of dyssocial or self-injurious behavior by adolescents.

Additionally, the learning of immediate reinforcing effects of a euphoriant agent in alleviating anxiety, depression, or abstinence symptoms has been well known since antiquity.

Yet another "psychological" view of an addictive syndrome and a treatment approach (Alcoholism, Alcoholics Anonymous) is the cybernetics-general systems theory proposed by Bateson (16). His analysis of the alcoholic interacting with sub- and suprasystems (notably, his bottle, the significant "other," and the larger systems perceived as "hitting bottom") provide a new viewpoint. Especially, the effectiveness of AA in dysfunction is explicated in terms of complimentarity and symmetry.

The Social Readjustment Scale developed by Holmes, Rahe, and others (17) has been applied to predict vulnerability to many conditions ranging from athletic injury to suicide. The 43-item SRS scale contains some items seen as direct losses and others potentially productive of lessened self-esteem, but all requiring coping energies. Drug-dependent subjects, including alcoholics, appear to incur an unusually large number of these situational stresses. Certainly in no other field of psychiatric practice are recurring interpersonal, vocational, and socio-legal crises encountered with such frequency. The diversion of psychic energies to cope with such stresses may well render the addict more vulnerable to depressive illness as well as psychophysiologic disorder.

## BIOCHEMICAL CORRELATES

Ethanol has been shown by many investigators to increase release and excretion of catecholamines in man. This process appears to be related to the intermediate ethanol metabolite, acetaldehyde, rather than to a direct effect of ethanol itself (13).

It is not determined whether brain concentrations of norepinephrine and dopamine are chronically lowered by alcohol-acetaldehyde action, or whether tolerance may develop. Where resynthesis of norepinephrine is decreased by disulfiram (Antabuse) inhibition of dopamine B. oxidase, acute depletion of brain norepinephrine does occur.

The role of ethanol or its metabolites in acute and chronic administration upon central catecholamine mechanisms appears complex, but is at least consistent with the catecholamine hypothesis of affective disorder.

Reviewing animal studies with narcotics, Schildkraut et al. (19) noted increased norepinephrine turnover during acute administration, but variable alterations in norepinephrine and MHPG levels with chronic administration and withdrawal. Their studies with human subjects during heroin administration and subsequent methadone detoxification showed elevated MHPG excretion during heroin administration (significant in only 4 of 9 subjects) with an "anticipatory" rise in MHPG in this subgroup occurring the day *before* heroin administration.

Inwange and Primm (20) have suggested that individuals with low capacity to synthesize biogenic amines may self-medicate against an "inherent affective disorder." They acknowledge, however, a basic difficulty in such theorizing; there is no way to ascertain baseline amine levels prior to a person's *first* use of addictive drugs.

## GENETIC THEORIES

Winokur et al. (21) have studied the families of women characterized as prototypes of "depression spectrum disease" and found a high incidence of male relatives (father, brother) who exhibit alcoholism or antisocial behavior. Also, the female relatives of index patients were frequently noted to have had depressive episodes. However, the complex interplay of a family system including alcoholic male and/or depressed female parents makes nature-nurture conclusions difficult.

## MANAGEMENT: EVALUATION AND DIAGNOSIS

Woodruff et al. (22) note the difficulty of thinking in precise diagnostic terms about patients with both depression and alcoholism. Directives of DSM-II (23) notwithstanding, it is often difficult to ascertain which syndrome began first and which is secondary or additional. Woodruff's group of depressed alcoholic patients manifested early behavioral disturbances (e.g., school difficulty, fighting) similar to those of a nondepressed alcoholic group and not present in a group of purely depressed patients.

## ASSESSMENT

The first step in planning treatment for the depressed, substance-dependent individual must be the collection of data necessary to assess the existence, nature, and severity of depression and addiction. When the patient acknowledges depression only, inquiry should be made regarding the use of alcohol and drugs in alleviating or aggravating mood changes. When addiction is the presenting complaint, pre-existing mood swings or recent life stresses and losses should be considered. We have found the Zung Self-Rating Depression Scale and the Holmes-Rahe Social Readjustment Scale (15) helpful as early screening tools in this assessment.

A decision to hospitalize is typically influenced by the patient population, availability of hospital resources, and philosophy of the physician concerning desirability of outpatient crisis management. In general, however, severe intoxication, significant immediate suicidal risk, and deficiency of environmental supports dictate hospital treatment. Similarly, when outpatient management fails to achieve significant abstinence, or when noncompliance with drug therapy occurs, hospitalization is indicated.

Abstinence syndromes are treated according to the drug of abuse; with the exception of alcohol and narcotics addiction withdrawals, which are managed with chlordiazepoxide and methadone, decreasing doses of the drug of abuse are employed after establishing probable daily requirement.

As the amelioration of abstinence symptoms is achieved, the patient is asked to engage with staff members in the definition of problem areas. We employ a structured problem inventory sheet which somewhat artificially categorizes problems as: I. Behavioral; II. Thinking; III. Feeling; IV. Social-

## Table 1. Example

| Outcome | Problem 1 | Problem 2 | Problem 3 | Problem 4 | Etc. |
|---|---|---|---|---|---|
| | Drug dependence heroin | Depression | Marital conflict | Unemployment | |
| Best Possible + 2 | Total abstinence | Total clearing without recurrence | "Happy" marriage | Steady employ- with advance- ment | |
| Expected Outcome 0 | | | | | |
| Worst Possible − 2 | Continual addiction, eventual death | Persistent severe depression | Divorce | Permanently unemployed | |

Environmental-Vocational; and V. Medical. This device is employed to confront the addict's well-known tendencies to deny problem areas other than those most overt and conspicuous. Also, this inventory aids staff in assuring that less apparent problems are not overlooked.

Following the identification of problems, treatment goals are formulated in behavioral terms along the dimensions of Goal Attainment Scaling or contract fulfillment analysis described by Kiresuk et al. (24,25).

This goal definition specifies a range of possible outcomes for each problem, and invites the patient to specify a predicted outcome as well as an estimate of current functional status.

In our experience, this particularizes outcome and serves useful functions for both patient and staff. The patient is encouraged to see outcome as a gradient rather than an all-or-none proposition with total abstinence or idyllic happiness as the only acceptable end points. This seems to mitigate somewhat the "failure"—guilt—depression—readdiction cycle. Also staff members experience less frustration when treatment plans are formulated with more realistic and achievable goals.

## TREATMENT

*General:* The goal-attainment and problem-oriented format enables the clinician to review problems independently as well as concurrently. Problems which are of vocational nature are assessed in totality, and appropriate corrective counseling, training, educative, or rehabilitative measures initiated.

Similarly, family therapy, marital counseling, or divorce counseling is directed toward construction of an optimal achievable climate in which the patient may combat his addiction and depression. Medical problems are identified, accorded levels of priority, and either treated or referred (with adequate patient instruction) for management elsewhere.

*Milieu:* The milieu of a hospital drug dependency unit should afford at least the following elements:

1. "Reasonable" security against the introduction of abused substances.

2. Problems of daily living comparable to those of the "outside world"; for this reason the unit has many structured regulations rather than a permissive climate.

3. A system of social reinforcement designed to diminish depressive and addictive behaviors and to enhance adaptive, nondependent behaviors.

4. A vehicle for the practice of self-government and the therapeutic illustration of authority-submission conflicts.

*Chemotherapy:* Our narcotic addiction treatment program complies with federal regulations for methadone programs. Those persons satisfying the two-year addiction requirement for methadone maintenance are instructed in detail concerning the statistical advantages of methadone vs. drug-free status on long-term abstinence. The obsessional-omnipotent fantasy of absolute self-control is confronted both to allow "forgiveness" for future relapse and to set the stage for more enthusiastic future compliance. We employ a low-dose methadone schedule as described by Jaffe (26) with usual daily dosages in the 20-to-70 mg range. In our experience it is more typical for the patient to request "detoxification" or discontinuing methadone than for the staff to recommend it. Premature discontinuance of methadone is viewed and interpreted as the probably unconscious wish to expose oneself to narcotic risk, thereby testing personal invulnerability. The wish is treated as a natural, even necessary step toward the recognition of human limits of control. When the clinician attempts to impose "you *should* continue" control over the treatment, a power struggle typically ensues and noncompliance usually results. In our experience a restatement of the "odds" against abstinence, acceptance of the need to "test" self-control, and the "it's your decision" attitude typically result in a return to compliance. The methadone side effects of constipation, weight gain, altered libido, insomnia, and sweating must be considered when evaluating physiologic features of depression. Alcoholic patients are encouraged to utilize disulfiram (Antabuse) in the manner of an "insurance policy." As pointed out by Fox (27), one is typically unable to employ insights gained in prior or current psychotherapy unless alcohol is interdicted.

The contraindications of serious heart disease, diphenylhydantoin (Dilantin), or antituberculosis chemotherapy are discussed and excluded by thorough medical and drug history. An "Antabuse Information Sheet" is reviewed with the patient, informing him of the nature and sequence of the alcohol-disulfiram toxic reaction. The risks are compared to the health and accident risks of continued alcohol consumption. If the patient accepts disulfiram therapy as a useful adjunct, he is asked to sign one copy and to retain a second in his billfold for identification purposes.

The abuser of sedative-hypnotic and psychostimulant drugs poses in our population a greater challenge than either pure narcotic or pure alcohol dependent persons. Because of the absence of effective antagonists, as well as the immaturity and diverse psychopathology, abstinence appears to require a lengthy reductive-naturational experience.

Tricyclic antidepressants are in our hospital and clinic generally reserved for patients scoring an SDS index of 60 or more on the Zung Scale or in excess of 25 on the Hamilton Scale. Depressions marked by prominent physiological equivalents (where these are determined not to be primarily due to drug or alcohol withdrawal or methadone administration) are the most likely to respond to antidepressant drugs in our combined addicted-depressed population.

Choice of tricyclic antidepressant is influenced by (1) history of previous favorable response (2) degree of nighttime sedation desired and (3) therapeutic response and side effects. We have ordinarily employed a single nighttime dose schedule except when a history of cardiac insufficiency or arrhythmia was obtained, or when side effects such as orthostatic hypotension intervened. Our method involved the initiation of imipramine or amitriptyline in doses of 50 mg daily (nightly) and increase by 50 mg nightly until a dosage of approximately 3.5 mg/kg was achieved (200-300 mg usual daily range), or until side effects precluded further increase.

Patients manifesting depressions with delusions, as described by Glassman elsewhere in this volume, are more likely to respond to electroconvulsive therapy (ECT). The importance of distinguishing the delusions of an alcohol- or drug-induced organic brain syndrome from the depressive variety when considering ECT will be clearly appreciated. Unilateral ECT with minimal convulsive voltage to the nondominant hemisphere may have an advantage in lessened memory impairment or avoiding aggravation of subclinical drug-induced organic changes.

It would be desirable to add an electroencephalogram to the usual (skull series, lumbar, spine, EKG) roentgenographic and cardiographic screen prior to ECT, especially when a history of drug-related alterations of consciousness or seizures is obtained.

Imipramine pretreatment has additionally been reported to ameliorate symptoms of morphine abstinence syndrome in rats (28) and alcohol withdrawal in man (29). Propranalol (Inderal) a B-adrenergic blocking agent, has been reported by Carlson and Johannson (30) to ameliorate tension and depression associated with alcohol withdrawal. Hollister and Prusmarck (31) in a subsequent controlled study reported little benefit from propranalol in the management of psychologic symptoms during opiate withdrawal.

*Psychotherapy:* Practical approaches of group psychotherapy dealing with current life problems have been advocated as more effective than intensive individual therapy for alcoholism (27).

A variety of group theories and techniques: The experience of Synanon, Daytop Village, Phoenix House and related residential programs have claimed encounter-type therapies to be effective vehicles for facilitating change in lifestyle and self-concept in motivated patients. That encounter group format and results vary greatly with the theoretical bias and personal style of the leader has been documented. Lieberman, Yalon, and Miles (32) noted 8-10% "casualties" and 32-34% positive change among 206 "normal" college students seeking a growth experience.

Their 17 groups utilized a variety of theoretical models including National Training Laboratories format, Gestalt, psychodrama, Synanon, psychoanalysis, and Transactional Analysis.

It seems reasonable to assume that similar variability in leadership styles could account for the differential outcomes seen in alcohol and drug abuse programs.

A more "quantifiable" approach is that proposed by Ross (33). This method utilizes an "intake record" to identify cues which precipitate drinking behavior and the circumstances and consequences of such behavior. The construction and negotiation of behavioral contracts serve to modify problem behaviors. The identification of interpersonal conflicts and their reconstruction by psychodramatic role-playing techniques is facilitated in the group setting. Equipped with problem list, goal attainment scales, and greater recognition of the determinants of behavior, patient and therapist are in a position to develop contracts for the shaping of more adaptive, non-addictive or -depressive behaviors. A similar holistic approach "utilizing all or any methods of therapy that seem appropriate" is advocated by Ewing (34).

*Adjunctive Therapies:* A variety of techniques including meditation, biofeedback, relaxation training, and cerebral electrotherapy have been employed to diminish anxiety and achieve a relaxed state. The learning of new methods of self-assertion and social skills are similarly helpful adjuncts to long-term rehabilitation. The achievement of a "natural high" has been advocated as an alternative to drug-induced euphoria.

## SUMMARY

The problems of addictive syndromes and depression occurring individually test the skill of the clinician. Together they require a multimodality treatment program with expertise in (*1*) problem definition, (2) behavioral descriptions of goals, (3) psychoactive drug actions and interactions and (*4*) flexible use of psychotherapeutic techniques. Outcome measurements for this significant group of patients are thus far limited to independent follow-up of abstinence or "global functioning" and remain in most cases anecdotal.

## REFERENCES

1. Fenichel, O. *The Psychoanalytic Theory of Neurosis.* New York: W. W. Norton, 1945, pp. 357-414.
2. Kraepelin, E. *Lectures on Clinical Psychiatry.* New York: Hafner Publishing Company, 1968.
3. Freud, S. Letter No. 79 (1897), in M. Bonaparte, A. Freud, and E. Kris, eds. *The Origins of Psychoanalysis: Letters to W. Fliess.* New York: Basic Books, 1954.
4. Sachs, H. Zur Genese der Perversioner. *Int. Z. Psychoanal.* 9:172-182, 1923.
5. Abraham, K. A short study of the development of the libido, viewed in the light of mental disorders (1924). In *Selected Papers of Karl Abraham.* London: Hogarth Press, 1948, p. 418.
6. Rado, S. The psychic effects of intoxicants: An attempt to evolve a psychoanalytic theory of morbid cravings. *Int. J. Psychoanalysis* 7:396-413, 1926.
7. Menninger, K. A. *Man Against Himself.* New York: Harcourt, Brace & World, 1938, pp. 160-184.
8. Menninger, K., Mayman, M., and Pruyser, P. *The Vital Balance.* New York: Viking, 1963.
9. Blum, E. M. Psychoanalytic views of alcoholism: A review. *Quarterly Journal of Studies on Alcohol,* 27:259-290, 1966.
10. Salzman, L. *The Obsessive Personality.* New York: Jason Aronson, Inc., 2nd ed., 1973, pp. 162-191.
11. Glasser, W. *Reality Therapy.* New York: Harper & Row, 1965.
12. Ellis, A. *Humanistic Psychotherapy: The Rational-Emotive Approach.* New York: Julian Press, 1973.
13. Lewinsohn, P. M., Weinstein, M. S., and Shaw, D. A. Depression: A clinical research approach, in R. Rulin, and C. Franks, eds. *Advances in Behavior Therapy.* New York: Academic Press, Inc., 1969.
14. Lieberman, R. P., and Raskin, D. E. Depression: A behavioral formulation. *Arch. Gen. Psychiat.* 24:515-523, June 1971.
15. Folsom, J. C. Attitude therapy and the team approach. *Ment. Hosp.* 16 (11) :307-323, November 1965.
16. Bateson, G. The cybernetics of self: A theory of alcoholism. *Psychiatry* 34:1-18, 1971.
17. Holmes, T. H., and Rahe, R. H. The Social Readjustment Scale. *J. Psychosomatic Research* 11:213-218, 1967.
18. Davies, V. E., and Walsh, M. J. Effect of ethanol on neuroamine metabolism, in Y.

Israel, and J. Mardones, eds. *Biological Basis of Alcoholism.* New York: Wiley, 1971, pp. 73-102.

19. Schildkraut, J. J., et al. The effects of heroin on catecholamine metabolism in man, in *Aminergic Hypotheses of Behavior: Reality or Cliché,* B. K. Bernard, ed. NIDA Research Monograph Series 3, November 1975, pp. 137-145.

20. Inwange, E. E., and Primm, B. J. 2, Phenylethylamine: Biochemical and Clinical Characterization of Narcotic Dependence and Gradual Methadone Withdrawal in Man, presented at National Drug Abuse Conference, New Orleans, April 1974.

21. Winokur, G., et al. Depressive disease: A genetic study. *Arch. Gen. Psychiat.* 24:135, 1971.

22. Woodruff, R. A., et al. Alcoholism and depression. *Arch. Gen. Psychiat.* 28:97-100, January 1973.

23. *Diagnostic and Statistical Manual II* of The American Psychiatric Assoc., 1968.

24. Kiresuk, T. J., and Sherman, R. E. Goal attainment scaling: A general method for evaluating community mental health programs. *Community Mental Health J.* 4:443-453, 1968.

25. Lombillo, J. R., Kiresuk, T. J., and Sherman, R. E. Evaluating a community mental health program: Contract fulfillment analysis. *Hospital and Community Psychiatry* 24 (11) :760-762, November 1973.

26. Jaffe, J. H. A review of the approaches to compulsive narcotics use, in *Drugs and Youth,* J. R. Wittebow, H. Brill, et al., eds. Springfield, Ill.: Charles C Thomas, 1969.

27. Fox, R. Alcoholism and reliance on drugs as depressive equivalents. *Am. J. Psychotherapy* 21:585-596, 1967.

28. Schwarz, A. S., and Eidelberg, E. Role of biogenic amines in morphine dependence in the rat. *Life Sciences* 9:613-624 (part I) , 1970.

29. Butterworth, A. T. Depression associated with alcohol withdrawal: Imipramine therapy compared with placebo. *Quarterly Journal of Studies on Alcohol* 32:343-348, 1971.

30. Carlson, C., and Johannson, T. The psychological effects of propranalol in the abstinence phase of chronic alcoholics. *Br. J. Psychiat.* 119:605-606, 1971.

31. Hollister, L. E., and Prusmarck, J. J. Propranalol in withdrawal from opiates. *Arch. Gen. Psychiat.* 31:695-700, 1974.

32. Lieberman, M. A., Yalon, T. D., and Miles, M. B. *Encounter Groups: First Facts.* New York: Basic Books, 1973.

33. Ross, S. M. Behavioral group therapy with alcohol abusers, in *Group Counseling and Therapy Techniques in Special Settings.* R. E. Hardy, and J. G. Cull, eds. Springfield, Ill.: Charles C Thomas, 1974.

34. Ewing, J. A. Behavioral approaches for problems with alcohol. *Int. J. of the Addictions* 9 (3) :389-399, 1974.

# Subject Index